Postmortem Toxicology of Abused Drugs

Postmortem Toxicology of Abused Drugs

Edited by

Steven B. Karch, MD, FFFLM

Consultant Pathologist and Toxicologist
Berkeley, California

CRC Press
Taylor & Francis Group
Boca Raton London New York

CRC Press is an imprint of the
Taylor & Francis Group, an informa business

CRC Press
Taylor & Francis Group
6000 Broken Sound Parkway NW, Suite 300
Boca Raton, FL 33487-2742

10 9 8 7 6 5 4 3 2 1

International Standard Book Number-13: 978-1-4200-5451-4 (Hardcover)

Library of Congress Cataloging-in-Publication Data

Postmortem toxicology of abused drugs / [edited by] Steven B. Karch.
p. ; cm.
"A CRC title."
Includes bibliographical references and index.
ISBN-13: 978-1-4200-5451-4 (alk. paper)
ISBN-10: 1-4200-5451-1 (alk. paper)
1. Forensic toxicology. 2. Drugs of abuse--Toxicology. 3. Autopsy. I. Karch, Steven B.
[DNLM: 1. Autopsy--methods. 2. Forensic Toxicology--methods. 3. Street Drugs--poisoning. W 825 P858 2007]

RA1228.P67 2007
614'.13--dc22 2007008111

Visit the Taylor & Francis Web site at
http://www.taylorandfrancis.com

and the CRC Press Web site at
http://www.crcpress.com

Contents

Chapter 1 Introduction to Postmortem Toxicology 1
W. Lee Hearn, Ph.D. and H. Chip Walls, B.S.

Chapter 2 Specimen Selection, Collection, Preservation, and Security 13
Bradford R. Hepler, Ph.D. and Daniel S. Isenschmid, Ph.D.

Chapter 3 Common Methods in Postmortem Toxicology 31
W. Lee Hearn, Ph.D. and H. Chip Walls, B.S.

Chapter 4 Strategies for Postmortem Toxicology Investigation 67
Edited and Revised by Henrik Druid, M.D., Ph.D.

Chapter 5 Quality Assurance in Postmortem Toxicology 95
Wilmo Andollo, B.S.

Chapter 6 Interpretation of Postmortem Drug Levels 113
Graham R. Jones, Ph.D., DABFT

Appendix I Glossary of Terms in Forensic Toxicology 131
Compiled by H. Chip Walls, B.S.

Appendix II Common Abbreviations 137
Compiled by H. Chip Walls, B.S.

Appendix III References for Methods of Drug Quantitative Analysis 141

Appendix IV Sample Calculations 181
Barry K. Logan, Ph.D. and Alan Wayne Jones, D.Sc.

Appendix V Predicted Normal Heart Weight (g) as a Function of Body Height in 392 Women and 373 Men 185

Index 187

Preface

Because of the continuous increase in availability and use of pharmaceuticals and illicit drugs, postmortem toxicology has become more and more important in death investigations. The introduction of new substances to the market requires a high awareness among pathologists and toxicologists and necessitates the development of methods that encompass the newcomers. Fortunately, many important achievements have been made in methodology, and the application of novel techniques, such as modifications of solid phase extraction and LC/MS techniques, now offers better conditions for efficient and sensitive analyses of numerous substances.

Many important contributions regarding the impact of various postmortem changes that may influence the toxicological results have been published. Pharmacogenetic analyses, e.g., to identify poor metabolizers, may now be applied on postmortem material and assist in the determination of the manner of death, and studies on postmortem redistribution of drugs have resulted in a widespread appreciation of the influence of the specimen type on the drug concentrations.

In recent years, the specific detection of many compounds and their metabolites in various matrices has improved substantially. However, the interpretation of their concentrations remains a difficult task. Hence, despite the progress in postmortem toxicology, information about previous drug use and the circumstances surrounding death, and the autopsy findings are still very important in order to arrive at correct conclusions when interpreting the analytical results. An intimate collaboration between toxicologists and pathologists is therefore desirable.

Traditionally, teachers of forensic science have always emphasized that the proper investigation of a drug-related death involves three elements: scene investigation, autopsy, and toxicological examination. The traditional approach is no longer valid because it assumes that the autopsy was complete. We now know that it has never been complete. Heart disease is not ruled out just because 25 sections of myocardium look normal. Poisoning is not proven just because blood morphine concentrations are very high. We now live in the age of the DNA microarray. Chips for measurement of CYP2D6 polymorphisms are already available commercially. Arrays for the measurement of the hundreds of genes involved in hypertrophic cardiomyopathy already exist in development labs. The sooner these new technologies are incorporated into forensic toxicology, the sooner the justice system will benefit.

Preface

The Editor

Steven B. Karch, M.D., FFFLM, received his undergraduate degree from Brown University. He attended graduate school in anatomy and cell biology at Stanford University. He received his medical degree from Tulane University School of Medicine. Dr. Karch did postgraduate training in neuropathology at the Royal London Hospital and in cardiac pathology at Stanford University. For many years he was a consultant cardiac pathologist to San Francisco's Chief Medical Examiner.

In the U.K., Dr. Karch served as a consultant to the Crown and helped prepare the cases against serial murderer Dr. Harold Shipman, who was subsequently convicted of murdering 248 of his patients. He has testified on drug abuse–related matters in courts around the world. He has a special interest in cases of alleged euthanasia, and in episodes where mothers are accused of murdering their children by the transference of drugs, either *in utero* or by breastfeeding.

Dr. Karch is the author of nearly 100 papers and book chapters, most of which are concerned with the effects of drug abuse on the heart. He has published seven books. He is currently completing the fourth edition of *Pathology of Drug Abuse*, a widely used textbook. He is also working on a popular history of Napoleon and his doctors.

Dr. Karch is forensic science editor for Humana Press, and he serves on the editorial boards of the *Journal of Cardiovascular Toxicology*, the *Journal of Clinical Forensic Medicine* (London), *Forensic Science, Medicine and Pathology*, and *Clarke's Analysis of Drugs and Poisons*.

Dr. Karch was elected a fellow of the Faculty of Legal and Forensic Medicine, Royal College of Physicians (London) in 2006. He is also a fellow of the American Academy of Forensic Sciences, the Society of Forensic Toxicologists (SOFT), the National Association of Medical Examiners (NAME), the Royal Society of Medicine in London, and the Forensic Science Society of the U.K. He is a member of The International Association of Forensic Toxicologists (TIAFT).

Contributors

Wilmo Andollo, B.S.
Quality Assurance Officer
Dade County Medical Examiner Toxicology Laboratory
Miami, Florida

Henrik Druid, M.D., Ph.D.
Associate Professor
Department of Forensic Medicine
Karolinska Institute
Stockholm, Sweden

W. Lee Hearn, Ph.D.
Director
Dade County Medical Examiner Toxicology Laboratory
Miami, Florida

Bradford R. Hepler, Ph.D.
Toxicology Laboratory
Wayne County Medical Examiner's Office
Detroit, Michigan

Daniel S. Isenschmid, Ph.D.
Toxicology Laboratory
Wayne County Medical Examiner's Office
Detroit, Michigan

Alan Wayne Jones, D.Sc.
Department of Forensic Toxicology
University Hospital
Linköping, Sweden

Graham R. Jones, Ph.D., DABFT
Office of the Chief Medical Examiner
Edmonton, Alberta, Canada

Barry K. Logan, Ph.D.
Director
Washington State Toxicology Laboratory
Department of Laboratory Medicine
University of Washington
Seattle, Washington

H. Chip Walls, B.S.
Department of Pathology
Forensic Toxicology Laboratory
University of Miami
Miami, Florida

CHAPTER 1

Introduction to Postmortem Toxicology

W. Lee Hearn, Ph.D.[1] and H. Chip Walls, B.S.[2]
[1] Director, Dade County Medical Examiner Toxicology Laboratory, Miami, Florida
[2] Department of Pathology, Forensic Toxicology Laboratory, University of Miami, Miami, Florida

CONTENTS

1.1 Medicolegal Death Investigation 1
 1.1.1 Role of Police and Medical Examiner Investigators 3
 1.1.2 Role of the Forensic Pathologist 3
1.2 Certification of Death 4
1.3 Role of Toxicology in Death Investigation 4
 1.3.1 Homicides 4
 1.3.2 Suicides 5
 1.3.3 Accidents 6
 1.3.4 Natural Deaths 6
 1.3.5 Unclassified, Undetermined, or Pending 7
 1.3.6 Pending Toxicology (Overdose) 7
1.4 The Toxicology Examination 7
 1.4.1 Poisons 8
 1.4.2 Comprehensive Toxicology Screening 8
 1.4.3 Case Review 8
 1.4.4 Quality Assurance 9
 1.4.5 The Toxicology Report 9
 1.4.6 Toxicological Interpretation 9
References 10

1.1 MEDICOLEGAL DEATH INVESTIGATION

The medical examiner's office investigates sudden, violent, unnatural, or unexpected deaths,[1–3] and the medical examiner, coroner, or pathologist is responsible for determining the cause and manner of death. The cause of death is the injury, intoxication, or disease that initiates a process leading to death, and if that initial event had not occurred, the individual would not have died. Death may follow years after the causal event. The manner of death is the circumstances in which the cause of death occurred. Five classifications are used to categorize the manner of death: homicide, suicide, accident, natural, and undetermined. Anatomic findings elicited at autopsy are often insufficient to determine the manner of death.

To determine the manner of death, all available information pertaining to a particular case, including the terminal events, scene investigation, police reports, social and medical history, autopsy findings, and results of histologic and toxicologic testing, must be considered. The question "Did alcohol, other drugs, or poisons cause or contribute to this person's death?" must always be answered. Success in arriving at the correct conclusion depends on the combined efforts of the pathologist, the investigators, and the toxicologist. The process of death investigation and the role of the laboratory are outlined in Figure 1.1.

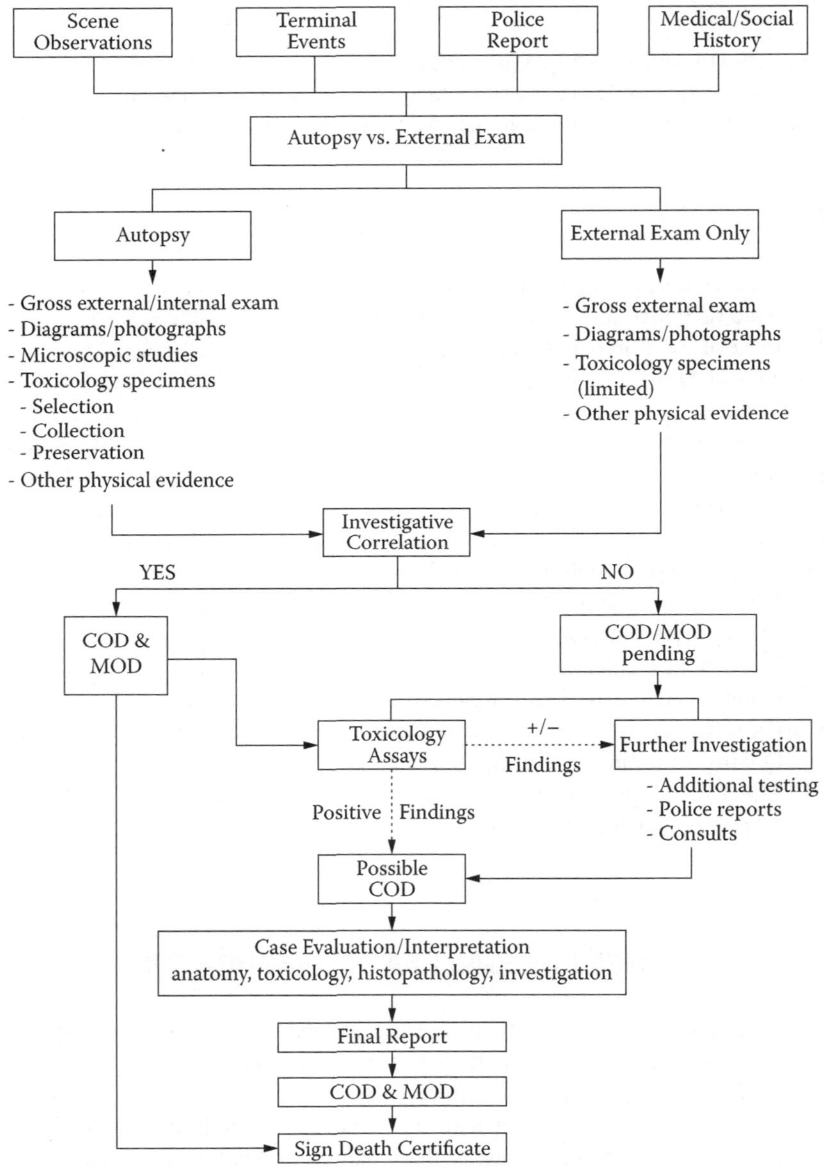

Figure 1.1 Overview of death investigation.

1.1.1 Role of Police and Medical Examiner Investigators

When a death is reported to the medical examiner's office, a case investigator will obtain certain information to determine whether the case falls under the jurisdiction of the medical examiner. The following is a list of important topics to consider, which may vary according to jurisdiction:

Cases Requiring Medicolegal Death Investigation

1. Any death where any form of violence, whether criminal, suicidal, or accidental, was directly responsible or contributory.
2. Any death caused by an unlawful act or criminal neglect.
3. Any death occurring in a suspicious, unusual, or unexplained fashion.
4. Any death where there is no attending physician.
5. Any death of a person confined to a public institution.
6. The death of any prisoner even though both the cause and manner appear to be natural.
7. Any death caused by or contributed to by drugs or other chemical poisoning or overdose.
8. Any sudden death of a person in apparent good health.
9. Any death occurring during diagnostic or therapeutic procedures.
10. Any fetal stillbirth in the absence of a physician.
11. Any death where there is insufficient medical information to explain the individual's demise.

An unnatural death is any death that is not a direct result of a natural, medically recognized disease process. Any death where an outside, intervening influence, either directly or indirectly, is contributory to the individual's demise, or accelerates and exacerbates an underlying disease process to such a degree as to cause death, would also fall into the category of unnatural death.

Investigators are the eyes and ears of the medical examiner, especially in cases where the body is removed prior to the pathologist's involvement. The importance of an adequate investigation into past social and medical history cannot be overemphasized.

Police reports and investigations provide scene documentation. Typically, a report will include a description and identification of the body, time and place of death, eyewitness accounts, drugs present, and photographs. Investigators assigned by the medical examiner collect all items and information pertaining to establishing the cause and manner of death. Investigators contact the family and friends of the deceased for information regarding, for example, past medical and social history and prescribed medications. Many cases have histories of prescription drugs to guide the investigation. All medication bottles should be verified as to content and count, in addition to performing a routine pharmacy check of the person's medication usage. Medical examiner investigators must also contact hospitals and treating physicians to obtain copies of medical records and police agencies to obtain arrest records. Progressively, a file is assembled that contains all of the relevant background information to assist the pathologist in understanding the medical and social history of the deceased.

The medicolegal systems in countries outside the U.S. vary, but the selection of cases subjected to a forensic pathology examination is usually similar. However, in several countries the police are responsible for the investigation even in noncriminal cases. It is therefore important that the pathologists and toxicologists stay in good contact with the investigating police officer to obtain all relevant information outlined above.

1.1.2 Role of the Forensic Pathologist

The principal role of the forensic pathologist is to investigate sudden, unexpected, and violent deaths in order to determine the cause and manner of death. In suspected drug-related deaths or poisonings, the pathologist must both exclude traumatic or pathological mechanisms as possible causes of death *and* select and preserve appropriate specimens for toxicologic analysis. After autopsy, cases can often be divided into two categories: those with an anatomical cause of death and those without. Few drugs leave telltale signs so obvious that the pathologist can determine a manner and cause of death without additional testing. Obvious exceptions include liver necrosis caused by acetaminophen, or the severely hemorrhagic gastric mucosa and smell from cyanide exposure, or coronary artery disease and cardiac enlargement in a cocaine user. Negative findings require toxicological analyses.

Approximately 10% of the cases submitted for toxicology do not have any guiding features. However, many of the thousands of potential compounds that could have caused death will have already been eliminated after history and autopsy results are correlated. Since the majority of drugs and poisons do not produce characteristic pathological lesions, their presence in the body can be demonstrated only by chemical methods.

Collection and preservation of appropriate specimens is a critical component of the autopsy examination.[4–9] Just what is collected depends, at least partly, on the policy and finances of the department. The utility of these specimens depends not only on the condition of the body, but also on the pathologist's technique. Specimens must be large enough, the correct preservative must be used, and they must be placed in appropriate, clearly and correctly labeled containers.

Specimen collection is the first link in the chain of custody. Sample integrity within the chain of custody is an essential requirement for the rest of the forensic investigation. In cases where autopsy fails to determine a cause of death, or where there is an incomplete investigation, it is imperative to collect an adequate variety of specimens. Subsequent findings may modify or narrow the field of search, and make it unnecessary to examine each specimen, but they can always be discarded. However, many toxins are completely lost in the embalming process, so if the appropriate specimens are not collected at the time of the initial postmortem examination, the cause of death may never be determined.

1.2 CERTIFICATION OF DEATH

Each state requires a medical and legal document known as the Death Certificate be filed with the Bureau of Vital Statistics. The certificate contains demographic information as well the cause and manner of death as determined by the medical examiner. Five different classifications are recognized: (1) homicide, (2) suicide, (3) accident, (4) natural, and (5) undetermined.

The results from toxicological analyses of postmortem specimens are applied to determine whether drugs or toxins are a cause of death, or whether they may have been a contributing factor in the death. Negative toxicological results may be equally important as positive results, and sometimes even more meaningful as in the case of antiseizure medicines not detected in a suspected seizure death as compared to a positive marijuana test in the urine of a shooting victim.

1.3 ROLE OF TOXICOLOGY IN DEATH INVESTIGATION

Most toxicology offices have established routines for specific types of cases, and the pathologist often provides some indication of what toxicological testing should be performed on each case (Figure 1.2). It would appear that cases of suspected homicide require much more thorough testing than obvious cases of accidental or natural death, but that is not really the case. Alcohol and other sedative hypnotic drugs, for example, are often detected in fire victims and may well have contributed to the cause of death.

1.3.1 Homicides

The relationship between intoxication and violence is well recognized.[10–12] Toxicological studies in cases of traumatic homicide should include tests for alcohol, prescribed medications, and

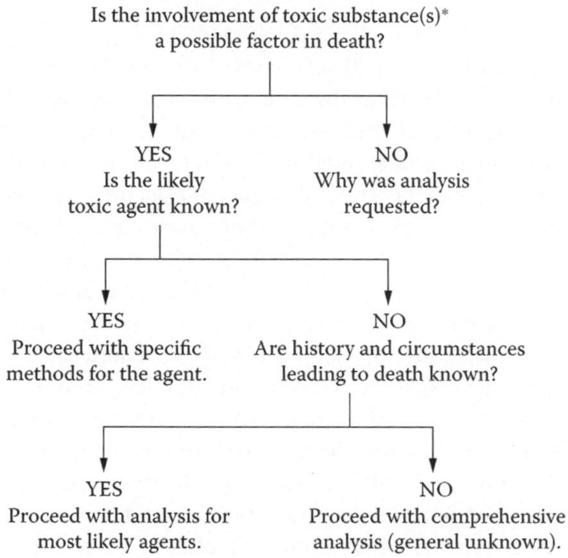

***Forensic Questions Relative to Poisoning:**

1. Was the death or illness due to a poison?
2. What toxin produced the illness?
3. Was the substance employed capable of producing death?
4. Was a sufficient quantity taken to produce death or toxic results?
5. When and how was the toxin taken?
6. Could a poisoning have occurred and the poison either be or have become undetectable?
7. Could the detected poison have an origin other than in poisoning?
8. Was the poisoning SUICIDAL, ACCIDENTAL, or HOMICIDAL?
9. Were the correct specimens collected and preserved, analyzed in such a manner to answer the question at hand?

Figure 1.2 Identification of a toxicology issue in the death investigation.

other drugs. Negative findings can be used in court to rebut assertions of self-defense against a "drug-crazed" attacker. Positive findings may help explain how the victim became involved in a physical altercation. In addition, results of drug screening provide information about the deceased's lifestyle that may prove useful to police as they search for the murderer. Toxicological investigations may also reveal evidence that a victim was drugged to incapacitation and then murdered.

1.3.2 Suicides

In cases of suicide, investigators try to discover an explanation for the act.[13–15] People may be driven to suicide by failing health, financial problems, loss of a loved one, severe mental depression, or other causes. Drugs that can potentiate or exacerbate depression are commonly detected in suicides. A well-recognized drawback with antidepressants is that they neutralize passivity and inhibition before they affect the mood, and thereby confer an increased risk for suicide during the first weeks of treatment.[16,17] Drugs commonly found in suicide victims include alcohol, sedatives (particularly benzodiazepines), analgesics, and hypnotics, and sometimes even illicit drugs. Therefore, toxicological investigations should encompass a large number of intoxicants. Occasionally, a suicide victim employs multiple means to reduce the chances of survival, implying that intake of drugs should not be overlooked even if another suicidal method is apparent.

1.3.3 Accidents

For fatal accidents, highway crashes immediately come to mind; however, accidental deaths occur in many other circumstances.[9,11,18–22] Drownings, falls, fires, electrocutions, boating accidents, and aircraft crashes, as well as accidental drug overdoses, are included in this classification. Accidents often result from carelessness or the impairment of mental or motor function on the part of the victim or another person. In apparent cases of accidental death, it is important to confirm or rule out alcohol- or other drug-induced impairment. Many insurance policies exclude death or injury resulting from the misuse of intoxicating substances, although in some cases quite the opposite is true. In those jurisdictions where drug deaths are considered accidents, double indemnity clauses may come into play. The families of victims dying from cocaine toxicity could, in some instances, be entitled to twice the face value of the decedent's life insurance.

Parties injured in an accident may litigate to recover damages. The sobriety or intoxication of the deceased can be a factor in efforts to assign blame. And, of course, apparent accidental deaths may actually turn out to be suicides, or they may be natural deaths occurring in circumstances that suggest an accident. When a driver becomes incapacitated by a heart attack, for example, and loss of control results in an accident, toxicological studies may play a part in the investigation. Detection of intoxicants, together with other evidence, may indicate that an apparent accident was actually intentional. For example, finding large quantities of a drug in a deceased person's stomach suggests that an overdose was intentional (i.e., suicide) rather than accidental.

If postmortem investigation fails to detect carbon monoxide in the blood of a burn victim, or soot in the airway, it may be that the victim had already died when the fire started. Such cases may be deaths from natural causes, or attempts to destroy evidence of a murder. Further investigation may discover evidence of illness or trauma. Workplace accidents must always be investigated for the possible involvement of alcohol or other drugs, since there are likely to be insurance claims against the employer. If the victim is shown to have intoxicants in the body, the employer may be held blameless. Another aspect of workplace-related accidents concerns exposure to toxic chemicals. The potential for such exposures varies with the nature of the business. If exposure to a toxic chemical is alleged or suspected, investigators should obtain a list of chemicals in the workplace, and the toxicology laboratory of the medical examiner should analyze for those chemicals whose toxicity is consistent with the circumstances of death.

1.3.4 Natural Deaths

Apparent natural deaths may or may not require toxicological study. If the autopsy clearly reveals the cause of death, and no history of drug or alcohol misuse is known, the pathologist may decide that further toxicological study is not necessary.[23,25] Sometimes studies are ordered to evaluate compliance with required pharmacotherapy, such as measurement of anticonvulsant drug levels in an person with epilepsy who has a seizure and then dies. When the apparent cause of death may be related to drug or alcohol misuse, testing should be done to determine whether or not relevant drugs are present. For example, acute myocardial infarctions, cerebral hemorrhages, ruptured berry aneurysms, and dissecting aortic aneurysms are often associated with recent cocaine use. Such cases should be tested for cocaine and other drugs, particularly when this occurs in young people or when there is a history of drug use. A diagnosis of alcoholism should call for a blood alcohol analysis.

The diagnosis of sudden infant death syndrome (SIDS) is a diagnosis of exclusion. All apparent SIDS cases should be tested for alcohol and other drugs. Child abuse can include drugging a restless infant, where even a small dose of drug may be fatal.

When there is any uncertainty regarding the cause of death, testing should be done to rule out an overdose. Terminally ill people sometimes commit suicide, and hospice patients are occasionally poisoned by their caregivers. When samples for apparent natural deaths are submitted to the toxicology laboratory for testing, unrecognized poisoning cases are sometimes discovered.

1.3.5 Unclassified, Undetermined, or Pending

When the cause or manner of death remains elusive at the completion of investigations and autopsy, the case is left unclassified, pending further studies.[4,23] Additional inquiries, microscopic examinations, and toxicological studies are initiated to find sufficient evidence for a diagnosis. The primary goal for the toxicology laboratory is to determine whether or not toxic substances are present in the deceased in sufficient quantities to kill. If a probable toxic cause of death is identified, the laboratory gathers additional evidence to assist the pathologist in deciding how it was administered, and estimating how much was used, and how long before death. The results of toxicology testing are considered along with other evidence to formulate an opinion regarding the manner of death.

1.3.6 Pending Toxicology (Overdose)

Death by poisoning or overdose may be accidental, suicidal, or homicidal.[15,20,23,25–27] Various clues indicating poisoning may be observed during the autopsy. In some cases, a large amount of partially degraded medicinal tablets is found in the stomach, esophagus, mouth, and nostrils, or a typical strong smell of alcohol is noticed. However, other unusual odors or abnormal colors of stomach contents, urine, or tissues, and specific lesions may suggest to the experienced forensic pathologist that a drug or poison was the cause of death. Evidence from the death scene, such as a suicide note or empty containers, may point to a poisoning or drug overdose in some cases. However, most drug-related deaths do not leave such telltale markers as those found in heart attacks, cancer, or trauma. Often the only clue from the autopsy is pulmonary congestion and edema. The pathologist calls upon the toxicology laboratory to confirm the suspicion by identifying the poison or poisons and gathering enough quantitative data to support a conclusion that the detected poison was sufficient to cause death.

In addition, the laboratory may sometimes be able to shed light on the issues of how much was taken and the route of administration. The assignment of manner of death is based on the totality of the evidence, including the pharmacology and toxicology of the substance, the route of administration and quantity taken, the social and medical history of the deceased, and evidence collected from the death scene.[7,20,28,29] Drug-related death certification is by a process of compilation and evaluation of all findings during the death investigation, where elimination of a number of other possible causes of death (COD) is as important as the detection of a toxic substance in sufficient concentrations to have caused or contributed to the death.[28]

1.4 THE TOXICOLOGY EXAMINATION

The toxicologic investigation typically begins with the preliminary identification of drugs or chemicals present in postmortem specimens.[30–39] Confirmatory testing is then performed to conclusively identify the substance(s) present in the postmortem specimens. In a forensic laboratory, positive identification must be established by at least two independent analyses, each based on a different analytic principle. The next step in the process is to determine the quantity of substance in the appropriate specimens. Identifying drugs in waste fluids, such as bile and urine, is a useful undertaking, but quantifying drugs in these fluids usually has limited interpretive value. Drug quantification in peripheral blood, along with quantification in samples from liver, gastric contents, or other specimens, as dictated by the case, provides more meaningful interpretive information.

Therapeutic and toxic ranges have been established for many compounds,[28] but it should be recognized that "therapeutic" concentrations rarely can be determined in the postmortem setting.[40]

All cases cannot be tested for all drugs. A number of factors, some not immediately obvious, determine what kind, and how many, tests will be done. The importance of the medicolegal classification of death and specimen collection has already been mentioned. But other factors, such as geographic patterns of drug use and laboratory capabilities, must also be considered.

Occasionally, mere detection of a drug is sufficient. But, in the case of some prescription medications, the actual amount present must be quantified. A request for "therapeutic" drug analysis may be made even if the autopsy has already determined the cause of death. If a history of seizure is obtained, the pathologist may request an antiepileptic drug screen to determine whether or not the person was taking any such medication. The same holds true for, e.g., theophylline in individuals with asthma. An individual who has committed suicide may have been prescribed therapeutic drugs for depression or other mental illness. A test for these drugs may indicate the degree of patient compliance. In forensic toxicology, a negative laboratory result carries the same weight as a positive result.

1.4.1 Poisons

Often the nature of a suspected toxin is unknown. This type of case is termed a "general unknown."[41,42] In cases of this nature, a full analysis of all available specimens by as many techniques as possible may be required to reach a conclusion. The most common approach involves first testing for volatile agents, and then performing drug screens. The drug screen is usually confined to those drugs that are commonly seen in the casework. When the most common substances have been ruled out, the laboratory proceeds to test for more exotic drugs and poisons.

1.4.2 Comprehensive Toxicology Screening

It is impossible to consider the topic of forensic toxicology without discussing analytical toxicology in detail.[43–46] Screening methods should provide presumptive identification, or at least class identification while also giving an indication of concentration. An adequate screening protocol, capable of detecting or eliminating the majority of the commonly encountered toxins, usually requires a combination of three or more chemically unrelated techniques. In general, some toxins are so common that, no matter the type of case, they should always be included for analysis; e.g., ethanol, salicylate, acetaminophen, sedatives, hypnotics, and other drugs such as cocaine, opiates, and antidepressants. All screening tests that are positive for substances relevant to the case must then be confirmed, and analytes of significance submitted for quantification in several tissues. Later sections in this chapter discuss testing methods and how they are combined to yield effective analytical strategies.

1.4.3 Case Review

During the toxicological investigation, each case is subjected to periodic review, its status evaluated, and the need for additional testing determined. Based on what is known about the death and the specimens available, a panel of screening tests is designed to quickly detect or rule out the most common drugs and, when appropriate, poisons.[33,37,38,43,47] New tests may be ordered to expand the initial search, or to confirm preliminary findings.

The flow of information in forensic toxicology must be in two directions[48] — from pathologist to laboratory, then back to the physician who will integrate all of the findings. Laboratory personnel must effectively communicate with the pathologist concerning the scope (and limitations) of the services they can provide, suggest the proper selection of specimens, and assist with interpretation of the results. In particular, when drug screens are used, the pathologist should know which drugs they cover — and which drugs will go undetected. To operate effectively, the toxicologist must be provided with enough information about the history and autopsy findings to rationally select the most appropriate tests.

1.4.4 Quality Assurance

Each laboratory must formulate and adhere to a quality assurance (QA) program. QA provides safeguards to ensure that the toxicology report contains results that are accurate and reproducible, and that the chain of custody has been preserved. A written QA plan sets out the procedures employed to ensure reliability, and provides the means to document that those procedures were correctly followed. The laboratory's strict adherence to a proper QA program induces confidence in the laboratory's work product and prevents or overcomes potential legal challenges. Before a new or improved method is introduced into a laboratory, it must be selected with care and its performance must be rigorously and impartially evaluated under laboratory conditions.

1.4.5 The Toxicology Report

When all toxicological testing is completed, the results are summarized in a report that is sent to the pathologist. This report becomes a part of the autopsy report. It specifies the name of the deceased, if known, and the medical examiner case number. The specimens tested, the substances detected in each specimen, and the measured concentrations of those substances are presented in tabular form. The report should also list substances tested for, but not found, especially if they were named in the toxicology request. If any drug was detected, but not confirmed, a note to that effect should be on the report. In addition, any information about the specimens, such as the date and time of collection of ante-mortem blood or any unusual condition of a specimen, should also be noted on the report. Because of the well-known difficulties associated with the postmortem redistribution of many drugs, the report should always indicate where in the body the blood specimen was obtained. Toxicology reports are usually signed or initialed by the issuing toxicologist, and in some jurisdictions may be signed by the pathologist as well.

1.4.6 Toxicological Interpretation

> All substances are poisons; there is none which is not a poison. The right dose differentiates a poison and a remedy.
>
> **Paracelsus (1493–1541)**

> Poisons and medicines are oftentimes the same substance given with different intents.
>
> **Peter Mere Latham (1789–1875)**

The significance of the reported results must be explained, often to a jury.[5,28,43,48–51] The pharmacology, toxicology, local patterns of drug abuse, and postmortem changes all can affect toxicological results. In any given case, a toxicologist may be asked the following questions (even though a definitive answer may not be possible in all instances):

1. What was taken, when, and how?
2. Was the drug or combination of drugs sufficient to kill or to affect behavior?
3. What are its effects on behavior?
4. Does the evidence indicate if a substance was taken for therapeutic purposes, as a manifestation of drug misuse, for suicidal purposes, or was it administered homicidally?
5. Was the deceased intoxicated at the time of the incident that caused death?

6. How would intoxication by the particular drug manifest?
7. Is there any alternative explanation for the findings?
8. What additional tests might shed light on the questions?

REFERENCES

1. Mason, J.K., Forensic medicine [review]. *Injury* 21: 325–327, 1990.
2. Prahlow, J.A. and Lantz, P.E., Medical examiner/death investigator training requirements in state medical examiner systems. *J. Forensic Sci.* 40: 55–58, 1995.
3. Gross, E.M., The Model Postmortem Examinations Act in the State of Connecticut, 1969–1974. *Legal Med. Annu.* 51–66, 1975.
4. Norton, L.E., Garriott, J.C., and DiMaio, V.J., Drug detection at autopsy: a prospective study of 247 cases. *J. Forensic Sci.,* 27: 66–71, 1982.
5. Margot, P.A., Finkle, B.S., and Peat, M.A., Analysis and problems of interpretation of digoxin in postmortem blood and tissues. *Proc. West. Pharmacol. Soc.* 26: 393–396, 1983.
6. Patel, F., Ancillary autopsy — forensic histopathology and toxicology. *Med. Sci. Law* 35: 25–30, 1995.
7. Prouty, R.W. and Anderson, W.H., The forensic science implications of site and temporal influences on postmortem blood-drug concentrations. *J. Forensic Sci.* 35: 243–270, 1990.
8. McCurdy, W.C., Postmortem specimen collection. *Forensic Sci. Int.* 35: 61–65, 1987.
9. Nagata, T., Significance of toxicological examination in the practice of forensic medicine [Japanese]. *Fukuoka Igaku Zasshi Fukuoka Acta Medica* 77: 173–177, 1986.
10. Garriott, J.C., Drug use among homicide victims. *Am. J. Forensic Med. Pathol.* 14: 234–237, 1993.
11. Ladewig, D. Drugs and violence [German]. *Ther. Umschau* 50: 194–198, 1993.
12. Poklis, A., Graham, M., Maginn, D., Branch, C.A., and Gantner, G.E., Phencyclidine and violent deaths in St. Louis, Missouri: a survey of medical examiners' cases from 1977 through 1986. *Am. J. Drug Alcohol Abuse* 16: 265–274, 1990.
13. Derby, L.E., Jick, H., and Dean, A.D., Antidepressant drugs and suicide. *J. Clin. Psychopharmacol.* 12: 235–240, 1992.
14. Nielsen, A.S., Stenager, E., and Brahe, U.B., Attempted suicide, suicidal intent, and alcohol. *Crisis* 14: 32–38, 1993.
15. Marzuk, P.M., Tardiff, K., and Leon, A.C., Final exit and suicide assessment in a forensic setting — reply. *Am. J. Psychiatry* 152: 1833, 1995.
16. Stahl, S.M., Nierenberg, A.A., and Gorman, J.M., Evidence of early onset of antidepressant effect in randomized controlled trials. *J. Clin. Psychiatry* 62(Suppl. 4): 17–23, discussion 37, 2001.
17. Licinio, J. and Wong, M.L., Depression, antidepressants and suicidality: a critical appraisal. *Nat. Rev. Drug Discov.* 4: 165–171, 2005.
18. Alleyne, B.C., Stuart, P., and Copes, R., Alcohol and other drug use in occupational fatalities. *J. Occup. Med.* 33: 496–500, 1991.
19. Caplan, Y.H., Ottinger, W.E., Park, J., and Smith, T.D., Drug and chemical related deaths: incidence in the state of Maryland — 1975 to 1980. *J. Forensic Sci.* 30: 1012–1021, 1985.
20. Hammersley, R., Cassidy, M.T., and Oliver, J., Drugs associated with drug-related deaths in Edinburgh and Glasgow, November 1990 to October 1992. *Addiction* 90: 959–965, 1995.
21. Marx, J., Alcohol and trauma. *Emerg. Med. Clin. North Am.* 8: 929–938, 1990.
22. Lewis, R.J. and Cooper, S.P., Alcohol, other drugs, and fatal work-related injuries. *J. Occup. Med.* 31: 23–28, 1989.
23. Mcginnis, J.M. and Foege, W.H., Actual causes of death in the United States [see comments]. *J. Am. Med. Assoc.* 270: 2207–2212, 1993.
24. Hanzlick, R., National Association of Medical Examiners Pediatric Toxicology (PedTox) Registry Report 3. *Am. J. Forensic Med. Pathol.* 16: 270–277, 1995.
25. Briglia, E.J., Davis, P.L., Katz, M., and Dal Cortivo, L.A., Attempted murder with pancuronium. *J. Forensic Sci.* 35: 1468–1476, 1990.
26. Bogan, J., Rentoul, E., Smith, H., and Weir, W.P., Homicidal poisoning by strychnine. *J. Forensic Sci. Soc.* 6: 166–169, 1966.

27. Moffat, A.C., Interpretation of post mortem serum levels of cardiac glycosides after suspected overdosage. *Acta Pharmacol. Toxicol.* 35: 386–394, 1974.
28. Stead, A.H. and Moffat, A.C., A collection of therapeutic, toxic and fatal blood drug concentrations in man. *Hum. Toxicol.* 2: 437–464, 1983.
29. Brettel, H.F. and Dobbertin, T., Multifactorial studies of 154 fatalities of psychotropic drug poisoning [German]. *Beitr. Gerichtl. Med.* 50: 127–130, 1992.
30. Sunshine, I., Basic toxicology. *Pediatr. Clin. North Am.* 17: 509–513, 1970.
31. Levine, B., Forensic toxicology [review]. *Anal. Chem.* 65: 272A–276A, 1993.
32. Jentzen, J.M., Forensic toxicology. An overview and an algorithmic approach. *Am. J. Clin. Pathol.* 92: S48–55, 1989.
33. Levine, B.S., Smith, M.L., and Froede, R.C., Postmortem forensic toxicology [review]. *Clin. Lab. Med.* 10: 571–589, 1990.
34. Flanagan, R.J., Widdop, B., Ramsey, J.D., and Loveland, M., Analytical toxicology [review]. *Hum. Toxicol.* 7: 489–502, 1988.
35. Chollet, D. and Kunstner, P., Fast systematic approach for the determination of drugs in biological fluids by fully automated high-performance liquid chromatography with on-line solid-phase extraction and automated cartridge exchange. *J. Chromatogr.* 577: 335–340, 1992.
36. Maurer, H.H., Systematic toxicological analysis of drugs and their metabolites by gas chromatography-mass spectrometry. *J. Chromatogr.* 580: 3–41, 1992.
37. Nagata, T., Fukui, Y., Kojima, T., Yamada, T., Suzuki, O., Takahama, K. et al., Trace analysis for drugs and poisons in human tissues [Japanese]. *Nippon Hoigaku Zasshi Jpn. J. Legal Med.* 46: 212–224, 1992.
38. Stewart, C.P. and Stollman, A., The toxicologist and his work, in *Toxicology: Mechanisms and Analytical Methods,* Stewart, C.P. and Stollman, A., Eds., Academic Press, New York, 1960, chap. 1.
39. Puopolo, P.R., Volpicelli, S.A., Johnson, D.M., and Flood, J.G., Emergency toxicology testing (detection, confirmation, and quantification) of basic drugs in serum by liquid chromatography with photodiode array detection. *Clin. Chem.* 37: 2124–2130, 1991.
40. Druid, H. and Holmgren, P., Compilations of therapeutic, toxic, and fatal concentrations of drugs, *J. Toxicol. Clin. Toxicol.* 36:133–134, 1998.
41. Wu Chen, N.B., Schaffer, M.I., Lin, R.L., Kurland, M.L, Donoghue, E.R., Jr., and Stein, R.J., The general toxicology unknown. I. The systematic approach. *J. Forensic Sci.* 28: 391–397, 1983.
42. Wu Chen, N.B., Schaffer, M.I., Lin, R.L., Kurland, M.L., Donoghue, E.R., Jr., and Stein, R.J., The general toxicology unknown. II. A case report: doxylamine and pyrilamine intoxication. *J. Forensic Sci.* 28: 398–403, 1983.
43. Osselton, M.D., Analytical forensic toxicology [review]. *Arch. Toxicol.* Suppl. 15: 259–267, 1992.
44. Drummer, O.H., Kotsos, A., and Mcintyre, I.M., A class-independent drug screen in forensic toxicology using a photodiode array detector. *J. Anal. Toxicol.* 17: 225–229, 1993.
45. Bailey, D.N., Comprehensive toxicology screening in patients admitted to a university trauma center. *J. Anal. Toxicol.* 10: 147–149, 1986.
46. Chen, J.S., Chang, K.J., Charng, R.C., Lai, S.J., Binder, S.R., and Essien, H., The development of a broad-spectrum toxicology screening program in Taiwan. *J. Toxicol. Clin. Toxicol.* 33: 581–589, 1995.
47. De Zeeuw, R.A., Procedures and responsibilities in forensic toxicology [letter]. *J. Forensic Sci.* 27: 749–753, 1982.
48. Stafford, D.T., Prouty, R.W., and Anderson, W.H., Current conundrums facing forensic pathologists and toxicologists [editorial]. *Am. J. Forensic Med. Pathol.* 4: 103–104, 1983.
49. Lokan, R.J., James, R.A., and Dymock, R.B., Apparent post-mortem production of high levels of cyanide in blood. *J. Forensic Sci. Soc.* 27: 253–259, 1987.
50. Heatley, M.K. and Crane, J., The blood alcohol concentration at post-mortem in 175 fatal cases of alcohol intoxication. *Med. Sci. Law* 30: 101–105, 1990.
51. Schulz, M. and Schmoldt, A., A compilation of therapeutic and toxic plasma drug concentrations. *Anaesthesist* 43: 835–844, 1994.

CHAPTER 2

Specimen Selection, Collection, Preservation, and Security

Bradford R. Hepler, Ph.D. and Daniel S. Isenschmid, Ph.D.
Toxicology Laboratory, Wayne County Medical Examiner's Office, Detroit, Michigan

CONTENTS

2.1 Chain of Custody 14
2.2 Specimen Collection 15
 2.2.1 Specimen Containers 15
 2.2.2 Specimen Preservatives 15
2.3 Sampling 16
 2.3.1 Blood 16
 2.3.2 Urine 17
 2.3.3 Bile 17
 2.3.4 Vitreous Humor 18
 2.3.5 Gastric Contents 18
 2.3.6 Hair 18
 2.3.7 Tissues 19
 2.3.8 Labeling 19
2.4 Selection of Postmortem Specimens 19
 2.4.1 Blood 20
 2.4.2 Urine 20
 2.4.3 Bile 21
 2.4.4 Vitreous Humor 21
 2.4.5 Gastric Contents 22
 2.4.6 Tissues 22
 2.4.7 Hair 23
 2.4.8 Bone and Bone Marrow 23
 2.4.9 Skeletal Muscle 24
 2.4.10 Larvae 24
 2.4.11 Meconium 25
 2.4.12 Other Specimens 25
2.5 Nonbiological Evidence 25
References 26

Specimen selection, collection, preservation, and security place unique demands on the postmortem forensic toxicologist. The quality of results expected from the postmortem laboratory today is high and reflects the research advances and continued improvements in instrumentation and analytical methods seen since the origins of modern forensic toxicology in the early 20th century.[1–3] However, it must be recognized that — even with technological advances — accurate, forensically defensible results are predicated on the quality and type of specimens provided, and the documentation of each specimen's origin and history. As important are issues relating to security and evidence control during the collection and storage process. Finally, in considering data available from publications and databases, it is important to recognize that the quality and the "comparability" of data between institutions are only as good as the consistency of approach in specimen collection, storage, and analysis between these organizations.

Many major references in forensic pathology have, each in its own manner, sought to provide information about specimen collection issues.[1,4–9] More recently, the literature has focused on novel and more intriguing issues such as postmortem release and/or redistribution of drugs from tissues into blood as mechanisms that can lead to legitimate debates about the meaning of a reported value.[10–17] Thus, even an analytically "accurate value" may be subject to misinterpretation when the drug concentration in a single blood specimen is used to explain the circumstances surrounding a drug intoxication death, particularly when the drug concentrations are not excessively high or low. This and other specimen collection and documentation issues are the subjects for discussion in this chapter.

2.1 CHAIN OF CUSTODY

One major difference between forensic and clinical toxicology is that institutions performing forensic work are held legally accountable for documenting the handling of specific evidence within the organization. This means that all evidence associated with a specific case must be kept in a secure area at all times and be accounted for during its lifetime by using a record or chain of custody (COC).

Documentation should include *who* handled the evidence, *what* evidence was handled, *when* and *why* the evidence was handled, and *where* the evidence was located at all times. This documentation is central to the demonstration that the evidence has remained intact, and not been adulterated, changed, mishandled, or misplaced in any fashion that would compromise its integrity. Evidence ties together people, places, actions, and things that have important impact on circumstances surrounding events in which individuals are held legally accountable. In criminal actions the importance of the evidence may truly involve a "life or death" determination, while in civil litigation large sums of money or property may be at stake.

The biological specimens collected during the autopsy are evidence and must be legally accounted for. Specimens must be maintained in secure, limited-access areas at all times with access restricted to only those individuals designated in the institution's standard operating procedure. Specimen handling has been and will continue to be legally scrutinized by the courts. Properly maintained COC documentation rules out any period of time in which a specimen may be left vulnerable to adulteration or tampering. Failure to properly document the COC may compromise not only the integrity of the specimen, but also the credibility of the institution handling the specimen.

Labor-intensive documentation can be tedious and a natural deterrent to the consistent maintenance of records, including the COC. The use of computers for documenting COC and other specimen transactions within the postmortem forensic toxicology laboratory has recently been demonstrated.[18–20] The ability of the computer to routinely maintain and monitor predictable and consistently occurring events makes it an ideal tool for tracking of forensic events.

2.2 SPECIMEN COLLECTION

2.2.1 Specimen Containers

There are several unique challenges to collecting postmortem forensic toxicology specimens compared with specimen collection in other forensic toxicology disciplines such as human performance toxicology and employment drug testing. Postmortem specimen quality can be quite variable, making specimen collection and subsequent reproducibility in aliquoting of the specimen difficult at times. Specimen quantity, or availability, will vary considerably from one case to another, yet the laboratory must attempt to provide a comprehensive toxicological analysis for a general unknown. In the latter regard, detection limits are pressed, and trace findings may have a major bearing on issues of compliance and proper patient care in hospitalized or extended care facilities and the potential for civil litigation. The use of appropriate specimen containers and preservatives can be critical in the toxicologists' ability to ultimately identify a substance in a given specimen.

Usually, the best container to utilize when collecting and storing postmortem biological fluids is glass.[1,9,21] Glass is inert, does not contain any plasticizer contaminants, and maximizes storage space. Plasticizer contamination is further reduced with Teflon-lined caps. If drug concentrations of less than 0.010 μg/mL are expected, silation of glassware may be indicated.[1] Disposable Pyrex glass culture tubes are suitable for long-term frozen storage and come in a variety of sizes. It is important that the container size chosen for each specimen will allow it to be as close to full as possible in order to minimize concerns about oxidative losses due to air trapped in the top of the container, volatile drug evaporation, and "salting-out" effects from preservatives that may be added to the tube.[1] Generally, 50-mL culture tubes represent the best choice for blood and urine specimens. Smaller tubes (e.g., 15, 20, and 30 mL) can be used for the collection of small amounts of blood, vitreous humor, and bile specimens.

Most types of plastic containers are suitable for the collection of solid tissue specimens and gastric contents. The nature of solid tissue reduces direct contact with the plastic container, and the relative amount of drug(s) present in gastric contents will minimize the influence of plasticizer interference.

The principal argument that can be made against glass containers is the possibility of breakage. However, this can be minimized by using appropriate storage racks and carrying totes. Some laboratories have successfully used plastic containers by identifying a product that reduces plasticizer contribution and adsorption of drug to the container. Nalgene® containers have been recommended for collection of postmortem biological fluids.[22] While drug stability in these containers was not determined to be a problem, the evaluation of contaminants was not reported. Whether a facility chooses glass or plastic, it is important that the laboratory carefully evaluate the container before routinely collecting specimens in it. The nature and potential for contamination can be evaluated by analyzing drug-negative biological fluids stored over time in the container. In addition, the plastic must be chosen carefully to ensure that it does not crack when frozen. For example, polystyrene is subject to cracking under these conditions whereas polypropylene is not.

2.2.2 Specimen Preservatives

Blood specimens should be preserved by adding 2% w/v sodium fluoride to the collection container. Sodium fluoride is added to inhibit microorganism conversion of glucose to ethanol, microorganism oxidation of ethanol,[23,24] postmortem conversion of cocaine to ecgonine methyl ester by cholinesterases,[25] and enzymatic loss of other esters such as 6-acetylmorphine.[1,26] Esters, subject to alkaline hydrolysis, are more stable in postmortem blood than ante-mortem blood because the pH of blood falls after death; therefore acidification of blood is not indicated. Some laboratories may choose to add an anticoagulant such as potassium oxalate, EDTA, or sodium citrate at a concentration of 5 mg/mL in addition to the fluoride preservative.[21,23,24] Preservatives and anticoagulants may be added to collection containers designated for blood ahead of time. However, if only a small amount of blood is collected, the excess fluoride may affect headspace volatile assays by altering the vapor pressure of the analyte.[11] Ideally, one preserved and one unpreserved blood specimen should be taken for comparison, if needed.[22]

Once collected, blood specimens should be stored in tightly sealed containers at low temperatures (4°C short term and –20°C long term). The low temperatures inhibit bacterial growth and generally slow reaction kinetics such as the conversion of ethanol to acetaldehyde.[25] In addition, an aliquot of preserved blood, sufficient in quantity to fill the secondary container, should be removed from the primary specimen at the time of specimen accessioning and stored at –20°C in a frost-free freezer. This aliquot should be saved for the quantitative confirmation of unstable analytes such as cocaine and olanzapine and for ethanol reanalysis, if needed.

Specimen preservatives are generally not required for other specimens (e.g., urine, bile, vitreous, tissues, etc.); however, to all samples subject to alcohol analysis, sodium (or potassium) fluoride should be added. As for blood, these specimens should be stored sealed at 4°C until testing is completed and then frozen at –20°C if long-term storage is required.

2.3 SAMPLING

Biological fluids are collected using new or chemically clean hypodermic syringes using appropriate needle gauges and lengths for the specimen to be collected. One needle and syringe should be used per specimen taken. If syringes and needles are to be reused, then care must be taken to scrupulously clean and disinfect these devices between uses. A typical cleansing procedure should include a minimum of 30 min of soaking in a disinfectant, e.g., 10% solution of household bleach in water (0.5% w/v sodium hypochlorite in water), followed by washing with a non-ionic detergent and rinsing with copious amounts of clean water. Additional disinfection can be performed using an autoclave operated under proper quality control guidelines. The College of American Pathologists recommends that instruments be autoclaved at the usual steam autoclave pressure of 15 lb for 45 min. These conditions are suitable for most pathogens; however, higher pressures and temperatures for longer times (approximately 2 h) are necessary if the rare Creutzfeldt–Jakob disease is of concern.[21] For all this effort, it would seem that disposable needles and syringes are the easiest and most time effective and efficient approach for sampling while reducing the possibility for specimen contamination.

Additionally, autopsy staff must maintain the cleanliness of the specimen container as they collect the specimen. All spillage on the outside of the container should be rinsed off and decontaminated using 10% bleach solution.

Collection techniques are discussed below by specimen type. Table 2.1 provides a summary of the information discussed in detail in the text.

2.3.1 Blood

Whenever possible, postmortem blood specimens from two sites, heart and peripheral, should be collected at every autopsy. If no autopsy is performed, then only peripheral blood should be collected.

Heart blood specimens should be taken by needle aspiration using a suitable hypodermic syringe. To obtain a proper cardiac specimen, the pericardial sack must be opened, the pericardium removed, the heart dried, and the blood specimen removed by syringe. Blood from the right chamber is preferable, but regardless from where blood is collected it is essential to label the site from which it was taken.[21] At least 50 mL should be collected — more if possible.

Table 2.1 Guide to the Collection of Routine Toxicology Specimens

Specimen	Amount	When to Obtain	Comments
Blood, heart	50–100 mL	Always	Identify source; preserve with 2% sodium fluoride and potassium oxalate; reserve an aliquot without preservative, if possible
Blood, peripheral	5–10 mL	For complete toxicology testing	Identify source; use femoral or subclavian blood if possible
Blood, clot	Whole clot	Trauma cases	
Urine	All	Always	Submit any quantity, even if <1 mL, for immunoassay screening
Bile	All	Always	Tie off gallbladder to reduce contamination; collect prior to liver
Vitreous humor	All	Always	Combine fluid from both eyes into a single tube
Gastric contents	All	For complete toxicology testing	Tie off stomach to prevent contamination of other viscera; note total volume
Liver	50 g	Always	Identify source; deep right lobe preferred
Kidney	50 g	Metals, ethylene glycol	
Spleen	50 g	CO, CN	Very useful when blood not available in fire deaths
Brain, fat	50 g	Lipophilic drugs	Brain may be especially useful in infant drug deaths
Lung	50 g	Volatile poisons	Collect in sealed container; collect tracheal air as well
Hair	Pen-sized bundle	Drug history, metals	Identify distal and proximal ends

Note: Biological specimens should be kept at refrigerated temperatures (4°C) for short-term storage (up to 2 weeks) and at frozen temperatures (–20°C) for long-term storage. An aliquot of preserved blood should be frozen immediately for analysis and preservation of less stable compounds.

Peripheral blood specimens are usually obtained from the femoral vein. Leg veins are preferred to veins of the head and neck due to the anatomical presence of a larger number of valves that resist blood movement from the intestines.[23] The peripheral blood specimen should be taken using a clean or new 10- to 20-mL hypodermic syringe. Do not "milk" the leg in order to increase specimen volume. If possible, up to 10 mL of peripheral blood should be collected. The source of the peripheral blood specimen should be noted on the specimen container.

As discussed elsewhere, blood clots should be collected in cases of head trauma or if other blood specimens are not available. Because of the strong possibility of contamination, thoracic and abdominal cavity blood should be avoided unless no other blood is available. If collected, they should clearly be labeled as to the source or origin.

2.3.2 Urine

During autopsy, urine specimens should be taken directly from the bladder by insertion of a clean/new hypodermic needle into the bladder. For non-autopsied cases the needle may be inserted directly through the lower abdominal wall, just above the pubic symphysis.[9] If possible, up to 100 mL of urine should be acquired. In cases where the bladder appears to be empty, it is important to aspirate as much urine as possible from the bladder and the ureter. Bladder washings using a minimum amount of clean water (or saline) would be desirable in the absence of any urine. The specimen container should clearly identify and indicate the nature of this specimen, and the amount of water/saline utilized. As little as 50 μl of urine can be useful for some applications such as chemical spot tests and immunoassay testing.

2.3.3 Bile

Following the removal of the organ block during the autopsy process, bile is aspirated from the gallbladder using a clean/new hypodermic syringe. If there is any possibility of contamination, the gallbladder should be tied off and removed from the organ block so that the bile may be collected away from the potential source of contamination. Up to 15 mL of bile should be collected and placed into a properly labeled screw-capped glass culture tube.

2.3.4 Vitreous Humor

Vitreous humor specimens are obtained by direct aspiration from each eye using a 5- to 10-mL syringe and 20-gauge needle. The needle should be inserted through the outer canthus, until its tip is placed centrally in the globe. Vitreous humor can be aspirated from the globe by application of gentle suction. Vacuum tubes and heavy suction should be avoided to prevent specimen contamination with retinal fragments and other tissue. With proper technique 2 to 3 mL of fluid can be removed from each eye in an adult, while up to about 1 mL of specimen may be removed from a newborn.[27] Once the vitreous specimen has been removed from the eye, an appropriate amount of saline can be injected back into the eye in order to reproduce the cosmetic integrity of the eye. Vitreous humor specimens obtained from both eyes may be combined in one properly labeled specimen container.

2.3.5 Gastric Contents

Because gastric contents are not homogeneous, and because the total volume of gastric fluid is critical in the interpretation of positive findings, the entire contents of the stomach should be collected. If this is not possible, then the total volume present must be noted and provided with the specimen to the laboratory. The prosector should tie off the stomach ends before removing it from the organ block. The stomach should be opened away from other specimens and tissues in a manner to avoid contamination of other viscera.

2.3.6 Hair

Hair is preferably collected from the posterior vertex or the back of the skull, where the average hair growth rate is fairly constant, and has been extensively studied.[28] The size of the sample to be collected is dependent on the purpose of the analysis. If a segmental analysis is desired, hair from a 1 × 2 cm area will typically yield about 50 mg of hair/cm segments, which is the amount used for many GC/MS or LC/MS methods reported. Additional samples have to be collected if several analyses with different extraction techniques are desired. One strategy is to collect one sample for screening, and additional samples for confirmation analyses,[29] should the screening come out positive.

In cases with a suspicion of a recent poisoning, analysis of plucked hair may be rewarding, since there is an interval for most drugs during which blood, urine, and cut hair may all be negative, but where the intradermal portion of the hair may harvest traces of the drug. The most common scenario is, however, that the hair analysis is used as a supplementary tool to disclose or confirm previous drug use. Cut hair is then usually preferable since hair roots, often containing high amounts of drugs from an acute intake, are then excluded. Unfortunately, it is difficult to avoid disalignment of a hair sample no matter how carefully the hair is cut from the scalp. An easy way to align the hair strands is to put the sample collected into a small Eppendorff tube with the cut end first and use tweezers to adjust the hair strands. If the time for exposure is not an issue, this procedure is not necessary, and further, smaller hair samples may suffice.

Directly after collection, a convenient means to preserve the alignment, and to keep control of the scalp end, is to put the sample into a small piece of aluminum foil that is folded once or twice. Putting hair into folded paper should be avoided, particularly regarding plucked hair, since the sticky hair roots will become fixed to the porous surface of the paper, and the strands will break at variable distances from the root. Hair that has been soaked with blood should first be washed with water and then dried before sampling. It is wise to make a note that such contamination has occurred if it turns out that the blood contains high levels of drugs.

2.3.7 Tissues

When collecting tissue, a minimum of 50 g should be collected. Each specimen collected should be put into its own properly labeled airtight container. If inhalants are suspected, it is important to collect and seal the specimen in a container as soon as possible after the body has been opened. Because of the possibility that portions of the liver can be contaminated by postmortem diffusion of drugs from the gastric contents, only liver from deep within the right lobe should be collected.[30] Additionally, bile should be collected prior to the liver specimen, to prevent specimen contamination.

2.3.8 Labeling

The first step in the specimen collection process (including evidence collection) is ensuring that the specimen containers are labeled appropriately. Without attention to this detail all other activities that occur with the specimen(s) are suspect. First, the collector must only be working with one specimen at a time. Second, specimens collected should *never* be placed into an unlabeled container. The collector must ensure that the container is labeled so that it can be read prior to the placement of the specimen into the container. As a minimum, the label should include the following information: (1) institutional case number identifier; (2) name or other identifier; (3) date and time of collection; (4) signature or initials of the collector; (5) specimen type (blood, liver, kidney, etc.) and where collected, when applicable (heart blood, femoral blood, etc.). Finally, tamper-resistant tape with the collector's initials and the collection date should be placed over the specimen lid and container to document specimen integrity. Alternatively, all of the samples collected for a given case may be placed in a tamper-evident container labeled with the case number and name. This protocol is particularly useful in institutions with larger caseloads where specimens may not immediately be transferred to the toxicology laboratory.

2.4 SELECTION OF POSTMORTEM SPECIMENS

The choice of specimens available in a postmortem forensic toxicology investigation can be numerous and variable. Specimens may be selected based on case history, institutional policy, and availability for a given case. Generally, the specimens routinely collected from cases in which an autopsy was performed include blood from both peripheral and cardiac sources, all urine and bile available, vitreous humor, all available gastric contents, and tissues (particularly liver).[2] However, because the autopsy allows a one-time opportunity to collect as many specimens as may be needed to complete the toxicological investigation, it is suggested that as many specimens be obtained as is feasible for the institution.

In cases where no autopsy is performed, only peripheral blood, urine, and vitreous humor are collected. Heart blood should be avoided due to the potential of contamination by esophageal contents when performing a blind stick.[31,32]

On some occasions a medical examiner or coroner's case may have had a significant survival time in the hospital prior to death. In cases where hospital survival time exceeds 24 to 48 h, the value of postmortem specimens diminishes considerably. This is especially true if there are allegations that a death may be drug related. Under these circumstances, hospital admission specimens (blood and urine) taken prior to significant therapeutic intervention can be invaluable in the documentation and support of this history. It is important that the postmortem toxicology laboratory physically obtain these specimens (under COC) for reanalysis, since the results available from the hospital are frequently unconfirmed screening results.

Decomposed, skeletonized, or embalmed cases present unique challenges for the forensic toxicologist. The possibilities for specimens in some of these cases are limited only by availability, analytical capabilities, and sometimes imagination, of the toxicology laboratory. Some of these unusual specimens are discussed later in this section.

2.4.1 Blood

Blood is the specimen of choice for detecting, quantifying, and interpreting drug concentrations in postmortem toxicology. Historically, most of the meaningful data derived from the literature was determined in blood.[33] Despite concerns about postmortem redistribution of drugs from tissues to blood, some aspects of interpretation remain straightforward. A negative result below a defined limit of detection for a given analyte can be readily interpreted as lack of acute exposure to that analyte or noncompliance in the case of therapeutic agents. Conversely, blood drug concentrations that exceed therapeutic (or, for some drugs, toxic) concentrations by 10 to 20 times are still consistent with intoxication or death (barring an obvious contamination problem). In addition, the higher the parent drug-to-metabolite ratio, the more likely acute intoxication is a factor. This is especially the case when multiple drug analytes are involved, and in cases involving ethanol.

Interpretation becomes especially difficult in cases where drug analytes known to undergo postmortem redistribution are determined to be present in a heart blood specimen at concentrations ranging between the upper therapeutic limit and the lower limit where intoxication or death has been reported. In these cases, analysis of a peripheral blood specimen may be critical in determining the role that the drug may have played in the decedent. Although drug concentrations in cardiac blood generally rise due to postmortem drug redistribution, and peripheral blood drug concentrations tend to remain constant, this is not always the case.[13,34,35] Thus, results from a single postmortem blood specimen, whether cardiac or peripheral, may be difficult if not impossible to interpret. Since cardiac blood is usually more plentiful than peripheral blood, many laboratories perform initial toxicological tests on cardiac blood, reserving the peripheral blood specimens for cases where additional context is needed for interpretation. Regardless of the blood samples available for analysis, it is important for the toxicologist to appreciate that the material collected as "blood" at autopsy is not the same specimen collected in an ante-mortem venipuncture and clinically based pharmacokinetic principles may not be applicable to postmortem cases.

Following injury or trauma to the head, blood clots from the brain cavity (subdural, subarachnoid, and/or epidural) should be collected in properly identified containers and saved for the laboratory. These materials are potential "time capsules," which are generally poorly perfused, and may reflect drug or alcohol concentrations closer to the time of injury. These specimens become more important as accurate knowledge of the post-injury survival time increases. Blood clots may also be useful for documenting preexisting drug use prior to hospital therapy. Most laboratories routinely analyze alcohol on these specimens, reserving analysis for additional drugs if indicated. Thoracic and abdominal cavity blood should be collected for analysis only if blood or uncontaminated blood clots cannot be obtained from any other area. These "blood" specimens tend to be contaminated by and contain large numbers of microbes. Additional contamination from gastric contents is also possible. Nevertheless, qualitative documentation of presence of given analytes is of importance and value in death investigations with respect to compliance and exposure issues.

2.4.2 Urine

Urine collected at autopsy has the greatest potential of any specimen to provide the toxicologist with qualitative ante-mortem drug-exposure information. The urine matrix is generally devoid of circulating serum proteins, lipids, and other related large-molecular-weight compounds due to the renal filtration process, simplifying preparation of the specimen for analysis. The accumulation of drugs and their metabolites in urine results in relatively high drug concentrations, facilitating detection of an exposure to a potential poison. Immunoassays and non-instrumental spot tests can be performed directly on the urine specimen for the analysis of certain drug classes. Detection times for drugs in urine can vary from 24 h to as long as a month, depending on the drug. Thus, except for acute drug deaths where survival time is less than an hour and drugs may not yet have been excreted into the urine, urine provides an ideal matrix for the detection for the widest variety of compounds.

Positive identification of drugs in the urine indicates past drug use, but does not indicate when or how much drug was ingested. To interpret the context of exposure, blood should be tested for the analytes found in the urine. In cases where death is suspected to have occurred rapidly due to drug ingestion, as might be suggested by the presence of a needle in the decedent's arm at the time of death, negative urine drug findings may be consistent if blood drug concentrations are very high.

2.4.3 Bile

Bile is another fluid that should be collected at autopsy as a matter of course since many drugs and drug metabolites have been demonstrated to accumulate in this specimen.[1,9,21,36,37] The qualitative finding of the presence of drug and/or metabolites in this specimen is important for documentation of historic exposures to specific agents and chronic drug-use history. In the absence of urine, bile has also been useful as an alternative specimen for alcohol analysis[38] and has been used in immunoassay screening after sample pretreatment[39] or without pretreatment using enzyme-linked immunosorbent immunoassays.[40] Historically, bile has most often been used in the determination of opiates in general and morphine in particular.[1,36,37] More recently, it has been noted that many drugs are found to accumulate at concentrations significantly higher then those in blood.[39] With an appropriate sample cleanup, bile is a useful specimen for the analysis of a wide variety of drugs and their metabolites, including benzodiazepines.

2.4.4 Vitreous Humor

Vitreous humor plays an important role in helping resolve many issues in a postmortem examination. Because of this, it should be collected in all cases when possible, including cases where no autopsy is performed. Vitreous humor, by virtue of its protected environment inside the eye, is less subject to contamination and bacterial decomposition. As a result it may be used to distinguish ante-mortem alcohol ingestion from postmortem alcohol formation and may provide the only opportunity to establish an ante-mortem ethanol concentration in embalmed bodies.[23,24,41–43] Additionally, because vitreous humor is contained in a peripheral compartment, there is a delay in both the uptake of drugs and alcohol into this fluid as well as a delay in the excretion process.

It has been observed that vitreous drug concentrations often reflect circulating blood concentrations 1 to 2 h prior to death and that any drug found in the blood will be detected in the corresponding vitreous specimen given analytical techniques of sufficient sensitivity.[9] Although these findings suggest that vitreous humor analysis following positive blood findings might be useful to aid in the interpretation of blood drug concentrations, more research needs to be performed. Studies comparing vitreous humor and blood ethanol concentrations yielded a wide variety of ratios of vitreous humor to blood ethanol.[42] If such diversity is seen for an analyte that demonstrates minimal postmortem redistribution effects, attempting to use vitreous humor drug concentrations to aid in interpreting heart blood drug concentrations may prove difficult.[11] Despite these concerns, vitreous humor is the best specimen from which to evaluate postmortem digoxin concentrations.[21] However, the analysis of femoral blood in addition to vitreous humor is still recommended to provide the best context for an appropriate interpretation of ante-mortem digoxin toxicity.[44]

Vitreous humor lacks the esterases that hydrolyze certain drugs and metabolites in blood and may be the specimen of choice to detect the metabolite of heroin, 6-acetylmorphine.[45–48] Because

6-acetylmorphine is quickly hydrolyzed *in vivo* and *in vitro* (especially without the presence of sodium fluoride) to morphine in blood, the analysis of vitreous humor may be helpful in establishing whether a death occurred after heroin use. Similarly, cerebrospinal fluid may also be useful.[48,49]

Vitreous humor has been shown to be particularly useful for the postmortem analysis of glucose, urea nitrogen, uric acid, creatinine, sodium, and chloride. Measuring these analytes is important for documenting diabetes, degree of hydration, electrolyte balance, and the state of renal function prior to death. A recent article has reviewed the extent and breadth of chemistry analyte analysis applied to vitreous fluid, among other postmortem specimens.[27]

2.4.5 Gastric Contents

Oral ingestion is still the major route of drug administration for prescribed drugs and therefore a major compartment for the investigation of a potential poisoning. Drug overdoses, whether by accident or by intent, may readily be discovered through the analysis of gastric contents. In many cases undissolved capsules or tablets may be discovered, which may be useful for identification. In addition, illicit drugs are frequently smuggled by ingestion of balloons or condoms filled with the contraband. If these devices burst and an acute drug death occurs, evidence of these items may be seen in the gastric contents at autopsy.[50]

A large quantity of the parent drug in the gastric content, relative to a prescription dose, is indicative of an oral drug overdose when supported by blood and/or tissue findings.[51] However, the toxicologist is cautioned that low concentrations of drug in the stomach, especially drug metabolites and weak bases, may represent passive diffusion and/or ion trapping from the blood back into the stomach contents and may not be indicative of a recent oral ingestion of these agents. It is important to make a record of the total volume of gastric contents present in the decedent in order to calculate the total amount of the analyte present in the stomach. Since the gastric content is not a homogeneous specimen, ideally the entire specimen should be submitted to the toxicology laboratory for mixing before aliquoting.

The odor of gastric contents can potentially point to a specific agent that might otherwise elude routine detection in the toxicology laboratory. Cyanide ingestions produce stomach contents with the odor of bitter or burned almonds. Although not everyone is able to discern this odor, its presence is almost certainly indicative of a cyanide intoxication, and may be potentially hazardous in close quarters. Other characteristic odors include the "fruity-like" odor of ethanol and its congeners; the odor of airplane glue (xylene, toluene); cleaning fluid (halogenated hydrocarbons); carrots (ethchlorvynol);[32] and garlic (organophosphate insecticides).[32]

2.4.6 Tissues

Tissues commonly collected for postmortem study include liver, kidney, brain, lung, and spleen. Tissues provide the best and most useful context with which to interpret blood findings. They may also be the only specimens available in decomposed cases. A large amount of data for drug findings in tissue exists, primarily for liver and kidney, and, to a lesser degree, brain and lung.[33] Comparison is most often between heart blood findings and those in the liver, the site where many drugs are metabolized and for which the greatest amount of reference data is available. For example, in cases where the concentration of basic drugs in blood is high and ratios of liver-to-blood drug concentration exceed 10, a drug fatality is strongly suggested if no other interceding cause of death is present. Smaller ratios, even with high heart blood concentrations, tend to suggest a greater potential for postmortem redistribution of drugs into the blood.

Analysis of tissue may be more appropriate than analysis of biological fluids for some analytes. In cases of heavy metal poisoning, kidney is a very useful specimen as heavy metals concentrate in it. In addition, structural damage to the kidney due to heavy metal or ethylene glycol exposure may be documented histologically. Spleen, an organ rich in blood, is useful for the analysis of compounds that bind to hemoglobin, such as carbon monoxide and cyanide. Frequently, in fire deaths where extensive charring is present, spleen may be the only useful specimen available to perform these assays. Lung tissue is particularly useful in cases where inhalation of volatile substances, such as solvents or Freon, is suspected. In addition, air may be collected directly from the trachea with a syringe and injected into a sealed vial to be used for headspace analysis.[52] Brain, due to its high fat content, tends to accumulate lipophilic substances, such as chlorinated hydrocarbons, and other organic volatiles. Additionally, there is evidence to suggest that ratios of brain to blood cocaine are high in cocaine fatalities; thus cocaine deaths may be more readily interpreted through the analysis of both matrices.[53] Finally, because the brain is in a protected environment, it also tends to be more resistant to postmortem decomposition.

The analysis of tissue is performed by weight. Usually, 1 to 5 g of tissue is shredded and homogenized with four parts of water (or saline) to generate a final dilution factor of 5. Recovery of drug from this homogenate has been found to be consistent with recovery of drug from postmortem blood.[54] Drilling through the tissue with a cork-borer allows tissue to be sampled and weighed while frozen.[55] This method is easier and more precise than sampling wet tissue and is less malodorous when handling decomposed specimens.

2.4.7 Hair

Hair has a long history as a useful specimen in forensic toxicology. Traditionally, hair, along with fingernails, was the specimen of choice in determining chronic heavy metal poisoning such as arsenic, mercury, and lead. Heavy metals bind to sulfhydryl groups on the cysteine molecule to form a covalent complex. Keratin, found in large amounts in hair and nails, is an excellent source of cysteine, and therefore an ideal specimen for determining chronic arsenic and mercury poisoning. Interpretation of positive findings can be augmented by segmentation of the hair strands to assist in determining the time of exposure.[56–58]

More recently, hair has been successfully used as a specimen from which chronic drug use may be determined.[59] Numerous drugs have been identified in hair including drugs of abuse[60,61] and, more recently, various therapeutic agents.[62,63] The usefulness of hair analysis in determining compliance remains controversial.[64] However, in postmortem toxicology, segmental analysis can offer a temporal mapping of the drug abuse pattern, and such information may prove useful to identify possible hazardous drug combinations and to detect periods of abstinence that might indicate reduced tolerance to particular groups of drugs. In extremely decomposed or skeletonized cases where no other specimens remain, positive findings for drugs in hair may at least corroborate a history of drug use. The use of hair in workplace drug testing is controversial due to issues such as environmental contamination,[65] washing techniques,[66] sex or ethnic bias,[67,68] the difficulty in performing quantitative analysis,[69] and establishing cutoff concentrations.[70] In the postmortem setting these issues are not critical, and drug analysis for both pharmaceutical and illicit drugs in hair will most likely become more frequently applied following a growing appreciation of the supplemental information that such analysis may add to the interpretation of the routine toxicological results.

2.4.8 Bone and Bone Marrow

Bone marrow has not received a great deal of consideration as an alternative specimen in postmortem toxicology. Because it is protected by bone, the highly vascularized tissue may be particularly useful when contamination of blood specimens is suspected in trauma cases. Research studies have been performed, primarily on rabbits, showing that linear relationships exist between bone marrow and peri-mortem blood drug concentrations for up to 24 h for many substances including tricyclic antidepressants, barbiturates, benzodiazepines, and ethyl alcohol.[71–74] However, these studies were performed when the bone marrow was still fresh and moist. Although putrefaction is delayed in bone marrow, usually bone marrow is not considered as an alternative specimen in postmortem toxicology unless other specimens are unavailable. Typically, at this stage of decomposition the bone marrow has transformed from spongy red marrow to a brown viscous liquid or paste-like substance, and it is unknown if any interpretation can be made from quantitative data.[75] However, drugs have even been identified in the bone marrow of skeletonized remains,[76,77] and heavy metals have been identified in the bone itself.[78]

2.4.9 Skeletal Muscle

Skeletal muscle is an often-overlooked specimen with many potential applications in postmortem forensic toxicology. It meets many of the criteria of an ideal forensic specimen: it is relatively homogeneous, almost always available, and not easily contaminated. Studies have shown that drug concentrations in thigh muscle reflect drug concentrations in blood for many common basic drugs and ethyl alcohol, except in cases of an acute drug death where muscle drug concentrations may be lower than blood due to inadequate time for tissue equilibration.[79] The analysis of thigh muscle may be especially useful in cases where drugs suspected of undergoing postmortem release are detected in the heart blood.[79] It is important that extremity muscle be collected, where possible, as drug concentrations in other muscles, such as abdominal muscle, increase with time while remaining constant in thigh muscle.[80,81]

Because skeletal muscle is often well preserved despite advanced decomposition of other tissue, it may be useful as an indicator of postmortem blood concentrations even in decomposed cases, although more studies need to be performed.[81,82] Surprisingly, even parent cocaine, which is known to be unstable in blood, has been identified in numerous cases of decomposed, dried skeletal muscle.[83]

The potentially useful data that may be obtained from the analysis of skeletal muscle have prompted some toxicologists to recommend that skeletal muscle be collected in all cases where drugs may be implicated in the cause of death.[81] One disadvantage to skeletal muscle is the need to homogenize the sample prior to analysis. However, this is true of many traditional specimens as well, such as liver and kidney. As more laboratories analyze skeletal muscle leading to the availability of additional data to aid in the interpretation of results, its potential advantages will outweigh any disadvantages.

2.4.10 Larvae

In cases of suspected poisoning where decomposition prevents traditional specimens from being obtained, homogenized fly larvae, usually of Calliphorid genus (blowfly), have proved to be useful alternative specimens in which drugs may be identified. Depending on temperature, larvae may be present as soon as 1 to 2 days after death. The first reported use of fly larvae in drug analysis occurred as recently as 1980 and involved a phenobarbital case.[84] Since then numerous drugs have been identified in fly larvae including barbiturates, benzodiazepines, and tricyclic antidepressants,[85] opiates,[86] cocaine,[87] and the organophosphate, malathion.[88]

The choice of where larvae are best collected from the body needs further study. Interpretation of positive findings seem to be most useful if the larvae are collected at the site of their food source, such as any remaining muscle or liver, under the premise that drugs detected in fly larvae feeding on a body can only have originated from the tissues of that body.[89] This assumption seems to be supported by one study where a quantitative relationship was suggested between the morphine concentrations in the larvae and the livers on which they fed.[90] By contrast, other studies suggest that the analysis of fly larvae provides only qualitative data.[85,86,91] However, in these studies larvae were collected from multiple sites and pooled before analysis. If larval drug concentrations are based on the tissue on which they fed,[89] these results are not surprising.

Studies using Calliphorid larvae have shown that the age of the larvae may also play a major role in determining whether drugs may be identified in them.[91,92] By collecting larvae over a period of up to 11 days in cases of known suicidal drug overdoses, it was demonstrated that drugs were readily detectable in larvae through the third instar stage, but a precipitous fall in drug concentration was associated with pupariation after their food ingestion ceases. Similarly, larvae that had been feeding on drug-laden muscle for 5 days demonstrated a significant loss in drug concentration within 1 day of being transferred to drug-free tissue. This suggests that Calliphorid larvae readily eliminate drugs when removed from a food source. Thus it appears to be critical that larvae collected for drug analysis from a decomposed body be frozen and analyzed as soon as possible after collection. Even under refrigerated conditions, when larvae are in a state of diapause, slow bio-elimination of drugs still occurs over the course of several weeks.[93] In addition, to eliminate surface contamination as a possible source of interpretive error, larvae should be washed with deionized water prior to analysis.

2.4.11 Meconium

Meconium, the first fecal matter passed by a neonate, has recently been given much attention because it is a useful specimen in which to determine fetal drug exposure. Issues relating to the screening and confirmation of most drugs of abuse in meconium have been reviewed.[94] While meconium analysis has principally been performed to assess *in utero* drug exposure in newborns so that treatment may begin as early after birth as possible, it may also be useful in determining drug exposure in stillborn infants. One study demonstrated the presence of cocaine in the meconium of a 17-week-old fetus, suggesting that fetal drug exposure can be determined early in gestation.[95]

Unlike urine, which allows the detection of fetal drug exposure for only 2 to 3 days before birth, meconium extends this window to about 20 weeks. Most postmortem toxicology laboratories are not currently performing meconium analysis. While potentially useful, there are several issues that must be considered. Because meconium forms layers in the intestine as it is being deposited, it is not a homogeneous specimen. As with other nonhomogeneous specimens, such as gastric contents, it is important that all available specimens be collected and thoroughly mixed before sampling. Consideration should also be given to the fact that infants do not metabolize some drugs the way adults do. If commercial immunoassay screening kits are used that target metabolites found in adult urine, the ability to detect some drugs in meconium may be compromised.[96]

2.4.12 Other Specimens

Many other specimens have been used in toxicological investigations. Any item with which a body or bodily fluid has been in contact is a potential candidate for the identification of drugs or poisons. Examples include tracheal air,[52] blood stains on clothing,[97] soil samples collected at the site of a skeleton or decomposed body,[98] and even cremation ash.[99] Even though positive findings in these specimens are qualitative, there is at least the potential that this information can be useful in determining the circumstances of a death.

2.5 NONBIOLOGICAL EVIDENCE

Evidence found at a scene may provide additional information to assist in the toxicological investigation. Drug paraphernalia (cocaine spoons, cookers, bhongs, syringes, poppers, whipped cream propellant canisters, butane lighters, etc.) is suggestive of a possible drug-related death, or at least a history of drug abuse. Prescription drugs at a scene may be useful for compiling a list of suspected drugs, attending physicians, and pharmacy phone numbers. However, this evidence may be misleading as drugs found at a scene are frequently old, may not have been taken for years due to patient compliance problems, or may be someone else's medication. Pain medication and tranquilizers, particularly important in drug deaths, are often prescribed to be taken on an as-needed basis, and thus subject to collecting in medicine cabinets. Counting the number of tablets or capsules in a prescription vial for consistency with the date of the prescription and dosage instructions may be useful, but has the potential for many variables including that of compliance. Additionally, empty medicine vials are not necessarily indicative of a drug overdose. Nevertheless, it is important that for a potential drug-related death, the role of the drugs found at the scene be ruled out by assaying for the agents of potential pharmacological significance.

Whether prescription vials are submitted to the toxicology laboratory is largely a matter of choice in a given jurisdiction. Since these items are evidence, it is often best that the police maintain them and provide a list to the laboratory. Unless the toxicology laboratory has specific experience in analyzing powders and syringes, or has jurisdiction over them, these items are best left for the crime laboratory to analyze, if needed.

In cases where poisoning is suspected, household products at the scene may provide key evidence for the toxicologist. Examples include aerosol containers in suspected inhalation deaths, rat and pest killers, insecticides and pesticides, caustics, windshield washer solvents, anti-freeze, Freon, etc. The garage, basement, or under-sink cabinets are common storage places for many of these items. Unlabeled containers holding solids or liquids, or more importantly, labeled containers that clearly hold a different product, may be the key to a poisoning case. These items, or an aliquot of them, should be provided to the toxicology laboratory, since they often contain analytes for which the toxicology laboratory does not test. The analysis of the product in question may provide mass spectral data and chromatographic information that can be correlated with findings in the biological matrix.

Suicide notes are often critical in determining whether drug intoxication is determined to be an accident or a suicide. However, the toxicologist is cautioned that if a suicide note identifies the suicidal agent or agents, toxicological analysis may reveal a different substance entirely.

REFERENCES

1. Moffat, A.C., Ed., *Clark's Isolation and Identification of Drugs in Pharmaceuticals, Body Fluids and Postmortem Material*, Pharmaceutical Press, London, 1986.
2. Levine, B.S., Smith, M.L., and Froede, R.C., Postmortem forensic toxicology, *Clin. Lab. Med.*, 10, 571–589, 1990.
3. Levine, B., Forensic toxicology, *Anal. Chem.*, 65, 272A–276A, 1993.
4. Adelson, L., *The Pathology of Homicide,* Charles C Thomas, Springfield, IL, 1974.
5. Stewart, C.P. and Stoleman, A., *Toxicology: Mechanisms and Analytical Methods,* Vol. I, Academic Press, New York, 1960.
6. Sunshine, I., Ed., *Methodology for Analytical Toxicology,* CRC Press, Cleveland, OH, 1975.
7. Spitz, W.U. and Fisher, R.S., *Medicolegal Investigation of Death,* 2nd ed., Charles C Thomas, Springfield, IL, 1980.
8. Klaassen, C.D., Amdur, M.O., and Doull, J., Eds., *Casarett and Doull's Toxicology: The Basic Science of Poisons,* 3rd ed., Macmillan, New York, 1986.
9. DiMaio, D.J. and DiMaio, V.J.M., *Forensic Pathology,* CRC Press, Boca Raton, FL, 1993.
10. Jones, G.R. and Pounder, D.J., Site dependence of drug concentrations in postmortem blood — a case study, *J. Anal. Toxicol.,* 11, 186–189, 1987.
11. Prouty, R.W. and Anderson, W.H., A comparison of postmortem heart blood and femoral blood ethyl alcohol concentrations, *J. Anal. Toxicol.,* 11, 191–197, 1987.
12. Prouty, R.W. and Anderson, W.H., The forensic science implications of site and temporal influences on postmortem blood-drug concentrations, *J. Forensic Sci.,* 35, 243–270, 1990.
13. Anderson, W.H. and Prouty, R.W., Postmortem redistribution of drugs, in *Advances in Analytical Toxicology,* Vol. II, Baselt, R.C., Ed., Year Book Medical Publishers, Boca Raton, FL, 1989, 71–102.
14. Levine, B., Wu, S.C., Dixon, A., and Smialek, J.E., Site dependence postmortem blood methadone concentrations, *Am. J. Forensic Med. Pathol.,* 16, 97–100, 1995.
15. Logan, B.K. and Smirnow, D., Postmortem distribution and redistribution of morphine in man, *J. Forensic Sci.,* 41, 37–46, 1996.

16. Pelissier-Alicot, A., Gaulier, J., Champsaur, P., and Marquet, P., Mechanisms underlying postmortem redistribution: a review, *J. Anal. Toxicol.*, 27, 533–544, 2003.
17. Hepler, B.R., Isenschmid, D.S., and Schmidt, C.J., Postmortem redistribution: practical considerations in death investigation, presented at the American Academy of Forensic Sciences, Abstract K-14, Dallas, TX, 2004.
18. Cechner, R.L., Hepler, B.R., and Sutheimer, C.A., Improving information management in a metropolitan coroner's office, part I: design and implementation of a cost effective minicomputer system with initial application for the toxicology laboratory, *J. Forensic Sci.*, 35, 375–390, 1990.
19. Cechner, R.L. Hepler, B.R., and Sutheimer, C.A., Expert systems in the forensic toxicology laboratory, *Diagn. Clin. Testing,* 27, 42–45, 1989.
20. Hepler, B.R., Monforte, J.R., and Cechner, R.L., Use of the Toxlab-pc® in alcohol and drug incidence in Wayne County, *Ther. Drug Monit. Clin. Toxicol. Newsl.,* 8, 2–4, 1993.
21. Hutchens, G.M., Ed., *An Introduction to Autopsy Technique,* College of American Pathologists, Northfield, IL, 1994.
22. McCurdy, W.C., Postmortem specimen collection, *Forensic Sci. Int.,* 35, 61–65, 1987.
23. Harper, D.R. and Couy, J.E.L., Collection and storage of specimens for alcohol analysis, in *Medicolegal Aspects of Alcohol Determination in Biological Samples,* Garriott, J.C., Ed., Year Book Medical Publishers, Boca Raton, FL, 1988, 145–169.
24. Caplan, Y.H., Blood, urine and other fluid and tissue specimens for alcohol analysis, in *Medicolegal Aspects of Alcohol Determination in Biological Samples,* Garriott, J.C., Ed., Year Book Medical Publishers, Boca Raton, FL, 1988, 74–86.
25. Isenschmid, D.S., Levine, B.S., and Caplan, Y.H., A comprehensive study of the stability of cocaine and its metabolites, *J. Anal. Toxicol.,* 13, 250–256, 1989.
26. Isenschmid, D.S. and Hepler, B.R., Unpublished data.
27. Coe, J.I., Postmortem chemistry update: emphasis on forensic application, *Am. J. Forensic Med. Pathol.,* 14, 91–117, 1993.
28. Pounder, D. and Davies, J., Zopiclone poisoning, letter to the editor, *J. Anal. Toxicol.,* 20, 273, 1996.
29. Harkey, M.R., Anatomy and physiology of hair, *Forensic Sci. Int.,* 63, 9–18, 1993.
30. Kronstrand, R., Nystrom, I., Strandberg, J., and Druid, H., Screening for drugs of abuse in hair with ion spray LC-MS-MS, *Forensic Sci. Int.,* 145,183–90, 2004.
31. Logan, B.K. and Lindholm, G., Gastric contamination of postmortem blood samples during blind stick sample collection, *Am. J.. Forensic Med. Pathol.,* 17, 109–111, 1996.
32. Monforte, J.R., Methodology and interpretation of toxicological procedures, in *Medicolegal Investigation of Death,* 2nd ed., Spitz, W.U. and Fisher, R.S., Eds., Charles C Thomas, Springfield, IL, 1980, 571–589.
33. Baselt, R. and Cravey, R., *Disposition of Drugs and Toxic Chemicals in Man,* 4th ed., Chemical Toxicology Institute, Foster City, CA, 1995.
34. Hearn, W.L., Keran, E.E., Wei, H., and Hime, G., Site-dependent postmortem changes in blood cocaine concentrations, *J. Forensic Sci.,* 36, 673–684, 1991.
35. Logan, B.K., Smirnow, D., and Gullberg, R.G., Time dependent changes and site dependent difference in postmortem concentration of cocaine, benzoylecgonine and cocaethylene, presented at the American Academy of Forensic Sciences, Abstract K-32, Nashville, TN, 1996.
36. Stajic, M., The general unknown, in *Introduction to Forensic Toxicology,* Cravey, R.C. and Baselt, R.C., Eds., Biomedical Publications, Davis, CA, 1981, 169–181.
37. Agarwal, A. and Lemoc, M., Significance of bile analysis in drug induced deaths, *J. Anal. Toxicol.,* 20, 61–62, 1996.
38. Baselt, R.C. and Danhof, I.E., Disposition of alcohol in man, in *Medicolegal Aspects of Alcohol Determination in Biological Samples,* Garriott, J.C., Ed., Year Book Medical Publishers, Boca Raton, FL, 1988, 55–73.
39. Hepler, B.R., Sutheimer, C.A., Sebrosky, G.F., and Sunshine, I., Combined enzyme immunoassay-LCEC method for the identification, confirmation and quantitation of opiates in biological fluids, *J. Anal. Toxicol.,* 8, 78, 1984.
40. Isenschmid, D.S., Patton, D.M., Hepler, B.R., and Schmidt, C.J., Use of the Immunalysis™ ELISA assays for the detection of drugs in postmortem specimens: a multiple matrix approach, presented at The International Association of Forensic Toxicologists, Poster Session 2, Paper 77, Melbourne, Australia, 2003.

41. O'Neal, C.L. and Poklis, A., Postmortem production of ethanol and factors that influence interpretation, *Am. J. Forensic Med. Pathol.,* 17, 8–20, 1996.
42. Caplan, Y.H. and Levine, B.S., Vitreous humor in the evaluation of postmortem blood ethanol concentrations, *J. Anal. Toxicol.,* 14, 305–307, 1990.
43. Scott, W., Root, I., and Sanborn, B., The use of vitreous humor for determination of ethyl alcohol in previously embalmed bodies, *J. Forensic Sci.,* 19, 913–196, 1974.
44. Vorpahl, T.E. and Coe, J.I., Correlation of antemortem and postmortem digoxin levels, *J. Forensic Sci.,* 23, 329–334, 1978.
45. Pragst, F., Spiegel, K., Leuschner, U., and Hager, A., Detection of 6-acetylmorphine in vitreous humor and cerebralspinal fluid — comparison with urinary analysis for proving heroin administration in opiate fatalities, *J. Anal. Toxicol.*, 23, 168–172, 1999.
46. Scott, K.S. and Oliver, J.S., Vitreous humor as an alternative sample to blood for the supercritical fluid extraction of morphine and 6-monoacetylmorphine, *Med. Sci. Law,* 39, 77–81, 1999.
47. Pearson, J.M. and Saady, J.J., Utility of vitreous humor in investigations of heroin-related deaths, *J. Anal. Toxicol.*, 27, 199, 2003.
48. Wyman, J. and Bultman, S., Post-mortem distribution of heroin metabolites in femoral blood, liver, cerebrospinal fluid, and vitreous humor, *J. Anal. Toxicol.*, 28, 260–263, 2004.
49. Jenkins, A.J. and Lavins, E.S., 6-Acetylmorphine detection in postmortem cerebrospinal fluid, *J. Anal. Toxicol.*, 22, 173–175, 1998.
50. Wetli, C.V. and Mittelman, R.E., The "body packer" syndrome — toxicity following ingestion of illicit drugs packaged for transportation, *J. Forensic Sci.,* 26, 492–500, 1981.
51. Freimuth, H.C., Guidelines for preservation of toxicological evidence, in *Medicolegal Investigation of Death,* 2nd ed., Spitz, W.U. and Fisher, R.S., Eds., Charles C Thomas, Springfield, IL, 1980, 556–564.
52. Isenschmid, D.S., Cassin, B.J., and Hepler, B.R., Acute tetrachloroethylene intoxication in an autoerotic fatality, presented at the American Academy of Forensic Sciences, Abstract K-20, Seattle, WA, 1995.
53. Karch, S.B., *The Pathology of Drug Abuse,* CRC Press, Boca Raton, FL, 1993, 42–43.
54. Hepler, B.R., Sutheimer, C.A., and Sunshine, I., Unpublished data.
55. Anderson, W.H. and Prouty, R.W., Personal communication.
56. Smith, H., Forshufvud, S., and Wassen, A., Distribution of arsenic in Napoleon's hair, *Nature,* 194, 725–726, 1962.
57. Grandjean, P., Lead poisoning: hair analysis shows the calendar of events, *Hum. Toxicol.*, 3, 223–228, 1984.
58. Poklis, A. and Saady, J.J., Arsenic poisoning: acute or chronic? *Am. J. Forensic Med. Pathol.,* 11, 236–232, 1990.
59. DuPont, R.L. and Baumgartner, W.A., Drug testing by urine and hair analysis: complementary features and scientific issues, *Forensic Sci. Int.,* 70, 63–76, 1995.
60. Baumgartner, W.A., Cheng, C., Donahue, T.D., Hayes, G.F., Hill, V.A., and Scholtz, H., Forensic drug testing by mass spectrometric analysis in hair, in *Forensic Applications of Mass Spectrometry,* Yinon, J., Ed., CRC Press, Boca Raton, FL, 1995, chap. 2.
61. Harkey, M.R. and Henderson, G.L., Hair analysis for drugs of abuse, in *Advances in Analytical Toxicology,* Vol. II, Baselt, R.C., Ed., Yearbook Medical Publishers, Chicago, 1989, chap. 10.
62. Couper, F.J., McIntyre, I.M., and Drummer, O.H., Detection of antidepressant and antipsychotic drugs in postmortem human scalp hair, *J. Forensic Sci.,* 40, 87–90, 1995.
63. Uematsu, T., Therapeutic drug monitoring in hair samples: principles and practice, *Clin. Pharmacokinetics*, 25, 83–87; 1993.
64. Tracqui, A., Kintz, P., and Mangin, P., Hair analysis: a worthless tool for therapeutic compliance monitoring, *Forensic Sci. Int.,* 70, 183–189, 1995.
65. Cone, E.J. and Wang, W.L., Testing human hair for drugs of abuse, IV, environmental cocaine contamination and washing effects, *Forensic Sci. Int.,* 70, 39–51, 1995.
66. Blank, D.L. and Kidwell, D.A., Decontamination procedures for drugs of abuse in hair: are they sufficient? *Forensic Sci. Int.,* 70, 13–38, 1995.
67. Joseph, R.E., Su, T., and Cone, E.J., Sex bias in hair testing for cocaine, presented at the American Academy of Forensic Sciences, Abstract K-10, Seattle, WA, 1995.

68. Joseph, R.E., Su, T., and Cone, E.J., Evaluation of *in vitro* binding of cocaine to lipids and melanin in hair, presented at the American Academy of Forensic Sciences, Abstract K-19, Nashville, TN, 1996.
69. Welch, M.J., Sniegoski, L.T., and Allgood, C.C., Interlaboratory comparison studies on the analysis of hair for drugs of abuse, *Forensic Sci. Int.,* 63, 295–303, 1993.
70. Kintz, P. and Mangin, P., What constitutes a positive result in hair analysis: proposal for the establishment of cut-off values, *Forensic Sci. Int.,* 70, 3–11, 1995.
71. Winek, C.L., Morris, E.M., and Wahba, W.W., The use of bone marrow in the study of postmortem redistribution of amitriptyline, *J. Anal. Toxicol.,* 17, 93, 1993.
72. Winek, C.L., Costantino, A.G., Wahba, W.W., and Collom, W.D., Blood versus bone marrow pentobarbital concentrations, *Forensic Sci. Int.,* 27, 15–24, 1985.
73. Winek, C.L. and Pluskota, M., Plasma versus bone marrow flurazepam concentrations in rabbits and humans, *Forensic Sci. Int.,* 19, 155–163, 1982.
74. Winek, C.L. and Esposito, F.M., Comparative study of ethanol levels in blood versus bone marrow, vitreous humor, bile and urine, *Forensic Sci. Int.,* 17, 27–36, 1981.
75. Winek, C.L., Matejczyk, R.J., and Buddie, E.G., Blood, bone marrow and eye fluid ethanol concentrations in putrefied rabbits, *Forensic Sci. Int.,* 22, 151–159, 1983.
76. Noguchi, T.T., Nakamura, G.R., and Griesemer, E.C., Drug analysis of skeletoninzing remains, *J. Forensic Sci.,* 23, 490–492, 1978.
77. Kojima, T., Okamoto, I., Miyazaki, T., Chikasue, F., Yashiki, M., and Nakamura, K., Detection of methamphetamine and amphetamine in a skeletonized body buried for 5 years, *Forensic Sci. Int.,* 31, 93–102, 1986.
78. Logemann, E., Krützfeldt, B., Kalkbrenner, G., and Schüle, W., Mercury in bones, presented at the Society of Forensic Toxicologists, Abstract 44, Tampa, FL, 1994.
79. Garriott, J.C., Skeletal muscle as an alternative specimen for alcohol and drug analysis, *J. Forensic Sci.,* 36, 60, 1991.
80. Kudo K., Nagata, T., Kimura, K., Imamura, T., and Urakawa, N., Postmortem changes of triazolam concentrations in body tissues, *Nippon Hoigaku Zasshi,* 46, 293, 1992.
81. Christensen, H., Steentoft, A., and Worm, K., Muscle as an autopsy material for evaluation of fatal cases of drug overdose, *J. Forensic Sci. Soc.,* 25, 191–206, 1985.
82. Garriot, J.C., Interpretive toxicology: drug abuse and drug abuse deaths, in *Forensic Pathology,* DiMaio, D.J. and DiMaio, V.J.M., Eds., CRC Press, Boca Raton, FL, 1993, chap. 21.
83. Manhoff, D.T., Hood, I., Caputo, F., Perry, J., Rosen, S., and Mirchandani, H.G., Cocaine in decomposed human remains, *J. Forensic Sci.,* 36, 1732, 1991.
84. Beyer, J.C., Enos, W.F., and Stajic, M., Drug identification through analysis of maggots, *J. Forensic Sci.,* 25, 411–413, 1980.
85. Kintz, P., Godelar, B., Tracqui, A., Mangin, P., Lugnier, A.A., and Chaumont, A.J., Fly larvae: a new toxicological method of investigation in forensic medicine, *J. Forensic Sci.,* 35, 204–207, 1990.
86. Kintz, P., Traqui, A., and Mangin, P., Analysis of opiates in fly larvae sampled on a putrefied cadaver, *J. Forensic Sci. Soc.,* 34, 95–97, 1994.
87. Nolte, K.B., Pinder, R.D., and Lord, W.D., Insect larvae used to detect cocaine poisoning in a decomposed body, *J. Forensic Sci.,* 37, 1179–1185, 1992.
88. Gunatilake, K. and Goff, L., Detection of organophosphate poisoning in a putrefying body analyzing arthropod larvae, *J. Forensic Sci.,* 34, 714–716, 1989.
89. Pounder, D.J., Forensic entomotoxicology, *J. Forensic Sci. Soc.,* 31, 469–472, 1991.
90. Introna, F., Lo Dico, C., Caplan, Y.H., and Smialek, J.E., Opiate analysis in cadaveric blowfly larvae as an indicator of narcotic intoxication, *J. Forensic Sci.,* 35, 118–122, 1990.
91. Kintz, P., Traqui, P., Ludes, B., Waller, J., Boukhabza, A., Mangin, P., Lugnier, A.A., and Chaumont, A.J., Fly larvae and their relevance in forensic toxicology, *Am. J. Forensic Med. Pathol.,* 11, 63–65, 1990.
92. Wilson, Z., Hubbard, S., and Pounder, D.J., Drug analysis in fly larvae, *Am. J. Forensic Med. Pathol.,* 14, 118–120, 1993.
93. Sadler, D.W., Fuke, C., Court, F., and Pounder, D.J., Drug accumulation and elimination in *Calliphora vicina* larvae, *Forensic Sci. Int.,* 71, 191–197, 1995.
94. Moore, C. and Negrusz, A., Drugs of abuse in meconium, *Forensic Sci. Rev.,* 7, 103–118, 1995.

95. Ostrea, E.M., Romero, A., Knapp, D.K., Ostrea, A.R., Lucena, J.E., and Utarnachitt, R.B., Postmortem drug analysis of meconium in early-gestation human fetuses exposed to cocaine, *J. Pediatr.,* 124, 477, 1994.
96. Steele, B.W., Bandstra, E.S., Wu, N.C., Hime, G.W., and Hearn, W.L., *m*-Hydroxy-benzoylecgonine: an important contributor to the immunoreactivity in assays for benzoylecgonine in meconium, *J. Anal. Toxicol.,* 17, 348–351, 1993.
97. Tracqui, A., Kintz, P., Ludes, B., Jamey, C., and Mangin, P., The detection of opiate drugs in nontraditional specimens (clothing): a report of ten cases, *J. Forensic Sci.,* 40, 263–265, 1995.
98. Monforte, J.R., Personal communication.
99. Barchet, R., Harzer, K., Helmers, E., and Wippler, K., Arsenic content in cremation ash after lethal arsenic poisoning, in *Proceedings of the 1994 Joint TIAFT/SOFT International Meeting*, Spiehler, V., Ed., Newport Beach, CA, 1995, 315–319.

CHAPTER 3

Common Methods in Postmortem Toxicology

W. Lee Hearn, Ph.D.[1] **and H. Chip Walls, B.S.**[2]
[1] Director, Dade County Medical Examiner Toxicology Laboratory, Miami, Florida
[2] Department of Pathology, Forensic Toxicology Laboratory, University of Miami, Miami, Florida

CONTENTS

3.1 Analytical Chemistry in Postmortem Toxicology 32
3.2 Simple Chemical Tests 33
3.2.1 Useful Color Tests 34
3.2.1.1 Trinder's Reagent 34
3.2.1.2 Fujiwara Test for Trichloro Compounds 34
3.2.1.3 Diphenylamine Test for Oxidizing Agents 34
3.2.1.4 Ethchlorvynol (Placidyl) Test 34
3.2.2 Other Color Tests That May Be Included in a Screen 34
3.3 Reinsch Test for Heavy Metals 34
3.4 Microdiffusion Tests 35
3.4.1 Cyanide Test 35
3.4.2 Carbon Monoxide 35
3.5 Other Simple Tests 35
3.5.1 Glucose, Ketones, Protein, and pH via a Diagnostic Reagent Strip (Dip-Stick) 35
3.5.2 Odor, Color, and pH of Gastric Contents 35
3.6 Immunoassays 35
3.6.1 Enzyme Immunoassay 37
3.6.1.1 General 37
3.6.1.2 CEDIA 37
3.6.1.3 ELISA 37
3.6.2 Fluoresence Polarization Immunoassay 37
3.6.3 Radioimmunoassay 38
3.6.4 Kinetic Interaction of Microparticles in Solution 38
3.6.5 Useful Immunoassays for Postmortem Toxicology Screening 38
3.6.5.1 Amphetamines (Class) 38
3.6.5.2 Barbiturates (Class) 38
3.6.5.3 Benzodiazepines (Class) 38
3.6.5.4 Benzoylecgonine 39

3.6.5.5 Opiates (Class) 39
3.6.5.6 Phencyclidine....... 39
3.6.5.7 Propoxyphene 39
3.6.5.8 Cannabinoids 39
3.6.5.9 Cyclic Antidepressants (Class)....... 39
3.7 Chromatography 39
3.7.1 Thin-Layer Chromatography 40
3.7.1.1 Toxi-Lab® TLC....... 40
3.7.2 Gas Chromatography 41
3.7.2.1 Flame Ionization Detector....... 42
3.7.2.2 Nitrogen/Phosphorus Detector 42
3.7.2.3 Electron Capture Detector....... 42
3.7.3 Gas Chromatography/Mass Spectrometry 42
3.7.4 High-Performance Liquid Chromatography 44
3.7.4.1 Ultraviolet Absorption Detectors 44
3.7.4.2 Diode Array Detectors 44
3.7.4.3 Fluorescence Detectors 44
3.7.4.4 Advantages and Disadvantages of HPLC....... 44
3.7.4.5 REMEDi HS™HPLC....... 45
3.8 Ultraviolet-Visible Spectrophotometry 45
3.9 Spectroscopic Methods for Analysis of Toxic Metals and Metaloids....... 46
3.10 Sample Preparation 46
3.10.1 Extraction Methods....... 46
3.10.1.1 Liquid–Liquid Extraction....... 46
3.10.1.2 Solid Phase Extraction 47
3.10.1.3 pH Adjustment for Extraction....... 48
3.10.2 Hydrolysis to Release Drugs in Sample Pretreatment....... 48
3.10.3 Applications 49
References 49

3.1 ANALYTICAL CHEMISTRY IN POSTMORTEM TOXICOLOGY

Analytical toxicology is an applied science.[1–4] Toxicologists must be familiar not only with the effects and toxic mechanisms involved in poisoning, but also with the metabolism of drugs, the chemical properties of parent drugs and their metabolites, and the composition of biological samples. The detection and measurement of toxicologically relevant concentrations of potent new drugs require the use of analytical techniques on the forefront of instrumental technology.[5–9]

Immunoassay technology, now a mainstay of drug screening protocols, first became commercially available only about 25 years ago.[10–14] At that time, classical thin-layer chromatography (TLC),[15–23] packed column gas chromatography,[24,25] strip chart recorders, and ultraviolet-visible spectrophotometry were the state of the art in toxicology laboratories.[26–29] Over the intervening years, capillary column gas chromatography,[30–44] solid-phase extraction technology,[46–53] nitrogen-phosphorus gas chromatography detectors,[42,43,54,55] high-performance liquid chromatography (HPLC),[56–74] ion trap mass spectrometry,[75–79] and computerized mass spectrometry have become essential to the practice of postmortem toxicology.[80,99]

New technology is continually being introduced. Mass spectrometry is evolving to tandem mass spectrometry, and is being interfaced to liquid chromatographs.[92,100–106] Chemical ionization, in both positive and negative ion modes, is increasingly used in the mass spectral analysis of drugs and poisons.[107–119] Robotic technology is used to increase efficiency of sample processing while maintaining and documenting sample integrity.[120–123] At the same time, the proliferation of ever more

Table 3.1 Comparison of Frequently Used Methods for Analysis of Biosamples

Method	Specificity	Sensitivity	Multiple Drugs	Identification: Structural Analysis (Qualitative)	Quantitative Analysis	Labor	Expertise
Color tests	+	+	Yes	+	Some	+	+
UV-VIS	+	+	No	++++	Yes	++	++
IA	++	++	Some	No	Some	+	+
GC	++	++	Yes	++	Yes	++	++
TLC	++	+	Yes	++	No	+++	+++
HPLC	++	++	Yes	++	Yes	++	++
GC/MS	++++	++++	Yes	++++	Yes	+++	++++
AAS	+++	+++	No	++	++++	+++	++++
ICP-MS	++++	++++	Yes	++++	++++	++++	++++

Key: Low = +; High = ++++; UV-VIS = ultraviolet-visible spectrophotometry; IA = immunoassay; GC = gas chromatography; TLC = thin-layer chromatography; HPLC = high performance liquid chromatography; GC/MS = gas chromatography mass spectrometry; AAS = atomic absorption spectrometry; ICP-MS = inductively coupled plasma mass spectrometry.

From Dolgin, J., Human clinical toxicology, in *CRC Handbook of Toxicology,* Derelanko, M.J. and Hollinger, M.A., Eds., CRC Press, Boca Raton, FL, 1995, 697.

powerful microcomputers, and sophisticated software applications, has vastly improved the processing and archiving of analytical data, control of instruments, laboratory management, and quality assurance monitoring.

While newer technologies have replaced many of the older, less sensitive, and less specific testing methods, some of the older tests, such as the microchemical tests, still have a place in the modern toxicology laboratory. But change is occurring so rapidly that today's technology may soon be obsolete. The best and most current guides to the innovations in testing methodologies are to be found in the scientific journals such as the *Journal of Forensic Science* and the *Journal of Analytical Toxicology*; the annual meetings of professional organizations such as the Society of Forensic Toxicologists and the American Academy of Forensic Sciences; and the annual meeting of the Pittsburgh Conference on Analytical Chemistry and Applied Spectroscopy. Table 3.1 compares the analytical techniques with respect to specificity, sensitivity, labor, cost, and applicability.

3.2 SIMPLE CHEMICAL TESTS

Chemical tests were once the mainstay of postmortem toxicology.[21,124–127] Today, many have been abandoned and replaced by automated broad range screening procedures. However, some are still useful as supplemental tests to rapidly and easily detect drugs and poisons that are not detected by the other screening tests.

Virtually all clinical and forensic toxicology laboratories utilize micro-color tests to indicate the possible presence of drugs or toxins — the so-called spot tests.[21,125,127–133] Micro-color tests are performed by adding a single or multiple reagents to a specimen or extract and observing the color produced. Color tests are specific examples of the more general method of qualitative organic chemistry, relying on functional group reactions with the reagents. These tests require some expertise and familiarity to use, but are inexpensive and relatively rapid. They are nonspecific. However, in conjunction with other confirmatory tests, they can be used as rapid diagnostic aids.

Color tests can be combined with visible or spectrophotometric methodologies for qualitative to semiquantitative answers. Drugs including phenothiazines, salicylates, acetaminophen, carbamates, ethchlorvynol, and imipramine may be detected by colorimetric methods. Positive test results are confirmed and quantified by another technique. The greatest advantage of color tests is their ease of use. They can be performed directly on urine or a protein-free filtrate of blood or tissues. A negative color test precludes the need for any further work on that drug, assuming the detection limit of the test is acceptable. For example, the color test for phenothiazines is useful if an overdose has occurred, but is not sensitive enough to test for patient compliance with the drug.

3.2.1 Useful Color Tests

Some or all of the following tests may be incorporated in a routine screening protocol or some may be reserved for cases requiring more comprehensive poison screening.

3.2.1.1 Trinder's Reagent

Trinder's test is a simple color test that detects salicylic acid in urine or serum. It does not detect acetylsalicylic acid in gastric contents without prior hydrolysis by boiling with dilute HCl. Trinder's reagent is a mixture of ferric nitrate and mercuric chloride in dilute hydrochloric acid. It immediately produces a violet color when mixed with an equal volume of sample containing salicylate. Phenothiazines also give a positive reaction.[125,126,129,133,134]

3.2.1.2 Fujiwara Test for Trichloro Compounds

A mixture of 1 mL 20% sodium hydroxide and 1 mL of pyridine at 100°C yields a red or pink color with chloral hydrate or other compounds with at least two halogens bound to one carbon.[124–126,131,135] Trichloroethanol gives a yellow color. Contamination of the laboratory atmosphere with chlorinated solvents will give "false" positive results. Metabolites of carbon tetrachloride may also give a positive result with this test, but carbon tetrachloride is only partially metabolized to trichloromethyl compounds and the test may fail to detect this agent. A blank sample and a control (trichloroacetic acid) should be tested at the same time, with both blank and control solutions treated in similar fashion to the sample.

3.2.1.3 Diphenylamine Test for Oxidizing Agents

A solution of 0.5% diphenylamine in 60% sulfuric acid added to the sample or sample filtrate in a porcelain spot plate or a test tube immediately gives an intense blue color if an oxidizing agent is present. This test detects hypochlorite, chlorate, bromate, iodate, chromate, dichromate, nitrate, nitrite, permanganate, vanadate, lead (IV), or manganese (III, IV, or VII).[125,126]

3.2.1.4 Ethchlorvynol (Placidyl) Test

In this test 1 mL of sample (urine or sample filtrate) is mixed with the reagent and allowed to stand for 20 min. If ethclorvynol is present, the solution turns red or pink. The reagent consists of 1 g diphenylamine dissolved in 50 mL concentrated sulfuric acid and added slowly with stirring to 100 mL of 50% (V/V) acetic acid. The test is sufficiently sensitive to detect therapeutic concentrations.[125,126,136]

3.2.2 Other Color Tests That May Be Included in a Screen

Other color tests that may be included in a screen can be found in various toxicology references.[124–128]

3.3 REINSCH TEST FOR HEAVY METALS

A spiral of copper wire is first cleaned with 35% nitric acid and washed. It is then immersed in 15 mL of sample, acidified with concentrated HCl (4 mL), heated for 1 h, and then examined. A silver colored deposit on the copper indicates mercury, while a dark colored or black deposit is produced by arsenic, antimony, bismuth, tellurium, selenium, and sulfur. Further differentiation can be made on the basis of color of the deposit, and its solubility characteristics in potassium cyanide solution.[128,137–141]

3.4 MICRODIFFUSION TESTS

3.4.1 Cyanide Test

In this test 2 mL of sample are placed in a screw cap culture tube. Disks are punched from a strip of Cyantesmo paper, available from Gallard-Schlessinger Chemical Mfg. Co. (Carle Place, New York), and one disk is stuck to the adhesive in the center of a 1-cm square of cellophane tape. The sample is acidified with H_2SO_4, the tape is placed over the mouth of the tube, with the adhesive and disk side down, and the tube is tightly capped. After 4 h at 35°C, the caps are removed and the color of the disk is compared with cyanide standards treated the same way. A pale green or yellow color is a negative result. Cyanide turns the disk blue in proportion to the concentration in the sample. Comparison of the color with standards from 0.2 to 5.0 mg/L cyanide can be used to estimate the concentration.

3.4.2 Carbon Monoxide

A simple test for carbon monoxide utilizes a procedure similar to the cyanide test described above, but using a disk of filter paper saturated with palladium chloride solution (1%) in 0.12 *N* HCl and dried. Carbon monoxide is released from hemoglobin by the addition of a solution containing lactic acid and potassium ferricyanide. Lead acetate is added to trap sulfide, which might interfere with the test. If carbon monoxide is present, the disk turns gray to black. While this test is simple, a faster and more effective method is to analyze the blood with a CO-Oximeter (Instrumentation Laboratories), which gives a result in % saturation of hemoglobin.

3.5 OTHER SIMPLE TESTS

3.5.1 Glucose, Ketones, Protein, and pH via a Diagnostic Reagent Strip (Dip-Stick)

Dip a strip briefly into the urine and read after 10 to 60 s. Elevated glucose may indicate diabetes. A positive result for ketones may indicate intoxication by acetone or isopropyl alcohol. This test may also be positive in starvation or in diabetic ketosis.

3.5.2 Odor, Color, and pH of Gastric Contents

Characteristic smells may indicate the presence of substances such as camphor, cresol, cyanide, ethanol and other organic solvents, ethchlorvynol, methyl salicylate, and paraldehyde. A high pH may indicate ingestion of alkali. A green or blue color suggests the presence of iron salts. Other colors may result from dissolution of colored pills or capsules. Intact tablets or capsules should be retrieved and examined separately.

3.6 IMMUNOASSAYS

Immunoassays for postmortem toxicology are sold commercially as kits. Often, they are exactly the same products as those used for urine drug screening in forensic urine drug testing programs.[142]

Such products are standardized and validated by the manufacturer, and are approved by the U.S. Food and Drug Administration (FDA). They are intended and approved for the analysis of particular specimen types, such as urine or serum. When urine cannot be obtained, other tissue may be used. A number of publications have described effective techniques for precipitating/extracting drugs from blood or tissue homogenates. Generally, the technique involves use of a solvent, such as acetone or acetonitrile, followed by evaporation of the solvent/water mixture and reconstitution in a suitable reagent for assay, according to the procedure for urine. However, application to specimens other than urine requires validation[143–156]

Immunoassays are based upon the principle that antibodies can be produced that recognize and bind to specific chemicals by interacting with unique structural features of their molecules. The interaction is analogous to that of a lock and key. Some antibodies are so selective that they bind to only one substance, such as methamphetamine. Others interact with a variety of compounds with similar structures, such as amphetamine, methamphetamine, phentermine, ephedrine, pseudoephedrine, and others, though not with structurally dissimilar compounds such as morphine. For postmortem screening, assays utilizing antibodies with broad selectivity for drugs within a particular class, such as sympathomimetic amines, are preferred over those with antibodies sensitive to one specific drug such as methamphetamine. Thus, a negative class selective assay can exclude all drugs with which it interacts, albeit with differing sensitivity for individual drugs. Conversely, a positive result requires further testing to distinguish among the possibilities. With few exceptions, all cross-reacting substances are of potential interest to the postmortem toxicology laboratory.

Immunoassays used for drug screening utilize a competitive interaction between the drug in the specimen and a labeled drug in the reagent, for sites on an antibody specific to the drug being tested. The drug is detected by its ability to displace or block binding of a fixed amount of chemically labeled drug molecules that are included in the reagent. The label can be an enzyme, a fluorescent molecule, a radioactive isotope, or some other substance that can be detected by instrumental means. The object of the assay is to measure either the amount of antibody-bound or the amount of free labeled drug, which is related to the concentration of the targeted drug in the sample.

Some assays can distinguish between bound and free labeled drug in a mixture and are referred to as homogeneous immunoassays. Others require physical separation of bound and free label prior to making the measurement. These are called heterogeneous immunoassays. In general, homogeneous immunoassays are more readily automated and, thus, less labor intensive than heterogeneous immunoassays.

Various types of immunoassays use different detection principles, such as enzyme immunoassay (EIA), fluorescence polarization immunoassay (FPIA), radioimmunoassay (RIA), kinetic interaction of microparticulates in solution (KIMS), and enzyme-linked immunosorbent assay (ELISA). Each type has advantages and disadvantages in terms of cost, throughput, and time for analysis in postmortem drug screening. The detection limit for various members of a class of drugs (e.g., opiates) or the degree of cross-reactivity for similar drugs (e.g., sympathomimetic amines) varies. Each manufacturer of immunoassay reagents should be consulted for specific information regarding detection limits for various drugs within a class.

These assays are easy to perform, the results are "semiquantitative" (higher or lower than a predetermined calibrator cutoff concentration) rather than subjective (e.g., TLC), and they generally have low detection limits (0.02 to 1.0 μg/mL). Several non-isotopic immunoassays (e.g., EMIT™, CEDIA®, and FPIA) have been automated for postmortem drug screening. Immunoassays complement chromatographic procedures (TLC and gas chromatography, GC) because they detect those drugs that would require hydrolysis prior to chromatography (e.g., morphine-3-glucuronide and oxazepam glucuronide), that may require a separate extraction (e.g., benzoylecgonine) or derivatization, or that have high TLC detection limits (e.g., phencyclidine). For abused drugs, immunoassays are the methods of choice for initial screening.

3.6.1 Enzyme Immunoassay

3.6.1.1 General

EIA reagents are available from several manufacturers. Spectrophotometric readings are used to measure the quantity of product produced by an enzyme-catalyzed reaction. The homogeneous EIAs are readily adaptable to automated clinical analyzers for rapid throughput of sample batches with minimal labor. Most are designed for screening urine samples, but they can be adapted for screening unhemolyzed serum or plasma. However, results depend on transmission of light through the reaction mixture, so these assays cannot be applied to turbid, highly colored, or opaque specimens, without first doing labor-intensive pre-extraction steps. The homogeneous EIA reagents are the most economical immunoassays for analysis of urine and stomach contents, although the extra labor required for their application to whole blood and other tissues may offset the reagent savings for those applications.[10–14,142,157–166]

3.6.1.2 CEDIA

CEDIA assays represent state-of-the-art technique, utilizing two genetically engineered enzymatically inactive fragments of beta-galactosidase as the basis for a homogeneous enzyme immunoassay.[167–173] Two separate genes are engineered to express two separate inactive polypeptide fragments: enzyme-donor (ED) and enzyme-acceptor (EA). These fragments can spontaneously recombine to form active beta-galactosidase enzyme. Ligands can be attached to the ED peptide in such a way that the degree of recombination is controlled by the binding of anti-ligand antibodies to the ED–ligand conjugate. CEDIA methodology is based on the competition between ligand in the sample and ED–ligand conjugate for a limited amount of antibody binding sites. The advantages of the CEDIA immunoassay system over conventional homogeneous EIAs include a linear calibration curve with high precision over the entire assay range, and lower limits of detection of analytes in human body fluids. Assay procedures can easily be automated and can be performed on most automated clinical chemistry analyzers.

3.6.1.3 ELISA

ELISA assays are heterogeneous enzyme immunoassays conducted in special multiwell (typically 96 wells) assay plates.[174–179] They are more labor intensive than the homogeneous EIAs if assayed manually, although robotic equipment is available to process plates in a semiautomated manner. They require specialized plate readers to measure the reaction products. Costs are somewhat higher than homogeneous EIA reagents; however, ELISA assays are manufactured for some drugs for which no other immunoassay is commercially available (e.g., haloperidol, methylphenidate, phenylbutazone, furosemide, phenothiazine, reserpine, and others). ELISA has the great advantage that it can be used with whole blood, typically diluted with water or buffer, and with proper validation even tissue homogenates.

3.6.2 Fluoresence Polarization Immunoassay

FPIA reagents were developed by Abbott Laboratories, and some are also available from Sigma Chemical Company.[99,149,161–164,166,180–194] They are homogeneous immunoassays that can be used only in specialized instruments that are capable of exciting the fluorescein label with polarized ultraviolet light, and then measuring the intensity of polarized fluorescent emissions. Because the sample is highly dilute in the reaction mixture and the instrument measures emitted, rather than transmitted, light, FPIA is less subject to interference by color or turbidity of the sample matrix than are EIAs.

Most hemolyzed or whole blood samples, as well as serum, plasma, and urine, can be analyzed directly without extraction. If the sample is too dark to be analyzed without pretreatment, it can usually be analyzed after diluting with buffer, although with less sensitivity. In addition to their application to drug screening, some of the FPIA assays can yield quantitative measurements because of the high specificity of their antibodies. The major drawbacks of FPIAs are the high price of reagents and the limited sample capacity of the instruments. The latter problem is being addressed with the introduction of a new high-capacity instrument (Abbott AxSYM™).

3.6.3 Radioimmunoassay

RIA reagents are available from several manufacturers. They are heterogeneous immunoassays and, as such, are not readily automated. However, some RIAs have the antibody bound to the inside of the assay tube, which simplifies the separation and wash procedures. Most RIA reagents that are used in toxicology have ^{125}I as the label, and require a gamma counter to measure either bound or unbound label. Reagents are available for many drugs and drug classes, cost is reasonable, and sensitivity is excellent. The major drawbacks of RIA relate to the use of radioactive materials, i.e., the need for radioactive materials licensure and radioactive waste disposal, and the relatively short shelf life of the reagents.[79,145,150–152,161,162,165,174,182,195–202]

3.6.4 Kinetic Interaction of Microparticles in Solution

KIMS (OnLine) reagents are available only from Roche Diagnostics. They are homogeneous assays with microscopic particles as the label. In the absence of drug, the labeled drug is bound by antibody, forming light-scattering aggregates. The intensity of light transmitted through the sample is measured spectrophotometrically in an automated clinical analyzer. Light transmission increases with concentration of unlabeled drug in the sample. Reagents are stable and sensitivity is good, although price remains somewhat higher than the EIA reagents.[161,165,166,203–205]

3.6.5 Useful Immunoassays for Postmortem Toxicology Screening

3.6.5.1 Amphetamines (Class)

Polyclonal immunoassays for sympathomimetic amines including amphetamine, methamphetamine, phenylpropanolamine, ephedrine, pseudoephedrine, methylenedioxymethamphetamine (MDMA), phentermine, and related compounds are preferred over monoclonal assays for postmortem toxicology. Approximate detection times are 12 h to 3 days. Administrative detection cutoffs are 300 to 1000 ng/mL in urine based on amphetamines or methamphetamine. They may be less sensitive for other drugs within the class.[13,144,167,187,194,203,206–217]

3.6.5.2 Barbiturates (Class)

Most assays detect pentobarbital, secobarbital, amobarbital, butalbital, phenobarbital, thiopental, and related compounds. Normal detection times are 6 h to 2 days after administration. Detection cutoffs are 300 to 8000 ng/mL in urine depending on cross-reactivity.[145,196,218–221]

3.6.5.3 Benzodiazepines (Class)

Most benzodiazepine immunoassays use antibodies directed to oxazepam. Their cross-reactivity for other benzodiazepines varies considerably, but most detect diazepam, oxazepam, flurazepam metabolites, chlordiazepoxide metabolites, alprazolam, triazolam, and related compounds. Lorazepam, flunitrazepam metabolites, and some others may not be detected by some immunoassays. Normal detection times are 3 h to 2 weeks. Administrative detection cutoffs are 300 to 3000 ng/mL in urine.[144,146,173,176,181,188,191,192,222–234]

3.6.5.4 Benzoylecgonine

The cocaine metabolite assays are designed to detect benzoylecgonine, the principal urinary metabolite of cocaine. Cocaine and ecgonine methyl ester may also be detected if present in sufficient concentrations. Normal detection times are 6 h to 5 days. Administrative detection cutoffs are 300 ng/mL in urine.[149,178,179,235–250]

3.6.5.5 Opiates (Class)

These assays detect a variety of opiates including morphine, morphine-glucuronide, hydromorphone, codeine, hydrocodone, and heroin metabolites. High concentrations of meperidine and oxycodone may give positive test results. Normal detection times are 6 h to 3 days. Administrative detection cutoffs are 300 to 3000 ng/mL in urine.[12,144,154–156,160,165,167,173,202,204,215,245,251–257]

3.6.5.6 Phencyclidine

The phencyclidine (PCP) assays detect only PCP metabolites. Normal detection times are 24 h. Administrative detection cutoffs are 25 ng/mL in urine.[156,173,221–265]

3.6.5.7 Propoxyphene

The propoxyphene assays detect the parent drug and the metabolite norpropoxyphene. In abuse situations, methadone (a close structural similarity) and chlorpromazine can produce a false positive. Normal detection time is 24 h. The administrative detection cutoff is 300 ng/mL in urine.[156,226]

3.6.5.8 Cannabinoids

The cannabinoid assays interact with at least ten of the non-active metabolites of tetrahydrocannabinol (THC). Normal detection times range from hours to weeks, depending on the frequency, potency, dose, and route of administration. Administrative detection cutoffs for the principal urinary metabolites are 20 to 100 ng/mL in urine, depending on the assay.[61,79,148,155,160,161,165,167,205,267–277]

3.6.5.9 Cyclic Antidepressants (Class)

The immunoassay for tricyclic antidepressants detects amitriptyline, nortriptyline, imipramine, desipramine, and their hydroxy metabolites, clomipramine, doxepin, protriptyline, cyclobenzaprine, and certain phenothiazines. Administrative detection cutoffs are 300 to 2000 ng/mL in urine.[278–283]

3.7 CHROMATOGRAPHY

Chromatographic drug screening techniques separate components of mixtures by partitioning them between a stationary phase, usually a solid or viscous liquid, and a mobile phase consisting of a gas or liquid. Under a given set of chromatographic conditions, the time required for a substance to traverse the chromatographic column (retention time) or the distance traveled on a TLC plate relative to the solvent front (R_f) is a constant. Separated analytes are detected and identified by a variety of techniques, and often quantitative measurements or semiquantitative estimates of analyte concentration may be made by reference to a standard curve. Chromatographic techniques that are currently used for screening purposes in postmortem toxicology include TLC, GC, and HPLC.

3.7.1 Thin-Layer Chromatography

TLC is a versatile procedure that requires no instrumentation and thus is relatively simple and inexpensive to perform.[16–21,23,82,284–293] However, its application to drug screening requires considerable skill to recognize drug and metabolite patterns and the various detection color hues. TLC techniques employ silica gel or a chemically modified silica gel as the stationary phase. The mobile phase consists of a mixture of organic solvents, often with a small quantity of acid or base to convert acidic or basic drugs to nonionic species. After extraction and specimen spotting, the TLC plates are developed with appropriate solvents to achieve chromatographic resolution. After the chromatogram is developed, drug spots are visualized by chemical modification to colored products or by absorption or fluorescence in ultraviolet light. Drug identifications are based on R_f values, color reactions, and presence of expected metabolite patterns. Standards are included on each plate to compensate for variations in R_f values.

With TLC, a large number of drugs may be detected, and presumptively identified, with a single analysis. TLC may be used to analyze serum, gastric contents, or urine. Urine, however, is the specimen of choice, since most drugs and drug metabolites are present in urine in relatively high concentrations. Although the detection limit varies for each drug, and with the conditions of extraction and detection, it is generally on the order of 0.5 to 4.0 μg/mL. TLC is less sensitive than immunoassay techniques, but its use is not restricted to the detection of only the drug or drugs for which antibodies are available. Literally hundreds of drugs can be detected and identified.

TLC can be used as either a screening or a confirmation procedure in toxicology tests. Many laboratories use TLC as a first screening step, because a wide variety of drugs/toxins can potentially be detected and presumptively identified. When used to screen, confirmation of TLC results can be made by using a variety of other procedures, including GC, GC/mass spectrometry (GC/MS), immunoassay, and HPLC. In some situations, the spot can be scraped from the TLC plate, extracted from the solid phase and injected directly into a GC or GC/MS for confirmation.

TLC will usually produce a spot for any organic drug/toxin that is present in sufficient concentration in urine or other body fluid. The major disadvantage of this technique is its insensitivity. In addition, when urine is the extracted specimen, drug metabolites are often present, and evaluation of a chromatogram containing several drugs and their metabolites can be complicated. However, the presence of known metabolites, when interpreted properly, adds support to the identification of the parent drug. TLC also has the drawback of being subjective in interpretation. A color-blind technologist will have difficulty interpreting the results.

3.7.1.1 Toxi-Lab® TLC

Over the last 20 years, classical TLC has been largely replaced in the postmortem toxicology laboratory by the Toxi-Lab® TLC system.[284,290–293] The Toxi-Lab system is a group of products produced by the AnaSys Corporation and marketed through major vendors of laboratory supplies and equipment. The Toxi-Lab TLC plates, Toxi-Grams®, are composed of glass fiber paper impregnated with silica gel or a C-8 (8 carbon aliphatic) reversed-phase sorbent. Drugs are extracted from urine, stomach contents, or other specimens in prepared Toxi-Tubes® containing buffer and an optimized extraction solvent mixture. Sample extracts are evaporated in disposable aluminum cups with small disks of the same material as the plates. As the evaporation proceeds, extracted drugs are adsorbed into the disk, which, when dry, is inserted into a matching hole at the bottom of the plate. Standards are contained in similar disks. Both prestandardized and unstandardized plates are available and standard impregnated disks are available separately.

The prepared plate is developed in a glass chamber with a solvent mixture designated by the manufacturer for each chromatography system. After developing, plates are dried, and then drugs are visualized by sequentially dipping the chromatogram into a series of tanks containing reagents and viewing under long-wave ultraviolet (UV) light. Colors and positions of spots are recorded at each visualization stage. Photographic illustrations of visualization stages and metabolite patterns are available in a compendium comprising more than 100 drugs with new drugs added as data are developed.

An available PC-compatible search program can help with data analysis, yielding statistical probability for identifications. Systems are available to screen for basic and neutral drugs, acidic and neutral drugs, tetrahydrocannabinol metabolites, and opiates, as well as the C-8 reversed-phase system that is used for further differentiating and confirming presumptive findings. In addition, confirmatory procedures for many drugs are described. The Toxi-Lab system is a powerful tool for screening urine and stomach contents. It is less effective for blood and other tissues due to interference from lipids and sensitivity limitations.

3.7.2 Gas Chromatography

GC is widely used for qualitative and quantitative drug analysis. It is relatively rapid, and capable of resolving a broad spectrum of drugs. Modern gas chromatography employs fused silica capillary columns that are coated on their inner wall with a liquid stationary phase consisting of a polymer chemically bonded to the silica.[45,80,294] The most common liquid phases are methyl silicones that contain 1, 5, or 50% phenyl side chains. The higher phenyl contents yield higher polarity liquid phases. Other polymers are used for special purposes.

The mobile phase is a gas, i.e., the carrier gas. Usually helium is used, although hydrogen, nitrogen, and gas mixtures may be preferred for some applications. The coiled column, which may be 10 to 60 m in length, is located in an oven having a precisely controlled programmable temperature capability. During a chromatographic analysis, the column temperature may be kept constant, raised at a selected constant rate, or programmed through a series of temperature ramps and isothermal intervals.

The separation capabilities of GC are determined by the polarity of the liquid phase, the flow rate and composition of the carrier gas, and the temperature program. Compounds are separated as a consequence of their different vapor pressures at the column temperature and their affinity for the liquid phase, which is related to their polarity.

In practice, the sample is injected manually or by an autosampler, either as an extract in a suitable organic solvent, or as a vapor of volatile analytes mixed with air or carrier gas. The sample is volatilized in the heated injection port and its constituents are swept into the column. As the analysis proceeds, some components move through the column faster than others, forming discrete bands that progress to the distal end and emerge into the detector, ideally in a pure state. GC detectors of various types recognize particular properties of substances, generating an electrical signal proportional to the quantity of the substance in the detector.

The resulting signal is electronically amplified and recorded on a moving chart or, more commonly, processed by a microcomputer to yield absolute and relative retention time, peak area, and height data for each detected component in the sample. Retention times of sample components, relative to a reference compound (internal standard) that is added to the sample, are constant for a given set of chromatographic conditions. Presumptive identifications are based on relative retention times corresponding with those produced by standards under identical conditions. For drug screening, some laboratories use dual column GCs with both columns originating at the same injection port. The sample is divided between the two columns and analyzed simultaneously on both. Agreement of relative retention times in two columns of differing polarities provides greater certainty of identification.

Some drugs do not chromatograph well with GC because they contain polar functional groups that adhere strongly to the liquid phase or depress the vapor pressure. Such problems can often be overcome by converting the active functional groups to less polar derivatives; such as esters from alcohols, phenols, or carboxylic acids, or amides from amines. Derivatives may be selected to give longer or shorter retention times while improving peak shape and sensitivity.[36,77,88,89,117,295–304]

Several types of detectors are used in postmortem toxicology laboratories. Each has characteristics that allow for detection and quantification of some, but not all, of the drugs and poisons that are of concern to the postmortem toxicologist.

3.7.2.1 Flame Ionization Detector

The flame ionization detector (FID) uses a hydrogen/air flame to oxidize sample components that emerge from the column. Substances containing carbon yield a charged plasma. Electrodes produce a high-voltage field that deflects the charged particles to a collector that produces an electric current with a magnitude proportional to the quantity of the component. The FID detects virtually all drugs that can be passed through the GC; however, lipids and other matrix-derived components interfere with the detection of drugs and limit practical sensitivity.

The FID, once the mainstay of GC in toxicology laboratories, is still used for the analysis of alcohols and other volatile substances in the GC equipped with an automated headspace sampler. Barbiturates and other acidic and neutral drugs are detected and quantified effectively with FID.[305–310] However, most GC basic drug screens typically employ nitrogen/phosphorus detectors (NPD), which provide better sensitivity and selectivity than FID.

3.7.2.2 Nitrogen/Phosphorus Detector

The NPD has some similarities to the flame ionization detector in that a hydrogen-air flame is used, but the collector is a ceramic bead coated with a rubidium salt. The NPD is insensitive to carbon when properly adjusted, but it responds with high sensitivity to compounds containing nitrogen or phosphorus. Furthermore, it can be tuned to maximize sensitivity to either element. The selectivity for nitrogen makes the NP detector ideal for screening basic drugs, which all contain amine functions.[30,42,43,55,311–314] Lipids and other non-nitrogenous matrix components do not interfere with the analysis.

3.7.2.3 Electron Capture Detector

The electron capture detector (ECD) contains a radioactive nickel-63 foil that emits high energy electrons (beta particles). The carrier gas is ionized by the radiation, forming anions that establish an ion current between two electrodes. Sample compounds, emerging from the GC column, extract electrons from the ionized gas, decreasing the current flow. The change in current is the signal produced by the detector.

Most substances do not capture electrons and are not detected by the ECD. However, the presence of two or more halogen atoms or a nitro or nitroso group in the molecule allows the substance to be detected. The outstanding sensitivity of the ECD for most polyhalogenated compounds is the reason for its use in the analysis of benzodiazepines.[232,315–317] A laboratory possessing a GC with ECD detector must have a radioactive materials license. A general license is sufficient for sealed detectors, but a specific license is required if the detector can be disassembled.

3.7.3 Gas Chromatography/Mass Spectrometry

GC/MS is a powerful analytical tool for identification of semivolatile organic compounds. It combines the separation efficiency of gas chromatography with the structure elucidating capabilities of mass spectrometry.[6,78–83,94,97,98,318–321] When it is used to identify unknown substances in a sample extract, the instrument may be programmed to automatically search for matches against a predefined library (target compound analysis) or it can acquire spectral data for later analysis. In the latter instance, the operator examines a chromatogram peak by peak, extracting background-subtracted spectra and searching spectral libraries by using a pattern-matching algorithm through the instrument's data system. If no acceptable match is found, the spectrum can be visually compared with printed compilations of mass spectral data. Considerable experience is required for effective and efficient substance identification by GC/MS. A chromatogram may consist of hundreds of peaks, most of which represent endogenous compounds. Recognition of frequently encountered patterns can save considerable time by avoiding unnecessary library searches. Conversely, the experienced operator will recognize the novel pattern as one that requires investigation. Nevertheless, a thorough search of a GC/MS data file can take an hour or more.

The price of GC/MS instrumentation has dropped to the point where many laboratories use it as a primary drug screening technique. However, some laboratories still rely on less definitive techniques such as TLC, GC, or class selective immunoassays for pre-screening.[80,255,256,269,297,319,322–324] When GC/MS is employed to identify unknown peaks from a GC analysis, the portion of the chromatogram that must be examined can be narrowed if the same type of column and same column temperature program are used in both instruments. The remaining extract from the GC analysis can be injected into the GC/MS. Knowing the relative retention time of the unknown, the operator can first locate the peak corresponding to the internal standard and then estimate the region of the GC/MS chromatogram where the unknown peak should be. That region is examined carefully to locate and identify a peak whose spectrum is inconsistent with expected endogenous compounds. With some instrumentation it is possible to simultaneously inject extracts onto a system with both MS and NP detector systems. This may be done either by connecting two columns to a single injector or by splitting the effluent from one column into two detectors (one MS, one NP).

In the identification of substances giving rise to unknown spots on TLC, an extract of the sample is analyzed in the GC/MS with a column temperature program extending from below the boiling point of the solvent to 300°C or higher. When the GC/MS run is complete, the entire chromatogram is examined. Time can be saved by initially examining the 20 or 30 largest peaks first. The GC/MS is much more sensitive than TLC, so any component that gives a visible spot should produce a large peak on the GC/MS. Alternatively, the operator may examine all peaks, and detect even substances missed by the TLC analysis. In most cases, such sensitivity is unnecessary for analyzing urine or gastric contents, but it can be useful when potent drugs such as fentanyl or haloperidol must be excluded.

An alternative approach to the identification of unknowns detected by TLC is to scrape the spot from a duplicate plate and analyze it by GC/MS. In practice, a second TLC plate is prepared and developed, but is not sprayed or dipped with color reagents. Instead, the area of the plate corresponding to the unknown spot is scraped (or cut from a Toxi-Gram), and the drug is eluted into a solvent. The solvent is evaporated, and the residue is redissolved and analyzed by GC/MS. This procedure should produce a single major peak on the GC/MS that corresponds to the unknown spot on the TLC plate. The spectrum of the major peak can then be searched to identify the unknown.

GC/MS is often used to identify the drug, or drugs, giving rise to a positive result in a class selective immunoassay test. Such analyses are most efficiently accomplished by methods that search an area of the chromatogram for patterns matching reference spectra in a computer library. The library is generated by analyzing a standard of each of the targeted drugs and storing a representative spectrum in the data system.[92,199,256,325] The search can be programmed to take place automatically at the end of each data file acquisition. However, the data must be reviewed by the operator before reporting.

GC/MS data can be used for both identification and confirmation in drug screening.[318,320,321,325–327] However, for it to serve as a final confirmation test, the GC/MS analysis should be performed on a separate aliquot or a different specimen from that which yields the initial presumptive finding.

3.7.4 High-Performance Liquid Chromatography

HPLC utilizes a column filled with microscopic particles of silica, or resin particles bonded with a polymer whose side chains have specific functional groups.[57,59,64,69,328–332] The polymer is the stationary phase in HPLC, and the nature of the side chains determines the type of interactions the column will have with analytes. Various normal phases and reverse phases are available. Normal phases are characterized by polar side chains such as silica, diol, amino, and cyano, whereas reverse phases have nonpolar side chains such as 8 carbon (C-8) and 18 carbon (C-18) aliphatic and phenyl moieties. Anion and cation exchange phases are also available.

The mobile phase in HPLC is a mixed solvent containing a buffer to suppress or induce ionization of analytes as required for the intended separation. The solvent composition may be kept constant (isocratic) or the percentages of components may be varied (gradient) during the analysis. For instance, in reverse-phase HPLC, the mobile phase will start at higher polarity. As the run proceeds, the polarity is decreased, enabling the removal of any remaining nonpolar substances from the nonpolar reverse phase column, while decreasing the tendency toward broad peaks near the end of a run.

3.7.4.1 Ultraviolet Absorption Detectors

The most common detection systems for HPLC are UV absorption detectors.[56,64,72,331,332] The less expensive detectors measure absorption at a single wavelength which may be fixed (e.g., at 254 or 280 nm) or variable over a range of 190 to over 340 nm. The variable wavelength detectors are set to a desired wavelength by the operator, and some can be programmed to change wavelengths during the analysis. However, the time required to change wavelengths precludes using variable wavelength detectors for spectral scanning of peaks.

3.7.4.2 Diode Array Detectors

Photo diode array detectors simultaneously measure absorbance at many small wavelength increments over a broad wavelength band.[46,57,58,64,69,70,73,74,333–348] The detector uses a diffraction grating to break the light beam into a spectrum that is focused onto an array of UV-sensitive photo diodes. Thus, UV spectra of individual peaks can be recorded. A data processing system enables the instrument to determine peak purity by comparing spectra at the leading and tailing ends of a peak and to create and search libraries of target analyte spectra. The sensitivity of the diode array detector is poorer than that of the fixed or variable wavelength, but the availability of spectral data makes it a valuable tool for drug screening.

3.7.4.3 Fluorescence Detectors

Fluorescence detectors, with variable excitation and emission wavelengths, provide high sensitivity and specificity for the detection and quantification of fluorescent compounds, but they are more useful for quantification than for screening. Fluorescence detection could be used to provide a sensitive screen to target a single substance or a group of substances with similar fluorescence characteristics and different retention times.[56–59]

3.7.4.4 Advantages and Disadvantages of HPLC

HPLC systems can be equipped with autosamplers, manual injectors, or both. In general, the greatest screening efficiency is achieved through automation. Increased applications of HPLC for drug screening are likely. Substantially more definitive drug identification can be achieved by the use of a mass spectrometer as the HPLC detector. The relatively high cost of these liquid chromatograph/mass spectrometer-coupled instruments limits their current usage for general drug screening or confirmation, although their use is becoming increasingly more common.

HPLC is a more expensive and labor intensive and less sensitive analytical technique than GC, so it is less commonly used for screening. However, it can be used to detect many drugs and poisons that are thermolabile, too polar, or lacking in sufficient volatility for analysis by GC. In addition to the qualitative information obtained from the chromatographic retention time, quantification can also be obtained. The signal generated by the detector is proportional to the amount of substance detected. Therefore, by preparing standards of known concentration and treating them in like fashion to the case specimen, the amount of toxin in the specimen can be quantified. The precision of the quantification can be enhanced by adding an internal standard at the beginning of the extraction. The internal standard is usually a compound with similar extraction and chromatographic characteristics to the analytes of interest. The presence of the internal standard permits the quantification to be based on the ratio of analyte to internal standard peak heights or areas. Because ratios are used instead of absolute amounts, the need for quantitative transfers in the extraction process is removed.

3.7.4.5 REMEDi HS™ HPLC

A commercial, completely automated HPLC system designed for drug screening is available (REMEDi HS; Bio-Rad Laboratories, Hercules, CA).[349–352] This system utilizes four columns in series and column switching techniques to extract, separate, and perform a spectral scan on eluted drugs. Identification of about 500 drugs and metabolites is based on computer matching of retention time and spectra with comparable data stored in the drug library.

Quantification of identified drugs may also be performed. REMEDi HS was developed for the clinical laboratory, but it can be adapted for postmortem drug screening. Urine, serum, and plasma can be analyzed directly, but whole blood and tissues require manual extraction prior to analysis. Sensitivity for many drugs is not as good as GC with NPD, but should be sufficient for screening urine or stomach contents. If REMEDi HS is applied to screening blood or tissues, sensitivity may not be adequate to detect therapeutic or intoxicating concentrations of some important drugs, but should be adequate for detecting lethal concentrations.

The REMEDi HS system can be complementary to other drug screening techniques, detecting drugs that would otherwise be overlooked and providing corroborative evidence to confirm identifications.

3.8 ULTRAVIOLET-VISIBLE SPECTROPHOTOMETRY

Ultraviolet-visible (UV-Vis) spectrophotometry was one of the earliest instrumental techniques used in postmortem forensic toxicology.[26–29] The use of ultraviolet and visible spectrophotometry as a screening tool is based on the fact that many drugs contain aromatic nuclei that absorb light in the UV and visible regions. Such drugs have absorption spectra with maxima and minima at characteristic wavelengths. Furthermore, the spectrum often changes with the ionization state of the drug in acidic or basic solutions. UV absorption maxima and entire spectra of drugs and poisons are available from various references.

Several limitations, however, affect the use of spectrophotometry. The major limitation is the lack of sensitivity required to detect many of today's therapeutic or misused drugs. Another drawback of spectrophotometry is the requirement that the drug be isolated in a form free from substances with overlapping spectra. Drug mixtures and impure extracts yield mixed spectra that may not be interpretable. In addition, spectrophotometry is not able to distinguish between the parent drug and metabolites. Some of a drug's metabolites may be active while others are inactive, and there is a need to distinguish between these compounds. In spite of these deficiencies, a role remains for spectrophotometric methods for some drug and toxicant analyses. UV spectrometry is especially useful for purity and concentration checks of primary and stock standards.

3.9 SPECTROSCOPIC METHODS FOR ANALYSIS OF TOXIC METALS AND METALOIDS

Toxicologists should be prepared to support investigations that involve toxic exposure to metals and metaloids. Proper sample collection and rigorous state-of-the-art analytical techniques are critical to prevent exogenous contamination.[353,354] A number of different techniques may be employed for the identification of such compounds: flame atomic absorption spectroscopy (FAAS),[355] graphite furnace atomic absorption spectroscopy (GF-AAS),[356,357] inductively coupled plasma-emission spectroscopy (ICPAES),[358] and inductively coupled plasma-mass spectrometry (ICP-MS)[358,359] may all be used. These are sensitive and specific techniques that provide the laboratory with the capability to measure a broad range of metals. An in-depth discussion of methods used for metal analysis is beyond the scope of this chapter.

3.10 SAMPLE PREPARATION

3.10.1 Extraction Methods

There are two approaches to the screening of biofluids for drugs or poisons. One is the direct analysis of the specimen for the presence of a specific analyte or its class, without isolation or purification. The other is isolation of the analyte from the sample followed by instrumental analysis of the concentrated extract. The most common example of this is liquid-liquid extraction of an appropriately buffered sample with an immiscible organic solvent.[21,23,25,43,65,66,71,314,360–371] The proper choice of sample, pH, and solvent will effectively remove the target analytes from the aqueous sample matrix.[21,25,362,371–373] Separation of an analyte from interfering substances usually will require more involved techniques.

3.10.1.1 Liquid–Liquid Extraction

The liquid–liquid extraction technique dates to the mid-19th century when Stas and Otto developed extraction schemes for nonvolatile organic compounds. The method utilizes differences in the pH and solubility characteristics of various analytes. A basic compound is in the non-ionized form in alkaline pH; an acidic compound is in the ionized form in a similar medium. A compound in its non-ionized form prefers the lipophilic environment of an organic solvent to the aqueous environment of the biologic sample. It is on this basis that the separation of drugs from the biologic matrix occurs. The specimen is buffered according to the pH characteristics of the analyte of interest and mixed with an immiscible organic solvent. Commonly used solvents are hexane, toluene, diethyl ether, chlorobutane, dichloromethane, chloroform, or mixtures of these. Ionized compounds and many of the biologic components such as proteins remain in the aqueous layer while the un-ionized drug molecules are transferred to the organic solvent.

The extraction process can be illustrated by taking as an example a basic drug of pK 8, present in plasma. If the plasma is brought to pH 10 using a suitable alkali or alkaline buffer and is shaken with a suitable organic solvent, the drug will be removed from the aqueous into the organic phase. Unfortunately, many endogenous bases and neutral compounds will also be extracted if they are soluble in the organic solvent. The organic phase is then separated from the aqueous phase (using a Pasteur pipette, for example). This is usually done after centrifugation, to completely separate the two phases.

For drugs that behave like strong acids and bases, a further purification step called back-extraction can be carried out. By shaking the organic phase with dilute acid, such as 0.1 *N* sulfuric, the basic drug will now be ionized and will no longer be as soluble in the organic phase: it will be extracted into the aqueous phase. Any neutral compounds will be left behind in the organic phase. Endogenous bases may also be co-extracted with the basic drug, but by carefully choosing the pH and the organic solvent the amounts of these bases can be reduced. The acidic aqueous phase is then made alkaline by the addition of a base, such as 2 *N* sodium hydroxide, and shaken with fresh organic solvent to take the drug into the organic phase. The organic phase can be separated, evaporated, reconstituted, and analyzed.

In many methods the organic phase, containing the drug, is washed with water, and the washings are discarded. This step must be carefully controlled. For example, if the drug is a moderate to strong base and the wash water is even slightly acidic, then some of the drug may be removed into the aqueous phase. If such a process takes place, then low and very erratic recoveries will result.

Before leaving the subject of solvent extraction a number of simple points should be emphasized:

1. In general the least polar solvent capable of extracting the drug in question should be used in order to reduce the possibility of co-extracting endogenous materials. The least polar solvents are the hydrocarbons, such as hexane, toluene, chlorinated hydrocarbons, and diethyl and related ethers. Ethyl acetate is more polar, and the short-chain alcohols are very polar and miscible with water to a greater or lesser degree.
2. Many drugs are so highly lipid soluble that they can be extracted into nonpolar solvents, even in the ionized state. For example, the β-adrenoreceptor blocking drug propranolol has a pK of about 9.5, and therefore in a pH 7.4 buffer it is more than 99% ionized. Since its partition coefficient, between *n*-octanol and pH 7.4 buffer at 37°C, is 20.2, this means that the ionized drug is highly soluble in *n*-octanol.
3. Many extraction procedures employ a ratio of solvent to aqueous phase greater than unity in order to reduce the possibility of emulsion formation during extraction. The ideal is a 10:1 solvent-to-sample ratio. There are, however, successful methods that use ratios very much less than unity. Troublesome emulsions can also be avoided or reduced by saturating the aqueous phase with an inorganic salt, such as sodium chloride, before extraction.
4. Recoveries can be increased by using mixed solvents such as hexane: butanol (9:1) or hexane-isoamyl alcohol (97:3). Such solvents are also mandatory to efficiently extract polar drugs or metabolites.
5. Extraction conditions should always be optimized using the relevant biological fluid. It should not be assumed that the extractability from water will exactly match that from blood or tissue homogenates.
6. When extraction conditions have been optimized, it is worthwhile to put a series of specimens through the complete procedure, half of them diluted approximately tenfold. Although this does not always succeed, it can result in cleaner extracts.
7. The multiple step liquid–liquid extraction process is quite effective in separating analytes from biologic specimens, but is also time-consuming. In an attempt to alleviate this time-related problem, solid-phase extraction (SPE) techniques have been developed.

3.10.1.2 Solid Phase Extraction

In SPE, the specimen is applied to a solid packing material, which is usually, but not exclusively, silica gel based. The sample is partitioned between the matrix and the solid phase, which provides the separation. The general process of SPE involves several steps: (1) column conditioning, (2) addition of specimen, (3) column washing with solvents to remove interfering substances, and (4) analyte elution.[46–53,55,57,59,63,69,70,72,82,91,308,374–391] Each individual step depends on the analyte of interest, or the type of extraction column, and method development frequently involves a significant amount of trial and error. SPE is utilized in a vast number of analytical methods developed for drug analysis in human postmortem materials.[392] The advantages of SPE procedures include decreased operator time, reduced solvent volumes, and increased extraction efficiency. In postmortem toxicology, the availability of automated SPE systems has made this extraction technique attractive to forensic laboratories with a high throughput of postmortem samples, where several extraction programs adjusted for different analytical methods can be run on the same system. For certain analyses, immunoaffinity SPE techniques may be employed, significantly improving the purity of the sample. This variant of the SPE technique has been used in the analysis of a large number of drugs.[393]

A little more than a decade ago, solid-phase microextraction (SPME) was introduced and the technique has since been extensively used in several areas, including analysis of drugs and endogenous compounds.[394,395] SPME has many advantages over other extraction methods; it is simple, rapid, efficient, and requires no solvent. All steps of sample preparation, i.e., extraction, concentration, derivatization, and transfer to the chromatograph, are integrated in one step and in one device. In forensic toxicology applications of this technique include analytical methods for barbiturates,[396] drug screening in hair,[397] organophosphates,[398] GHB,[399] and certain pharmaceutical drugs.[400] SPME is typically followed by GC/MS or LC/MS analysis, but may be combined with other methods. Recently, SPME has been applied in a methodological approach to determine the binding parameters of drugs to human serum albumin. From these parameters the concentrations of albumin, free drug, and total drug can be calculated in unknown mixtures.[401]

A closely related technique is solid-phase dynamic extraction (SPDE), based on an inside needle capillary absorption trap. An automated HS-SPDE-GC-MS procedure was developed and applied for analysis of drugs of abuse in hair, and was found to provide, compared with SPME, a higher extraction rate, in addition to a faster automated operation and greater stability of the device.[402]

Summing up, the development of the several different modifications of solid-phase extraction techniques in recent years is impressive, and is comparable to the rapid innovations in LC/MS instrumentation. It seems likely that we will face a large number of new methodological concepts and applications of SPE techniques that will resolve several analytical problems in forensic toxicology.

3.10.1.3 pH Adjustment for Extraction

Weakly acidic drugs, such as barbiturates, primidone, and phenytoin, can be separated from the specimen by using a liquid–liquid or solid-phase extraction at pH 5. This extraction also removes some neutral drugs, such as meprobamate, glutethimide, and carbamazepine. After solvent concentration, these drugs can be identified by TLC, GC, or HPLC.

The largest group of drugs that are normally encountered in the postmortem laboratory are the organic bases. These include antiarrhythmics, antidepressants, antihistamines, benzodiazepines, cocaine, narcotic analgesics, nicotine, phencyclidine, phenothiazines, and sympathomimetic amines. These drugs all extract under alkaline conditions.

Amphoteric drugs such as morphine and benzoylecgonine require careful adjustment of pH for their efficient extraction by liquid–liquid procedures. Amphoteric compounds contain both acidic and basic functional groups. If the aqueous phase is too acidic or too basic, one of the functional groups will be ionized, and extraction will be inefficient. The pH must be close to the isoelectric point for high recovery by liquid–liquid extraction. Such compounds may be isolated by solid phase techniques, if a column with ion exchange functions is used. The pH is adjusted to completely ionize one of the functional groups in the analyte. The appropriate solid phase will capture ionized analyte as the sample passes through. The sorbent is washed to remove impurities, and then the analyte is recovered in either an acidic or basic elution solvent in order to reverse its ionization.

3.10.2 Hydrolysis to Release Drugs in Sample Pretreatment

Before extraction, tissues may be homogenized with a blender or an ultrasonic disruptor, or they may be hydrolyzed by enzymes such as Subtilysin Carlsburg or Protease K to produce a homogeneous fluid sample.[39,365,378,403] Conjugates can be cleaved by gentle but time-consuming enzymatic hydrolysis, or by rapid acid hydrolysis.[34,53,117,224,227,404,405] However, the formation of artifacts during the latter procedure must be considered.

3.10.3 Applications

Universal liquid–liquid extraction procedures are preferable for general unknown analysis because substances with very different physicochemical properties must be isolated from heterogeneous matrices. On the other hand, solid-phase extraction is preferable if target compounds must be selectively isolated from relatively homogeneous samples, such as urine for confirmation of a single drug, or metabolite, or a group of drugs with similar extraction properties.

REFERENCES

1. Jackson, J.V., Forensic toxicology, in *Clarke's Isolation and Identification of Drugs in Pharmaceuticals, Body Fluids, and Post-Mortem Material*, 2nd ed., Moffatt, A.C., Ed., Pharmaceutical Press, London, 1986, 35.
2. Jentzen, J.M., Forensic toxicology. An overview and an algorithmic approach, *Am. J. Clin. Pathol.*, 92, S48–55, 1989.
3. Stewart, C.P. and Martin, G.J., The mode of action of poisons, in *Toxicology: Mechanisms and Analytical Methods*, Vol. 2, Stewart, C.P. and Stolman, A., Eds., Academic Press, New York, 1960, 1–15.
4. Stewart, C.P. and Stolman, A., The toxicologist and his work, in *Toxicology: Mechanisms and Analytical Methods*, Vol. 1, Stewart, C.P. and Stolman, A., Eds., Academic Press, New York, 1960, 1–22.
5. Garriott, J.C., Drug analysis in postmortem toxicology, *Chem. Anal.* (New York), 85, 353–376, 1986.
6. Costello, C.E., GC/MS analysis of street drugs, particularly in the body fluids of overdose victims, in *Street Drug Analysis and Its Social and Clinical Implications*, John Wiley & Sons, New York, 1974, 67–78.
7. Walker, S. and Johnston, A., Laboratory screening of body fluids in self poisoning and drug abuse, *Ann. Acad. Med. Singapore,* 20, 91–94, 1991.
8. Duncan, W.P. and Deutsch, D.G., The use of GC/IR/MS for high-confidence identification of drugs, *Clin. Chem.,* 35, 1279–1281, 1989.
9. Kinberger, B., Holmen, A., and Wahrgren, P., A strategy for drug analysis in serum and urine. An application to drug screening of samples from drivers involved in traffic accidents, *Anal. Lett.,* 15, 937–951, 1982.
10. Rowley, G.L., Armstrong, T.A., Crowl, C.P., Eimstad, W.M., Hu, W.M., Kam, J.K., et al., Determination of THC and its metabolites by EMIT homogeneous enzyme immunoassay: a summary report, *NIDA Res. Monogr.,* 7, 28–32, 1976.
11. Walberg, C.B., Correlation of the "EMIT" urine barbiturate assay with a spectrophotometric serum barbiturate assay in suspected overdose, *Clin. Chem.,* 20, 305–306, 1974.
12. Cavanagh, K., Draisey, T.F., and Thibert, R.J., Assessment of the EMIT technique as a screening test for opiates and methadone for a methadone maintenance clinic and its calibration by Bayesian statistics, *Clin. Biochem.,* 11, 210–213, 1978.
13. Oellerich, M., Kulpmann, W.R., and Haeckel, R., Drug screening by enzyme immunoassay (EMIT) and thin-layer chromatography (Drug Skreen), *J. Clin. Chem. Clin. Biochem.,* 15, 275–283, 1977.
14. Fletcher, S.M., Urine screening for drugs by EMIT, *J. Forensic Sci. Soc.,* 21, 327–332, 1981.
15. Davidow, B., Li Petri, N., and Quame, B., A thin-layer chromatographic screening procedure for detecting drug abuse, *Tech. Bull. Registry Med. Technol.,* 38, 298–303, 1968.
16. Kaistha, K.K. and Jaffe, J.H., TLC techniques for identification of narcotics, barbiturates, and CNS stimulants in a drug abuse urine screening program, *J. Pharm. Sci.,* 61, 679–689, 1972.
17. Siek, T., Thin-layer and gas chromatography as identification aids in forensic science, *Analabs (Res. Notes),* 13, 1–15, 1973.
18. Davidow, B., Quame, B., Abell, L.L., and Lim, B., Screening for drug abuse, *Health Lab. Sci.,* 10, 329–334, 1973.

19. Davidow, B. and Fastlich, E., The application of thin-layer chromatography and of other methods for the detection of drug abuse, *Prog. Clin. Pathol.,* 5, 85–98, 1973.
20. Masoud, A.N., Systematic identification of drugs of abuse. II. TLC, *J. Pharm. Sci.,* 65, 1585–1589, 1976.
21. Hackett, L.P. and Dusci, L.J., Rapid identification of drugs in the overdosed patient, *Clin. Toxicol.,* 11, 341–352, 1977.
22. Sunshine, I., *CRC Handbook Series in Clinical Laboratory Science: Section B: Toxicology,* Vol. I, CRC Press, West Palm Beach, FL, 1978, 3–269.
23. Warfield, R.W. and Maickel, R.P., A generalized extraction-TLC procedure for identification of drugs, *J. Appl. Toxicol.,* 3, 51–57, 1983.
24. Foerster, E.H., Hatchett, H., and Garriott, J.C., A rapid, comprehensive screening procedure for basic drugs in blood or tissues by gas chromatography, *J. Anal. Toxicol.,* 2, 50–55, 1978.
25. Dusci, L.J. and Hackett, L.P., The detection of some basic drugs and their major metabolites using gas-liquid chromatography, *Clin. Toxicol.,* 14, 587–593, 1979.
26. Siek, T.J. and Osiewicz, R.J., Identification of drugs and other toxic compounds from their ultraviolet spectra. II. Ultraviolet absorption properties of thirteen structural groups, *J. Forensic Sci.,* 20, 18–37, 1975.
27. Siek, T.J., Osiewicz, R.J., and Bath, R.J., Identification of drugs and other toxic compounds from their ultraviolet spectra. III. Ultraviolet absorption properties of 22 structural groups, *J. Forensic Sci.,* 21, 525–551, 1976.
28. Feldstein, M., Spectrum analysis: B. Absorption spectra Part 1: The use of ultraviolet spectra in toxicological analysis, in *Toxicology: Mechanisms and Analytical Methods*, Vol. 1, Stewart, C.P. and Stolman, A., Eds., Academic Press, New York, 1960, 464–506.
29. Curry, S., Spectrum analysis: B. Absorption spectra Part 2: Ultraviolet spectrophotometry, in *Toxicology: Mechanisms and Analytical Methods*, Vol. 1, Stewart, C.P. and Stolman, A., Eds., Academic Press, New York, 1960, 507–555.
30. Demedts, P., De Waele, M., Van der Verren, J., and Heyndrickx, A., Application of the combined use of fused silica capillary columns and NPD for the toxicological determination of codeine and ethylmorphine in a human overdose case, *J. Anal. Toxicol.,* 7, 113–115, 1983.
31. Anderson, W.H. and Archuleta, M.M., The capillary gas chromatographic determination of trazodone in biological specimens, *J. Anal. Toxicol.,* 8, 217–219, 1984.
32. Francom, P., Andrenyak, D., Lim, H.K., Bridges, R.R., Foltz, R.L., and Jones, R.T., Determination of LSD in urine by capillary column gas chromatography and electron impact mass spectrometry, *J. Anal. Toxicol.,* 12, 1–8, 1988.
33. Feng, N., Vollenweider, F.X., Minder, E.I., Rentsch, K., Grampp, T., and Vonderschmitt, D.J., Development of a gas chromatography-mass spectrometry method for determination of ketamine in plasma and its application to human samples, *Ther. Drug Monit.,* 17, 95–100, 1995.
34. Meatherall, R., GC/MS confirmation of urinary benzodiazepine metabolites, *J. Anal. Toxicol.,* 18, 369–381, 1994.
35. Taylor, R.W., Greutink, C., and Jain, N.C., Identification of underivatized basic drugs in urine by capillary column gas chromatography, *J. Anal. Toxicol.,* 10, 205–208, 1986.
36. Christophersen, A.S., Biseth, A., Skuterud, B., and Gadeholt, G., Identification of opiates in urine by capillary column gas chromatography of two different derivatives, *J. Chromatogr.,* 422, 117–124, 1987.
37. Lee, X.P., Kumazawa, T., and Sato, K., Rapid extraction and capillary gas chromatography for diazine herbicides in human body fluids, *Forensic Sci. Int.,* 72, 199–207, 1995.
38. Seno, H., Suzuki, O., Kumazawa, T., and Hattori, H., Rapid isolation with Sep-Pak C18 cartridges and wide-bore capillary gas chromatography of benzophenones, the acid-hydrolysis products of benzodiazepines, *J. Anal. Toxicol.,* 15, 21–24, 1991.
39. Turcant, A., Premel-Cabic, A., Cailleux, A., and Allain, P., Screening for neutral and basic drugs in blood by dual fused-silica column chromatography with nitrogen-phosphorus detection [published erratum appears in *Clin. Chem.* 34(11), 2370, 1988], *Clin. Chem.,* 34, 1492–1497, 1988.
40. Watts, V.W. and Simonick, T.F., Screening of basic drugs in biological samples using dual column capillary chromatography and nitrogen-phosphorus detectors, *J. Anal. Toxicol.,* 10, 198–204, 1986.

41. Anderson, W.H. and Fuller, D.C., A simplified procedure for the isolation, characterization, and identification of weak acid and neutral drugs from whole blood, *J. Anal. Toxicol.,* 11, 198–204, 1987.
42. Cox, R.A., Crifasi, J.A., Dickey, R.E., Ketzler, S.C., and Pshak, G.L., A single-step extraction for screening whole blood for basic drugs by capillary GC/NPD, *J. Anal. Toxicol.,* 13, 224–228, 1989.
43. Fretthold, D., Jones, P., Sebrosky, G., and Sunshine, I., Testing for basic drugs in biological fluids by solvent extraction and dual capillary GC/NPD, *J. Anal. Toxicol.,* 10, 10–14, 1986.
44. Perrigo, B.J., Peel, H.W., and Ballantyne, D.J., Use of dual-column fused-silica capillary gas chromatography in combination with detector response factors for analytical toxicology, *J. Chromatogr.,* 341, 81–88, 1985.
45. Bogusz, M., Bialka, J., Gierz, J., and Klys, M., Use of short, wide-bore capillary columns in GC toxicological screening, *J. Anal. Toxicol.,* 10, 135–138, 1986.
46. Theodoridis, G., Papadoyannis, I., Tsoukali-Papadopoulou, H., and Vasilikiotis, G., A comparative study of different solid phase extraction procedures for the analysis of alkaloids of forensic interest in biological fluids by RP-HPLC/diode array, *J. Liquid Chromatogr.,* 18, 1973–1995, 1973.
47. Taylor, R.W., Jain, N.C., and George, M.P., Simultaneous identification of cocaine and benzoylecgonine using solid phase extraction and gas chromatography/mass spectrometry, *J. Anal. Toxicol.,* 11, 233–234, 1987.
48. Casas, M., Berrueta, L.A., Gallo, B., and Vicente, F., Solid phase extraction conditions for the selective isolation of drugs from biological fluids predicted using liquid chromatography, *Chromatographia,* 34, 79–82, 1992.
49. Platoff, G.E., Jr. and Gere, J.A., Solid phase extraction of abused drugs from urine, *Forensic Sci. Rev.,* 3, 117–133, 1992.
50. Chen, X.H., Hommerson, A.L., Zweipfenning, P.G., Franke, J.P., Harmen-Boverhof, C.W., Ensing, K., et al., Solid phase extraction of morphine from whole blood by means of Bond Elut Certify columns, *J. Forensic Sci.,* 38, 668–676, 1993.
51. Dixit, V. and Dixit, V.M., Solid phase extraction of phencyclidine with GC/MS confirmation, *Indian J. Chem. Sect. B,* 30, 164–168, 1991.
52. Marko, V. and Bauerova, K., Study of the solid phase extraction of pentoxifylline and its major metabolite as a basis of their rapid low concentration gas chromatographic determination in serum, *Biomed. Chromatogr.,* 5, 256–261, 1991.
53. Huang, W., Andollo, W., and Hearn, W.L., A solid phase extraction technique for the isolation and identification of opiates in urine, *J. Anal. Toxicol.,* 16, 307–310, 1992.
54. Kintz, P., Tracqui, A., Mangin, P., Lugnier, A., and Chaumont, A., Subnanogram GC/NPD method for the determination of sparteine in biological fluids, *Methods Findings Exp. Clin. Pharmacol.,* 11, 115–118, 1989.
55. Taylor, R.W., Le, S.D., Philip, S., and Jain, N.C., Simultaneous identification of amphetamine and methamphetamine using solid-phase extraction and GC/NPD or GC/MS, *J. Anal. Toxicol.,* 13, 293–295, 1989.
56. Binder, S.R., Analysis of drugs of abuse in biological fluids by liquid chromatography, in *Advances in Chromatography,* Vol. 36, Brown, P. and Grushka, E., Eds., Marcel Dekker, New York, 1996.
57. Akerman, K.K., Jolkkonen, J., Parviainen, M., and Penttila, I., Analysis of low-dose benzodiazepines by HPLC with automated solid-phase extraction, *Clin. Chem.,* 42, 1412–1416, 1996.
58. Clauwaert, K.M., Vanbocxlaer, J.F., Lambert, W.E., and Deleenheer, A.P., Analysis of cocaine, benzoylecgonine, and cocaethylene in urine by HPLC with diode array detection, *Anal. Chem.,* 68, 3021–3028, 1996.
59. Bourque, A.J., Krull, I.S., and Feibush, B., Automated HPLC analyses of drugs of abuse via direct injection of biological fluids followed by simultaneous solid-phase extraction and derivatization with fluorescence detection, *Biomed. Chromatogr.,* 8, 53–62, 1994.
60. Gill, R., Moffat, A.C., Smith, R.M., and Hurdley, T.G., A collaborative study to investigate the retention reproducibility of barbiturates in HPLC with a view to establishing retention databases for drug identification, *J. Chromatogr. Sci.,* 24, 153–159, 1986.
61. Bogusz, M., Hill, D.W., and Rehorek, A., Comparability of RP-HPLC retention indices of drugs in three databases, *J. Liquid Chromatogr. Relat. Technol.,* 19(8), 1291–1316, 1996.

62. Law, B., Williams, P.L., and Moffat, A.C., The detection and quantification of cannabinoids in blood and urine by RIA, HPLC/RIA and GC/MS, *Vet. Hum. Toxicol.,* 21, 144–147, 1979.
63. Moore, C., Browne, S., Tebbett, I., and Negrusz, A., Determination of cocaine and its metabolites in brain tissue using high-flow solid-phase extraction columns and HPLC, *Forensic Sci. Int.,* 53, 215–219, 1992.
64. Wong, A.S., An evaluation of HPLC for the screening and quantitation of benzodiazepines and acetaminophen in post mortem blood, *J. Anal. Toxicol.,* 7, 33–36, 1983.
65. Bernal, J.L., Delnozal, M.J., Rosas, V., and Villarino, A., Extraction of basic drugs from whole blood and determination by HPLC, *Chromatographia,* 38, 617–623, 1994.
66. Pawula, M., Barrett, D.A., and Shaw, P.N., An improved extraction method for the HPLC determination of morphine and its metabolites in plasma, *J. Pharm. Biomed. Anal.,* 11, 401–406, 1993.
67. Bogusz, M., Influence of elution conditions on HPLC retention index values of selected acidic and basic drugs measured in the 1-nitroalkane scale, *J. Anal. Toxicol.,* 15, 174–178, 1991.
68. Bogusz, M. and Erkens, M., Influence of biological matrix on chromatographic behavior and detection of selected acidic, neutral, and basic drugs examined by means of a standardized HPLC-DAD system, *J. Anal. Toxicol.,* 19, 49–55, 1995.
69. Logan, B.K., Stafford, D.T., Tebbett, I.R., and Moore, C.M., Rapid screening for 100 basic drugs and metabolites in urine using cation exchange solid-phase extraction and HPLC with diode array detection, *J. Anal. Toxicol.,* 14, 154–159, 1990.
70. Musshoff, F. and Daldrup, T., A rapid solid-phase extraction and HPLC/DAD procedure for the simultaneous determination and quantification of different benzodiazepines in serum, blood and postmortem blood, *Int. J. Legal Med.,* 105, 105–109, 1992.
71. Mayer, F., Kramer, B.K., Ress, K.M., Kuhlkamp, V., Liebich, H.M., Risler, T., et al., Simplified, rapid and inexpensive extraction procedure for a high-performance liquid chromatographic method for determination of disopyramide and its main metabolite mono-*N*-dealkylated disopyramide in serum, *J. Chromatogr.,* 572, 339–345, 1991.
72. Ferrara, S.D., Tedeschi, L., Frison, G., and Castagna, F., Solid-phase extraction and HPLC-UV confirmation of drugs of abuse in urine, *J. Anal. Toxicol.,* 16, 217–222, 1992.
73. Bogusz, M. and Wu, M., Standardized HPLC/DAD system, based on retention indices and spectral library, applicable for systematic toxicological screening [published erratum appears in *J. Anal. Toxicol.,* 16(3), 16A, 1992], *J. Anal. Toxicol.,* 15, 188–197, 1991.
74. Tracqui, A., Kintz, P., and Mangin, P., Systematic toxicological analysis using HPLC/DAD, *J. Forensic Sci.,* 40, 254–262, 1995.
75. Wu, A.H., Onigbinde, T.A., Wong, S.S., and Johnson, K.G., Evaluation of full-scanning GC/ion trap MS analysis of NIDA drugs-of-abuse urine testing in urine, *J. Anal. Toxicol.,* 16, 202–206, 1992.
76. Schuberth, J., Volatile compounds detected in blood of drunk drivers by headspace/capillary gas chromatography/ion trap mass spectrometry, *Biol. Mass Spectrom.,* 20, 699–702, 1991.
77. McCurdy, H.H., Lewellen, L.J., Callahan, L.S., and Childs, P.S., Evaluation of the Ion Trap Detector for the detection of 11-nor-delta 9-THC-9-carboxylic acid in urine after extraction by bonded-phase adsorption, *J. Anal. Toxicol.,* 10, 175–177, 1986.
78. Hernandez, A., Andollo, W., and Hearn, W.L., Analysis of cocaine and metabolites in brain using solid phase extraction and full-scanning gas chromatography/ion trap mass spectrometry, *Forensic Sci. Int.,* 65, 149–156, 1994.
79. Moody, D.E., Rittenhouse, L.F., and Monti, K.M., Analysis of forensic specimens for cannabinoids. I. Comparison of RIA and GC/MS analysis of blood, *J. Anal. Toxicol.,* 16, 297–301, 1992.
80. Pettersen, J.E. and Skuterud, B., Application of combined GC/MS as compared to a conventional analytical system for identification of unknown drugs in acute drug intoxications, *Anal. Chem. Symp. Ser.,* 13, 111–129, 1983.
81. Ullucci, P.A., Cadoret, R., Stasiowski, D., and Martin, H.F., A comprehensive GC/MS drug screening procedure., *J. Anal. Toxicol.,* 2, 33–35, 1978.
82. Lillsunde, P. and Korte, T., Comprehensive drug screening in urine using solid-phase extraction and combined TLC and GC/MS identification, *J. Anal. Toxicol.,* 15, 71–81, 1991.
83. Finkle, B.S., Foltz, R.L., and Taylor, D.M., A comprehensive GC/MS reference data system for toxicological and biomedical purposes., *J. Chromatogr. Sci.,* 12, 304–328, 1974.
84. Clouette, R., Jacob, M., Koteel, P., and Spain, M., Confirmation of 11-nor-delta 9-tetrahydrocannabinol in urine as its t-butyldimethylsilyl derivative using GC/MS, *J. Anal. Toxicol.,* 17, 1–4, 1993.

85. Bellanca, J.A., Davis, P.L., Donnelly, B., Dal Cortivo, L.A., and Weinberg, S.B., Detection and quantitation of multiple volatile compounds in tissues by GC and GC/MS, *J. Anal. Toxicol.*, 6, 238–240, 1982.
86. Fehn, J. and Megges, G., Detection of O6-monoacetylmorphine in urine samples by GC/MS as evidence for heroin use, *J. Anal. Toxicol.*, 9, 134–138, 1985.
87. Dunemann, L. and Hajimiragha, H., Development of a screening method for the determination of volatile organic compounds in body fluids and environmental samples using purge and trap GC/MS, *Anal. Chim. Acta*, 283, 199–204, 1993.
88. West, R. and Ritz, D., GC/MS analysis of five common benzodiazepine metabolites in urine as tert-butyl-dimethylsilyl derivatives, *J. Anal. Toxicol.*, 17, 114–116, 1993.
89. Wimbish, G.H. and Johnson, K.G., Full spectral GC/MS identification of delta 9-carboxy-tetrahydrocannabinol in urine with the Finnigan ITS40, *J. Anal. Toxicol.*, 14, 292–295, 1990.
90. Zune, A., Dobberstein, P., Maurer, K.H., and Rapp, U., Identification of drugs using a gas chromatography-mass spectrometry system equipped with electron impact-chemical ionization and electron impact-field ionization field desorption combination sources, *J. Chromatogr.*, 122, 365–371, 1976.
91. Liu, R.H., McKeehan, A.M., Edwards, C., Foster, G., Bensley, W.D., Langner, J.G., et al., Improved GC/MS analysis of barbiturates in urine using centrifuge-based solid-phase extraction, methylation, with d5-pentobarbital as internal standard, *J. Forensic Sci.*, 39, 1504–1514, 1994.
92. Van Vyncht, G., Gaspar, P., DePauw, E., and Maguin-Rogister, G., Multi-residue screening and confirmatory analysis of anabolic steroids in urine by GC/MS/MS, *J. Chromatogr., A*, 683, 67–74, 1994.
93. Maurer, H.H., On the metabolism and the toxicological analysis of methylenedioxyphenyl-alkylamine designer drugs by gas chromatography mass spectrometry, *Ther. Drug Monit.*, 18, 465–470, 1996.
94. Saady, J.J., Narasimhachari, N., and Blanke, R.V., Rapid, simultaneous quantification of morphine, codeine, and hydromorphone by GC/MS, *J. Anal. Toxicol.*, 6, 235–237, 1982.
95. Wu Chen, N.B., Cody, J.T., Garriott, J.C., Foltz, R.L., Peat, M.A., and Schaffer, M.I., Recommended guidelines for forensic GC/MS procedures in toxicology laboratories associated with offices of medical examiners and/or coroners, *J. Forensic Sci.*, 35, 236–242, 1990.
96. Moeller, M., Doerr, G., and Warth, S., Simultaneous quantitation of delta-9-tetrahydrocannabinol (THC) and 11-nor-9-carboxy-delta-9-tetrahydrocannabinol (THC-COOH) in serum by GC/MS using deuterated internal standards and its application to a smoking study and forensic cases, *J. Forensic Sci.*, 37, 969–983, 1992.
97 Gibb, R.P., Cockerham, H., Goldfogel, G.A., Lawson, G.M., and Raisys, V.A., Substance abuse testing of urine by GC/MS in scanning mode evaluated by proficiency studies, TLC/GC, and EMIT, *J. Forensic Sci.*, 38, 124–133, 1993.
98. Maurer, H.H., Systematic toxicological analysis of drugs and their metabolites by gas chromatography-mass spectrometry [review], *J. Chromatogr.*, 580, 3–41, 1992.
99. Maurer, H.H. and Kraemer, T., Toxicological detection of selegiline and its metabolites in urine using fluorescence polarization immunoassay (FPIA) and gas chromatography-mass spectrometry (GC/MS) and differentiation by enantioselective GC/MS of the intake of selegiline from abuse of methamphetamine or amphetamine, *Arch. Toxicol.*, 66, 675–678, 1992.
100. Covey, T.R., Lee, E.D., and Henion, J.D., High-speed LC/MS/MS for the determination of drugs in biological samples, *Anal. Chem.*, 58, 2453–2460, 1986.
101. Brotherton, H.O. and Yost, R.A., Determination of drugs in blood serum by MS/MS, *Anal. Chem.*, 55, 549–553, 1983.
102. Phillips, W.H., Jr., Ota, K., and Wade, N.A., Tandem mass spectrometry (MS/MS) utilizing electron impact ionization and multiple reaction monitoring for the rapid, sensitive, and specific identification and quantitation of morphine in whole blood, *J. Anal. Toxicol.*, 13, 268–273, 1989.
103. Kerns, E., Lee, M.S., Mayol, R., and Klunk, L.J., Comparison of drug metabolite identification methods: rapid MS/MS screening versus isolation and GC/MS analysis, presented at 38th ASMS Conference, Tucson, AZ, 1990.
104. Gilbert, J.D., Greber, T.F., Ellis, J.D., Barrish, A., Olah, T.V., Fernandez-Metzler, C., et al., The development and cross-validation of methods based on radioimmunoassay and LC/MS/MS for the quantification of the class III antiarrhythmic agent, MK-0499, in human plasma and urine, *J. Pharm. Biomed. Anal.*, 13, 937–950, 1995.

105. Henion, J., Crowthers, J., and Covey, T., An improved thermospray LC/MS system for determining drugs in urine, *Proc. ASMS,* 32, 203–204, 1984.
106. Verheij, E.R., van der Greef, J., La Vos, G.F., van der Pol, W., and Niessen, W.M., Identification of diuron and four of its metabolites in human postmortem plasma and urine by LC/MS with a moving-belt interface, *J. Anal. Toxicol.,* 13, 8–12, 1989.
107. Koves, E.M. and Yen, B., The use of gas chromatography/negative ion chemical ionization mass spectrometry for the determination of lorazepam in whole blood, *J. Anal. Toxicol.,* 13, 69–72, 1989.
108. Leloux, M. and Maes, R., The use of electron impact and positive chemical ionization mass spectrometry in the screening of beta blockers and their metabolites in human urine, *Biomed. Environ. Mass Spectrom.,* 19, 137–142, 1990.
109. Cailleux, A. and Allain, P., Superiority of chemical ionization on electron impact for identification of drugs by GC/MS, *J. Anal. Toxicol.,* 3, 39–41, 1979.
110. Harkey, M.R., Henderson, G.L., and Zhou, C., Simultaneous quantitation of cocaine and its major metabolites in human hair by gas chromatography/chemical ionization mass spectrometry, *J. Anal. Toxicol.,* 15, 260–265, 1991.
111. Ohno, Y. and Kawabata, S., Rapid detection of illicit drugs by direct inlet chemical ionization mass spectrometry, *Kanzei Chuo Bunsekishoho,* 27, 7–15, 1987.
112. Mulvana, D.E., Duncan, G.F., Shyu, W.C., Tay, L.K., and Barbhaiya, R.H., Quantitative determination of butorphanol and its metabolites in human plasma by gas chromatography electron capture negative-ion chemical ionization mass spectrometry, *J. Chromatogr. B Biomed. Appl.,* 682, 289–300, 1996.
113. Milne, G.W.A., Foles, H.M., and Axenrod, T., Identification of dangerous drugs by isobutane chemical ionization mass spectrometry, *Anal. Chem.,* 43, 1815–1820, 1971.
114. Wu, W.S., Szklar, R.S., and Smith, R., Gas chromatographic determination and negative-ion chemical ionization mass spectrometric confirmation of 4,4′-methylenebis(2-chloroaniline) in urine via thin-layer chromatographic separation, *Analyst,* 121, 321–324, 1996.
115. Saferstein, R., Manura, J.J., and De, P.K., Drug detection in urine by chemical ionization-mass spectrometry, *J. Forensic Sci.,* 23, 29–36, 1978.
116. Wolen, R.L., Ziege, E.A., and Gruber, C., Jr., Determination of propoxyphene and norpropoxyphene by chemical ionization mass fragmentography, *Clin. Pharmacol. Ther.,* 17, 15–20, 1975.
117. Fitzgerald, R.L., Rexin, D.A., and Herold, D.A., Benzodiazepine analysis by negative chemical ionization gas chromatography-mass spectrometry, *J. Anal. Toxicol.,* 17, 342–347, 1993.
118. Suzuki, O., Hattori, H., and Asano, M., Detection of methamphetamine and amphetamine in a single human hair by gas chromatography-chemical ionization mass spectrometry, *J. Forensic Sci.,* 29, 611–617, 1984.
119. Sosnoff, C.S., Ann, Q., Bernert, J.T., Jr., Powell, M.K., Miller, B.B., Henderson, L.O., et al., Analysis of benzoylecgonine in dried blood spots by liquid chromatography — atmospheric pressure chemical ionization tandem mass spectrometry, *J. Anal. Toxicol.,* 20, 179–184, 1996.
120. Vidal, D.L., Ting, E.J., Perez, S.L., Taylor, R.W., and Le, S.D., Robotic method for the analysis of morphine and codeine in urine, *J. Forensic Sci.,* 37(5), 1283–1294, 1992.
121. Lloyd, T.L., Perschy, T.B., Gooding, A.E., and Tomlinson, J.J., Robotic solid phase extraction and high performance liquid chromatographic analysis of ranitidine in serum or plasma, *Biomed. Chromatogr.,* 6, 311–316, 1992.
122. Taylor, R.W. and Le, S.D., Robotic method for the analysis of cocaine and benzoylecgonine in urine, *J. Anal. Toxicol.,* 15, 276–278, 1991.
123. de Kanel, J. and Korbar, T., Robotics and the analysis of drugs of abuse, in *Analysis of Addictive and Misused Drugs*, Adamovics, J.A., Ed., Marcel Dekker, New York, 1995, 267–294.
124. Clarke, E. and Williams, M., Microcolor tests in toxicology, *J. Pharm. Pharmacol.,* 7, 255–262, 1955.
125. Stevens, H.M., Color tests, in *Clarke's Isolation and Identification of Drugs in Pharmaceuticals, Body Fluids and Postmortem Material*, Moffat, A.C., Ed., Pharmaceutical Press, London, 1986, 28–147.
126. Widdop, B., Hospital toxicology and drug abuse screening, in *Clarke's Isolation and Identification of Drugs in Pharmaceuticals, Body Fluids and Postmortem Material,* Moffat, A.C., Ed., Pharmaceutical Press, London, 1986, 4–6.
127. Masoud, A.N., Systematic identification of drugs of abuse. I. Spot tests, *J. Pharm. Sci.,* 64, 841–844, 1975.

128. Berry, D.J. and Grove, J., Emergency toxicological screening for drugs commonly taken in overdose, *J. Chromatogr.,* 80, 205–220, 1973.
129. Trinder, P., Rapid determination of salicylates in biological materials, *Biochem. J.,* 57, 1954.
130. King, J.A., Storrow, A.B., and Finkelstein, J.A., Urine Trinder spot test: a rapid salicylate screen for the emergency department, *Ann. Emerg. Med.,* 26, 330–333, 1995.
131. Stair, E.L. and Whaley, M., Rapid screening and spot tests for the presence of common poisons, *Vet. Hum. Toxicol.,* 32, 564–566, 1990.
132. Hepler, B.R., Sutheimer, C.A., and Sunshine, I., The role of the toxicology laboratory in emergency medicine. II. Study of an integrated approach, *J. Toxicol. Clin. Toxicol.,* 22, 503–528, 1984.
133. Decker, W.J. and Treuting, J.J., Spot tests for rapid diagnosis of poisoning, *Clin. Toxicol.,* 4, 89–97, 1971.
134. Asselin, W.M. and Caughlin, J.D., A rapid and simple color test for detection of salicylate in whole hemolyzed blood, *J. Anal. Toxicol.,* 14, 254–255, 1990.
135. Reith, J.F., Ditmarsh, W.C., and DeRuiter, T., An improved procedure for application of the Fujiwara reaction in the determination of organic halides, *Analyst,* 99, 652–656, 1974.
136. Frings, C.S. and Cohen, S., Rapid colorimetric method for the quantitative determination of ethchlorvynol (placidyl) in serum and urine, *Am. J. Clin. Pathol.,* 54, 833, 1970.
137. Kaye, S., Arsenic, in *Methodology for Analytical Toxicology,* Vol. I, Sunshine, I., Eds., CRC Press, Boca Raton, FL, 1984, 30–31.
138. Stolham, A., Chemical tests for metallic poisons, in *Toxicology: Mechanisms and Analytical Methods,* Stewart, C.P. and Stolman, A., Eds., Academic Press, New York, 1960, 640–678.
139. Stollman, A. and Stewart, C.P., Metallic poisons, in *Toxicology: Mechanisms and Analytical Methods,* Vol. 1, Stewart, C.P. and Stolman, A., Eds., Academic Press, New York, 1960, 202–222.
140. Kaye, S., Simple procedure for the detection of arsenic in body fluids, *Am. J. Clin. Pathol.,* 14, 36, 1944.
141. Gettler, A.O., Simple tests for mercury in body fluids and tissues, *Am. J. Clin. Pathol. (Tech. Suppl.),* 7, 13, 1937.
142. Aziz, K., Drugs-of-abuse testing. Screening and confirmation [review], *Clin. Lab. Med.,* 10, 493–502, 1990.
143. Slightom, E.L., The analysis of drugs in blood, bile, and tissue with an indirect homogeneous enzyme immunoassay, *J. Forensic Sci.,* 23, 292–303, 1978.
144. Bogusz, M., Aderjan, R., Schmitt, G., Nadler, E., and Neureither, B., The determination of drugs of abuse in whole blood by means of FPIA and EMIT-dau immunoassays — a comparative study, *Forensic Sci. Int.,* 48, 27–37, 1990.
145. Mason, P.A., Law, B., Pocock, K., and Moffat, A.C., Direct radioimmunoassay for the detection of barbiturates in blood and urine, *Analyst,* 107, 629–633, 1982.
146. Goddard, C.P., Stead, A.H., Mason, P.A., Law, B., Moffat, A.C., McBrien, M., et al., An iodine-125 radioimmunoassay for the direct detection of benzodiazepines in blood and urine, *Analyst,* 111, 525–529, 1986.
147. Lewellen, L.J. and McCurdy, H.H., A novel procedure for the analysis of drugs in whole blood by homogeneous enzyme immunoassay (EMIT), *J. Anal. Toxicol.,* 12, 260–264, 1988.
148. Perrigo, B.J. and Joynt, B.P., Optimization of the EMIT immunoassay procedure for the analysis of cannabinoids in methanolic blood extracts, *J. Anal. Toxicol.,* 13, 235–237, 1989.
149. Maier, R.D., Erkens, M., Hoenen, H., and Bogusz, M., The screening for common drugs of abuse in whole blood by means of EMIT-ETS and FPIA-ADx urine immunoassays, *Int. J. Legal Med.,* 105, 115–119, 1992.
150. Henderson, L.O., Powell, M.K., Hannon, W.H., Miller, B.B., Martin, M.L., Hanzlick, R.L., et al., Radioimmunoassay screening of dried blood spot materials for benzoylecgonine, *J. Anal. Toxicol.,* 17, 42–47, 1993.
151. Appel, T.A. and Wade, N.A., Screening of blood and urine for drugs of abuse utilizing Diagnostic Products Corporation's Coat-A-Count radioimmunoassay kits, *J. Anal. Toxicol.,* 13, 274–276, 1989.
152. Spiehler, V. and Brown, R., Unconjugated morphine in blood by radioimmunoassay and gas chromatography/mass spectrometry, *J. Forensic Sci.,* 32, 906–916, 1987.
153. Asselin, W.M. and Leslie, J.M., Modification of EMIT assay reagents for improved sensitivity and cost effectiveness in the analysis of hemolyzed whole blood, *J. Anal. Toxicol.,* 16, 381–388, 1992.

154. Gjerde, H., Christophersen, A.S., Skuterud, B., Klemetsen, K., and Morland, J., Screening for drugs in forensic blood samples using EMIT urine assays, *Forensic Sci. Int.*, 44, 179–185, 1990.
155. Blum, L.M., Klinger, R.A., and Rieders, F., Direct automated EMIT d.a.u. analysis of *N,N*-dimethylformamide-modified serum, plasma, and postmortem blood for benzodiazepines, benzoylecgonine, cannabinoids, and opiates, *J. Anal. Toxicol.*, 13, 285–288, 1989.
156. Asselin, W.M., Leslie, J.M., and McKinley, B., Direct detection of drugs of abuse in whole hemolyzed blood using the EMIT d.a.u. urine assays [published erratum appears in *J. Anal. Toxicol.*, 12(6), 16A, 1988], *J. Anal. Toxicol.*, 12, 207–215, 1988.
157. Fraser, A.D., Clinical evaluation of the EMIT salicylic acid assay, *Ther. Drug Monit.*, 5, 331–334, 1983.
158. Gooch, J.C., Caldwell, R., Turner, G.J., and Colbert, D.L., Cost effective EMIT assays, for drugs of abuse in urine, using the Eppendorf EPOS analyser, *J. Immunoassay,* 13, 85–96, 1992.
159. Poklis, A., Jortani, S., Edinboro, L.E., and Saady, J.J., Direct determination of benzoylecgonine in serum by EMIT d.a.u. cocaine metabolite immunoassay, *J. Anal. Toxicol.*, 18, 419–422, 1994.
160. Armbruster, D.A., Schwarzhoff, R.H., Pierce, B.L., and Hubster, E.C., Method comparison of EMIT 700 and EMIT II with RIA for drug screening, *J. Anal. Toxicol.*, 18, 110–117, 1994.
161. Armbruster, D.A., Schwarzhoff, R.H., Hubster, E.C., and Liserio, M.K., Enzyme immunoassay, kinetic microparticle immunoassay, radioimmunoassay, and fluorescence polarization immunoassay compared for drugs-of-abuse screening [see comments], *Clin. Chem.*, 39, 2137–2146, 1993.
162. Camara, P.D., Velletri, K., Krupski, M., Rosner, M., and Griffiths, W.C., Evaluation of the Boehringer Mannheim ES 300 immunoassay analyzer and comparison with enzyme immunoassay, fluorescence polarization immunoassay, and radioimmunoassay methods, *Clin. Biochem.*, 25, 251–254, 1992.
163. Fraser, A.D., Bryan, W., and Isner, A.F., Urinary screening for alpha-OH triazolam by FPIA and EIA with confirmation by GC/MS, *J. Anal. Toxicol.*, 16, 347–350, 1992.
164. Meenan, G.M., Barlotta, S., and Lehrer, M., Urinary tricyclic antidepressant screening: comparison of results obtained with Abbott FPIA reagents and Syva EIA reagents, *J. Anal. Toxicol.*, 14, 273–276, 1990.
165. Armbruster, D.A., Schwarzhoff, R.H., Pierce, B.L., and Hubster, E.C., Method comparison of EMIT II and online with RIA for drug screening [see comments], *J. Forensic Sci.*, 38, 1326–1341, 1993.
166. Kintz, P., Machart, D., Jamey, C., and Mangin, P., Comparison between GC/MS and the EMIT II, Abbott ADx, and Roche OnLine immunoassays for the determination of THCCOOH, *J. Anal. Toxicol.*, 19, 304–306, 1995.
167. Armbruster, D.A., Hubster, E.C., Kaufman, M.S., and Ramon, M.K., Cloned enzyme donor immunoassay (CEDIA) for drugs-of-abuse screening, *Clin. Chem.*, 41, 92–98, 1995.
168. Coty, W.A., Loor, R., Bellet, N., Khanna, P.L., Kaspar, P., and Baier, M., CEDIA — homogeneous immunoassays for the 1990s and beyond [review], *Wiener Klin. Wochenschr. Suppl.*, 191, 5–11, 1992.
169. Engel, W.D. and Khanna, P.L., CEDIA *in vitro* diagnostics with a novel homogeneous immunoassay technique. Current status and future prospects, *J. Immunol. Methods,* 150, 99–102, 1992.
170. Fleisher, M., Eisen, C., and Schwartz, M.K., An evaluation of a non-isotopic homogeneous enzyme immunoassay (CEDIA assay) for cortisol and its clinical utility, *Wiener Klin. Wochenschr. Suppl.*, 191, 77–80, 1992.
171. Henderson, D.R., Friedman, S.B., Harris, J.D., Manning, W.B., and Zoccoli, M.A., CEDIA, a new homogeneous immunoassay system, *Clin. Chem.*, 32, 1637–1641, 1986.
172. Klein, G., Collinsworth, W., Courbe, A., Diez, O., Domke, I., Hanseler, E., et al., Results of the multicenter evaluation of the CEDIA Phenobarbital assay, *Wiener Klin. Wochenschr. Suppl.*, 191, 43–47, 1992.
173. Wu, A.H., Forte, E., Casella, G., Sun, K., Hemphill, G., Foery, R., et al., CEDIA for screening drugs of abuse in urine and the effect of adulterants, *J. Forensic Sci.*, 40, 614–618, 1995.
174. Gosling, J.P., A decade of development in immunoassay methodology, *Clin. Chem.*, 36, 1408–1427, 1990.
175. Roberts, C.J. and Jackson, L.S., Development of an ELISA using a universal method of enzyme-labelling drug-specific antibodies, *J. Immunol. Methods,* 181, 157–166, 1995.
176. Laurie, D., Mason, A.J., Piggott, N.H., Rowell, F.J., Seviour, J., Strachan, D., et al., Enzyme linked immunosorbent assay for detecting benzodiazepines in urine, *Analyst,* 121, 951–954, 1996.
177. Makowski, G.S., Richter, J.J., Moore, R.E., Eisma, R., Ostheimer, D., Onoroski, M., et al., An enzyme-linked immunosorbent assay for urinary screening of fentanyl citrate abuse, *Ann. Clin. Lab. Sci.*, 25, 169–178, 1995.

178. Aoki, K., Yoshida, T., and Kuroiwa, Y., Forensic immunochemistry, *Forensic Sci. Int.,* 80, 163–173, 1996.
179. Cone, E.J., Validity testing of commercial urine cocaine metabolite assays. III, *J. Forensic Sci.,* 34, 991–995, 1989.
180. Oeltgen, P.R., Shank, W., Jr., Blouin, R.A., and Clark, T., Clinical evaluation of the Abbott TDx fluorescence polarization immunoassay analyzer, *Ther. Drug Monit.,* 6, 360–367, 1984.
181. Becker, J., Correll, A., Koepf, W., and Rittner, C., Comparative studies on the detection of benzodiazepines in serum by means of immunoassays (FPIA), *J. Anal. Toxicol.,* 17, 103–108, 1993.
182. Alvarez, J.S., Sacristan, J.A., and Alsar, M.J., Comparison of a monoclonal antibody fluorescent polarization immunoassay with monoclonal antibody radioimmunoassay for cyclosporin determination in whole blood, *Ther. Drug Monit.,* 14, 78–80, 1992.
183. De la Torre, R., Badia, R., Gonzalez, G., Garcia, M., Pretel, M.J., Farre, M., et al., Cross-reactivity of stimulants found in sports drug testing by two fluorescence polarization immunoassays, *J. Anal. Toxicol.,* 20, 165–170, 1996.
184. Ferrara, S.D., Tedeschi, L., Frison, G., Brusini, G., Castagna, F., Bernardelli, B., et al., Drugs-of-abuse testing in urine: statistical approach and experimental comparison of immunochemical and chromatographic techniques, *J. Anal. Toxicol.,* 18, 278–291, 1994.
185. Karnes, H.T. and Beightol, L.A., Evaluation of fluorescence polarization immunoassay for quantitation of serum salicylates, *Ther. Drug Monit.,* 7, 351–354, 1985.
186. Beutler, D., Molteni, S., Zeugin, T., and Thormann, W., Evaluation of instrumental, nonisotopic immunoassays (fluorescence polarization immunoassay and enzyme-multiplied immunoassay technique) for cyclosporine monitoring in whole blood after kidney and liver transplantation, *Ther. Drug Monit.,* 14, 424–432, 1992.
187. Przekop, M.A., Manno, J.E., Kunsman, G.W., Cockerham, K.R., and Manno, B.R., Evaluation of the Abbott ADx Amphetamine/Methamphetamine II abused drug assay: comparison to TDx, EMIT, and GC/MS methods, *J. Anal. Toxicol.,* 15, 323–326, 1991.
188. Fraser, A.D. and Bryan, W., Evaluation of the Abbott TDx serum benzodiazepine immunoassay for the analysis of lorazepam, adinazolam, and N-desmethyladinazolam, *J. Anal. Toxicol.,* 19, 281–284, 1995.
189. AlFares, A.M., Mira, S.A., and el-Sayed, Y.M., Evaluation of the fluorescence polarization immunoassay for quantitation of digoxin in serum, *Ther. Drug Monit.,* 6, 454–457, 1984.
190. Caplan, Y.H., Levine, B., and Goldberger, B., Fluorescence polarization immunoassay evaluated for screening for amphetamine and methamphetamine in urine, *Clin. Chem.,* 33, 1200–1202, 1987.
191. Huang, W., Moody, D.E., Andrenyak, D.M., and Rollins, D.E., Immunoassay detection of nordiazepam, triazolam, lorazepam, and alprazolam in blood, *J. Anal. Toxicol.,* 17, 365–369, 1993.
192. Beck, O., Lafolie, P., Odelius, G., and Boreus, L.O., Immunological screening of benzodiazepines in urine: improved detection of oxazepam intake, *Toxicol. Lett.,* 52, 7–14, 1990.
193. Wong, S.H., Methodologies for antidepressant monitoring [review], *Clin. Lab. Med.,* 7, 415–433, 1987.
194. Ensslin, H.K., Kovar, K.A., and Maurer, H.H., Toxicological detection of the designer drug 3,4-methylenedioxyethylamphetamine (MDE, Eve) and its metabolites in urine by gas chromatography-mass spectrometry and fluorescence polarization immunoassay, *J. Chromatogr. B: Biomed. Appl.,* 683, 189–197, 1996.
195. Castro, A. and Malkus, H., Radioimmunoassays of drugs of abuse in humans: a review [review], *Res. Commun. Chem. Pathol. Pharmacol.,* 16, 291–309, 1977.
196. Budd, R.D., Yang, F.C., and Utley, K.O., Barbiturates — structure versus RIA reactivity, *Clin. Toxicol.,* 18, 317–352, 1981.
197. Weaver, M.L., Gan, B.K., Allen, E., et al., Correlations on RIA, FPIA, and EIA of *Cannabis* metabolites with GC/MS analysis of 11-nor-D9-THC acid in urine specimens, *Forensic Sci. Int.,* 49, 43–56, 1991.
198. Moeller, M.R. and Mueller, C., The detection of 6-monoacetylmorphine in urine, serum and hair by GC/MS and RIA, *Forensic Sci. Int.,* 70, 125–133, 1995.
199. Abercrombie, M.L. and Jewell, J.S., Evaluation of EMIT and RIA high volume test procedures for THC metabolites in urine utilizing GC/MS confirmation, *J. Anal. Toxicol.,* 10, 178–180, 1986.
200. Watts, V.W. and Caplan, Y.H., Evaluation of the Coat-A-Count 125I fentanyl RIA: comparison of ^{125}I RIA and GC/MS-SIM for quantification of fentanyl in case urine specimens, *J. Anal. Toxicol.,* 14, 266–272, 1990.

201. Kintz, P., Cirimele, V., Edel, Y., Jamey, C., and Mangin, P., Hair analysis for buprenorphine and its dealkylated metabolite by RIA and confirmation by LC/ECD, *J. Forensic Sci.,* 39, 1497–1503, 1994.
202. Budd, R.D., Leung, W.J., and Yang, F.C., RIA opiates: structure versus reactivity, *Clin. Toxicol.,* 17, 383–393, 1980.
203. Baker, D.P., Murphy, M.S., Shepp, P.F., Royo, V.R., Caldarone, M.E., Escoto, B., et al., Evaluation of the Abuscreen ONLINE assay for amphetamines on the Hitachi 737: comparison with EMIT and GC/MS methods, *J. Forensic Sci.,* 40, 108–112, 1995.
204. Hailer, M., Glienke, Y., Schwab, I.M., and von Meyer, L., Modification and evaluation of Abuscreen OnLine assays for drug metabolites in urine performed on a COBAS FARA II in comparison with EMIT d.a.u. Cannabinoid 20, *J. Anal. Toxicol.,* 19, 99–103, 1995.
205. Moody, D.E. and Medina, A.M., OnLine kinetic microparticle immunoassay of cannabinoids, morphine, and benzoylecgonine in serum, *Clin. Chem.,* 41, 1664–1665, 1995.
206. Budd, R.D., Amphetamine EMIT — structure versus reactivity, *Clin. Toxicol.,* 18, 91–110, 1981.
207. Bailey, D.N., Amphetamine detection during toxicology screening of a university medical center patient population, *J. Toxicol. Clin. Toxicol.,* 25, 399–409, 1987.
208. Budd, R.D., Amphetamine radioimmunoassay — structure versus reactivity, *Clin. Toxicol.,* 18, 299–316, 1981.
209. Kunsman, G.W., Manno, J.E., Cockerham, K.R., and Manno, B.R., Application of the Syva EMIT and Abbott TDx amphetamine immunoassays to the detection of 3,4-methylene-dioxymethamphetamine (MDMA) and 3,4-methylene-dioxyethamphetamin (MDEA) in urine, *J. Anal. Toxicol.,* 14, 149–153, 1990.
210. Turner, G.J., Colbert, D.L., and Chowdry, B.Z., A broad spectrum immunoassay using fluorescence polarization for the detection of amphetamines in urine, *Ann. Clin. Biochem.,* 28, 588–594, 1991.
211. D'Nicuola, J., Jones, R., Levine, B., and Smith, M.L., Evaluation of six commercial amphetamine and methamphetamine immunoassays for cross-reactivity to phenylpropanolamine and ephedrine in urine [see comments], *J. Anal. Toxicol.,* 16, 211–213, 1992.
212. Cody, J.T. and Schwarzhoff, R., Fluorescence polarization immunoassay detection of amphetamine, methamphetamine, and illicit amphetamine analogues, *J. Anal. Toxicol.,* 17, 23–33, 1993.
213. Levine, B.S. and Caplan, Y.H., Isometheptene cross reacts in the EMIT amphetamine assay, *Clin. Chem.,* 33, 1264–1265, 1987.
214. Poklis, A. and Moore, K.A., Response of EMIT amphetamine immunoassays to urinary desoxyephedrine following Vicks Inhaler use, *Ther. Drug Monit.,* 17, 89–94, 1995.
215. Braithwaite, R.A., Jarvie, D.R., Minty, P.S., Simpson, D., and Widdop, B., Screening for drugs of abuse. I. Opiates, amphetamines and cocaine [review], *Ann. Clin. Biochem.,* 32, 123–153, 1995.
216. Poklis, A. and Moore, K.A., Stereoselectivity of the TDx/ADx/FLx amphetamine/methamphetamine II immunoassay — response of urine specimens following nasal inhaler use, *J. Toxicol. Clin. Toxicol.,* 33, 35–41, 1995.
217. Moore, F.M., Jarvie, D.R., and Simpson, D., Urinary amphetamines, benzodiazepines and methadone: cost-effective detection procedures, *Med. Lab. Sci.,* 49, 27–33, 1992.
218. Law, B. and Moffat, A.C., The evaluation of an homogeneous enzyme immunoassay (EMIT) and radioimmunoassay for barbiturates, *J. Forensic Sci. Soc.*, 21, 55–66, 1981.
219. Spector, S. and Flynn, E.J., Barbiturates: radioimmunoassay, *Science,* 174, 1036–1038, 1971.
220. Jain, N.C., Mass screening and confirmation of barbiturates in urine by RIA/gas chromatography, *Clin. Toxicol.,* 9, 221–233, 1976.
221. Caplan, Y.H. and Levine, B., Abbott phencyclidine and barbiturates abused drug assays: evaluation and comparison of ADx FPIA, TDx FPIA, EMIT, and GC/MS methods, *J. Anal. Toxicol.,* 13, 289–292, 1989.
222. Frazer, A.D., Urinary screening for alprazolam, triazolam, and their metabolites with the EMIT d.a.u. benzodiazepine metabolite assay, *J. Anal. Toxicol.,* 11, 263–266, 1987.
223. Budd, R.D., Benzodiazepine structure versus reactivity with EMIT oxazepam antibody, *Clin. Toxicol.*, 18, 643–655, 1981.
224. Meatherall, R., Benzodiazepine screening using EMIT II and TDx: urine hydrolysis pretreatment required, *J. Anal. Toxicol.,* 18, 385–390, 1994.
225. Fitzgerald, R., Rexin, D., and Herold, D., Detecting benzodiazepines: immunoassays compared with negative chemical ionization gas chromatography/mass spectrometry, *Clin. Chem.,* 40, 373–380, 1994.

226. Beck, O., Lafolie, P., Hjemdahl, P., Borg, S., Odelius, G., and Wirbing, P., Detection of benzodiazepine intake in therapeutic doses by immunoanalysis of urine: two techniques evaluated and modified for improved performance, *Clin. Chem.,* 38, 271–275, 1992.
227. Simonsson, P., Liden, A., and Lindberg, S., Effect of beta-glucuronidase on urinary benzodiazepine concentrations determined by fluorescence polarization immunoassay, *Clin. Chem.,* 41, 920–923, 1995.
228. Manchon, M., Verdier, M.F., Pallud, P., Vialle, A., Beseme, F., and Bienvenu, J., Evaluation of EMIT-TOX Enzyme Immunoassay for the analysis of benzodiazepines in serum: usefulness and limitations in an emergency laboratory, *J. Anal. Toxicol.,* 9, 209–212, 1985.
229. Valentine, J.L., Middleton, R., and Sparks, C., Identification of urinary benzodiazepines and their metabolites — comparison of automated HPLC and GC/MS after immunoassay screening of clinical specimens, *J. Anal. Toxicol.,* 20, 416–424, 1996.
230. Huang, W. and Moody, D.E., Immunoassay detection of benzodiazepines and benzodiazepine metabolites in blood, *J. Anal. Toxicol.,* 19, 333–342, 1995.
231. Beyer, K.H. and Martz, S., [Immunologic studies of benzodiazepine — the effect of structural characteristics on cross-reactivity] [in German], *Arch. Pharm.,* 324, 933–935, 1991.
232. Schutz, H., Modern screening strategies in analytical toxicology with special regard to new benzodiazepines, *Z. Rechtsmed. J. Legal Med.,* 100, 19–37, 1988.
233. Fraser, A.D., Bryan, W., and Isner, A.F., Urinary screening for alprazolam and its major metabolites by the Abbott ADx and TDx analyzers with confirmation by GC/MS, *J. Anal. Toxicol.,* 15, 25–29, 1991.
234. Borggaard, B. and Joergensen, I., Urinary screening for benzodiazepines with radioreceptor assay: comparison with EMIT dau, *J. Anal. Toxicol.,* 18, 243–246, 1994.
235. Schramm, W., Craig, P.A., Smith, R.H., and Berger, G.E., Cocaine and benzoylecgonine in saliva, serum, and urine, *Clin. Chem.,* 39, 481–487, 1993.
236. Martinez, F., Poet, T.S., Pillai, R., Erickson, J., Estrada, A.L., and Watson, R.R., Cocaine metabolite (benzoylecgonine) in hair and urine of drug users, *J. Anal. Toxicol.,* 17, 138–142, 1993.
237. Foltz, R.L., Botelho, C., Reuschel, S.A., Kuntz, D.J., Moody, D.E., and Bristow, G.M., Comparison of immunoassays for semi-quantitative measurement of benzoylecgonine in urine, in NIDA Research Monograph 126, U.S. Government Printing Office, Rockville, MD, 1995, 110–117.
238. Moore, F.M. and Simpson, D., Detection of benzoylecgonine (cocaine metabolite) in urine: a cost-effective low risk immunoassay procedure, *Med. Lab. Sci.,* 47, 85–89, 1990.
239. Peterson, K.L., Logan, B.K., and Christian, G.D., Detection of cocaine and its polar transformation products and metabolites in human urine, *Forensic Sci. Int.,* 73, 183–196, 1995.
240. Poklis, A., Evaluation of TDx cocaine metabolite assay, *J. Anal. Toxicol.,* 11, 228–230, 1987.
241. Baugh, L.D., Allen, E.E., Liu, R.H., Langner, J.G., Fentress, J.C., Chadha, S.C., et al., Evaluation of immunoassay methods for the screening of cocaine metabolites in urine, *J. Forensic Sci.,* 36, 79–85, 1991.
242. De Kanel, J., Dunlap, L., and Hall, T.D., Extending the detection limit of the TDx fluorescence polarization immunoassay for benzoylecgonine in urine, *Clin. Chem.,* 35, 2110–2112, 1989.
243. Yee, H.Y., Nelson, J.D., and Papa, V.M., Measurement of benzoylecgonine in whole blood using the Abbott ADx analyzer, *J. Anal. Toxicol.,* 17, 84–86, 1993.
244. Steele, B.W., Bandstra, E.S., Wu, N.C., Hime, G.W., and Hearn, W.L., *m*-Hydroxybenzoylecgonine: an important contributor to the immunoreactivity in assays for benzoylecgonine in meconium, *J. Anal. Toxicol.,* 17, 348–352, 1993.
245. McCord, C.E. and McCutcheon, J.R., Preliminary evaluation of the Abbott TDx for benzoylecgonine and opiate screening in whole blood, *J. Anal. Toxicol.,* 12, 295–297, 1988.
246. Robinson, K. and Smith, R.N., Radioimmunoassay of benzoylecgonine in samples of forensic interest, *J. Pharm. Pharmacol.,* 36, 157–162, 1984.
247. Cone, E.J., Menchen, S.L., Paul, B.C., Mell, L.D., and Mitchell, J., Validity testing of commercial urine cocaine metabolite assays: I. *J. Forensic Sci.,* 34, 15–31, 1989.
248. Cone, E.J. and Mitchell, J., Validity testing of commercial urine cocaine metabolite assays. II. Sensitivity, specificity, accuracy, and confirmation by gas chromatography/mass spectrometry, *J. Forensic Sci.,* 34, 32–45, 1989.
249. Cone, E.J., Yousefnejad, D., and Dickerson, S.L., Validity testing of commercial urine cocaine metabolite assays. IV. Evaluation of the EMIT d.a.u. cocaine metabolite assay in a quantitative mode for detection of cocaine metabolite, *J. Forensic Sci.,* 35, 786–791, 1990.

250. Cone, E.J., Menchen, S.L., and Mitchell, J., Validity testing of the TDx Cocaine Metabolite Assay with human specimens obtained after intravenous cocaine administration, *Forensic Sci. Int.*, 37, 265–275, 1988.
251. Van der Slooten, E.P. and van der Helm, H.J., Comparison of the EMIT (enzyme multiplied immunoassay technique) opiate assay and a gas-chromatographic–mass-spectrometric determination of morphine and codeine in urine, *Clin. Chem.*, 22, 1110–1111, 1976.
252. Smith, M.L., Hughes, R.O., Levine, B., Dickerson, S., Darwin, W.D., and Cone, E.J., Forensic drug testing for opiates. VI. Urine testing for hydromorphone, hydrocodone, oxymorphone, and oxycodone with commercial opiate immunoassays and gas chromatography-mass spectrometry, *J. Anal. Toxicol.*, 19, 18–26, 1995.
253. Cone, E.J., Dickerson, S., Paul, B.D., and Mitchell, J.M., Forensic drug testing for opiates. V. Urine testing for heroin, morphine, and codeine with commercial opiate immunoassays, *J. Anal. Toxicol.*, 17, 156–164, 1993.
254. Cone, E.J., Dickerson, S., Paul, B.D., and Mitchell, J.M., Forensic drug testing for opiates. IV. Analytical sensitivity, specificity, and accuracy of commercial urine opiate immunoassays, *J. Anal. Toxicol.*, 16, 72–78, 1992.
255. Mitchell, J.M., Paul, B.D., Welch, P., and Cone, E.J., Forensic drug testing for opiates, *J. Anal. Toxicol.*, 15, 49–53, 1991.
256. Spiehler, V.R. and Sedgwick, P., Radioimmunoassay screening and GC/MS confirmation of whole blood samples for drugs of abuse, *J. Anal. Toxicol.*, 9, 63–66, 1985.
257. Lee, J.W., Pedersen, J.E., Moravetz, T.L., Dzerk, A.M., Mundt, A.D., and Shepard, K.V., Sensitive and specific radioimmunoassays for opiates using commercially available materials, *J. Pharm. Sci.*, 80, 284–288, 1991.
258. Weingarten, H.L. and Trevias, E.C., Analysis of phencyclidine in blood by gas chromatography, radioimmunoassay, and enzyme immunoassay, *J. Anal. Toxicol.*, 6, 88–90, 1982.
259. Heveran, J.E., Anthony, M., and Ward, C., Determination of phencyclidine by radioimmunoassay, *J. Forensic Sci.*, 25, 79–87, 1980.
260. Fyfe, M.J., Chand, P., McCutchen, C., Long, J.S., Walia, A.S., Edwards, C., et al., Evaluation of enzyme immunoassay performance characteristics — phencyclidine example, *J. Forensic Sci.*, 38, 156–164, 1993.
261. Sneath, T.C. and Jain, N.C., Evaluation of phencyclidine by EMIT d.a.u. utilizing the ETS analyzer and a 25-ng/mL cutoff, *J. Anal. Toxicol.*, 16, 107–108, 1992.
262. Ragan, F., Jr., Hite, S.A., Samuels, M.S., Garey, R.E., Daul, G., and Schuler, R.E., Extended EMIT-DAU phencyclidine screen, *J. Clin. Psychiatry*, 47, 194–195, 1986.
263. Levine, B., Goldberger, B.A., and Caplan, Y.H., Evaluation of the Coat-a-Count radioimmunoassay for phencyclidine, *Clin. Chem.*, 34, 429, 1988.
264. Cary, P.L., Johnson, C.A., Folsom, T.M., and Bales, W.R., Immunoassay method validation for a modified EMIT phencyclidine assay, *J. Anal. Toxicol.*, 16, 48–51, 1992.
265. Budd, R.D., Phencyclidine (PCP)-structure versus reactivity, *Clin. Toxicol.*, 18, 1033–1041, 1981.
266. Kintz, P. and Mangin, P., Abbott propoxyphene assay: evaluation and comparison of TDx FPIA and GC/MS methods, *J. Anal. Toxicol.*, 17, 222–224, 1993.
267. Frederick, D.L., Green, J., and Fowler, M.W., Comparison of six cannabinoid metabolite assays, *J. Anal. Toxicol.*, 9, 116–120, 1985.
268. Budgett, W.T., Levine, B., Xu, A., and Smith, M.L., Comparison of Abbott fluorescence polarization immunoassay (FPIA) and Roche radioimmunoassay for the analyses of cannabinoids in urine specimens, *J. Forensic Sci.*, 37, 632–635, 1992.
269. Kaeferstein, H., Sticht, G., and Staak, M., Comparison of various immunological methods with GC/MS analysis in the detection of cannabinoids in urine, *Beitr. Gerichtl. Med.*, 47, 115–122, 1989.
270. Moore, F.M.L. and Simpson, D., Detection of cannabinoids in urine: a cost-effective low risk immunoassay procedure, *Med. Lab. Sci.*, 48, 76–79, 1991.
271. Colbert, D.L., Sidki, A.M., Gallacher, G., and Landon, J., Fluoroimmunoassays for cannabinoids in urine, *Analyst*, 112, 1483–1486, 1987.
272. McBurney, L.J., Bobbie, B.A., and Sepp, L.A., GC/MS and EMIT analyses for delta 9-tetrahydrocannabinol metabolites in plasma and urine of human subjects, *J. Anal. Toxicol.*, 10, 56–64, 1986.

273. King, D.L., Martel, P.A., and O'Donnell, C.M., Laboratory detection of cannabinoids [review], *Clin. Lab. Med.,* 7, 641–653, 1987.
274. Moyer, T.P., Palmen, M.A., Johnson, P., Charlson, J.R., and Ellefson, P.J., Marijuana testing — how good is it? *Mayo Clin. Proc.,* 62, 413–417, 1987.
275. Cook, C.E., Seltzman, H.H., Schindler, V.H., Tallent, C.R., Chin, K.M., and Pitt, C.G., Radioimmunoassays for cannabinoids, *NIDA Res. Monogr.,* 42, 19–32, 1982.
276. Gjerde, H., Screening for cannabinoids in blood using EMIT: concentrations of delta-9-tetrahydrocannabinol in relation to EMIT results, *Forensic Sci. Int.,* 50, 121–124, 1991.
277. Goodall, C.R. and Basteyns, B.J., A reliable method for the detection, confirmation, and quantitation of cannabinoids in blood, *J. Anal. Toxicol.,* 19, 419–426, 1995.
278. Ernst, R., Williams, L., Dalbey, M., Collins, C., and Pankey, S., Homogeneous enzyme immunoassay (EMIT) protocol for monitoring tricyclic antidepressants on the COBAS-BIO centrifugal analyzer, *Ther. Drug Monit.,* 9, 85–90, 1987.
279. Asselin, W.M. and Leslie, J.M., Direct detection of therapeutic concentrations of tricyclic antidepressants in whole hemolyzed blood using the EMITtox serum tricyclic antidepressant assay, *J. Anal. Toxicol.,* 15, 167–173, 1991.
280. Benitez, J., Dahlqvist, R., Gustafsson, L.L., Magnusson, A., and Sjoqvist, F., Clinical pharmacological evaluation of an assay kit for intoxications with tricyclic antidepressants, *Ther. Drug Monit.,* 8, 102–105, 1986.
281. Dorey, R.C., Preskorn, S.H., and Widener, P.K., Results compared for tricyclic antidepressants as assayed by liquid chromatography and enzyme immunoassay, *Clin. Chem.,* 34, 2348–2351, 1988.
282. Nebinger, P. and Koel, M., Specificity data of the tricyclic antidepressants assay by fluorescent polarization immunoassay, *J. Anal. Toxicol.,* 14, 219–221, 1990.
283. Vandel, S., Vincent, F., Prudhon, F., Nezelof, S., Bonin, B., and Bertschy, G., Results compared for tricyclic antidepressants as assayed by gas chromatography and enzyme immunoassay, *Therapie,* 47, 41–45, 1992.
284. Brunk, S.D., Thin-layer chromatography using Toxi-lab system, in *Analysis of Addictive and Misused Drugs*, Adamovics, J.A., Ed., Marcel Dekker, New York, 1995, 41–50.
285. Guebitz, G. and Wintersteiger, R., Identification of drugs of abuse by high-performance thin-layer chromatography, *J. Anal. Toxicol.,* 4, 141–144, 1980.
286. Singh, A.K., Granley, K., Ashraf, M., and Misha, U., Drug screening and confirmation by thin layer chromatography, *J. Planar Chromatogr. Mod. TLC,* 2, 410–419, 1989.
287. Wilson, J.F., Williams, J., Walker, G., Toseland, P.A., Smith, B.L., Richens, A., et al., Sensitivity and specificity of techniques used to detect drugs of abuse in urine, in *Recent Developments in Therapeutic Drug Monitoring and Clinical Toxicology*, Sunshine, I., Ed., Marcel Dekker, New York, 1992, 527–535.
288. Bogusz, M., Klys, M., Wijsbeek, J., Franke, J.P., and de Zeeuw, R.A., Impact of biological matrix and isolation methods on detectability and interlaboratory variations of TLC Rf-values in systematic toxicological analysis, *J. Anal. Toxicol.,* 8, 149–154, 1984.
289. Wolff, K., Sanderson, M.J., and Hay, A.W., A rapid horizontal TLC method for detecting drugs of abuse, *Ann. Clin. Biochem.,* 27, 482–488, 1990.
290. Jarvie, D.R. and Simpson, D., Drug screening: evaluation of the Toxi-Lab TLC system, *Ann. Clin. Biochem.,* 23, 76–84, 1986.
291. Nishigami, J., Ohshima, T., Takayasu, T., Kondo, T., Lin, Z., and Nagano, T., [Forensic toxicological application of TOXI-LAB screening for biological specimens in autopsy cases and emergency cares], *Nippon Hoigaku Zasshi Jpn. J. Legal Med.,* 47, 372–379, 1993.
292. Nadkarni, S., Faye, S., and Hay, A., Experience with the use of the Toxi-Lab TLC system in screening for morphine/heroin abuse, *Ann. Clin. Biochem.,* 24, 211–212, 1987.
293. Plavsic, F., Barbaric, V., Parag, M., Arambasin, M., Gjerek, J., and Stavljenic, A., Increased possibilities for detecting drugs by the Toxi-Lab screening test, *Ann. Clin. Biochem.,* 22, 324–326, 1985.
294. Caldwell, R. and Challenger, H., A capillary column GC method for the identification of drugs of abuse in urine samples, *Ann. Clin. Biochem.,* 26, 430–443, 1989.
295. Grinstead, G.F., A closer look at acetyl and pentafluoropropionyl derivatives for quantitative analysis of morphine and codeine by gas chromatography–mass spectrometry, *J. Anal. Toxicol.,* 15, 293–298, 1991.

296. Kataoka, H., Derivatization reactions for the determination of amines by gas chromatography and their applications in environmental analysis, *J. Chromatogr. A,* 733, 19–34, 1996.
297. Lho, D., Hong, J., Paek, H., Lee, J., and Park, J., Determination of phenolalkylamines, narcotic analgesics, and beta-blockers by gas chromatography-mass spectrometry, *J. Anal. Toxicol.,* 14, 77–83, 1990.
298. Sanchez, M.C., Colome, J., and Gelpi, E., Electron capture and multiple ion detection of benzodiazepine esters in pharmacokinetic studies, *J. Chromatogr.,* 126, 601–613, 1976.
299. Beck, O. and Faull, K.F., Extractive acylation and mass spectrometric assay of 3-methoxytyramine, normetanephrine, and metanephrine in cerebrospinal fluid, *Anal. Biochem.,* 149, 492–500, 1985.
300. Jain, N.C., Sneath, T.C., Budd, R.D., and Leung, W.J., Gas chromatographic/thin-layer chromatographic analysis of acetylated codeine and morphine in urine, *Clin. Chem.,* 21, 1486–1489, 1975.
301. Czarny, R.J. and Hornbeck, C.L., Quantitation of methamphetamine and amphetamine in urine by capillary GC/MS. II. Derivatization with 4-carbethoxyhexafluorobutyryl chloride, *J. Anal. Toxicol.,* 13, 257–262, 1989.
302. Bowie, L.J. and Kirkpatrick, P.B., Simultaneous determination of monoacetylmorphine, morphine, codeine, and other opiates by GC/MS, *J. Anal. Toxicol.,* 13, 326–329, 1989.
303. Toyo'oka, T., Use of derivatization to improve the chromatographic properties and detection selectivity of physiologically important carboxylic acids, *J. Chromatogr. B Biomed. Appl.,* 671, 91–112, 1995.
304. Zamecnik, J., Use of cyclic boronates for GC/MS screening and quantitation of beta-blockers and some bronchodilators, *J. Anal. Toxicol.,* 14, 132–136, 1990.
305. Liu, F., Liu, Y.T., Feng, C.L., and Luo, Y., Determination of methaqualone and its metabolites in urine and blood by UV, GC/FID and GC/MS, *Yao Hsueh Hsueh Pao Acta Pharm. Sin.,* 29, 610–616, 1994.
306. Michalek, R.W., Rejent, T.A., and Spencer, R.A., Disopyramide fatality: case report and GC/FID analysis, *J. Anal. Toxicol.,* 6, 255–257, 1982.
307. Kintz, P., Mangin, P., Lugnier, A.A., and Chaumont, A.J., A rapid and sensitive gas chromatographic analysis of meprobamate or carisoprodol in urine and plasma, *J. Anal. Toxicol.,* 12, 73–74, 1988.
308. Qiu, F.H., Liu, L., Guo, L., Luo, Y., and Lu, Y.Q., [Rapid identification and quantitation of barbiturates in plasma using solid-phase extraction combined with GC-FID and GC/MS method], *Yao Hsueh Hsueh Pao Acta Pharm. Sin.,* 30, 372–377, 1995.
309. Kageura, M., Hara, K., Hieda, Y., Takamoto, M., Fujiwara, Y., Fukuma, Y., et al., [Screening of drugs and chemicals by wide-bore capillary gas chromatography with flame ionization and nitrogen phosphorus detectors]. [Japanese], *Nippon Hoigaku Zasshi Jpn. J. Legal Med.,*43(2), 161–165, 1989.
310. Ghittori, S., Fiorentino, M.L., and Imbriani, M., [Use of gas chromatography with flame ionization (GC-FID) in the measurement of solvents in the urine], *Giorn. Ital. Med. Lavoro,* 9, 21–24, 1987.
311. Verebey, K., Jukofsky, D., and Mule, S.J., Confirmation of EMIT benzodiazepine assay with GLC/NPD, *J. Anal. Toxicol.,* 6, 305–308, 1982.
312. Trinh, V. and Vernay, A., Evaluation of sample treatment procedure for the routine identification and determination at nanogram level of *O*-monoacetylmorphine in urine by capillary GC and dual NPD-FID, *J. High Resolution Chromatogr.,* 13, 162–166, 1990.
313. Verebey, K. and DePace, A., Rapid confirmation of enzyme multiplied immunoassay technique (EMIT) cocaine positive urine samples by capillary gas-liquid chromatography/nitrogen phosphorus detection (GLC/NPD), *J. Forensic Sci.,* 34, 46–52, 1989.
314. Balkon, J. and Donnelly, B., Determination of basic drugs in post mortem tissues: a microextraction technique utilizing GLC/NPD of effluents, *J. Anal. Toxicol.,* 6, 181–184, 1982.
315. Gaillard, Y., Gay-Montchamp, J.P., and Ollagnier, M., Simultaneous screening and quantitation of alpidem, zolpidem, buspirone and benzodiazepines by dual-channel gas chromatography using electron-capture and nitrogen-phosphorus detection after solid-phase extraction, *J. Chromatogr.,* 622, 197–208, 1993.
316. Japp, M., Garthwaite, K., Geeson, A.V., and Osselton, M.D., Collection of analytical data for benzodiazepines and benzophenones, *J. Chromatogr.,* 439, 317–339, 1988.
317. Lillsunde, P. and Seppala, T., Simultaneous screening and quantitative analysis of benzodiazepines by dual-channel gas chromatography using electron-capture and nitrogen-phosphorus detection, *J. Chromatogr.,* 533, 97–110, 1990.
318. Kokanovich, J.D., Simonick, T.F., and Watts, V.W., High speed analysis of underivatized drugs by GC/MS, *J. High Resolution Chromatogr.,* 12, 45–48, 1989.

319. Lillsunde, P. and Korte, T., Thin-layer chromatographic screening and GC/MS confirmation in analysis of abused drugs, in *Analysis of Addictive and Misused Drugs*, Adamovics, J.A., Ed., Marcel Dekker, New York, 1995, 221–265.
320. Maurer, H. and Pfleger, K., Screening procedure for detection of antidepressants and their metabolites in urine using a computerized GC/MS technique, *J. Chromatogr.,* 305, 309–323, 1984.
321. Siren, H., Saarinen, M., Hainari, S., Lukkari, P., and Riekkola, M.L., Screening of beta-blockers in human serum by ion-pair chromatography and their identification as methyl or acetyl derivatives by GC/MS, *J. Chromatogr.,* 632, 215–227, 1993.
322. Needleman, S.B. and Porvaznik, M., Identification of parent benzodiazepines by gas chromotography/mass spectroscopy (GC/MS) from urinary extracts treated with B-glucuronidase, *Forensic Sci. Int.,* 73, 49–60, 1995.
323. Maurer, H. and Pfleger, K., Screening procedure for detection of phenothiazines and analogous neuroleptics and their metabolites in urine using a computerized GC/MS technique, *J. Chromatogr.,* 306, 125–145, 1984.
324. Fraser, A.D., Bryan, W., and Isner, A.F., Urinary screening for midazolam and its major metabolites with the Abbott ADx and TDx analyzers and the EMIT dau benzodiazepine assay with confirmation by GC/MS, *J. Anal. Toxicol.,* 15, 8–12, 1991.
325. Masse, R., Ayotte, C., and Dugal, R., An integrated GC/MS screening method for anabolic steroid urinary metabolites in man, in *Developments in Analytical Methods in Pharmaceutical, Biomedical, and Forensic Sciences,* Quebec, Canada, 1986.
326. Maurer, H.H., Identification and differentiation of barbiturates, other sedative-hypnotics and their metabolites in urine integrated in a general screening procedure using computerized GC/MS, *J. Chromatogr.,* 530, 307–326, 1990.
327. Maurer, H. and Pfleger, K., Identification and differentiation of alkylamine antihistamines and their metabolites in urine by computerized gas chromatography, mass spectrometry, *J. Chromatogr.,* 430, 31–41, 1988.
328. Gill, R., Lopes, A.A., and Moffat, A.C., Analysis of barbiturates in blood by high-performance liquid chromatography, *J. Chromatogr.,* 226, 117–123, 1981.
329. Kleinschnitz, M., Herderich, M., and Schreier, P., Determination of 1,4-benzodiazepines by high performance liquid chromatography electrospray tandem mass spectrometry, *J. Chromatogr. B Biomed. Appl.,* 676, 61–67, 1996.
330. Mangin, P., Lugnier, A.A., and Chaumont, A.J., A polyvalent method using HPLC for screening and quantification of 12 common barbiturates in various biological materials, *J. Anal. Toxicol.,* 11, 27–30, 1987.
331. Hill, D.W. and Langner, K.J., Screening with high performance liquid chromatography, in *Analytical Aspects of Drug Testing*, Deutsch, D.G., Ed., John Wiley & Sons, New York, 1989, 129–148.
332. Ng, L.L., Sample preparation by salts precipitation and quantitation by HPLC with UV detection of selected drugs in biological fluids, *J. Chromatogr.,* 257, 345–353, 1983.
333. Foukaridis, G.N., Muntingh, G.L., and Osuch, E., Application of diode array detection for the identification of poisoning by traditional medicines, *J. Ethnopharmacol.,* 41, 135–146, 1994.
334. Lambert, W.E., Piette, M., Van Peteghem, C., and De Leenheer, A.P., Application of high-performance liquid chromatography to a fatality involving azide, *J. Anal. Toxicol.,* 19, 261–264, 1995.
335. Dipietra, A.M., Gatti, R., Andrisano, V., and Cavrini, V., Application of high-performance liquid chromatography with diode-array detection and on-line post-column photochemical derivatization to the determination of analgesics, *J. Chromatogr.,* 729, 355–361, 1996.
336. Puopolo, P.R., Volpicelli, S.A., Johnson, D.M., and Flood, J.G., Emergency toxicology testing (detection, confirmation, and quantification) of basic drugs in serum by liquid chromatography with photodiode array detection, *Clin. Chem.,* 37, 2124–2130, 1991.
337. Koves, E.M. and Wells, J., Evaluation of a photodiode array/HPLC-based system for the detection and quantitation of basic drugs in postmortem blood, *J. Forensic Sci.,* 37, 42–60, 1992.
338. Tracqui, A., Kintz, P., and Mangin, P., High-performance liquid chromatographic assay with diode-array detection for toxicological screening of zopiclone, zolpidem, suriclone and alpidem in human plasma, *J. Chromatogr.,* 616, 95–103, 1993.
339. Balikova, M. and Vecerkova, J., High-performance liquid chromatographic confirmation of cocaine and benzoylecgonine in biological samples using photodiode-array detection after toxicological screening, *J. Chromatogr. B Biomed. Appl.,* 656, 267–273, 1994.

340. Wielbo, D., Bhat, R., Chari, G., Vidyasagar, D., Tebbett, I.R., and Gulati, A., High-performance liquid chromatographic determination of morphine and its metabolites in plasma using diode-array detection, *J. Chromatogr.,* 615, 164–168, 1993.
341. Li, S., Gemperline, P.J., Briley, K., and Kazmierczak, S., Identification and quantitation of drugs of abuse in urine using the generalized rank annihilation method of curve resolution, *J. Chromatogr. B Biomed. Appl.,* 655, 213–223, 1994.
342. Overzet, F., Rurak, A., van der Voet, H., Drenth, B.F., Ghijsen, R.T., and de Zeeuw, R.A., On-line diode array UV-visible spectrometry in screening for drugs and drug metabolites by high-performance liquid chromatography, *J. Chromatogr.,* 267, 329–345, 1983.
343. Balikova, M., Selective system of identification and determination of antidepressants and neuroleptics in serum or plasma by solid-phase extraction followed by high-performance liquid chromatography with photodiode-array detection in analytical toxicology, *J. Chromatogr.,* 581, 75–81, 1992.
344. Tracqui, A., Kintz, P., Kreissig, P., and Mangin, P., A simple and rapid method for toxicological screening of 25 antidepressants in blood or urine using high performance liquid chromatography with diode-array detection, *Ann. Biol. Clin.,* 50, 639–647, 1992.
345. Puopolo, P.R., Pothier, M.E., Volpicelli, S.A., and Flood, J.G., Single procedure for detection, confirmation, and quantification of benzodiazepines in serum by liquid chromatography with photodiode-array detection, *Clin. Chem.,* 37, 701–706, 1991.
346. Turcant, A., Premel-Cabic, A., Cailleux, A., and Allain, P., Toxicological screening of drugs by microbore high-performance liquid chromatography with photodiode-array detection and ultraviolet spectral library searches, *Clin. Chem.,* 37, 1210–1215, 1991.
347. Stanke, F., Jourdil, N., Lauby, V., and Bessard, G., Zopiclone and zolpidem quantification in human plasma by high performance liquid chromatography with photodiode-array detection, *J. Liquid Chromatogr. Relat. Technol.,* 19, 2623–2633, 1996.
348. Law, B. and Stafford, L.E., The use of ultraviolet spectra and chromatographic retention data as an aid to metabolite identification, *J. Pharm. Biomed. Anal.,* 11, 729–736, 1993.
349. Demedts, P., Wauters, A., Franck, F., and Neels, H., Evaluation of the REMEDi drug profiling system, *Eur. J. Clin. Chem. Clin. Biochem.,* 32, 409–417, 1994.
350. Ohtsuji, M., Lai, J.S., Binder, S.R., Kondo, T., Takayasu, T., and Ohshima, T., Use of REMEDi HS in emergency toxicology for a rapid estimate of drug concentrations in urine, serum, and gastric samples, *J. Forensic Sci.,* 41, 881–886, 1996.
351. Patel, V., McCarthy, P.T., and Flanagan, R.J., Disopyramide analysis using REMEDi: comparison with EMIT and conventional high performance liquid chromatographic methods, *Biomed. Chromatogr.,* 5, 269–272, 1991.
352. Poklis, A. and Edinboro, L.E., REMEDi drug profiling system readily distinguishes between cyclobenzaprine and amitriptyline in emergency toxicology urine specimens [letter], *Clin. Chem.,* 38, 2349–2350, 1992.
353. Christensen, J.M., Human exposure to toxic metals: factors influencing interpretation of biomonitoring results, *Sci. Total Environ.,* 166, 89–135, 1995.
354. Flanagan, R.J., The poisoned patient: the role of the laboratory [review], *Br. J. Biomed. Sci.,* 52, 202–213, 1995.
355. Van Ormer, D.G., Atomic absorption analysis of some trace metals of toxicological interest, *J. Forensic Sci.,* 20, 595–623, 1975.
356. Sotera, J.J., Dulude, G.R., and Stux, R.L., Determination of toxic elements in biological materials by furnace atomic absorption spectrometry, *Sci. Total Environ.,* 71, 45–48, 1988.
357. Solomons, E.T. and Walls, H.C., Analysis of arsenic in forensic cases utilizing a rapid, non-ashing technique and furnace atomic absorption, *J. Anal. Toxicol.,* 7, 220–222, 1983.
358. Yoshinaga, J., [Inductively coupled plasma atomic emission spectrometry and ICP mass spectrometry], *Nippon Rinsho Jpn. J. Clin. Med.,* 54, 202–206, 1996.
359. Kalamegham, R. and Ash, K.O., A simple ICP-MS procedure for the determination of total mercury in whole blood and urine, *J. Clin. Lab. Anal.,* 6, 190–193, 1992.
360. Inoue, T. and Suzuki, S., Comparison of extraction methods for methamphetamine and its metabolites in tissue, *J. Forensic Sci.,* 31, 1102–1107, 1986.
361. Bush, M.T., Design of solvent extraction methods, *Methods Enzymol.,* 77, 353–372, 1981.

362. Dusaci, L.J. and Hackett, L.P., Direct extraction procedure for the analysis of neutral drugs in tissue, *Clin. Toxicol.,* 11, 353–358, 1977.
363. Brooks, K.E. and Smith, N.B., Efficient extraction of basic, neutral, and weakly acidic drugs from plasma for analysis by gas chromatography-mass spectrometry [published erratum appears in *Clin. Chem.* 38(2), 323, 1992], *Clin. Chem.,* 37, 1975–1978, 1991.
364. Hyde, P.M., Evaluation of drug extraction procedures from urine, *J. Anal. Toxicol.,* 9, 269–272, 1985.
365. Osselton, M.D., Hammond, M.D., and Watchett, P.J., The extraction and analysis of benzodiazepines in tissues by enzymatic digestion and HPLC, *J. Pharm. Pharmacol.,* 29, 460–462, 1977.
366. Bailey, D.N. and Kelner, M., Extraction of acidic drugs from water and plasma: study of recovery with five different solvents, *J. Anal. Toxicol.,* 8, 26–28, 1984.
367. Chiarotti, M., Overview on extraction procedures [review], *Forensic Sci. Int.,* 63, 161–170, 1993.
368. Ford, B., Vine, J., and Watson, T.R., A rapid extraction method for acidic drugs in hemolyzed blood, *J. Anal. Toxicol.,* 7, 116–118, 1983.
369. Moore, C.M. and Tebbett, I.R., Rapid extraction of anti-inflammatory drugs in whole blood for HPLC analysis, *Forensic Sci. Int.,* 34, 155–158, 1987.
370. Stoner, R.E. and Parker, C., Single-pH extraction procedure for detecting drugs of abuse, *Clin. Chem.,* 20, 309–311, 1974.
371. Hackett, L.P. and Dusci, L.J., The use of buffered celite columns in drug extraction techniques and their proposed application in forensic toxicology, *J. Forensic Sci.,* 22, 376–382, 1977.
372. Siek, T.J., Effective use of organic solvents to remove drugs from biologic specimens, *Clin. Toxicol.,* 13, 205–230, 1978.
373. Dusci, L.J. and Hackett, L.P., A comparison of the borate-celite column screening technique with other extraction methods in forensic toxicology, *J. Forensic Sci.,* 22, 545–549, 1977.
374. Chen, X.H., Franke, J.P., Wijsbeek, J., and de Zeeuw, R.A., Isolation of acidic, neutral, and basic drugs from whole blood using a single mixed-mode solid-phase extraction column, *J. Anal. Toxicol.,* 16, 351–355, 1992.
375. Black, D.A., Clark, G.D., Haver, V.M., Garbin, J.A., and Saxon, A.J., Analysis of urinary benzodiazepines using solid-phase extraction and gas chromatography-mass spectrometry [see comments], *J. Anal. Toxicol.,* 18, 185–188, 1994.
376. Lensmeyer, G.L., Wiebe, D.A., and Darcey, B.A., Application of a novel form of solid-phase sorbent (Empore membrane) to the isolation of tricyclic antidepressant drugs from blood, *J. Chromatogr. Sci.,* 29, 444–449, 1991.
377. Chen, X.H., Franke, J.P., Wijsbeek, J., and de Zeeuw, R.A., Determination of basic drugs extracted from biological matrices by means of solid-phase extraction and wide-bore capillary gas chromatography with nitrogen-phosphorus detection, *J. Anal. Toxicol.,* 18, 150–153, 1994.
378. Huang, Z.P., Chen, X.H., Wijsbeek, J., Franke, J.P., and Dezeeuw, R.A., An enzymic digestion and solid-phase extraction procedure for the screening for acidic, neutral, and basic drugs in liver using gas chromatography for analysis, *J. Anal. Toxicol.,* 20, 248–254, 1996.
379. Leloux, M.S., de Jong, E.G., and Maes, R.A., Improved screening method for beta-blockers in urine using solid-phase extraction and capillary gas chromatography-mass spectrometry, *J. Chromatogr.,* 488, 357–367, 1989.
380. Anderson, R.E. and Nixon, G.L., Isolation of benzoylecgonine from urine using solid-phase extraction, *J. Anal. Toxicol.,* 17, 432–433, 1993.
381. Cosbey, S.H., Craig, I., and Gill, R., Novel solid-phase extraction strategy for the isolation of basic drugs from whole blood, *J. Chromatogr. B Biomed. Appl.,* 669, 229–235, 1995.
382. Matyska, M. and Golkiewicz, W., Quantitation of benzodiazepine hydrolysis products in urine using solid-phase extraction and high performance liquid chromatography, *J. Liquid Chromatogr.,* 14, 2769–2778, 1991.
383. Wright, A.W., Watt, J.A., Kennedy, M., Cramond, T., and Smith, M.T., Quantitation of morphine, morphine-3-glucuronide, and morphine-6-glucuronide in plasma and cerebrospinal fluid using solid-phase extraction and high-performance liquid chromatography with electrochemical detection, *Ther. Drug Monit.,* 16, 200–208, 1994.
384. Bouquillon, A.I., Freeman, D., and Moulin, D.E., Simultaneous solid-phase extraction and chromatographic analysis of morphine and hydromorphone in plasma by high-performance liquid chromatography with electrochemical detection, *J. Chromatogr.,* 577, 354–357, 1992.

385. Pocci, R., Dixit, V., and Dixit, V.M., Solid-phase extraction and GC/MS confirmation of barbiturates from human urine, *J. Anal. Toxicol.,* 16, 45–47, 1992.
386. Chen, X.-H., Franke, J.-P., and de Zeeuw, R.A., Solid-phase extraction for systematic toxicological analysis, *Forensic Sci. Rev.,* 4, 147–159, 1992.
387. Casas, M., Berrueta, L.A., Gallo, B., and Vicente, F., Solid-phase extraction of 1,4-benzodiazepines from biological fluids, *J. Pharm. Biomed. Anal.,* 11, 277–284, 1993.
388. Dixit, V., Solid-phase extraction of amphetamine and methamphetamine, *Am. Clin. Lab.,* 11, 6, 1992.
389. Scheurer, J. and Moore, C.M., Solid-phase extraction of drugs from biological tissues — a review, *J. Anal. Toxicol.,* 16, 264–269, 1992.
390. Chen, X.H., Franke, J.P., Wijsbeek, J., and de Zeeuw, R.A., Study of lot-to-lot reproducibilities of Bond Elut Certify and Clean Screen DAU mixed-mode solid-phase extraction columns in the extraction of drugs from whole blood, *J. Chromatogr.,* 617, 147–151, 1993.
391. Nakamura, G.R., Meeks, R.D., and Stall, W.J., Solid-phase extraction, identification, and quantitation of 11-nor-delta-9-tetrahydrocannabinol-9-carboxylic acid, *J. Forensic Sci.,* 35, 792–796, 1990.
392. Scheurer, J. and Moore, C.M., Solid-phase extraction of drugs from biological tissues — a review, *J. Anal. Toxicol.,* 16, 264–269, 1992.
393. Delaunay-Bertoncini, N. and Hennion, M.C., Immunoaffinity solid-phase extraction for pharmaceutical and biomedical trace-analysis-coupling with HPLC and CE-perspectives, *J. Pharm. Biomed. Anal.*, 34, 717–736, 2004.
394. Ulrich, S., Solid-phase microextraction in biomedical analysis, *J. Chromatogr. A,* 902, 167–194, 2000.
395. Pawliszyn, J., Solid phase microextraction, *Adv. Exp. Med. Biol.*, 488, 73–87, 2001.
396. Iwai, M., Hattori, H., Arinobu, T., Ishii, A., Kumazawa, T., Noguchi, H., Noguchi, H., Suzuki, O., and Seno, H., Simultaneous determination of barbiturates in human biological fluids by direct immersion solid-phase microextraction and gas chromatography-mass spectrometry, *J. Chromatogr. B Anal. Technol. Biomed. Life Sci.*, 806, 65–73, 2004.
397. Lachenmeier, D.W., Kroener, L., Musshoff, F., and Madea, B., Application of tandem mass spectrometry combined with gas chromatography and headspace solid-phase dynamic extraction for the determination of drugs of abuse in hair samples, *Rapid Commun. Mass Spectrom.*, 17, 472–478, 2003.
398. Musshoff, F., Junker, H., and Madea, B., Simple determination of 22 organophosphorous pesticides in human blood using headspace solid-phase microextraction and gas chromatography with mass spectrometric detection, *J. Chromatogr. Sci.*, 40, 29–34, 2002.
399. Frison, G., Tedeschi, L., Maietti, S., and Ferrara, S.D., Determination of gamma-hydroxybutyric acid (GHB) in plasma and urine by headspace solid-phase microextraction and gas chromatography/positive ion chemical ionization mass spectrometry, *Rapid Commun. Mass Spectrom.*, 14, 2401–2407, 2000.
400. Frison, G., Tedeschi, L., Maietti, S., and Ferrara, S.D., Determination of midazolam in human plasma by solid-phase microextraction and gas chromatography/mass spectrometry, *Rapid Commun. Mass Spectrom.*, 15, 2497–2501, 2001.
401. Musteata, F.M. and Pawliszyn, J., Study of ligand-receptor binding using SPME: investigation of receptor, free, and total ligand concentrations, *J. Proteome Res.*, 4, 789–800, 2005.
402. Musshoff, F., Lachenmeier, D.W., Kroener, L., and Madea, B., Automated headspace solid-phase dynamic extraction for the determination of cannabinoids in hair samples, *Forensic Sci. Int.*, 133, 32–38, 2003.
403. Bogusz, M., Bialka, J., and Gierz, J., Enzymic digestion of biosamples as a method of sample pretreatment before XAD-2 extraction, *Z. Rechtsmed. J. Legal Med.,* 87, 287–295, 1981.
404. Bogusz, M., Bialka, J., and Gierz, J., Enzymic hydrolysis of tissues before XAD-2 extraction in poisoning cases, *Forensic Sci. Int.,* 20, 27–33, 1982.
405. Romberg, R.W. and Lee, L., Comparison of the hydrolysis rates of morphine-3-glucuronide and morphine-6-glucuronide with acid and beta-glucuronidase, *J. Anal. Toxicol.,* 19, 157–162, 1995.

CHAPTER 4

Strategies for Postmortem Toxicology Investigation

Edited and Revised by Henrik Druid, M.D., Ph.D.
Associate Professor, Department of Forensic Medicine, Karolinska Institute, Stockholm, Sweden

From the original by W. Lee Hearn, Ph.D.
Director, Dade County Medical Examiner Toxicology Laboratory, Miami, Florida

CONTENTS

4.1 Screening Strategy 68
4.2 General Concepts 68
4.3 Basic Strategies 69
4.3.1 Amphetamines 70
4.3.2 Barbiturates 70
4.3.3 Benzodiazepines 71
4.3.4 Cocaine 71
4.3.5 Opiates 71
4.3.6 Phencyclidine 71
4.3.7 Immunoassays for Other Illegal Drugs 71
4.3.8 Chromatographic Methods 72
4.3.8.1 ToxiLab A for Urine and Gastric Contents 72
4.3.8.2 Alternatives to ToxiLab 72
4.3.9 Gastric Contents vs. Urine 72
4.3.10 Screening with Gas Chromatography 73
4.3.11 Screening with Liquid Chromatography 74
4.4 The General Unknown 74
4.5 Confirmation 75
4.5.1 What Confirmation Is Necessary, and Why? 75
4.5.2 When Is Confirmation Necessary? 78
4.5.3 When Is Confirmation Unnecessary? 78
4.6 Gas Chromatography-Mass Spectrometry 78
4.6.1 Qualitative GC/MS-SIM Determination Criteria 79
4.6.2 Potential Problems with GC/MS Analyses 80

4.7 Liquid Chromatography-Mass Spectrometry....80
4.8 Method Validation....81
4.9 Quantification of Drugs and Poisons....81
4.9.1 What Should Be Quantified?....82
4.9.2 Specimens for Quantification of Drugs and Poisons....82
4.9.3 Quantification: Procedural Issues....83
4.9.3.1 Instruments....83
4.9.3.2 Sample Preparation....83
4.9.3.3 Internal Standard....84
4.10 The Review Process....84
4.11 Pending Toxicology Conference....84
References....84

4.1 SCREENING STRATEGY

The first step in any case is to review the case history and autopsy findings. If the pathologist makes no specific requests for analysis, then responsibility for deciding which tests to do falls exclusively to the professional judgment of the toxicologist.[1–9]

Obviously, cases of suspected drug intoxication require the most comprehensive testing, typically on samples of blood, liver, gastric contents, and urine or bile.[10,11] Tests in the case of a drug-related homicide may include a blood-ethanol analysis, and a standard drug-of-abuse screen on urine, with the concentration of any identified drug being quantified in the blood.[12–18] Fatalities involving motor vehicle drivers require a blood-ethanol determination, and a comprehensive urine screen with any positive drug concentration quantified in the blood.[19–23] Fatalities resulting from a fire require blood-carbon monoxide and sometimes cyanide analyses in addition to alcohol and other drugs.[24–26]

4.2 GENERAL CONCEPTS

Screening protocols should include tests capable of detecting as many drugs as possible, within the constraints imposed by the available specimens, the laboratory's workload, and requirements specific to the case (Figure 4.1).[5–9,27] Most laboratories lack the resources required to treat every case as a general unknown, applying test after test until all possible drugs and poisons are ruled out. Such an approach may occasionally be warranted when there is a high suspicion of poisoning, but usually several standardized protocols can be used to eliminate most of the substances that can realistically be expected in a sample.

A broad-spectrum screen, capable of detecting or eliminating most of the common drugs, usually requires a combination of three or more techniques.[1,2,11,28–88] Additional tests can be combined with standardized screening protocols, thereby expanding the screening capability to encompass additional drugs of concern based upon the specifics of the case. Table 4.1 shows test panels commonly employed for screening various types of cases.

The most effective strategies employ a combination of immunoassays, with chromatographic techniques, and chemical tests, in order to detect a wide range of substances. Immunoassays are used to test for classes of drugs with similar structures, while the chromatographic tests detect large groups of drugs with similar extraction characteristics, polarities, and detection characteristics. Chemical tests are selective for the chemical reactivity of substances with similar structures. The type of analysis required also depends on the type of biologic specimen to be analyzed. A putrefied liver specimen, for example, will require greater sample preparation than would a fresh urine specimen. Some drugs are present in much smaller concentrations than others and thus require more sophisticated detection techniques.

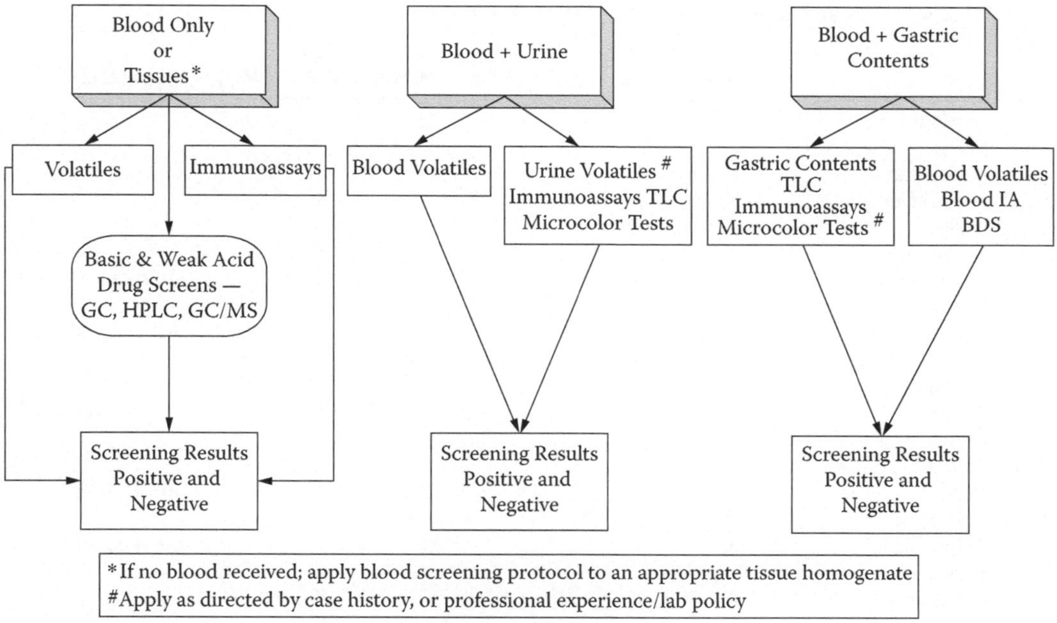

Figure 4.1 Postmortem forensic toxicology screening protocols.

It is impossible to design a single analytical scheme that is capable of detecting all the available drugs and poisons while being suitable for the wide variety of specimen combinations that may be submitted. In general, a collection of about a dozen standard general screening methods is supplemented with as many special methods as required. Because the main objective is qualitative detection rather than quantification, general screening methods are usually more flexible than special methods and can therefore be applied to a wider variety of materials. A good general method will provide a provisional identification, which can then be confirmed by the application of a quantitative directed analysis.

Often, the nature of a suspected toxin is unknown. The classic example is a person who has expired under suspicious circumstances and where the history, scene, and autopsy fail to disclose a definitive cause of death. In such cases, the screening strategy must be more extensive, since thousands of toxic drugs and chemicals are available on the market worldwide. A systematic procedure that allows the simultaneous detection of as many toxicants in biosamples as possible is necessary for a comprehensive toxicological analysis.[1,2,4,5,89–91]

4.3 BASIC STRATEGIES

In laboratories with small caseloads, each case may be reviewed individually by the director who assigns specific tests. Testing large numbers of samples proceeds more efficiently, and in a more organized fashion, when standardized assay panels are performed on batches of samples. Blood and urine are the specimens of choice to screen for drugs and poisons. Depending on the circumstances of the case, other samples include liver, stomach contents, or bile.

The blood volatiles screen detects and quantifies ethanol while simultaneously screening for methanol, isopropanol, and acetone as well as other volatiles, such as halogenated and non-halogenated hydrocarbons that are sometimes inhaled for purposes of intoxication.[46,70,92–95] Each of the immunoassay tests is used to detect substances that cannot easily be included in one or two chromatographic procedures, for which routine chromatographic tests may be too insensitive, or where specialized extraction or derivatization conditions may be required.

Table 4.1 Case Management by Manner of Death

	Volatiles	IA B/U	CO/ CN	BDS	WAN	TOXI-A/B	MCT	Specials
Accident								
MVA-pedestrian	X	X				X		
MVA-driver	X	X	X			X	X	
MVA-passenger	X	X	X			X		
Workplace	X	X	X			X	X	As required
Police investigation	X	X				X		As required
Aviation-crew	X	X	X	X	X	X		
Fire/smoke	X	X	X			X	X	
Other	X	X	X			X	X	As required
Natural								
With a COD	X	X				X		
SIDS	X	X				X		APAP, ASA
Epileptics	X	X			X	X		
Asthmatics	X					X		As required
Homicides								
Active role	X	X				X	X	
Innocent victim	X	X				X		
Unknown role	X	X				X	X	
Suicide (non-drug)								
Trauma	X	X				X		
CO	X	X	X			X		As required
Pending pathology	X	X				X		
Pending toxicology	X	X	X	X	X	X	X	As required

Immunoassays imply the use of urine; however, if a urine specimen is unavailable, or "indicates the presence of" a drug, a blood analysis should follow. At a minimum, perform amphetamines, barbiturates, benzodiazepines, cocaine, opiates, PCP, and others as required by case type and history.

CO (carbon monoxide): Between the months of September and May, request on all MEO (medical examiner office) cases involving apparent natural death and pending cases occurring indoors.

MCTs: Require urine and gastric contents.

Key: IA = immunoassays; B/U = blood and/or urine; CO/CN = carbon monoxide and cyanide; BDS = basic drug screen; WAN = weak acid neutral drug screen; TOXI-A/B = commercial thin-layer chromatography acids and bases; MCT = microcolor tests; MVA = motor vehicle accident; COD = cause of death; SIDS = sudden infant death syndrome; APAP = acetaminophen; ASA = salicylates.

4.3.1 Amphetamines

The amphetamines are relatively volatile, and can be lost by evaporation if the extract is not first acidified. In addition, they tend to give tailing peaks unless the gas chromatography (GC) columns are well maintained, or the amphetamines are derivatized. However, ToxiLab can effectively detect and differentiate the sympathomimetic amines in urine, so the amphetamines immunoassay could be omitted if ToxiLab is used. If an amphetamines immunoassay is used, it should be one of broad class selectivity, not one of the newer and more specific monoclonal antibody assays, so that is has the chance of detecting the maximum number of amphetamines and related drugs (e.g., ephedrine, pseudoephedrine).[96–98]

4.3.2 Barbiturates

An immunoassay for barbiturates can eliminate the need for labor-intensive chromatographic screens of weakly acidic and neutral drugs in the majority of cases. Only those cases testing positive, or where phenytoin is indicated, need the chromatographic screen. The ToxiLab B system can help to differentiate barbiturates in urine, or the testing can proceed directly to a GC, HPLC, or GC-MS screen on an acidic drug extract of blood to identify the specific barbiturate(s) present in the body.[99–104]

4.3.3 Benzodiazepines

The benzodiazepines comprise a large class of drugs that are often detected in postmortem cases. ToxiLab does not ordinarily detect them in urine at therapeutic doses, and a basic drug GC screen rarely detects the more potent drugs in this class, except in cases of overdose. Available immunoassays can yield positive results in urine for metabolites from most of the common benzodiazepines. Exceptions are lorazepam and flunitrazepam. GC with electron capture detection, or GC/mass spectrometry (GC/MS), may be applied to urine or blood to differentiate benzodiazepines and to detect those that are missed by immunoassays.[105–117] Whether or not to use these more labor intensive chromatographic tests in the absence of a positive immunoassay depends upon the potential significance of a benzodiazepine, if it were to be found, and on any indications from the investigation that one may have been taken. Several methods have also been published for the detection of a wide range of benzodiazepines by LC/MS or LC/MS/MS.

4.3.4 Cocaine

Cocaine should always be included in a postmortem toxicology screen. Even infants and elderly individuals occasionally test positive. The most efficient way to screen for cocaine is to use an immunoassay for benzoylecgonine.[118–121] Although both ToxiLab A and basic drug GC screens can actually detect cocaine itself, special procedures are required for the chromatographic detection of benzoylecgonine. Cocaine may not always be found in the urine with benzoylecgonine, although benzoylecgonine is almost always found whenever cocaine is present.

4.3.5 Opiates

The common opiates include morphine, 6-monoacetylmorphine, codeine, hydromorphone, hydrocodone, and oxycodone. Routine ToxiLab A or basic drug GC screens detect codeine, hydrocodone, and oxycodone. These methods are less effective for morphine and hydromorphone, which are usually found in the urine as water-soluble conjugates of glucuronic acid. Immunoassays can detect both parent drug and metabolites. Differentiation of opiates is usually accomplished by GC/MS, using procedures that include hydrolysis of conjugates and derivatization for maximum sensitivity and specificity, or by LC/MS.[122–124]

4.3.6 Phencyclidine

Phencyclidine (PCP) is more commonly encountered in some regions, while not in others. It is a powerful dissociative anesthetic with significant effects on behavior at low doses, and should be included as part of the postmortem drug screen. Both thin-layer chromatography (TLC) and GC detect PCP, although they may be insufficiently sensitive to reliably rule it out. Immunoassays capable of detecting PCP in urine down to 25 ng/mL provide a reliable screening test.[125,126]

4.3.7 Immunoassays for Other Illegal Drugs

Immunoassays have been developed to screen for the presence of other illegal drugs, including cannabinoids, LSD, and prescription drugs such as propoxyphene, methadone, and methaqualone. With the exception of cannabinoids and LSD, all of the analytes are readily detected by either ToxiLab A or GC basic drug screens. Cannabinoid and LSD assays may be included in a standard screening protocol or may be reserved for cases involving an issue of possible behavioral toxicity, since those are not known to contribute to either fatal intoxications or deaths attributable to natural causes.

4.3.8 Chromatographic Methods

Chromatographic methods are used to expand the range of a drug screen beyond those drugs detectable by the immunoassays. The extraction system should be selective for basic drugs, and neutral substances will also be extracted.[47,58,62,71–76,127–130]

4.3.8.1 ToxiLab A for Urine and Gastric Contents

The ToxiLab A system for basic drug detection is a powerful tool for drug screening in urine or gastric contents.[55–57,131] The four-stage visualization process, combined with R_f and detection of metabolite patterns, adds considerably to the confidence in drug identification. Sensitivity for many drugs is on the order of 0.5 to 1.0 mg/L, which is satisfactory for screening urine or gastric samples. The ToxiLab A can detect nearly 150 drugs and their metabolites.

4.3.8.2 Alternatives to ToxiLab

A screen for basic and neutral drugs by CG with a nitrogen/phosphorus detector (NPD) is an alternative to ToxiLab TLC for a laboratory having sufficient GC capacity.[47,71,74–76,82,127] GC is much more sensitive than TLC, having limits of detection on the order of 0.01 to 0.10 mg/L from 1 mL of sample. GC can be calibrated to presumptively identify hundreds of drugs and drug metabolites, and the NPD data can reveal other unidentified nitrogen-containing substances that may be characterized by additional analysis of the extract by GC/MS.

The Trinders test is added to the screen to detect salicylate from aspirin, a common drug and one that is sometimes taken for suicidal purposes. It may be eliminated if the screen is intended only to evaluate potential behavioral toxicity. The chemical tests for ethchlorvynol and chloral hydrate fill another gap in the screening protocol, since these drugs are not detected by immunoassay or in chromatographic screens for basic drug or volatiles. Figure 4.2 illustrates the analytical scheme for routine cases with both urine and blood submitted to the laboratory.

4.3.9 Gastric Contents vs. Urine

Often, urine is not available for testing because the bladder was empty at the time of autopsy. In such cases, an extract or filtrate of gastric contents may be substituted. However, a gastric drug screen alone may not be sufficient to exclude all potentially relevant substances. Drugs that are typically administered parenterally, smoked, or insufflated may not diffuse into the stomach in detectable amounts, so blood or plasma analysis with immunoassays for opiates and benzoylecgonine is often required to detect those substances.

Drugs taken hours before death may not remain in the stomach. However, some quantity of a basic drug will diffuse into the stomach from blood and become ionized, and thus remains there. The resulting concentration in the stomach contents is determined in part by the drug's concentration in blood and in part by its pKa. For optimum sensitivity, a gastric content drug screen may be combined with immunoassays on plasma, vitreous humor, or blood for barbiturates, benzodiazepines, benzoylecgonine, opiates, and a basic drug screen of blood by GC-NPD. The following protocols, which employ tests on gastric contents and blood (or plasma), can be used in place of a urine drug screen. The same blood test panel may be used when gastric contents are not available, or applied to tissue homogenates when blood is not available.

Immunoassays can usually be performed directly on unhemolyzed plasma or vitreous humor. Even hemolyzed plasma and postmortem whole blood can be tested directly if FPIA or RIA is

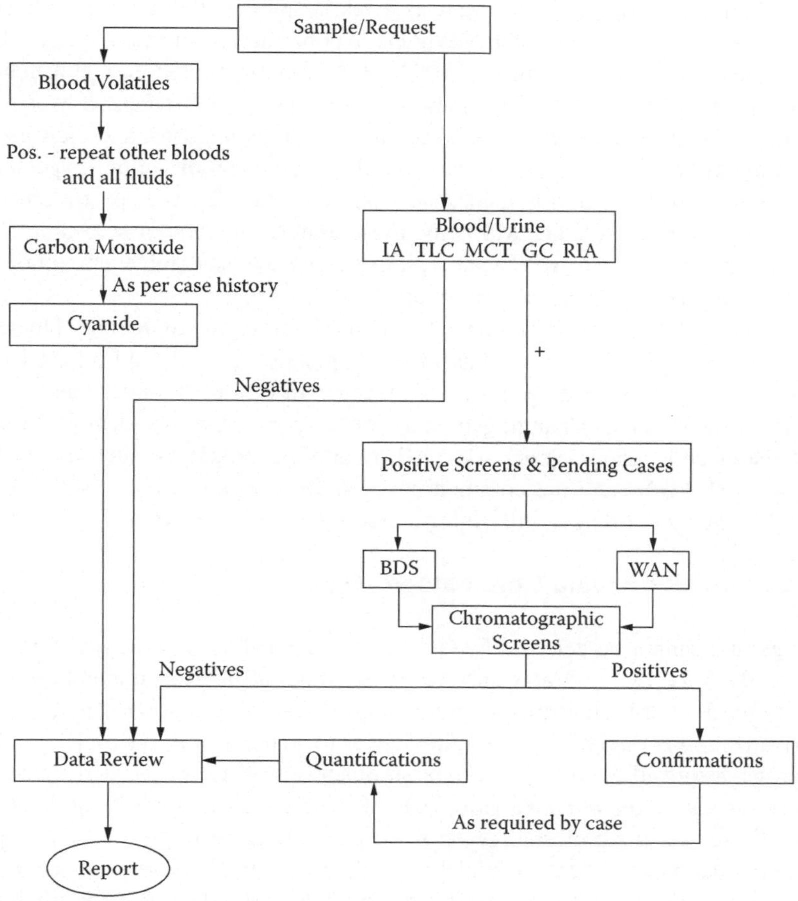

Figure 4.2 Flowchart for routine toxicology cases.

used.[50,52,132–145] If results are unsatisfactory, simple dilution with an equal volume of assay buffer is often sufficient to render an analyzable sample. If FPIA or RIA is not available in the laboratory, blood may be screened with spectrophotometry-based immunoassays, although hemoglobin and other proteins must first be precipitated by addition of acetone, methanol, or acetonitrile. The centrifuged supernatant from such treatment can be assayed against similarly prepared calibrators.[49–52,146–154] When applied to blood, plasma, or vitreous humor, immunoassays should be calibrated to a lower cutoff threshold than that used for urine screening. Cutoffs, on the order of 50 ng/mL (500 ng/mL for barbiturates), will yield some false positives. Considering the variations in cross-reactivity for analytes of interest (e.g., benzodiazepines), some false-positive immunoassay results may be acceptable in the interest of minimizing false negatives. Any positive immunoassay result must, of course, be confirmed if it is to be reported. If the case may involve lethal toxicity, immunoassays for acetaminophen and salicylate should be added to the panel.

4.3.10 Screening with Gas Chromatography

GC for basic drugs in blood is more sensitive than a basic drug screen on gastric contents, but is also more labor intensive. It may be included in a general drug screen whenever urine is not available or it may be reserved for cases where intoxication is indicated by the investigation, and gastric contents yield negative screening results. Figure 4.1 illustrates general screening protocols for various combinations of postmortem samples.

When initial chromatographic screening tests reveal an unidentified spot on TLC or a response from GC that does not match any standard, extracts may be further screened by GC/MS in the full scan electron-impact ionization mode.[80,82,83,100,155–163] Reconstructed ion chromatograms are inspected for spectra that indicate exogenous (i.e., xenobiotic) substances. Suspect spectra are compared with the instrument's computerized libraries of drugs, poisons, and their metabolites. In addition, spectra may be visually compared with published compilations of mass spectral data.[164–169] Whenever a tentative identification is made, the unknown and reference spectra must be visually compared to verify their identity. GC/MS is the most complex method of screening for drugs and poisons, and also the most expensive. The analyst must have a considerable amount of training and experience to reliably perform GC/MS screening.

To provide adequate support for a medical examiner's office the toxicology laboratory should periodically assess the prevalence of drugs in the population served, and adjust its offering of routine tests accordingly. Certain drugs are more prevalent in various localities due to supply routes, ethnic practices, and demand. Changing patterns of drug use may be identified through crime laboratory statistics and various epidemiological monitoring programs, such as the Drug Abuse Warning Network (DAWN) and the community-based Drug Epidemiology Network. In Europe, the www.emcdda Web site offers similar information for the EU countries.

4.3.11 Screening with Liquid Chromatography

Many drugs that cannot be detected by GC can be detected by high-performance liquid chromatography (HPLC). HPLC separates analytes in solution, at or near ambient temperature, and therefore can be used for drugs that are too thermolabile or polar to be analyzed by GC. Furthermore, chemical derivatization is rarely, if ever, required prior to analysis of drugs by HPLC. While most, but not all, drugs absorb ultraviolet (UV) light sufficiently well to be detected by a UV detector, a UV spectrum usually does not give sufficient information on its own for a forensically valid identification. Therefore, the preferred detector increasingly is becoming the mass spectrometer. However, LC/MS has not yet become widely accepted as a useful screening technique for two reasons. First, LC/MS instrumentation continues to cost approximately twice as much as a GC/MS instrument. Second, and more important, it has been very difficult to generate reference libraries that are universally useful. Although, perhaps arguably more useful than UV spectra, most LC/MS spectra lack the detail of typical electron impact (EI) GC/MS spectra, and worse, relative abundances across the spectrum can vary with pH and ionic strength.

4.4 THE GENERAL UNKNOWN

Cases in which a toxic cause of death is suspected but where a specified toxic agent is not known are referred to as general unknowns, and require an open-ended search for poisons. The first step in investigating a general unknown is to carefully examine the medical records, case history, autopsy findings, and scene observations for evidence of specific toxins, or of a toxic mechanism.[1–3,5–9,30,170,171]

The case history and medical records may describe symptoms characteristic of a particular pharmacologic category. Cardiac rhythm disturbances, respiratory rate and pattern, pupil size and responsiveness, condition of reflexes, convulsions, and any other pre-mortem symptoms may suggest a toxic mechanism that excludes some toxins from a long list of possible agents.

Autopsy findings may also provide guidance. The condition of the gastric and esophageal mucosa may suggest or exclude corrosive poisons. The presence of massive pulmonary edema may indicate preterminal respiratory depression. Hepatic necrosis may indicate acetaminophen or *Amanita* mushroom toxicity, among other agents. Needle punctures and, especially, "track marks" indicate possible intravenous drug overdose. These and other observations, properly interpreted, can narrow the focus of the analytical search.

Consideration of the place where death occurred, or where the terminal symptoms appeared, may suggest toxic agents. Scene investigation can yield valuable clues. For example, the death of a jewelry store employee may have resulted from exposure to cyanide, which is used in jewelry manufacture. Other employment settings have associated chemical hazards that should be recognized when planning a strategy for investigation of a workplace death.

In the home, other toxic exposures are more likely. Drugs, pesticides, and other chemical products for household use are possible agents. Also, drug misuse at home can result in accidents or fatal intoxication. Reports of witnesses can also give valuable clues. What was the deceased doing at the onset of illness? When was the deceased last seen alive? Was the deceased behaving normally, or was intoxication indicated? Was there a complaint of feeling sick? Eliciting such observations may make it possible to shorten the list of possible drugs.

The volatiles screen by headspace GC, and while designed to test for the common alcohols and acetone, can also detect other volatile chemicals such as toluene and other solvents and volatile anesthetics. Drug screening tests are essential to rule out drug intoxication, and chromatographic screens can detect many other chemical substances besides drugs. GC/MS is a mainstay of screening protocols for general unknowns. Semivolatile organic compounds can be identified by computerized comparison of their mass spectra with libraries containing over 50,000 spectra of pesticides, drugs, and industrial chemicals. Figure 4.3 illustrates a strategy for analysis of cases where classification is pending the outcome of toxicology testing.

Tests for drugs and poisons not detected by the basic strategy can be added to the protocol for general unknowns. Selective immunoassays are available to test for cardiac glycosides, LSD, fentanyls, haloperidol, aminoglycoside antibiotics, and anticonvulsants. Clinical laboratories can provide assistance with tests for potassium, lithium, iron, and insulin or C-peptide. Toxic metals and nonmetals can be detected by atomic absorption spectrophotometry, and classical inorganic qualitative tests can be used to screen for toxic anions on a dialysate of urine, blood, or stomach contents. Other drugs that do not chromatograph well by GC may be detected by HPLC.

The following guidelines should be observed in approaching the general unknown:

1. If specimen selection and quantity are not limiting factors, then the objective should be the broadest screen possible with available technology.
2. The blood and vitreous fluid alcohol content should be determined before or simultaneously with other analyses.
3. Blood alcohol analyses should be performed by headspace GC, utilizing an internal standard. This does not preclude possible confirmation by some other procedure.
4. If carbon monoxide is to be determined, this should also be done prior to drug screening procedures.
5. In the absence of background information on a given case, the selected analytical scheme should provide the best chances of successfully finding a drug or poison. That is, the more commonly encountered drugs and poisons should be sought before the more rarely encountered ones are considered.
6. In the event that specimen selection and quantity are limited, it will be necessary to plan assays more carefully. Immunoassay procedures should be applied early in the scheme if proper samples are available.
7. All assays should be considered with the intent of subsequently confirming positive findings by another independent procedure. This means, for example, that if specimen size is a limiting factor, then different stages of a general screen should be performed sequentially rather than in parallel.

4.5 CONFIRMATION

4.5.1 What Confirmation Is Necessary, and Why?

Courts require that the opinions expressed by toxicologists be of a "reasonable scientific probability," that the identity of reported substances be known with "scientific certainty," and that

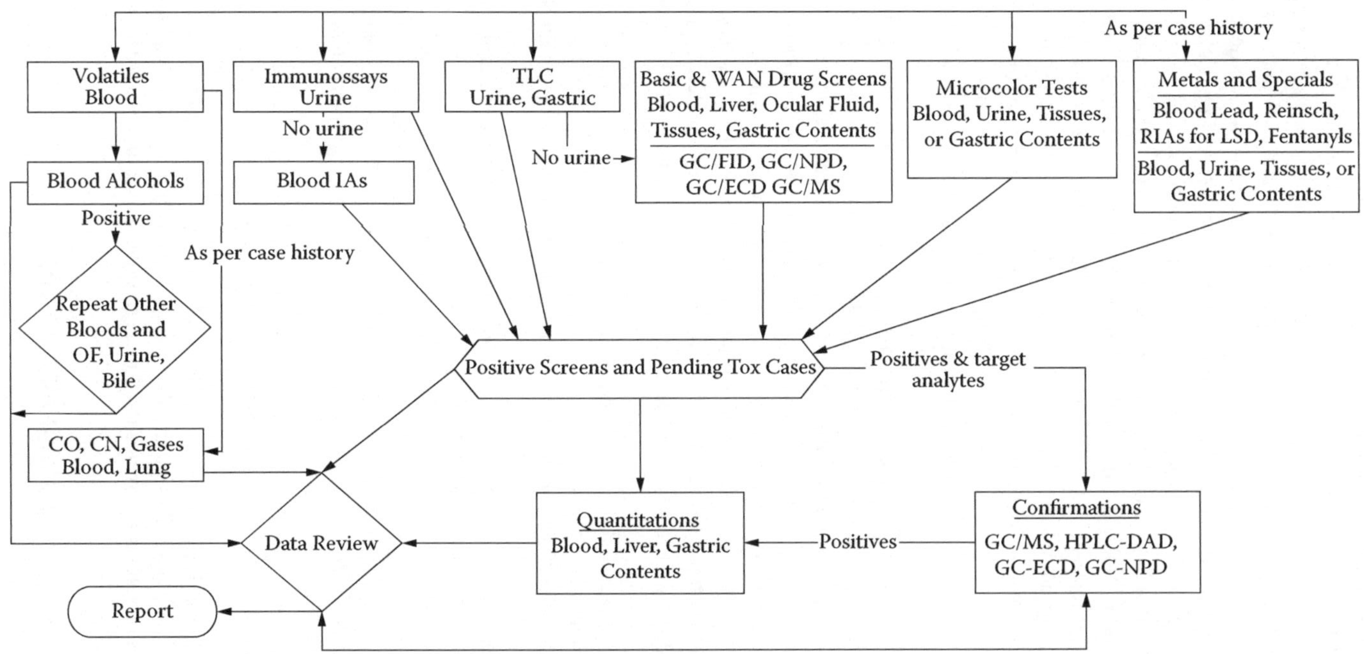

Figure 4.3 Analytical strategies for postmortem toxicology screening in the pending tox case.

quantitative values be accurate to a stated statistical probability. Screening tests provide tentative identification of drugs and poisons. The forensic standard for conclusive identification requires that their identity be confirmed by additional tests.[172]

The first analytical indication of the presence of a particular drug is usually obtained from an immunoassay, a chromatographic screen (e.g., TLC), or a spot test. The initial test may point to a particular drug, or class of drugs, such as barbiturates, benzodiazepines, or opiates. The confirmatory test must clearly identify the specific drug and/or its metabolite(s). Confirmatory methods may include gas chromatography with flame ionization (GC-FID), electron capture (GC-ECD), and nitrogen-phosphorus (GC-NPD) detectors, HPLC, UV spectroscopy, GC/MS, and other hyphenated techniques such as MS/MS coupled to either a GC or LC sample introduction system.

Any chemical test can be subject to errors that may cause a false-positive result. Immunoassays can cross-react with substances other than the target drug. Chromatographic methods can have interfering substances that produce a signal or spot at the same time and place as a target analyte. Even GC/MS can yield false-positive results if a sample is mislabeled or contaminated in process, or by carryover from a preceding injection, or if the spectrum does not have a unique fragmentation pattern. For example, amitriptyline and cyclobenzaprine have similar retention times and yield fragmentation patterns that are nearly identical. They may be confused if the molecular ion cannot be discerned.

In recognition of the possibility of a false-positive result from a single test, it is necessary that all potentially significant results be confirmed. Confirmation requires at least one additional test based on a different chemical detection principle, with high specificity and sensitivity at least equal to the initial test.[172] The essence of confirmation is to assemble a sufficient body of evidence such that a technically competent independent reviewer would agree with the conclusion.

The requirement for two or more chemically distinct methodologies is based on the concern that chemical similarity could cause a false-positive result in one type of test, and may also influence another test with a similar chemical principle. A radioimmunoassay cannot confirm enzyme immunoassay results since the chemical properties responsible for antibody binding may affect the antibodies in both tests similarly. Likewise, two similar GC columns such as 1 and 5% phenylmethylsilicone (DB-1 and DB-5) would not serve to confirm one another, because the polarities of the two liquid phases and, hence, the elution orders of most drugs are similar.

A combination of less specific chromatographic procedures (e.g., TLC, GC-NPD/ECD, or HPLC) can be used to confirm screening results from immunoassay or spot test results. A second chromatographic method based on a different chemical principle may be used to confirm a presumptive finding from a chromatographic screening test (e.g., TLC and GLC or HPLC and GC-NPD/EC). Derivatization of the presumptively identified drug can alter its chromatographic behavior sufficiently to permit confirmation by reanalysis in the same chromatographic system. Some screening procedures, such as GC/MS, identify specific compounds. Even here, a second test on a separate aliquot should be performed to "verify" the analyte and ensure that no human error in sample handling or analyses has occurred. Re-injection of the same extract would not be sufficient. An exception to this rule would be limited sample volume precluding repeat analyses.

In postmortem toxicology, confirmation tests are often applied to specimens other than the one used for screening. By employing a quantitative confirmatory method, the analyte is simultaneously confirmed and quantified. For example, a presumptive finding of diphenhydramine in urine by TLC may be confirmed by a quantitative GC procedure applied to blood.

Some additional illustrative examples of confirmation follow:

1. An immunoassay positive for opiates in urine, followed by a GC/MS analysis of urine to identify the specific drug(s).
2. An immunoassay positive for benzodiazepines in urine, followed by an analysis of blood by GC-ECD to identify the specific drug(s).

3. A drug such as amitriptyline detected by TLC in urine or gastric contents followed by GC-NPD analysis of blood with relative retention times matching the suspected drug, ideally on two columns of differing liquid phase. A quantification of the drug by HPLC would give additional confirmatory evidence as would detection of metabolites of the presumptively identified drug by TLC or GC.
4. Immunoassay positive for cocaine metabolite in urine or blood with detection of parent cocaine in blood by GC-NPD.
5. In some cases, such as blood volatiles analysis, GC headspace analysis can be correlated as relative retention times on two GC columns of differing polarity (giving a different elution order) to confirm an identification. However, novel or rarely detected analytes such as toluene or 1,1,1,-trichloroethane may require further confirmation by headspace GC/MS.

4.5.2 When Is Confirmation Necessary?

In general, any finding that could reasonably be questioned, or adversely affect insurance coverage or the reputation of the deceased, should be confirmed before it is reported. The greater the significance of a finding to the case, the more important it becomes to confirm that finding to absolute certainty by GC/MS, if possible.

- When the substance is potentially related to the cause and manner of death
- When the detected substance is an illicit drug such as marijuana, cocaine, methamphetamine, or PCP, since labeling an individual a possible drug abuser has serious sociologic and legal implications[173–176]
- Any prescription drug that is not known to have been prescribed for the deceased

4.5.3 When Is Confirmation Unnecessary?

When the substance presumptively detected has no relationship to the cause or manner of death, and when the detected substance carries no stigma, if reported, confirmation may not be needed. Over-the-counter medications, with no behavioral toxicity, usually do not require confirmation except when it is suspected that they may have contributed to toxicity. For example, salicylate or acetaminophen need not be confirmed in traumatic death cases, but should be confirmed in cases pending toxicology or suicidal intoxications.

Medications commonly administered during resuscitation, such as lidocaine and atropine, do not need confirmation if the deceased received such treatment before being pronounced dead. Prescribed medications that the deceased had been taking, and which are not related to the cause or manner of death, may not require confirmation either, since their presence in biological specimens is consistent with the history. Any substance reported without confirmation should be identified in the report as an unconfirmed presumptive finding.

4.6 GAS CHROMATOGRAPHY-MASS SPECTROMETRY

Today, GC/MS is generally accepted as unequivocal identification for most drugs, providing the best confirmatory information when performed correctly.[177,178] However, GC/MS assays can be performed in many ways, depending on the specific requirements and use of the results. Pharmacokinetic studies generally employ chemical ionization with single-ion monitoring to obtain optimum sensitivity. In such studies, the target drug is expected to be present, so criteria for identification need not be so rigorous, but single-ion monitoring is not usually considered sufficient for forensic purposes. GC/MS methods for the confirmation of illegal drugs of abuse in urine most often use electron impact ionization and multiple-ion monitoring to obtain conclusive results.[177–181] The more traditional MS identification criterion calls for matching retention times and full-scan electron impact mass spectra of the unknown with a standard.

Whether forensic samples should be analyzed by full-scan data acquisition, or by selected ion monitoring, is a matter of contention. The debate really comes down to one underlying question: How much spectral and chromatographic information is needed to provide a scientifically and legally defensible identification? Is a full-scan spectrum necessary? If selected ion monitoring is acceptable, how many ions must be monitored? Unfortunately, there are no simple answers. A good-quality, full-scan mass spectrum that matches a reference spectrum clearly constitutes a more definitive identification than ion current profiles of a few selected ions at the correct retention time.

Cody and Foltz have stated that the specificity of a GC/MS assay depends on many factors, including:

1. Choice of internal standard. The role of the internal standard in the overall analytical process cannot be overemphasized.[182–187]
2. Selectivity of the extraction procedure.
3. Choice of derivative, where appropriate.[188–190]
4. Efficiency of the GS separation.
5. Method of ionization.
6. Relative uniqueness of the analyte's mass spectrum or the chosen ions to be monitored.
7. Signal-to-noise ratio of the detected ions.[192]

Using GC/MS in the scanning mode, as both a screening and definitive identification methodology, has become quite common.[163] If the drug is an unknown, full-scan mode is the method of choice. Further comparison of the unknown's full mass spectrum with reference spectra will be necessary. Mass spectra are tentatively identified by a computerized library search and visually compared by an experienced analyst.[80,81,161–163]

GC/MS with selected ion monitoring (GC/MS-SIM) is commonly used to confirm the presence of drugs and/or metabolites in postmortem samples.[180,191] A well-designed assay, involving the selected ion monitoring of three or more abundant and structurally diagnostic ions, combined with specific requirements for the analyte's retention time relative to a suitable internal standard or calibrator, is regarded as a reliable identification.[192] Even fewer ions can provide an acceptable identification if the assay employs a highly selective extraction procedure or selective mode of ionization, such as ammonia chemical ionization.

GC/MS-SIM assays are extremely useful to confirm or exclude the presence of a suspected analyte that may have been indicated by history or screening results. However, target compound analyses such as GC/MS-SIM will detect, or exclude, only a limited number of related chemical compounds or classes of drugs. A reference standard and control materials of the target analyte must be analyzed within the same batch. Selected ion monitoring typically provides signal intensities that are 10- to 100-fold greater than those from full-scan analysis performed on quadrupole instruments. SIM analyses are therefore better adapted for quantitative measurements. Selected ion monitoring is generally less susceptible to interferences from co-eluting compounds than an assay employing full-scan recording. However, unlike full-scan spectral acquisition, a selected ion monitoring assay will not detect unsuspected drugs that may be of toxicological significance.

Standards adopted for conclusive drug identification include (1) the appearance of the monitored ions at a correct retention time, and (2) acceptable intensity ratios among those ions. The retention time and ion intensity ratios observed in the test sample are compared with those established from the calibrator(s) containing the target analyte, at a suitable concentration, incorporated in the same analytical batch.

4.6.1 Qualitative GC/MS-SIM Determination Criteria

To qualitatively identify a compound by selected ion monitoring (SIM), ion chromatograms are obtained from the reference compound for the primary ion and two or more qualifier ions. The criteria below must be met for a qualitative identification of an unknown:

1. The characteristic ions of the compound must be found at maxima in the same scan or within one scan of each other.
2. The retention time of the unknown compound's mass spectrum must be within ±2% of the retention time of the authentic compound or deuterated internal standard.
3. The ratios of the SIM peak areas must agree within ±20% with the ratios of the relative intensities for those ions in a reference mass spectrum from a calibrator analyzed on the same run by the GC/MS system.

These criteria should be kept in mind when making compound identification decisions. In addition Dr. Rodger Foltz has proposed the following helpful guidelines:[160,192–194]

1. Agreement among the relative ion intensities within a small mass range is more important than for those encompassing a wide mass range.
2. The higher mass ions are generally more diagnostic than those occurring at low mass.
3. No prominent ions in either spectrum (those with relative intensities above 10%) should be totally missing from the other spectrum, unless they can be attributed to an impurity.

4.6.2 Potential Problems with GC/MS Analyses

Several problems may be encountered in GC/MS analysis. The mass spectral library may give erroneous identifications when concentrations near the detection limit are analyzed, when chromatographically interfering substances are present, or when isomers are analyzed. Even MS with a full fragmentation pattern may not provide adequate confirmation, either because several drugs have very similar fragmentation patterns, as the barbiturates, for example, or because the drug may exhibit only one major peak consisting of a low mass fragment ion in its mass spectrum, such as the tricyclic antidepressants.

When using the SIM mode, a considerable gain in GC/MS sensitivity can be achieved by focusing on the most abundant ion, and two or more other characteristic ions. However, many illegal drugs or metabolites (and numerous other commonly used drugs, e.g., antihistamines, local anesthetics, some beta-blocking agents, etc.) have similar El mass spectra, showing a common base peak and weak molecular ion signals. Many elute over a wide range of retention times; others may have closely related retention indices.

The complexity of biological matrices encountered in postmortem cases, such as "blood," tissues, gastric contents, and hair/nails, necessitates well-designed, and often multistep, sample treatment procedures.[195] This is especially true when utilizing procedures based on physicochemical properties of drug/metabolites. Suitable sample preparation is the most important prerequisite in the GC/MS of typical postmortem samples. It involves isolation and, if necessary, cleavage of conjugates and/or derivatization of the drugs and their metabolites. Derivatization steps are necessary if relatively polar compounds such as metabolites are to be screened or confirmed.

4.7 LIQUID CHROMATOGRAPHY-MASS SPECTROMETRY

LC/MS is fast becoming an important technique in forensic toxicology, despite its increased cost over GC/MS.[225–230] For a long time, the combination of HPLC and MS was not an alternative because of interface problems. Now when this obstacle has been overcome by different innovations, LC/MS has become increasingly popular both for screening purposes and for sensitive and specific confirmation analyses. Many drugs cannot be analyzed by GC/MS because they are either thermolabile or are too polar or insufficiently volatile to chromatograph well, if at all. In contrast, virtually any drug can be analyzed by LC/MS after development of a suitable method. Other than the issue of cost, the only disadvantage of LC over GC is that LC separations usually require more development time than GC separations. The comments in Section 4.6 generally apply to LC/MS analysis, especially in regard to SIM analysis. As with GC/MS, so-called "hyphenated" techniques may be used, such as LC/MS/MS. Tandem MS-MS instruments have the enormous advantage of being able to provide a much higher degree of specificity than LC/MS alone. The first mass spectrometer in the LC/MS/MS system generates a conventional mass spectrum. One specific mass is then allowed to pass through into a separate collision cell where it can be ionized further. Either the entire mass spectrum of that chosen ion may be displayed, or a single ion isolated in SIM mode. Tandem MS techniques such as LC/MS/MS are particularly useful for postmortem forensic work because they minimize interference from endogenous compounds such as putrefactive products. LC/MS/MS-TOF (time-of-flight) instruments offer a further degree of specificity because of the increased specificity imparted by the medium to high mass resolution of TOF instruments. Of course, the major drawbacks of LC/MS/MS and LC/MS/MS-TOF instruments are considerably increased cost, and complexity of operation, often requiring a dedicated operator. Having stated that, the development of a method for a particular analyte is generally easier with LC/MS than with GC/MS because standards with reference compounds can be directly injected and calibration curves can readily be constructed. A special feature that the operator must keep in mind is that a change in pH to adjust the chromatography will also affect the charge of the compounds at the time for ionization, and hence influence the mass spectrometric detection.

Different interface systems are available. The most utilized alternative is atmospheric pressure-positive electrospray ionization (API-ES), and a number of applications in forensic toxicology with this methodology have been reported.[231–235] Alternatively, atmospheric pressure-chemical ionization (APCI) can be used. Both these variants of LC/MS instrumentation cover a wider spectrum of polar and nonpolar drugs than GC/MS analysis can offer, and API-ES also allows for analysis of molecules with higher masses. APCI MS/MS has been shown to be useful for sensitive screening of certain classes of drugs such as benzodiazepines and hypnotics,[236] and beta-blockers.[237]

4.8 METHOD VALIDATION

Bioanalytical methods, based on a variety of physicochemical and biological techniques, such as chromatography, immunoassay, and mass spectrometry, must all be individually validated prior to and during use to generate confidence in the results.[196–210] Method validation is discussed in Chapter 5.

4.9 QUANTIFICATION OF DRUGS AND POISONS

When you can measure what you are speaking about and express it in numbers, you know something about it; but when you cannot express it in numbers, your knowledge is of meagre and unsatisfactory kind.

— Lord Kelvin (1824–1907)

Screening and confirmation (qualitative) tests establish the presence of a specific substance; quantitative tests measure the amount of that substance in a particular specimen. Qualitative information alone can demonstrate that the deceased was exposed to the substance before death, and may even enable the toxicologist to offer an opinion regarding the ante-mortem interval in which the exposure probably took place. However, quantitative information is often required to form an opinion whether or not the exposure was sufficient to cause behavioral toxicity or death. Drug concentrations in postmortem tissues, or fluids, must be related to reference values derived from other cases.[5,211–215]

4.9.1 What Should Be Quantified?

Substances should be quantified only when necessary for interpretation. Most quantitative assays are separate, labor-intensive procedures that measure only one drug or group of similar compounds. Quantifying substances that, by their nature, could have no conceivable bearing on the issues of the case is a waste of time and resources. For example, drugs with no psychoactivity, such as acetaminophen, should not be quantified in a motor vehicle accident driver victim, while diphenhydramine, an antihistamine with sedative side effects, should. On the other hand, if the victim were a passenger, diphenhydramine would not require quantification. In deaths from asthma or epilepsy, the laboratory should quantify theophylline or anticonvulsant, respectively, to determine whether or not they were within or below the therapeutic concentration range.

In general, substances that can cause behavioral toxicity should be quantified. In most natural deaths, it is important to know that the concentration of a prescribed or therapeutic drug is not excessive. Semiquantitative information, derived from blood screening tests, is often sufficient to make the assessment. Only if the concentration estimate indicates an excessive amount would a quantitative assay be required. Poisons such as carbon monoxide, cyanide, and heavy metals should always be quantified in appropriate specimens. Tests for ethanol usually yield both qualitative and quantitative data, which should be reported if above the laboratory's administrative cutoff (usually 0.01%).

Cocaine should always be quantified. Its concentration is usually important and its instability in storage may prevent subsequent analysis if it is not quantified soon after detection. Other drugs or poisons that are unstable in storage should be quantified before their decomposition renders the analysis unreliable. In a case that is pending the outcome of toxicology testing, any detected drugs or poisons and their metabolites should be quantified, unless it is clear from the circumstances of the case that a particular substance did not play a role in the cause or manner of death.

When resuscitation has been attempted, lidocaine and atropine may be detected in postmortem blood. Unless a medication error is suspected, or the quantity appears to be excessive, it is not necessary to quantify them. Nor is there any need to quantify caffeine and nicotine, unless toxicity is suspected or screening tests indicate that an abnormally large amount of either is present.

In most cases a drug's metabolites are just as important to quantify as the parent compound. The ratio of parent drug to its metabolite often indicates the state of pharmacokinetics in the individual case. For example, a ratio greater than 1 for amitriptyline/nortriptyline may indicate an acute ingestion or short interval from ingestion to death, while a ratio of 0.3 in a propoxyphene/norpropoxyphene case may indicate a chronic exposure.

Active or toxic metabolites of a drug or poison are always measured, but inactive metabolites may also be important. Their presence may shed light on the pattern of drug use. High concentrations of benzoylecgonine indicate accumulations from multiple doses. Low concentrations suggest that only a few doses were taken or that there has been a long interval since the last dose. Furthermore, there is some evidence that benzoylecgonine may be a vasoconstrictor, so it may contribute to the hypertensive effects of cocaine use.

4.9.2 Specimens for Quantification of Drugs and Poisons

The choice of the sample for quantitative analysis is very important.[216] Often it is sufficient to quantify drugs or poisons in blood only. If toxicity is not suspected, a blood quantification can verify that the drug was present, and that its concentration was consistent with therapeutic use. Also, when a drug concentration is clearly in the lethal range, and poisoning or overdose is suspected, a blood determination may be sufficient. It may not be necessary to quantify brain morphine levels in an intravenous heroin user, found dead with syringe, tourniquet, and "cooker" present, with autopsy evidence of pulmonary edema, and a high concentration of morphine in the blood, to support a conclusion that death was caused by a heroin overdose. Likewise, a 15-mg/L blood amitriptyline concentration, in a case accompanied by a suicide note, is sufficient to define overt toxicity, regardless of potential postmortem diffusion.[216] Carbon monoxide should be measured in blood, its site of action. Other specimens are likely to give negative results. One exception, not related to drug abuse, is the analysis of skeletal muscle specimens for carbon monoxide to assist in the differentiation between entrance and exit gunshot wounds.

Tissues that selectively take up a particular drug class may have a much higher concentration than that found in blood. For example, volatile anesthetics, cocaine, marijuana, tricyclic antidepressants, and other lipid-soluble substances are preferentially absorbed into the fatty tissues of the brain and liver, while digoxin and other cardiac glycosides are taken up by cardiac muscle. Figures 4.2 and 4.3 show the relationship of quantifications to the overall process of postmortem toxicology analysis.

4.9.3 Quantification: Procedural Issues

4.9.3.1 Instruments

Many of the instruments used for screening tests can also provide accurate quantitative data. Immunoassays designed for therapeutic drug monitoring (TDM) (e.g., serum assays for phenobarbital, theophylline, and phenytoin) are specific, and yield accurate results with most postmortem specimens.[144,217] GC, HPLC, GC/MS, and LC/MS are readily adapted for quantification. Spectrophotometric methods are useful for some analytes, such as ethchlorvynol and heavy metals.[1] However, their utility is limited because many drugs have metabolites or breakdown products with similar spectra (e.g., phenothiazines), so relative contributions of the parent drug, and active and inactive metabolites, to the signal cannot be segregated and assessed.

4.9.3.2 Sample Preparation

Blood and other fluids are usually extracted with no pretreatment other than dilution. GC screening tests can provide an estimate of the concentration of the analyte. If the estimated concentration is above the upper limit of linearity of the assay, the sample must be diluted with water, buffer, or negative control matrix and thoroughly mixed to bring the analyte concentration into the dynamic range of the assay. Homogenates of tissue samples are prepared in a blender or a tissue homogenizer in water or a buffer usually in a 1:2 to a 1:5 ratio. These homogenates deteriorate rapidly so they are usually used within 2 weeks or less, and the remainder discarded. Gastric contents are weighed or measured by volume, homogenized, and appropriately diluted.

With the exception of some immunoassays, samples are usually extracted with organic solvent to isolate the compounds of interest from the biological matrix. Often, liquid–liquid extraction is used, with back-extraction to eliminate lipid interference. Recent advances in solid-phase extraction technology have made possible the application of these techniques to the analysis of blood and tissues. The speed and efficiency of solid-phase extractions make them an attractive alternative to liquid–liquid extraction procedures, and their use is expanding in postmortem toxicology. However, lot-to-lot inconsistencies in solid-phase extraction columns can cause quantitative methods to fail, due to poor recovery of analytes. Therefore, it is extremely important to evaluate each new batch of columns before risking wastage of, sometimes limited, samples.

Duplicate samples should be analyzed through the entire procedure to demonstrate the reproducibility of the result. If the difference between duplicate analyses is greater than the two standard deviations for the method, the analyst should suspect that an error occurred in one or both. Additional analyses should be performed to determine an accurate result with acceptable precision.

4.9.3.3 Internal Standard

Most quantitative procedures employ one or more internal standards to compensate for variations in extraction efficiency, injection volume, and changes in detector sensitivity. An internal standard is a substance with chemical properties similar to the target analyte. It is added in identical quantity to each sample and standard before the extraction process. The internal standard is extracted along with the analyte, so that any loss of analyte in the extraction process will be compensated for by a proportional loss of internal standard. The assumption is that the ratio of analyte to internal standard does not change. Selection and evaluation of the internal standards is a critical component for the development of a quantitative procedure.[184,218–222] Method development and validation and the selection of internal standards are discussed in Chapter 5.

4.10 THE REVIEW PROCESS

Individual cases should be reviewed periodically to assess the status of the investigation and the quality of the acquired data. Reassessment may suggest the need for additional tests. Before a report is issued, the entire case file must be reviewed to ensure that results are forensically acceptable and that sufficient data have been gathered to determine whether, and to what extent, drugs or poisons influenced the cause and manner of death. When testing has been completed, the toxicologist reviews the file one final time to ensure that nothing has been overlooked.

4.11 PENDING TOXICOLOGY CONFERENCE

In cases where the cause of death is not obvious, and determinations have been put on hold pending the results of toxicological testing, the toxicologist and pathologist together review the investigation, autopsy, and toxicology results. When both are satisfied that the toxicology results answer the questions pertinent to the case, a final toxicology report is issued. The need for communication and teamwork for an effective system cannot be overemphasized.[1–5,223,224] Refer to Figure 4.3 summarizing the analytic strategies for drug screening in "pending tox cases."

REFERENCES

1. Curry, A.S., Outline of a systematic search for an unknown poison in viscera, in *Mechanisms and Analytical Methods*, Vol. 1, Stewart, C.P. and Stolman, A., Eds., Academic Press, New York, 1960, 257–283.
2. Freimuth, H.C., Isolation and separation of poisons from biological material, in *Mechanisms and Analytical Methods*, Vol. 1, Stewart, C.P. and Stolman, A., Eds., Academic Press, New York, 1960, 285–302.
3. Stewart, C.P. and Martin, G.J., The mode of action of poisons, in *Mechanisms and Analytical Methods*, Vol. 2, Stewart, C.P. and Stolman, A., Eds., Academic Press, New York, 1960, 1–15.
4. Stewart, C.P. and Stolman, A., The toxicologist and his work, in *Toxicology: Mechanisms and Analytical Methods*, Vol. 1, Stewart, C.P. and Stolman, A., Eds., Academic Press, New York, 1960, 1–22.
5. Jackson, J.V., Forensic toxicology, in *Clarke's Isolation and Identification of Drugs in Pharmaceuticals, Body Fluids, and Post-Mortem Material*, 2nd ed., Moffatt, A.C., Ed., Pharmaceutical Press, London, 1986, 35.
6. Finkle, B.S., Forensic toxicology in the 1980's: the role of the analytical chemist, *Anal. Chem.*, 54, 433A–438A, 1982.
7. Levine, B., Forensic toxicology [review], *Anal. Chem.*, 65, 272A–276A, 1993.
8. Levine, B.S., Smith, M.L., and Froede, R.C., Postmortem forensic toxicology [review], *Clin. Lab. Med.*, 10(3), 571–589, 1990.

9. Osselton, M.D., Analytical forensic toxicology [review], *Arch. Toxicol. Suppl.,* 15, 259–267, 1992.
10. Kasantikul, V. and Kasantikul, D., Death following intentional overdose of psychotropic drugs, *J. Med. Assoc. Thailand,* 72, 109–111, 1989.
11. Costello, C.E., GC/MS analysis of street drugs, particularly in the body fluids of overdose victims, in *Street Drug Analysis and Its Social and Clinical Implications*, Marshman, J.A., Ed., Addiction Research Foundation, Toronto, 1974, 67–78.
12. Nashelsky, M.B., Dix, J.D., and Adelstein, E.H., Homicide facilitated by inhalation of chloroform, *J. Forensic Sci.,* 40, 134–138, 1995.
13. Tardiff, K., Marzuk, P.M., Leon, A.C., Hirsch, C.S., Stajic, M., Portera, L., et al., Cocaine, opiates, and ethanol in homicides in New York City: 1990 and 1991, *J. Forensic Sci.,* 40, 387–390, 1995.
14. Bailey, D.N. and Shaw, R.F., Cocaine- and methamphetamine-related deaths in San Diego County (1987): homicides and accidental overdoses, *J. Forensic Sci.,* 34, 407–422, 1989.
15. Budd, R.D., The incidence of alcohol use in Los Angeles County homicide victims, *Am. J. Drug Alcohol Abuse,* 9, 105–111, 1982.
16. Garriott, J.C., Di Maio, V.J., and Rodriguez, R.G., Detection of cannabinoids in homicide victims and motor vehicle fatalities, *J. Forensic Sci.,* 31, 1274–1282, 1986.
17. Garriott, J.C., Drug use among homicide victims, *Am. J. Forensic Med. Pathol.,* 14, 234–237, 1993.
18. Poklis, A., Graham, M., Maginn, D., Branch, C.A., and Gantner, G.E., Phencyclidine and violent deaths in St. Louis, Missouri: a survey of medical examiners' cases from 1977 through 1986, *Am. J. Drug Alcohol Abuse,* 16, 265–274, 1990.
19. Gerostamoulos, J. and Drummer, O.H., Incidence of psychoactive cannabinoids in drivers killed in motor vehicle accidents, *J. Forensic Sci.,* 38, 649–656, 1993.
20. Marzuk, P.M., Tardiff, K., Leon, A.C., Stajic, M., Morgan, E.B., and Mann, J.J., Prevalence of recent cocaine use among motor vehicle fatalities in New York City [see comments], *J. Am. Med. Assoc.,* 263, 250–256, 1990.
21. Perez-Reyes, M., Hicks, R.E., Bumberry, J., Jeffcoat, A.R., and Cook, C.E., Interaction between marihuana and ethanol: effects on psychomotor performance, *Alcohol. Clin. Exp. Res.,* 12, 268–276, 1988.
22. Garriott, J.C., DiMaio, V.J., Zumwalt, R.E:, and Petty, C.S., Incidence of drugs and alcohol in fatally injured motor vehicle drivers, *J. Forensic Sci.,* 22, 383–389, 1977.
23. Deveaux, M., Marson, J.C., Goldstein, P., Lhermitte, M., Gosset, D., and Muller, P.H., [Alcohol and psychotropic drugs in fatal traffic accidents (the Nord-Pas-de-Calais region, France)] [in French], *Acta Med. Legal. Socialis,* 40, 61–70, 1990.
24. Balkon, J., Results of a multilaboratory checksample analysis program for carbon monoxide and cyanide, *J. Anal. Toxicol.,* 15, 232–236, 1991.
25. Risser, D. and Schneider, B., Carbon monoxide-related deaths from 1984 to 1993 in Vienna, Austria, *J. Forensic Sci.,* 40, 368–371, 1995.
26. Nowak, R. and Sachs, H., [Development of carbon monoxide and hydrocyanic acid in automobile fires and their forensic significance], *Versicherungsmedizin,* 45, 20–22, 1993.
27. Jentzen, J.M., Forensic toxicology. An overview and an algorithmic approach, *Am. J. Clin. Pathol.,* 92, S48–S55, 1989.
28. Taylor, R.L., Cohan, S.L., and White, J.D., Comprehensive toxicology screening in the emergency department: an aid to clinical diagnosis, *Am. J. Emerg. Med.,* 3, 507–511, 1985.
29. Stair, E.L. and Whaley, M., Rapid screening and spot tests for the presence of common poisons, *Vet. Hum. Toxicol.,* 32, 564–566, 1990.
30. Bailey, D.N., Comprehensive toxicology screening: the frequency of finding other drugs in addition to ethanol, *J. Toxicol. Clin. Toxicol.,* 22, 463–471, 1984.
31. Berry, D.J. and Grove, J., Emergency toxicological screening for drugs commonly taken in overdose, *J. Chromatogr.,* 80, 205–219, 1973.
32. Kinberger, B., Holmen, A., and Wahrgren, P., A strategy for drug analysis in serum and urine. An application to drug screening of samples from drivers involved in traffic accidents, *Anal. Lett.,* 15, 937–951, 1982.
33. Ueki, M., [Drug screening in clinical toxicology and analytical doping control in sports] [review] [5 refs] [in Japanese], *Nippon Rinsho Jpn. J. Clin. Med.,* 1, 904–906, 1995.
34. Howarth, A.T. and Clegg, G., Simultaneous detection and quantitation of drugs commonly involved in self-administered overdoses, *Clin. Chem.,* 24, 804–807, 1978.

35. Jatlow, P.I., UV spectrophotometry for sedative drugs frequently involved in overdose emergencies, in *Methodology for Analytical Toxicology,* Vol. I, Sunshine, I., Ed., CRC Press, Boca Raton, FL, 1984, 414.
36. Christophersen, A.S. and Morland, J., Drug analysis for control purposes in forensic toxicology, workplace testing, sports medicine and related areas [review], *Pharmacol. Toxicol.,* 74, 202–210, 1994.
37. Chen, J.S., Chang, K.J., Charng, R.C., Lai, S.J., Binder, S.R., and Essien, H., The development of a broad-spectrum toxicology screening program in Taiwan, *J. Toxicol. Clin. Toxicol.,* 33, 581–589, 1995.
38. Bailey, D.N., Results of limited versus comprehensive toxicology screening in a university medical center [see comments], *Am. J. Clin. Pathol.,* 105, 572–575, 1996.
39. Tilson, H.A. and Moser, V.C., Comparison of screening approaches [review], *Neurotoxicology,* 13, 1–13, 1992.
40. Gambaro, V., Lodi, F., Mariani, R., Saligari, E., Villa, M., and Marozzi, E., Systematic generic chemico-toxicological testing in forensic toxicology. IV. Application of a computer in a generic survey of substances of toxicological interest [in Italian], *Farm. Ed. Pratica,* 38, 133–172, 1983.
41. Crouch, D.J., Peat, M.A., Chinn, D.M., and Finkle, B.S., Drugs and driving: a systematic analytical approach, *J. Forensic Sci.,* 28, 945–956, 1983.
42. Masoud, A.N., Systematic identification of drugs of abuse. I. Spot tests, *J. Pharm. Sci.,* 64, 841–844, 1975.
43. Schepers, P.G., Franke, J.P., and de Zeeuw, R.A., System evaluation and substance identification in systematic toxicological analysis by the mean list length approach, *J. Anal. Toxicol.,* 7, 272–278, 1983.
44. Wennig, R., Evaluation of a systematic analysis scheme used in clinical toxicology. Evaluation of 4 years' experience in a national health laboratory [in French], *Rech. Eur. Toxicol.,* 5, 277–280, 1983.
45. Marozzi, E., Cozza, E., Pariali, A., Gambaro, V., Lodi, F., and Saligari, E., Generic systematic chemico-toxicological research in forensic toxicology [in Italian], *Farm. Ed. Pratica,* 33, 195–207, 1978.
46. Tagliaro, F., Lubli, G., Ghielmi, S., Franchi, D., and Marigo, M., Chromatographic methods for blood alcohol determination [review], *J. Chromatogr.,* 580, 161–190, 1992.
47. Cox, R.A., Crifasi, J.A., Dickey, R.E., Ketzler, S.C., and Pshak, G.L., A single-step extraction for screening whole blood for basic drugs by capillary GC/NPD, *J. Anal. Toxicol.,* 13, 224–228, 1989.
48. Simpson, D., Jarvie, D.R., and Heyworth, R., An evaluation of six methods for the detection of drugs of abuse in urine, *Ann. Clin. Biochem.,* 26, 172–181, 1989.
49. Gjerde, H., Christophersen, A.S., Skuterud, B., Klemetsen, K., and Morland, J., Screening for drugs in forensic blood samples using EMIT urine assays, *Forensic Sci. Int.,* 44, 179–185, 1990.
50. Maier, R.D., Erkens, M., Hoenen, H., and Bogusz, M., The screening for common drugs of abuse in whole blood by means of EMIT-ETS and FPIA-ADx urine immunoassays, *Int. J. Legal Med.,* 105, 115–119, 1992.
51. Diosi, D.T. and Harvey, D.C., Analysis of whole blood for drugs of abuse using EMIT d.a.u. reagents and a Monarch 1000 Chemistry Analyzer, *J. Anal. Toxicol.,* 17, 133–137, 1993.
52. Bogusz, M., Aderjan, R., Schmitt, G., Nadler, E., and Neureither, B., The determination of drugs of abuse in whole blood by means of FPIA and EMIT-dau immunoassays — a comparative study, *Forensic Sci. Int.,* 48, 27–37, 1990.
53. Masoud, A.N., Systematic identification of drugs of abuse. II. TLC, *J. Pharm. Sci.,* 65, 1585–1589, 1976.
54. Machata, G., Thin layer chromatography in systematic, toxicologic analysis processes [in German], *Dtsch. Z. Ges. Gerichtl. Med.,* 59, 181–185, 1967.
55. Brunk, S.D., Thin-layer chromatography using Toxi-Lab system, in *Analysis of Addictive and Misused Drugs,* Adamovics, J.A., Ed., Marcel Dekker, New York, 1995, 41–50.
56. Jarvie, D.R. and Simpson, D., Drug screening: evaluation of the Toxi-Lab TLC system, *Ann. Clin. Biochem.,* 23, 76–84, 1986.
57. Nishigami, J., Ohshima, T., Takayasu, T., Kondo, T., Lin, Z., and Nagano, T., Forensic toxicological application of TOXI-LAB screening for biological specimens in autopsy cases and emergency cares [in Japanese], *Nippon Hoigaku Zasshi Jpn. J. Legal Med.,* 47, 372–379, 1993.
58. Warfield, R.W. and Maickel, R.P., A generalized extraction-TLC procedure for identification of drugs, *J. Appl. Toxicol.,* 3, 51–57, 1983.
59. Whitter, P.D. and Cary, P.L., A rapid method for the identification of acidic, neutral, and basic drugs in postmortem liver specimens by Toxi-Lab, *J. Anal. Toxicol.,* 10, 68–71, 1986.

60. Hackett, L.P., Dusci, L.J., and McDonald, I.A., Extraction procedures for some common drugs in clinical and forensic toxicology, *J. Forensic Sci.,* 21, 263–274, 1976.
61. Chen, X.H., Wijsbeek, J., van Veen, J., Franke, J.P., and de Zeeuw, R.A., Solid-phase extraction for the screening of acidic, neutral and basic drugs in plasma using a single-column procedure on Bond Elut Certify, *J. Chromatogr.,* 529, 161–166, 1990.
62. Chen, X.H., Franke, J.P., Wijsbeek, J., and de Zeeuw, R.A., Isolation of acidic, neutral, and basic drugs from whole blood using a single mixed-mode solid-phase extraction column, *J. Anal. Toxicol.,* 16, 351–355, 1992.
63. Foerster, E.H., Hatchett, C., and Garriott, J.C., A rapid, comprehensive screening procedure for basic drugs in blood or tissues by gas chromatography, *J. Anal. Toxicol.,* 2, 50–55, 1978.
64. Midha, K.K., Charette, C., McGilveray, I.J., Webb, D., and McLean, M.C., Application of GLC-alkali FID and GLC-MS procedures to analysis of plasma in suspected cases of psychotropic drug overdose, *Clin. Toxicol.,* 18, 713–729, 1982.
65. Griffiths, W.C., Oleksyk, S.K., and Diamond, I., A comprehensive gas chromatographic drug screening procedure for the clinical laboratory, *Clin. Biochem.,* 6, 124–131, 1973.
66. Eklund, A., Jonsson, J., and Schuberth, J., A procedure for simultaneous screening and quantification of basic drugs in liver, utilizing capillary gas chromatography and nitrogen sensitive detection, *J. Anal. Toxicol.,* 7, 24–28, 1983.
67. Marozzi, E., Gambaro, V., Lodi, F., and Pariali, A., [General systematic chemico-toxicological research in forensic toxicology. I. Considerations on the gas-chromatographic test in the general chemico-toxicological research] [in Italian], *Farm. Ed. Pratica,* 31, 180–211, 1976.
68. Drummer, O.H., Kotsos, A., and McIntyre, I.M., A class-independent drug screen in forensic toxicology using a photodiode array detector, *J. Anal. Toxicol.,* 17, 225–229, 1993.
69. Ojanpera, I., Rasanen, I., and Vuori, E., Automated quantitative screening for acidic and neutral drugs in whole blood by dual-column capillary gas chromatography, *J. Anal. Toxicol.,* 15, 204–208, 1991.
70. Premel-Cabic, A., Cailleux, A., and Allain, P., [A gas chromatographic assay of fifteen volatile organic solvents in blood (author's transl)] [in French], *Clin. Chim. Acta,* 56, 5–11, 1974.
71. Drummer, O.H., Horomidis, S., Kourtis, S., Syrjanen, M.L., and Tippett, P., Capillary gas chromatographic drug screen for use in forensic toxicology, *J. Anal. Toxicol.,* 18, 134–138, 1994.
72. Taylor, R.W., Greutink, C., and Jain, N.C., Identification of underivatized basic drugs in urine by capillary column gas chromatography, *J. Anal. Toxicol.,* 10, 205–208, 1986.
73. Ehresman, D.J., Price, S.M., and Lakatua, D.J., Screening biological samples for underivatized drugs using a splitless injection technique on fused silica capillary column gas chromatography, *J. Anal. Toxicol.,* 9, 55–62, 1985.
74. Turcant, A., Premel-Cabic, A., Cailleux, A., and Allain, P., Screening for neutral and basic drugs in blood by dual fused-silica column chromatography with nitrogen-phosphorus detection [published erratum appears in *Clin. Chem.,* 34(11), 2370, 1988], *Clin. Chem.,* 34, 1492–1497, 1988.
75. Watts, V.W. and Simonick, T.F., Screening of basic drugs in biological samples using dual column capillary chromatography and nitrogen-phosphorus detectors, *J. Anal. Toxicol.,* 10, 198–204, 1986.
76. Fretthold, D., Jones, P., Sebrosky, G., and Sunshine, I., Testing for basic drugs in biological fluids by solvent extraction and dual capillary GC/NPD, *J. Anal. Toxicol.,* 10, 10–14, 1986.
77. Chia, D.T. and Gere, J.A., Rapid drug screening using Toxi-Lab extraction followed by capillary gas chromatography/mass spectroscopy, *Clin. Biochem.,* 20, 303–306, 1987.
78. Fiers, T., Maes, V., and Sevens, C., Automation of toxicological screenings on a Hewlett Packard Chemstation GC/MS System, *Clin. Biochem.,* 29, 357–361, 1996.
79. Pettersen, J.E. and Skuterud, B., Application of combined GC/MS as compared to a conventional analytical system for identification of unknown drugs in acute drug intoxications, *Anal. Chem. Symp. Ser.,* 13, 111–129, 1983.
80. Maurer, H.H., Systematic toxicological analysis of drugs and their metabolites by gas chromatography-mass spectrometry [review], *J. Chromatogr.,* 580, 3–41, 1992.
81. Neill, G.P., Davies, N.W., and McLean, S., Automated screening procedure using gas chromatography-mass spectrometry for identification of drugs after their extraction from biological samples, *J. Chromatogr.,* 565, 207–224, 1991.

82. Brooks, K.E. and Smith, N.B., Efficient extraction of basic, neutral, and weakly acidic drugs from plasma for analysis by gas chromatography-mass spectrometry [published erratum appears in *Clin. Chem.,* 38(2), 323, 1992], *Clin. Chem.,* 37, 1975–1978, 1991.
83. Cailleux, A., Turcant, A., Premel-Cabic, A., and Allain, P., Identification and quantitation of neutral and basic drugs in blood by gas chromatography and mass spectrometry, *J. Chromatogr. Sci.,* 19, 163–176, 1981.
84. Maurer, H.H., Identification and differentiation of barbiturates, other sedative-hypnotics and their metabolites in urine integrated in a general screening procedure using computerized GC/MS, *J. Chromatogr.,* 530, 307–326, 1990.
85. Lambert, W.E., Meyer, E., Xue-Ping, Y., and De Leenheer, A.P., Screening, identification, and quantitation of benzodiazepines in postmortem samples by HPLC with photodiode array detection, *J. Anal. Toxicol.,* 19, 35–40, 1995.
86. Bogusz, M. and Wu, M., Standardized HPLC/DAD system, based on retention indices and spectral library, applicable for systematic toxicological screening [published erratum appears in *J. Anal. Toxicol.,* 16(3), 16A, 1992], *J. Anal. Toxicol.,* 15, 188–197, 1991.
87. Maier, R.D. and Bogusz, M., Identification power of a standardized HPLC/DAD system for systematic toxicological analysis, *J. Anal. Toxicol.,* 19, 79–83, 1995.
88. Chollet, D. and Kunstner, P., Fast systematic approach for the determination of drugs in biological fluids by fully automated high-performance liquid chromatography with on-line solid-phase extraction and automated cartridge exchange. Application to cebaracetam in human urine, *J. Chromatogr.,* 577, 335–340, 1992.
89. Wu Chen, N.B., Schaffer, M.I., Lin, R.L., Kurland, M.L., Donoghue, E.R., Jr., and Stein, R.J., The general toxicology unknown. I. The systematic approach, *J. Forensic Sci.,* 28, 391–397, 1983.
90. Wu Chen, N.B., Schaffer, M.I., Lin, R.L., Kurland, M.L., Donoghue, E.R., Jr., and Stein, R.J., The general toxicology unknown. II. A case report: doxylamine and pyrilamine intoxication, *J. Forensic Sci.,* 28, 398–403, 1983.
91. Maurer, H.H., Detection of anticonvulsants and their metabolites in urine within a "general unknown" analytical procedure using computerized GC/MS, *Arch. Toxicol.,* 64, 554–561, 1990.
92. Oliver, J.S. and Watson, J.M., Abuse of solvents "for kicks," *Lancet,* 1, 84–86, 1977.
93. Astier, A., Chromatographic determination of volatile solvents and their metabolites in urine for monitoring occupational exposure, *J. Chromatogr.,* 643, 389–398, 1993.
94. Jones, A.W., A rapid method for blood alcohol determination by headspace analysis using an electrochemical detector, *J. Forensic Sci.,* 23, 283–291, 1978.
95. Ghittori, S., Fiorentino, M.L., and Imbriani, M., [Use of gas chromatography with flame ionization (GC-FID) in the measurement of solvents in the urine], *Giorn. Ital. Med. Lavoro,* 9, 21–24, 1987.
96. Turner, G.J., Colbert, D.L., and Chowdry, B.Z., A broad spectrum immunoassay using fluorescence polarization for the detection of amphetamines in urine, *Ann. Clin. Biochem.,* 28, 588–594, 1991.
97. Kunsman, G.W., Manno, J.E., Cockerham, K.R., and Manno, B.R., Application of the Syva EMIT and Abbott TDx amphetamine immunoassays to the detection of 3,4-methylenedioxymethamphetamine (MDMA) and 3,4-methylenedioxyethamphetamine (MDEA) in urine, *J. Anal. Toxicol.,* 14, 149–153, 1990.
98. D'Nicuola, J., Jones, R., Levine, B., and Smith, M.L., Evaluation of six commercial amphetamine and methamphetamine immunoassays for cross-reactivity to phenylpropanolamine and ephedrine in urine [see comments], *J. Anal. Toxicol.,* 16, 211–213, 1992.
99. Mule, S. and Casella, G., Confirmation and quantitation of barbiturates in human urine by gas chromatography/mass spectrometry, *J. Anal. Toxicol.,* 13, 13–16, 1989.
100. Maurer, H.H., Identification and differentiation of barbiturates, other sedative-hypnotics and their metabolites in urine integrated in a general screening procedure using computerized gas chromatography-mass spectrometry, *J. Chromatogr.,* 530, 307–326, 1990.
101. Liu, R., McKeehan, A., Edwards, C., Foster, G., Bensley, W., Langner, J., et al., Improved gas chromatography-mass spectrometry analysis of barbiturates in urine using centrifuge-based solid-phase extraction, methylation, with d5-pentobarbital as internal standard, *J. Forensic Sci.,* 39, 1504–1514, 1994.
102. Mangin, P., Lugnier, A.A., and Chaumont, A.J., A polyvalent method using HPLC for screening and quantification of 12 common barbiturates in various biological materials, *J. Anal. Toxicol.,* 11, 27–30, 1987.

103. Jain, N.C., Mass screening and confirmation of barbiturates in urine by RIA/gas chromatography, *Clin. Toxicol.,* 9, 221–233, 1976.
104. Gill, R., Stead, A.H., and Moffat, A.C., Analytical aspects of barbiturate abuse: identification of drugs by the effective combination of gas-liquid, high-performance liquid and thin-layer chromatographic techniques, *J. Chromatogr.,* 204, 275–284, 1981.
105. Valentine, J.L., Middleton, R., and Sparks, C., Identification of urinary benzodiazepines and their metabolites — comparison of automated HPLC and GC/MS after immunoassay screening of clinical specimens, *J. Anal. Toxicol.,* 20, 416–424, 1996.
106. Schutz, H., Modern screening strategies in analytical toxicology with special regard to new benzodiazepines, *Z. Rechtsmed. — J. Legal Med.,* 100, 1937, 1988.
107. Black, D.A., Clark, G.D., Haver, V.M., Garbin, J.A., and Saxon, A.J., Analysis of urinary benzodiazepines using solid-phase extraction and gas chromatography-mass spectrometry [see comments], *J. Anal. Toxicol.,* 18, 185–188, 1994.
108. Jones, C.E., Wians, F.H., Jr., Martinez, L.A., and Merritt, G.J., Benzodiazepines identified by capillary gas chromatography-mass spectrometry, with specific ion screening used to detect benzophenone derivatives, *Clin. Chem.,* 35, 1394–1398, 1989.
109. Sioufi, A. and Dubois, J.P., Chromatography of benzodiazepines [review], *J. Chromatogr.,* 531, 459–480, 1990.
110. Drouet-Coassolo, C., Aubert, C., Coassolo, P., and Cano, J.P., Capillary GC/MS method for the identification and quantification of some benzodiazepines and their unconjugated metabolites in plasma, *J. Chromatogr.,* 487, 295–311, 1989.
111. Japp, M., Garthwaite, K., Geeson, A.V., and Osselton, M.D., Collection of analytical data for benzodiazepines and benzophenones, *J. Chromatogr.,* 439, 317–339, 1988.
112. Moore, C., Long, G., and Marr, M., Confirmation of benzodiazepines in urine as trimethylsilyl derivatives using gas chromatography-mass spectrometry, *J. Chromatogr. B Biomed. Appl.,* 655, 132–137, 1994.
113. Fitzgerald, R., Rexin, D., and Herold, D., Detecting benzodiazepines: immunoassays compared with negative chemical ionization gas chromatography-mass spectrometry, *Clin. Chem.,* 40, 373–380, 1994.
114. Joern, W.A., Confirmation of low concentrations of urinary benzodiazepines, including alprazolam and triazolam, by GC/MS: an extractive alkylation procedure, *J. Anal. Toxicol.,* 16, 363–367, 1992.
115. Needleman, S.B. and Porvaznik, M., Identification of parent benzodiazepines by gas chromotography-mass spectroscopy (GC/MS) from urinary extracts treated with B-glucuronidase, *Forensic Sci. Int.,* 73, 49–60, 1995.
116. McIntyre, I., Syrjanen, M., Crump, K., Horomidis, S., Peace, A., and Drummer, O., Simultaneous HPLC gradient analysis of 15 benzodiazepines and selected metabolites in postmortem blood, *J. Anal. Toxicol.,* 17, 202–207, 1993.
117. Lillsunde, P. and Seppala, T., Simultaneous screening and quantitative analysis of benzodiazepines by dual-channel gas chromatography using electron-capture and nitrogen-phosphorus detection, *J. Chromatogr.,* 533, 97–110, 1990.
118. Baugh, L.D., Allen, E.E., Liu, R.H., Langner, J.G., Fentress, J.C., Chadha, S.C., et al., Evaluation of immunoassay methods for the screening of cocaine metabolites in urine, *J. Forensic Sci.,* 36, 79–85, 1991.
119. Cone, E.J. and Mitchell, J., Validity testing of commercial urine cocaine metabolite assays. II. Sensitivity, specificity, accuracy, and confirmation by gas chromatography-mass spectrometry, *J. Forensic Sci.,* 34, 32–45, 1989.
120. Moore, F.M. and Simpson, D., Detection of benzoylecgonine (cocaine metabolite) in urine: a cost-effective low risk immunoassay procedure, *Med. Lab. Sci.,* 47, 85–89, 1990.
121. Mueller, M.A., Adams, S.M., Lewand, D.L., and Wang, R.I., Detection of benzoylecgonine in human urine, *J. Chromatogr.,* 144, 101–107, 1977.
122. Smith, M.L., Hughes, R.O., Levine, B., Dickerson, S., Darwin, W.D., and Cone, E.J., Forensic drug testing for opiates. VI. Urine testing for hydromorphone, hydrocodone, oxymorphone, and oxycodone with commercial opiate immunoassays and gas chromatography-mass spectrometry, *J. Anal. Toxicol.,* 19, 18–26, 1995.
123. Huang, W., Andollo, W., and Hearn, W.L., A solid phase extraction technique for the isolation and identification of opiates in urine, *J. Anal. Toxicol.,* 16, 307–310, 1992.

124. Cone, E.J., Dickerson, S., Paul, B.D., and Mitchell, J.M., Forensic drug testing for opiates. V. Urine testing for heroin, morphine, and codeine with commercial opiate immunoassays, *J. Anal. Toxicol.,* 17, 156–164, 1993.
125. Fyfe, M.J., Chand, P., McCutchen, C., Long, J.S., Walia, A.S., Edwards, C., et al., Evaluation of enzyme immunoassay performance characteristics — phencyclidine example, *J. Forensic Sci.,* 38, 156–164, 1993.
126. Ragan, F., Jr., Hite, S.A., Samuels, M.S., Garey, R.E., Daul, G., and Schuler, R.E., Extended EMIT-DAU phencyclidine screen, *J. Clin. Psychiatry,* 47, 194–195, 1986.
127. Chen, X.H., Franke, J.P., Wijsbeek, J., and de Zeeuw, R.A., Determination of basic drugs extracted from biological matrices by means of solid-phase extraction and wide-bore capillary gas chromatography with nitrogen-phosphorus detection, *J. Anal. Toxicol.,* 18, 150–153, 1994.
128. Balkon, J. and Donnelly, B., Determination of basic drugs in post mortem tissues: a microextraction technique utilizing GLC/NPD of effluents, *J. Anal. Toxicol.,* 6, 181–184, 1982.
129. Sharp, M.E., Evaluation of a screening procedure for basic and neutral drugs: *n*-Butyl chloride extraction and megabore capillary gas chromatography, *J. Can. Soc. Forensic Sci.,* 19, 83–101, 1986.
130. Hyde, P.M., Evaluation of drug extraction procedures from urine, *J. Anal. Toxicol.,* 9, 269–272, 1985.
131. Plavsic, F., Barbaric, V., Parag, M., Arambasin, M., Gjerek, J., and Stavljenic, A., Increased possibilities for detecting drugs by the Toxi-Lab screening test, *Ann. Clin. Biochem.,* 22, 324–326, 1985.
132. Moody, D.E., Rittenhouse, L.F., and Monti, K.M., Analysis of forensic specimens for cannabinoids. I. Comparison of RIA and GC/MS analysis of blood, *J. Anal. Toxicol.,* 16, 297–301, 1992.
133. Law, B., Williams, P.L., and Moffat, A.C., The detection and quantification of cannabinoids in blood and urine by RIA, HPLC/RIA and GC/MS, *Vet. Hum. Toxicol.,* 21, 144–147, 1979.
134. Clatworthy, A., Oon, M., Smith, R., and Whitehouse, M., Gas chromatographic-mass spectrometric confirmation of radioimmunoassay results for cannabinoids in blood and urine, *Forensic Sci. Int.,* 46, 219–230, 1990.
135. Mason, P.A., Law, B., Pocock, K., and Moffat, A.C., Direct radioimmunoassay for the detection of barbiturates in blood and urine, *Analyst,* 107, 629–633, 1982.
136. Lafisca, S., Bolelli, G., Mosca, R., and Zanon, C., Radioimmunoassay of morphine and morphine-like substances in biological fluids and human tissues, *Ric. Clin. Lab.,* 7, 179–190, 1977.
137. Spiehler, V. and Brown, R., Unconjugated morphine in blood by radioimmunoassay and gas chromatography/mass spectrometry, *J. Forensic Sci.,* 32, 906–916, 1987.
138. Altunkaya, D. and Smith, R., Evaluation of a commercial radioimmunoassay kit for the detection of lysergide (LSD) in serum, whole blood, urine and stomach contents, *Forensic Sci. Int.,* 47, 113–121, 1990.
139. Owens, S.M., McBay, A.J., Reisner, H.M., and Perez-Reyes, M., 125I radioimmunoassay of delta-9-tetrahydrocannabinol in blood and plasma with a solid-phase second-antibody separation method, *Clin. Chem.,* 27, 619–624, 1981.
140. Teale, J.D., Forman, E.J., King, L.J., Piall, E.M., and Marks, V., The development of a radioimmunoassay for cannabinoids in blood and urine, *J. Pharm. Pharmacol.,* 27, 465–472, 1975.
141. Goddard, C.P., Stead, A.H., Mason, P.A., Law, B., Moffat, A.C., McBrien, M., et al., An iodine-125 radioimmunoassay for the direct detection of benzodiazepines in blood and urine, *Analyst,* 111, 525–529, 1986.
142. Yee, H.Y., Nelson, J.D., and Papa, V.M., Measurement of benzoylecgonine in whole blood using the Abbott ADx analyzer, *J. Anal. Toxicol.,* 17, 84–86, 1993.
143. Appel, T.A. and Wade, N.A., Screening of blood and urine for drugs of abuse utilizing Diagnostic Products Corporation's Coat-A-Count radioimmunoassay kits, *J. Anal. Toxicol.,* 13, 274–276, 1989.
144. Caplan, Y.H. and Levine, B., Application of the Abbott TDx lidocaine, phenytoin, and phenobarbital assays to postmortem blood specimens, *J. Anal. Toxicol.,* 12, 265–267, 1988.
145. Alvarez, J.S., Sacristan, J.A., and Alsar, M.J., Comparison of a monoclonal antibody fluorescent polarization immunoassay with monoclonal antibody radioimmunoassay for cyclosporin determination in whole blood, *Ther. Drug Monit.,* 14, 78–80, 1992.
146. Peel, H.W. and Perrigo, B.J., Detection of cannabinoids in blood using EMIT, *J. Anal. Toxicol.,* 5, 165–167, 1981.
147. Slightom, E.L., Cagle, J.C., McCurdy, H.H., and Castagna, F., Direct and indirect homogeneous enzyme immunoassay of benzodiazepines in biological fluids and tissues, *J. Anal. Toxicol.,* 6, 22–25, 1982.

148. Blum, L.M., Klinger, R.A., and Rieders, F., Direct automated EMIT d.a.u. analysis of *N,N*-dimethylformamide-modified serum, plasma, and postmortem blood for benzodiazepines, benzoylecgonine, cannabinoids, and opiates, *J. Anal. Toxicol.,* 13, 285–288, 1989.
149. Lewellen, L.J. and McCurdy, H.H., A novel procedure for the analysis of drugs in whole blood by homogeneous enzyme immunoassay (EMIT), *J. Anal. Toxicol.,* 12, 260–264, 1988.
150. Asselin, W.M., Leslie, J.M., and McKinley, B., Direct detection of drugs of abuse in whole hemolyzed blood using the EMIT d.a.u. urine assays [published erratum appears in *J. Anal. Toxicol.,* 12(6), 16A, 1988], *J. Anal. Toxicol.,* 12, 207–215, 1988.
151. Asselin, W.M. and Leslie, J.M., Direct detection of therapeutic concentrations of tricyclic antidepressants in whole hemolyzed blood using the EMITtox serum tricyclic antidepressant assay, *J. Anal. Toxicol.,* 15, 167–173, 1991.
152. Perrigo, B.J. and Joynt, B.P., Optimization of the EMIT immunoassay procedure for the analysis of cannabinoids in methanolic blood extracts, *J. Anal. Toxicol.,* 13, 235–237, 1989.
153. Collins, C., Muto, J., and Spiehler, V., Whole blood deproteinization for drug screening using automatic pipettors, *J. Anal. Toxicol.,* 16, 340–342, 1992.
154. Slightom, E.L., The analysis of drugs in blood, bile, and tissue with an indirect homogeneous enzyme immunoassay, *J. Forensic Sci.,* 23, 292–303, 1978.
155. Klein, M., Mass spectrometry of drugs and toxic substances in body fluids, in *Forensic Mass Spectrometry,* Yinon, J., Ed., CRC Press, Boca Raton, FL, 1987, 51–86.
156. Gudzinowicz, B.J. and Gudzinowicz, M., *Analysis of Drugs and Metabolites by GC/MS,* Vol. 7, Marcel Dekker, New York, 1980.
157. Cone, E.J., Analysis of drugs in biological samples by combined GC/MS, *Drugs Pharm. Sci.,* 11A, 143–227, 1981.
158. Foltz, R.L., Applications of GC/MS in clinical toxicology, *Spectra,* 10, 8–10, 1985.
159. Finkle, B.S., Foltz, R.L., and Taylor, D.M., A comprehensive GC/MS reference data system for toxicological and biomedical purposes, *J. Chromatogr. Sci.,* 12, 304–328, 1974.
160. Wu Chen, N.B., Cody, J.T., Garriott, J.C., Foltz, R.L., Peat, M.A., and Schaffer, M.I., Recommended guidelines for forensic GC/MS procedures in toxicology laboratories associated with offices of medical examiners and/or coroners, *J. Forensic Sci.,* 35, 236–242, 1990.
161. Smith, N.B., Automated identification by computer of the mass spectra of drugs in urine or serum extracts, *J. Anal. Toxicol.,* 18, 16–21, 1994.
162. Ardrey, R.E., Mass spectrometry, in *Clarke's Isolation and Identification of Drugs in Pharmaceuticals, Body Fluids, and Post-Mortem Material,* 2nd ed., Moffatt, A.C., Ed., Pharmaceutical Press, London, 1986.
163. Gibb, R.P., Cockerham, H., Goldfogel, G.A., Lawson, G.M., and Raisys, V.A., Substance abuse testing of urine by GC/MS in scanning mode evaluated by proficiency studies, TLC/GC, and EMIT, *J. Forensic Sci.,* 38, 124–133, 1993.
164. Mills, T., Roberson, J.D., McCurdy, H.H., and Wall, W.H., *Instrumental Data for Drug Analysis* (5 vols.), 2nd ed., Elsevier, New York, 1992.
165. Pfleger, K., Maurer, H.H., and Weber, A., *Mass Spectral and GC Data of Drugs, Poisons, Pesticides, Pollutants and Their Metabolites,* 2nd ed., Vols. 1–3, 1992, Vol. 4, 2000, Wiley-VCH, New York, 2000.
166. Sunshine, I. and Caplis, M., *CRC Handbook of Mass Spectra of Drugs,* CRC Press, Boca Raton, FL, 1981.
167. Ardrey, R.E., Bal, T.S., Joyce, J.R., and Moffat, A.C., *Pharmaceutical Mass Spectra,* Pharmaceutical Press, London, 1985.
168. Hites, R.A., *Handbook of Mass Spectra of Environmental Contaminants,* 2nd ed., Lewis Publishers, Boca Raton, FL, 1992.
169. Cornu, A. and Massot, R., *Compilation of Mass Spectral Data,* Heyden & Son, London, 1966.
170. Reys, L.L. and Santos, J.C., Importance of information in forensic toxicology, *Am. J. Forensic Med. Pathol.,* 13, 33–36, 1992.
171. Stafford, D.T. and Logan, B.K., Information resources useful in forensic toxicology, *Fundam. Appl. Toxicol.,* 15, 411–419, 1990.
172. Forensic Toxicology Laboratory Guidelines, Society of Forensic Toxicologists/American Academy of Forensic Sciences, 2002. Available from the SOFT Web site http://www.soft-tox.org.
173. Osterloh, J.D. and Becker, C.E., Chemical dependency and drug testing in the workplace, *J. Psychoactive Drugs,* 22, 407–417, 1990.

174. Ng, T.L., Dope testing in sports: scientific and medico-legal issues [review], *Ann. Acad. Med. Singapore,* 22, 48–53, 1993.
175. DeCresce, R., Mazura, A., Lifshitz, M., and Tilson, J., *Drug Testing in the Workplace,* ASCP Press, Chicago, 1989.
176. McCunney, R.J., Drug testing: technical complications of a complex social issue, *Am. J. Indust. Med.,* 15, 589–600, 1989.
177. Gough, T.A., The analysis of drugs of abuse, in *The Analysis of Drugs of Abuse*, Gough, T.A., Ed., John Wiley & Sons, Chichester, U.K., 1991, 628.
178. Deutsch, D.G., Gas chromatography/mass spectrometry using tabletop instruments, in *Analytical Aspects of Drug Testing*, Deutsch, D.G., Ed., John Wiley & Sons, New York, 1989, 87–128.
179. Baselt, R.C., Ed., *Advances in Analytical Toxicology,* Vol. 1, Biomedical Publications, Foster City, CA, 1984, 275.
180. Lehrer, M., Application of gas chromatography-mass spectrometry instrument techniques to forensic urine drug testing, *Clin. Lab. Med.,* 10, 271–288, 1990.
181. Garland, W.A. and Powell, M.L., Quantitative selected ion monitoring (QSIM) of drugs and/or metabolites in biological matrices, *J. Chromatogr. Sci.,* 19, 392–434, 1981.
182. Gelpi, E., Bioanalytical aspects on method validation, *Life Sci.,* 41, 849–852, 1987.
183. Troost, J.R. and Olavesen, E.Y., Gas chromatographic-mass spectrometric calibration bias, *Anal. Chem.,* 68, 708–711, 1996.
184. ElSohly, M.A., Little, T.L., Jr., and Stanford, D.F., Hexadeutero-11-nor-delta 9-tetrahydrocannabinol-9-carboxylic acid: a superior internal standard for the GC/MS analysis of delta 9-THC acid metabolite in biological specimens, *J. Anal. Toxicol.,* 16, 188–191, 1992.
185. Giovannini, M.G., Pieraccini, G., and Moneti, G., Isotope dilution mass spectrometry: definitive methods and reference materials in clinical chemistry, *Ann. Istituto Superiore Sanita,* 27, 401–410, 1991.
186. Needleman, S.B. and Romberg, R.W., Limits of linearity and detection for some drugs of abuse, *J. Anal. Toxicol.,* 14, 34–38, 1990.
187. Liu, R.H., Foster, G., Cone, E.J., and Kumar, S.D., Selecting an appropriate isotopic internal standard for gas chromatography-mass spectrometry analysis of drugs of abuse — pentobarbital example, *J. Forensic Sci.,* 40, 983–989, 1995.
188. Carreras, D., Imaz, C., Navajas, R., Garcia, M.A., Rodriguez, C., Rodriguez, A.F., et al., Comparison of derivatization procedures for the determination of diuretics in urine by gas chromatography-mass spectrometry, *J. Chromatogr. A,* 683, 195–202, 1994.
189. Anderegg, R.J., Derivatization for GC/MS analysis, *Mass Spectrom. Rev.,* 7, 395, 1988.
190. Melgar, R. and Kelly, R.C., A novel GC/MS derivatization method for amphetamines, *J. Anal. Toxicol.,* 17, 399–402, 1993.
191. Goldberger, B.A. and Cone, E.J., Confirmatory tests for drugs in the workplace by gas chromatography-mass spectrometry, *J. Chromatogr. A,* 674, 73–86, 1994.
192. Cody, J.T. and Foltz, R.L., GC/MS analysis of body fluids for drugs of abuse, in *Forensic Applications of Mass Spectrometry,* Yinon, J., Ed., CRC Press, Boca Raton, FL, 1995, 1–59.
193. Foltz, R.L., Fentiman, A.F., Jr., and Foltz, R.B., GC/MS assays for abused drugs in body fluids [review], *NIDA Res. Monogr.,* 32, 1–198, 1980.
194. Foltz, R.L., High sensitivity quantitative analysis of drugs and metabolites by GC/MS, in *31st Annual Conference on Mass Spectrometry and Allied Topics*, Boston, May 8–13, 1983.
195. Bogusz, M., Wijsbeek, J., Franke, J.P., de Zeeuw, R.A., and Gierz, J., Impact of biological matrix, drug concentration, and method of isolation on detectability and variability of retention index values in gas chromatography, *J. Anal. Toxicol.,* 9, 49–54, 1985.
196. Hartmann, C., Massart, D.L., and McDowall, R.D., An analysis of the Washington Conference Report on bioanalytical method validation, *J. Pharm. Biomed. Anal.,* 12, 1337–1343, 1994.
197. Shah, V.P., Midha, K.K., Dighe, S., McGilveray, I.J., Skelly, J.P., Yacobi, A., et al., Analytical methods validation: bioavailability, bioequivalence and pharmacokinetic studies. Conference report, *Eur. J. Drug Metab. Pharmacokinet.,* 16, 249–55, 1991.
198. Mesley, R.J., Pocklington, W.D., and Walker, R.F., Analytical quality assurance — a review, *Analyst,* 116, 975–990, 1991.

199. Dadgar, D., Burnett, P.E., Choc, M.G., Gallicano, K., and Hooper, J.W., Application issues in bioanalytical method validation, sample analysis and data reporting [review], *J. Pharm. Biomed. Anal.,* 13, 89–97, 1995.
200. Pachla, L.A., Wright, D.S., and Reynolds, D.L., Bioanalytic considerations for pharmacokinetic and biopharmaceutic studies, *J. Clin. Pharmacol.,* 26, 332–335, 1986.
201. Karnes, H.T. and March, C., Calibration and validation of linearity in chromatographic biopharmaceutical analysis, *J. Pharm. Biomed. Anal.,* 9, 911–918, 1991.
202. Lang, J.R. and Bolton, S., A comprehensive method validation strategy for bioanalytical applications in the pharmaceutical industry. 2. Statistical analyses, *J. Pharm. Biomed. Anal.,* 9, 435–442, 1991.
203. Arnoux, P. and Morrison, R., Drug analysis of biological samples. A survey of validation approaches in chromatography in the UK pharmaceutical industry, *Xenobiotica,* 22, 757–764, 1992.
204. Passey, R.B. and Maluf, K.C., Foundations for validation of quantitative analytical methods in the clinical laboratory, *Arch. Pathol. Lab. Med.,* 116, 732–738, 1992.
205. Edwardson, P.A., Bhaskar, G., and Fairbrother, J.E., Method validation in pharmaceutical analysis, *J. Pharm. Biomed. Anal.,* 8, 929–933, 1990.
206. Buick, A.R., Doig, M.V., Jeal, S.C., Land, G.S., and McDowall, R.D., Method validation in the bioanalytical laboratory, *J. Pharm. Biomed. Anal.,* 8, 629–637, 1990.
207. Cardone, M.J., Willavize, S.A., and Lacy, M.E., Method validation revisited: a chemometric approach, *Pharm. Res.,* 7, 154–160, 1990.
208. Wieling, J., Hendriks, G., Tamminga, W.J., Hempenius, J., Mensink, C.K., Oosterhuis, B., et al., Rational experimental design for bioanalytical methods validation. Illustration using an assay method for total captopril in plasma, *J. Chromatogr. A,* 730, 381–394, 1996.
209. Braggio, S., Barnaby, R.J., Grossi, P., and Cugola, M., A strategy for validation of bioanalytical methods [review], *J. Pharm. Biomed. Anal.,* 14, 375–388, 1996.
210. Karnes, H.T., Shiu, G., and Shah, V.P., Validation of bioanalytical methods [review], *Pharm. Res.,* 8, 421–426, 1991.
211. Stead, A.H., Hook, W., Moffat, A.C., and Berry, D., Therapeutic, toxic and fatal blood concentration ranges of antiepileptic drugs as an aid to the interpretation of analytical data, *Hum. Toxicol.,* 2, 135–147, 1983.
212. Caplan, Y.H., Ottinger, W.E., and Crooks, C.R., Therapeutic and toxic drug concentrations in post mortem blood: a six year study in the State of Maryland, *J. Anal. Toxicol.,* 7, 225–230, 1983.
213. Baselt, R.C., Wright, J.A., and Cravey, R.H., Therapeutic and toxic concentrations of more than 100 toxicologically significant drugs in blood, plasma, or serum: a tabulation [review], *Clin. Chem.,* 21, 44–62, 1975.
214. Stead, A.H. and Moffat, A.C., A collection of therapeutic, toxic and fatal blood drug concentrations in man, *Hum. Toxicol.,* 2, 437–464, 1983.
215. Balselt, R.C. and Cravey, R.H., *Disposition of Toxic Drugs and Chemicals in Man*, 4th ed., Chemical Toxicology Institute, Foster City, CA, 1995.
216. Prouty, R.W. and Anderson, W.H., The forensic science implications of site and temporal influences on postmortem blood-drug concentrations, *J. Forensic Sci.,* 35, 243–270, 1990.
217. Othman, S., al-Turk, W.A., Awidi, A.S., Daradkeh, T.K., and Shaheen, O., Comparative determination of phenytoin in plasma by fluorescence polarization immunoassay and high performance liquid chromatography, *Drug Design Delivery,* 2, 41–47, 1987.
218. Valtier, S. and Cody, J.T., Evaluation of internal standards for the analysis of amphetamine and methamphetamine, *J. Anal. Toxicol.,* 19, 375–380, 1995.
219. Smith, N.B., Internal standards in gas-chromatographic analyses for ethylene glycol in serum [letter; comment], *Clin. Chem.,* 39, 2020, 1993.
220. Thomas, L.C. and Weichmann, W., Quantitative measurements via co-elution and dual-isotope detection by gas chromatography-mass spectrometry, *J. Chromatogr.,* 587, 255–262, 1991.
221. Pollak, P.T., A systematic review and critical comparison of internal standards for the routine liquid chromatographic assay of amiodarone and desethylamiodarone, *Ther. Drug Monit.,* 18, 168–178, 1996.
222. Claeys, M., Markey, S.P., and Maenhaut, W., Variance analysis of error in selected ion monitoring assays using various internal standards. A practical study case, *Biomed. Mass Spectr.,* 4, 122–128, 1977.

223. Tilstone, W.J., Pharmacokinetics metabolism, and the interpretation of results, in *Clarke's Isolation and Identification of Drugs in Pharmaceuticals, Body Fluids, and Postmortem Material,* 2nd ed., Moffatt, A.C., Ed., Pharmaceutical Press, London, 1986, 276.
224. Toseland, P.A., Samples and sampling, in *Clarke's Isolation and Identification of Drugs in Pharmaceuticals, Body Fluids, and Post-Mortem Material*, 2nd ed., Moffatt, A.C., Ed., Pharmaceutical Press, London, 1986, 111.
225. Bogusz, M.J., Hyphenated liquid chromatographic techniques in forensic toxicology, *J. Chromatogr. B,* 733, 65–91, 1999.
226. Lips, A.G. et al., Methodology for the development of a drug library based upon collision-induced fragmentation for the identification of toxicologically relevant drugs in plasma samples, *J. Chromatogr. B*, 759, 191–207, 2001.
227. Marquet, P., Is LC-MS suitable for a comprehensive screening of drugs and poisons in clinical toxicology? *Ther. Drug Monit.*, 24, 125–133, 2002.
228. Saint-Marcoux, F., Lachatre, G., and Marquet, P., Evaluation of an improved general unknown screening procedure using liquid chromatography-electrospray-mass spectrometry by comparison with gas chromatography and high-performance liquid-chromatography — diode array detection, *J. Am. Soc. Mass Spectrom.*, 14, 14–22, 2003.
229. Marquet, P. et al., Comparison of a preliminary procedure for the general unknown screening of drugs and toxic compounds using a quadrupole-linear ion-trap mass spectrometer with a liquid chromatography-mass spectrometry reference technique, *J. Chromatogr. B*, 789, 9–18, 2003.
230. Venisse, N. et al., A general unknown screening procedure for drugs and toxic compounds in serum using liquid chromatography-electrospray-single quadrupole mass spectrometry, *J. Anal. Toxicol.*, 27, 7–14, 2003.
231. Politi, L., Groppi, A., and Polettini, A., Applications of liquid chromatography-mass spectrometry in doping control, *J. Anal. Toxicol.*, 29(1), 1–14, 2005.
232. Maurer, H.H., Advances in analytical toxicology: the current role of liquid chromatography-mass spectrometry in drug quantification in blood and oral fluid, *Anal. Bioanal. Chem.,* 381, 110–118, 2005.
233. Weinmann, W., Schaefer, P., Thierauf, A., Schreiber, A., and Wurst, F.M., Confirmatory analysis of ethylglucuronide in urine by liquid-chromatography/electrospray ionization/tandem mass spectrometry according to forensic guidelines, *J. Am. Soc. Mass Spectrom.*, 15, 188–193, 2004.
234. Saint-Marcoux, F., Lachâtre, G., and Marquet, P., Evaluation of an improved general unknown screening procedure using liquid chromatography-electrospray-mass spectrometry by comparison with gas chromatography and high-performance liquid-chromatography — diode array detection, *J. Am. Soc. Mass Spectrom.,* 14, 14–22, 2003.
235. Marquet, P. and Lachâtre, G., Liquid chromatography-mass spectrometry: potential in forensic and clinical toxicology, *J. Chromatogr. B Biomed. Sci. Appl.,* 733, 93–118, 1999.
236. Kratzsch, C., Tenberken, O., Peters, F.T., Weber, A.A., Kraemer, T., and Maurer, H.H., Screening, library-assisted identification and validated quantification of 23 benzodiazepines, flumazenil, zaleplone, zolpidem and zopiclone in plasma by liquid chromatography/mass spectrometry with atmospheric pressure chemical ionization, *J. Mass Spectrom.,* 39(8), 856–872, 2004.
237. Maurer, H.H., Tenberken, O., Kratzsch, C., Weber, A.A., and Peters, F.T., Screening for library-assisted identification and fully validated quantification of 22 beta-blockers in blood plasma by liquid chromatography-mass spectrometry with atmospheric pressure chemical ionization, *J. Chromatogr. A,* 1058(1–2), 169–181, 2004.

CHAPTER 5

Quality Assurance in Postmortem Toxicology

Wilmo Andollo, B.S.
Quality Assurance Officer, Dade County Medical Examiner Toxicology Laboratory, Miami, Florida

CONTENTS

5.1 Introduction 96
5.2 Standard Operating Procedures 96
5.3 Personnel 97
5.3.1 Continuing Education 97
5.4 Measuring Devices 97
5.5 Reagents 97
5.6 Reference Materials 98
5.6.1 Calibrators 98
5.6.1.1 Multilevel Calibration 99
5.6.1.2 Method of Additions 100
5.6.2 Internal Standards 101
5.6.3 Controls 102
5.7 Samples and Sampling 104
5.8 Analytical Methods and Procedures 104
5.8.1 Quality of an Analytical Procedure 104
5.8.1.1 Limit of Detection 105
5.8.1.2 Sensitivity and Linearity 105
5.8.1.3 Precision 105
5.8.1.4 Accuracy 105
5.8.1.5 Selectivity and Specificity 106
5.8.2 Qualitative Methods 106
5.8.3 Quantitative Methods 106
5.8.4 Method Development and Validation 107
5.9 Instruments 107
5.9.1 Installation 108
5.9.2 Preventive Maintenance 108
5.9.3 Pre-Analysis Checklist 108
5.10 Data 108
5.10.1 Chain-of-Custody Data 109

5.10.2 Analytical Data 109
5.10.3 Quality Control Data 109
5.11 Reports 110
5.12 Proficiency Programs 110
5.13 Accreditation Programs 111
References 111

5.1 INTRODUCTION

The essence of the postmortem forensic analysis is to characterize a subject's biological tissue in terms of toxic chemical content. Based on the analytical result, an opinion can then be formed about the influence the toxic substance may have had on the subject. Since the result of any chemical analysis carries with it an uncertainty that is inherent in all measurements, an attempt must be made to control and measure the factors that influence that uncertainty. Only when these factors are measured and controlled can the analytical results be deemed reliable.

The quality assurance program is established to ensure the public that the results generated by the laboratory are reliable. This is crucial in a forensic toxicology laboratory since the analytical results are closely scrutinized in a court of law, where truth and impartiality must be authenticated for the public good. A comprehensive quality assurance program will provide an expert witness with details concerning the measurable factors that affect the analytical result. These factors include personnel, the implements of measurement; the quality of materials used; the sample; the analytical method; the analytical instruments; data handling; and reporting.

The *quality assurance* program describes the steps taken to *document* the execution of the quality control procedures; the traceability of reported data to raw data; instrument status during analysis; quality control status; description of the analytical method; qualifications of the analysts; sample integrity and chain of custody; and the corrective actions undertaken for out-of-control situations. The *quality control* program sets forth the procedures to be taken to *measure* and *control* all sources of random and systematic errors so that limits of accuracy and precision can be established for all analytical methods. It also describes the technical operations undertaken to assure that the data obtained are within the established limits.

5.2 STANDARD OPERATING PROCEDURES

The standard operating procedure is a written document that outlines in detail the mode of operation of the laboratory. It addresses the relationship of the laboratory with the institutions that it serves, the organizational structure of the laboratory, the quality assurance program, and the chemical hygiene plan. It must address every facet of the laboratory's operation and be available to all laboratory personnel and the public for consultation and review.

The standard operating procedures should address, as a minimum, the following aspects of the laboratory operation:

- Table of organization
- Personnel qualifications
- Precision implements
- Materials
- Sampling
- Analytical methods
- Instruments
- Data

- Reporting
- Proficiency program

The standard operating procedures manual is to be kept up to date and reviewed on a yearly basis to ensure that it typifies the actual operation and that it meets the needs of the laboratory. It is important to archive any old procedures, whether modified or omitted from the manual, so that they can be retrieved for future reference.

The rest of this chapter is devoted to expanding on the subjects that are deemed indispensable in a comprehensive quality assurance program and standard operating procedure manual.

5.3 PERSONNEL

The table of organization should be represented by means of a flowchart or schematic diagram. It should include all positions in order of hierarchy, name of persons occupying each position, and accountability of each individual.

The subject of personnel in forensic toxicology laboratories is covered in detail in the SOFT/AAFS Forensic Laboratory Guidelines.[1]

5.3.1 Continuing Education

The laboratory director is responsible for providing access to continuing education to all employees. Continuing education is essential to the development of the laboratory in maintaining the reliability and integrity necessary in an ever-challenging field. New and more potent drugs are being continuously developed along with more advanced analytical techniques and equipment necessary for their detection and identification. Keeping abreast of the new information, be it pharmacological or analytical, is of outmost importance for the subsistence of the forensic laboratory. Membership in professional forensic organizations, such as the American Academy of Forensic Sciences (AAFS), the Society of Forensic Toxicologists (SOFT), the California Association of Toxicologists (CAT), and The International Association of Forensic Toxicologists (TIAFT), provide the venue by which continuing education is not only available but relevant to the forensic laboratory.

5.4 MEASURING DEVICES

Regardless of their simplicity, burets, pipettes, volumetric flasks, pipettors, pipettor-diluters, and the analytical balance are used in one way or another in nearly every chemical analysis. They impart the first sources of systematic errors in the analysis. For this reason, it is imperative that their quality, maintenance, and calibration be addressed in the standard operating procedures.

The selection and maintenance of chemical measuring devices and instruments are beyond the scope of this section, but are covered in detail in textbooks of quantitative chemical analysis and instrumental analysis.[2,3]

5.5 REAGENTS

Chemicals, reagents, solvents, and gases used in the process of executing the analytical procedures must meet minimum quality criteria as required by the analytical method. They should be properly stored, according to manufacturers' specifications or good chemical hygiene practice, in order to maintain their integrity and safety. Special care must be taken to record the receipt date and consider the stability of the reagent before use.

The determination of trace amounts of analytes in complex biological fluids or tissues often requires concentration of organic solvent extracts, which must be analyzed by very sensitive instruments. This circumstance creates a need for high-purity solvents, reagents, and gases to avoid introducing significant amounts of interferences during the analytical process. Commercially available solvents have been developed with special qualities applicable to specific purposes. Examples include solvents possessing low ultraviolet absorption, used in high-performance liquid chromatography and spectrophotometry, as well as solvents with negligible halogenated organic content, required for electron capture detectors or negative ion chemical ionization mass spectrometry. A postmortem toxicology laboratory should procure the highest quality of reagent possible to minimize the potential for interferences with its analytical methods.

The use of inert, high-purity gases for gas-liquid chromatographs has been an essential part of the operation of gas chromatography since its inception as an analytical tool. The fragile nature of liquid phases in the presence of oxygen (air) at high temperatures and the development of very sensitive detectors such as nitrogen-phosphorus, electron capture, and mass spectrometers, among others, have made the gas quality a priority issue in the operation of the laboratory. Gases with 99.999% purities containing subpart-per-million quantities of air, moisture, and organic compounds are readily available at moderate cost. There are also a variety of products designed to remove or "scrub" contaminants from the gas stream before their introduction into the instrument, which can be utilized if high-purity gases are not readily available. These gas scrubbers should be monitored periodically for proper operation as part of the standard operating procedures.

The preparation of reagents, buffers, and mixtures should be conducted according to the specific instructions in the procedures manual. A reagent log book containing the preparation instructions for the most common solutions provides a convenient way to record their preparation with traceable information such as date of preparation, preparer, stock reagent lot number, and expiration date. This information should always be included in the reagent flask label along with the identification of the solution, its concentration, and any applicable safety recommendation.

5.6 REFERENCE MATERIALS

The accuracy of any quantitative analytical procedure depends directly on the purity of the standard used for calibrating the method. Therefore, the analyst must ascertain that the standards, or reference materials, used to prepare the calibrators are chemically pure. The subject of reference materials is discussed in the SOFT/AAFS Forensic Toxicology Laboratory Guidelines.[1]

5.6.1 Calibrators

Calibrators are materials with which the sample is compared in order to determine the concentration or other quantity.[6] Methods known to have acceptable accuracy because physical or matrix effects are negligible may be calibrated with certified reference solutions. However, procedural constraints and complex matrix effects of biological samples make the use of certified reference solutions impossible in many routine methods. The calibrators selected for such methods must simulate the physical and chemical properties of the samples in order to compensate for matrix effects during analysis and to be sensitive to important changes in analytical error conditions.

Assay values assigned to calibrators must be sufficiently accurate for the intended use. The uncertainty interval for the assigned concentration value must be small compared to the analytical precision of the method to be calibrated. That is, the absolute error calculated for the assigned value using dimensional analysis must be smaller than the absolute error obtained when the calibrator is analyzed multiple times by the method.[7]

In the forensic laboratory, three types of calibrators may be encountered. The first is use of a reference standard solution as a calibrator when the method has no procedural constraints and matrix effects are virtually non-existent. Certified standard solutions for this type of method can be obtained commercially or prepared in the laboratory with reference materials. This type of method, although rare in the forensic laboratory, can best be exemplified by the analysis of volatiles using headspace techniques with gas chromatography, and the percent purity determination of drug exhibits using ultraviolet spectrometry.

The second type of calibrators includes those obtained from commercial sources as kits to be used in self-contained analytical systems. They are matrix specific and manufactured in bulk under strict quality control. They are carefully designed to perform a specific task under rigorously controlled conditions and are provided with lot numbers and expiration dates. Assays of this type include quantitative techniques by radioactive, enzymatic, and fluorescent immunoassays.

The last type of calibrators encountered in the forensic laboratory are of most concern because they assume the most uncertainty. They are usually employed in analytical assays involving multistep extractions, concentration, derivatization, and complex instruments of analysis and data reduction. These working standards must be prepared in the laboratory from pure reference materials, be diluted with blank sample matrix to resemble the biological sample, and remain accurate enough to convey a reliable measurement when a sample is compared to them. For this reason, every effort should be made to ensure the quality of reference material, the proper maintenance of volumetric implements and balances, and the application of good analytical skills.

The preparation of a calibrator, or working standard, begins with the preparation of a stock solution from the reference drug material. A water-soluble organic solvent that readily dissolves the drug material without adverse reaction is the solvent of choice. Solvents that are not water soluble can be used, but they require additional steps to remove the solvent when further dilutions are made into aqueous biological fluids. A concentration of 1 mg of the un-ionized form of the drug per milliliter of solvent is convenient and adequate for most drugs analyzed. To keep the uncertainty of the calibrator below the variance of the method, it is desirable to know the exact concentration of the stock standard to at least three significant figures. The solutions stored in capped amber vials at –20°C can have long shelf lives if care is taken to allow the solutions to reach room temperature before opening, thus avoiding moisture condensation in the solution. The stability of these solutions must be established periodically. Calibration standards are discussed in the *CRC Handbook of Clinical Chemistry.*[7]

5.6.1.1 Multilevel Calibration

The calibration scheme used for the purpose of carrying out quantifications of unknown specimens is done with the preparation of a calibration graph that includes a minimum of three different concentrations and a blank. The concentrations of analyte used to prepare the graph must include the lower and upper limits of required linear response, since linearity must be demonstrated in every assay.

The recommended scheme for the preparation of a set of calibrators has been discussed in the Research Monograph Series of the National Institute on Drug Abuse.[8]

To control for the influence of matrix effects, it is recommended to add the same volume of working stock solution to each aliquot of biological matrix when preparing the calibrators. To do this, a fresh set of working stock solutions is prepared by serial dilutions from the stock solution. Mixtures of drugs and metabolites can also be included in the working stock solution sets.

The calibration graph is obtained by plotting the detector response against the assigned concentration of analyte in the working standard. Chromatographic assays that use internal standards are calibrated by plotting the detector response ratio of analyte to internal standard against the assigned concentration of analyte in the working standard. Using the statistical method of linear regression, the straight line that best fits the points can be determined. The slope of the line and the y-intercept are used to calculate the quantity of analyte in an unknown sample based on its detector response. Figure 5.1 shows a representative calibration curve for

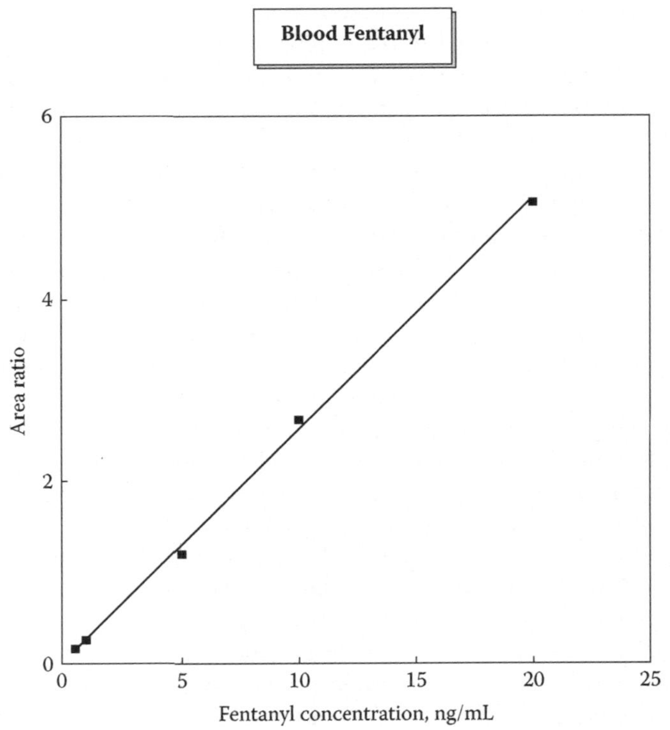

Figure 5.1 Multilevel calibration.

the analysis of fentanyl. Some calibrations are inherently nonlinear, and therefore it is acceptable to apply a quadratic curve fit rather than force a linear fit to data that is clearly not linear. It is up to the analyst, or as a matter of policy the laboratory, to determine when the degree of nonlinearity is clearly unacceptable. Furthermore, it is good practice for evaluation of the calibration to include reading each calibrator against the established curve. Most calibrators should read within ±20% of the target with perhaps a wider margin as the calibration approaches the origin.

5.6.1.2 Method of Additions

The method of additions is a very powerful calibration technique because the accuracy is independent of matrix effects. The technique requires that replicates of the specimen, instead of blank matrix, be fortified with the different levels of calibrators, along with an unspiked replicate of the specimen serving as the "blank." All the samples are analyzed by the analytical method as usual. A calibration graph is generated by plotting the detector response of the analyte (or response ratio if using internal standard) against the concentration of the calibrators and plotting the response of the unfortified specimen on the y-axis ($x = 0$). Using the statistical method of linear regression, the straight line that best fits the points is determined and the absolute value of the x-intercept represents the calculated concentration of the specimen. Figure 5.2 shows the calculation of azide in blood by the method of additions.

A disadvantage encountered in forensic analysis when using the method of additions is the requirement that multiple aliquots of the specimen be used when forensic samples are inherently limited in size. The use of this method of calibration, therefore, should be limited to situations where a rare analysis is being considered, controls are not available, or when dealing with a particularly difficult matrix.

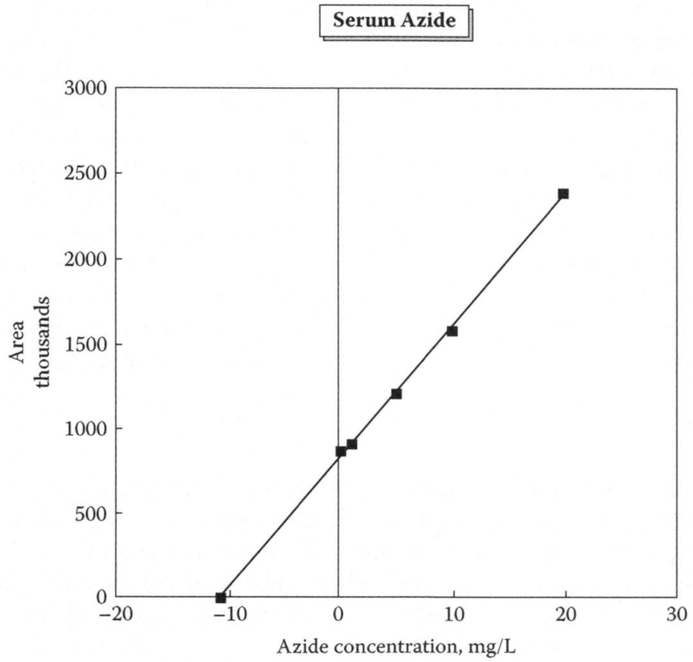

Figure 5.2 Calibration by method of additions.

5.6.2 Internal Standards

A suitable internal standard should be used in chromatographic assays such as gas chromatography, high-performance liquid chromatography, and gas chromatography-mass spectrometry. The internal standard can be defined as a substance that is added to all samples (specimens, standards, and controls) in a given assay before processing begins to correct for the many variations that occur in the manipulation of the samples during the entire analysis. Systematic errors affecting the quantity of analyte isolated from the sample will also affect the quantity of the internal standard in the same proportion. Therefore, the ratio of analyte to internal standard at the beginning of the procedure will remain unchanged throughout. For this concept to hold true, the internal standard must comply with certain qualifications.

First, the internal standard must have chemical and physical characteristics very similar to the analyte of interest. This quality ensures that extraction partition coefficients, formation of derivatives, chromatographic characteristics, and detector response are similar enough not to alter their weight ratio significantly. A compound such as difluorococaine, for example, is not a good internal standard choice for cocaine because its enhanced lipophilicity imparts a very different extraction partition ratio, a different chromatographic characteristic, and a dissimilar response to a nitrogen-phosphorus detector. A compound such as propylbenzoylecgonine, an analogue of cocaine containing a propyl ester instead of a methyl ester, is chemically and physically more satisfactory. From the point of view of extraction and derivatization properties the most appropriate internal standard is an analogue of the analyte that has been labeled with a stable isotope. These substances have identical chemical and physical characteristics to the analyte, so their weight ratio is not affected during the analysis. However, unless the chromatographic system can resolve the two components, these are only useful in analyses by gas chromatography-mass spectrometry.

In addition, it is important to add precisely the same amount of internal standard to each sample. It is not necessary to know exactly the weight amount added as long as it is exactly the same amount. The normal practice is to decide in advance the approximate quantity of internal standard to be added to each sample, since the ratio of analyte to internal standard can be measured most accurately when they are present in similar concentrations. The quantity of internal standard added to the samples, then, should give a concentration intermediate between the lowest and highest expected analyte concentrations. This concentration should be such that the lowest anticipated weight ratio of analyte to internal standard should approximately equal the inverse of the highest anticipated ratio. So, if one desires to measure concentrations of a drug over the range 1 to 1000 ng/mL, the amount of internal standard added should give a concentration of approximately 32 ng/mL (1:32 ~ 32:1000). Some analysts may favor the use of a lower concentration of internal standard to facilitate more accurate measurements of low levels of the drug, since low levels are more difficult to measure than high levels. On the other hand, higher amounts of internal standard can be used to act as a "carrier" to minimize losses of analyte due to adsorption at active sites on the surface of extraction vessels and within the chromatographic column.[9]

5.6.3 Controls

A control is a test sample of known concentration that is analyzed along with every batch of specimen to make certain that the analytical procedure performs within the expected limits of variation. Three types of controls can be defined: (1) the negative control, which is drug free and analyzed in qualitative and quantitative methods to show that the method is not introducing a contaminant that may construe a false positive, (2) a positive control, containing the drug at a concentration near the limit of detection and used in qualitative methods to demonstrate adequate performance, and (3) the analytical control(s), containing the drug at a meaningful level(s) and used to monitor the performance of the quantitative method. The intended use of controls is to monitor the performance of a method over a long period of time in an internal quality control program, never to calibrate a procedure. The level chosen for the analytical control should be of clinical and/or forensic importance, such as the significant therapeutic concentration of a drug or the legal intoxication level of ethanol. For assays where many samples are being analyzed, controls should be evenly distributed throughout the run, and one should be included at the end.

Control materials are useful only if applicable to the analytical method used. As is the case with calibrators, the control must simulate the physical and chemical properties of the samples to compensate for matrix effects during analysis and to monitor the performance characteristics of the method. They must be homogeneous to be sensitive to analytical imprecision and stable enough to detect system errors for meaningful periods of time.

The source of control materials and their applications have been discussed extensively in the literature as it pertains to clinical chemistry.[10–15] The principles discussed, although applicable to some extent to forensic analysis, do not conform to the unique complexity of the specimens encountered in postmortem work, such as nails, hair, decomposed tissue, and unstable analytes. However, the need to measure the quality of the method's performance during an analysis is still imperative, and these obstacles must be overcome with analytically sound ingenuity and thorough documentation.

Commercial immunoassays and commercial thin-layer chromatography kits are provided with control materials specifically designed to be used for their intended purpose. These control materials are manufactured in bulk under strict quality control and are conveniently provided with the expected value, acceptable limits of variation, lot number, and expiration dates. However, it is good laboratory practice, where practical, to include at least one independently prepared positive control.

Control materials may be obtained from commercially available sources, although the cost can be high, especially if this is to be done for the very wide range of drugs typically analyzed by a typical postmortem toxicology laboratory. These are usually supplied in the form of urine or lyophilized serum or plasma, with target concentrations, lot numbers, and expiration dates. Their stability may be short (5 to 30 days) once they have been reconstituted, but they remain stable for months if refrigerated in their lyophilized state. The drug selection available usually incorporates common drugs of abuse and of clinical therapeutic interest, which, albeit adequate, leaves the forensic laboratory with unaddressed needs. The matrices of these materials may not appropriately simulate the typical forensic sample under specific analytical conditions. Therefore, the suitability of these commercial control materials must be ascertained by evaluating them against properly selected calibrators under controlled conditions.

A reasonable source of control material is the pooling of excess laboratory specimens. This source is not very dependable, however, because of difficulties in obtaining unique drug selectivity, the uncontrolled degradation of biological fluids and drugs, biohazards, and increasing legal concerns regarding the use of human fluids and tissues for purposes other than strict determination of cause and manner of death of the individual from whom the specimens were collected.

An alternative is the preparation of controls in the laboratory using outdated whole blood or plasma from blood banks, voided urine, and tissue homogenates prepared from drug free sources. Some analysts in the field have successfully used bovine blood after adjusting the hematocrit to simulate human levels by diluting with water.[16] The only concern about "homemade" controls is that there is no independent way of qualifying the process. For this reason, every effort should be made to ensure the quality of reference material, the proper maintenance of volumetric implements and balances, and the execution of good analytical skills in the preparation of the in-house control.

The process begins with the preparation of a stock solution from a certified reference drug material. This stock solution must be distinct from the one used to prepare the calibrators. It is axiomatic that if the same reference solution is used to prepare both, the control is invalid. A water-soluble organic solvent that readily dissolves the drug material without adverse reaction is the solvent of choice. Solvents that are not water soluble can be used, but they require additional steps to remove the solvent when further dilutions are made into aqueous biological fluids. A concentration of 1 mg of the un-ionized form of the drug per milliliter of solvent is convenient and adequate for most drugs analyzed. The solutions stored in capped amber vials at –20°C can have long shelf lives if care is taken to allow the solutions to reach room temperature before opening, thus avoiding moisture condensation in the solution. The stability of these solutions should be established periodically as described earlier in this chapter.

A decision must be made whether to prepare batches of control material for future use or to prepare a working stock solution from which fresh controls can be fashioned at the time of analysis. The decision to prepare large batches of control material for future use rests on the requirements that (1) the drug be stable for a reasonable period of time in the appropriately preserved matrix of choice, and (2) the control be used frequently enough to merit the effort of establishing the limits of variation for the batch. For example, assays that are used frequently, such as blood ethanol, are good candidates for this type of control material. An assay that is performed about two or three times a year does not merit a batch preparation, even if the control material is deemed stable for a period of years in a frozen state.

A batch is simply prepared by making a proper dilution of the stock solution into the desired volume of biological fluid and adding the required preservatives as outlined in the procedures manual for the specimens being simulated. The control material can be dispensed into labeled vials containing working aliquots and stored until needed under the same protocols used for samples.

Control materials fashioned at the time of analysis are preferred for many postmortem toxicology analyses. They are prepared fresh at the time of analysis by spiking an aliquot of a working stock solution into the required amount of blank matrix. Hence, any fluid or tissue homogenate can be fortified with the control before processing, allowing the performance of the assay to be monitored for any tissue. The working stock solutions may remain stable for long periods of time because they are prepared in organic solvents. Therefore, a single working stock solution may be used repeatedly to monitor performance even for infrequently performed analyses. However, precautions must be taken to prevent or minimize evaporation of the solvent.

The working stock solution is prepared by diluting the stock solution to an intermediate concentration so that a small aliquot added to the required amount of blank matrix yields the desired control concentration. The solvent used must be water soluble and care must be taken that the volume of control solution chosen to spike the blank does not affect the matrix significantly. Keeping the solvent concentration of the matrix well below 10% is advisable to avoid protein precipitation.

Once a control material has been procured, it is identified with a lot number and, if applicable, an expiration date. Using control materials, the assay is evaluated to determine accuracy and precision expressed as standard deviation and coefficient of variation, which are evaluated by standard statistical methods. Where practical, this requires that the control be analyzed 20 to 30 times over a period of several days by all analysts who perform the assay using the variety of measuring devices that could conceivably be used to perform the assay. A smaller number of analyses may be more practical where the analyte is not routinely performed.

Occasionally, the forensic laboratory needs to perform a rare analysis for which a control has not been established (e.g., yohimbine, estazolam) or one for which a control is impractical to maintain (e.g., toluene, cyanide). In these situations, one can perform a "spike recovery" study to verify that the calculated result was not influenced by matrix differences between the specimen and the calibrators. This is accomplished by spiking a replicate of the specimen with one of the working stock calibrator solutions. The solution is chosen so that the amount added is not less than one tenth the existing concentration, nor more than ten times the existing concentration, and that the addition does not produce a concentration higher than the limits of linearity. The spiked sample is analyzed and the result is used to calculate the percent recovery as follows.

Recoveries that are outside the 20% margin allowed by this principle indicate that matrix effects are abnormally high and that the original concentration calculated for the specimen is inaccurate. If this is the case, the method of additions discussed in Section 5.6.1.2 can be pursued in the quest for an accurate result.

5.7 SAMPLES AND SAMPLING

Sampling is often called the basis of analysis because the analytical result is never better than the sample from which it is derived. The purpose of sampling is to provide the analyst with a representative part of the "object" that is suitable for the analysis. In forensic work, an appreciation of how the analytes may decompose and how contaminants may be introduced are important factors to consider.[17,18] The subject of samples and sampling is discussed in Chapter 2. The subject of safe handling of infectious materials has been treated in detail elsewhere.[19]

5.8 ANALYTICAL METHODS AND PROCEDURES

The analytical method is the set of instructions detailing the entire procedure by which a particular analysis is performed. The instructions describe the preparation of reagents, standards, controls, and sample; the steps to isolate and concentrate the analyte; the instrumental requirements; and the data manipulation. It is in the execution of the method that most of the sources of error are introduced, so strict guidelines must be followed to control them.

5.8.1 Quality of an Analytical Procedure

An analytical challenge is approached by selecting the method that is most appropriate in terms of its quality features to tackle the chemical problem. The factors that govern the quality of an analytical procedure are the limit of detection, sensitivity, dynamic linear range, precision, accuracy, and selectivity. An in-depth discussion on the subject of quality of analytical procedures has been provided by Kateman and Pijpers.[20]

5.8.1.1 Limit of Detection

The limit of detection can be defined as the smallest detector response given by the analyte that can be reliably differentiated from background noise produced by the instrument or the procedure. This signal is not necessarily quantifiable, since most detectors are not linear at low response levels.

The classical determination for the method detection limit involves statistical analysis of the probability that the signal is produced by the analyte, and not the instrument, with given confidence limits. These methods, which have been treated extensively in the literature, are involved and require that the background noise be consistent from sample to sample.[21–23]

In methodologies that render irregular background noise from sample to sample it is commonly accepted to determine a signal-to-noise ratio of at least 3:1 to consider the signal as being produced by the analyte. Establishment of a higher signal-to-noise ratio as a decision guideline increases the confidence that the analyte is present at the expense of deciding it is absent at lower ratios. The benefit of doubt imparted to the decision at higher signal-to-noise ratios can be comforting from a forensic viewpoint.

5.8.1.2 Sensitivity and Linearity

The sensitivity of a method can be defined as the change in detector response given by a change in concentration. The detector response is composed of a part that depends on the concentration and a part that is independent of it (the blank). In addition, the detector response is not linearly proportional to the concentration over the entire range of possible values. The range of values for which the sensitivity is constant is called the "linear dynamic range," and methods should be developed so that this range is as large as possible.

The linear dynamic range, or linearity, is limited at the lower level by concentration values whose detector response cannot be distinguished from the detector noise, or by ambiguous values of sensitivity. The linear range is limited at the upper level by saturation of the detector signal.

5.8.1.3 Precision

Precision is a measure of the dispersion of results when an analytical procedure is repeated on one sample. Although the dispersion of results may be caused by many sources, it is usually implied that it is caused by random fluctuations in the procedure. If no bias exists, the results usually scatter around the expected value in a normal distribution, described by a Gaussian curve (Figure 5.3). The normal distribution of the population of results is characterized by the position of the mean (x) and the standard deviation (s). The precision of an analytical method is often expressed as the standard deviation or coefficient of variation (CV), and it is calculated and monitored by analysis of control materials (Section 5.6.3).

5.8.1.4 Accuracy

Although the concept of accuracy is vague and difficult to interpret, it has been defined as the difference (error or bias) between an individual result, or the mean of a set of results, and the value that is accepted as the true or correct value for the quantity measured.[24]

An accurate measurement is one that is free of bias, does not scatter when repeated, and results in the "true value." The true value, however, is unknown because it must be measured, and measurements are biased and imprecise. Nevertheless, the accuracy can be estimated by measuring properties that are related to the concept of "accurate." Precision can be measured and bias can be estimated. Youden[25] stated that the mean of the results obtained by a number of independent

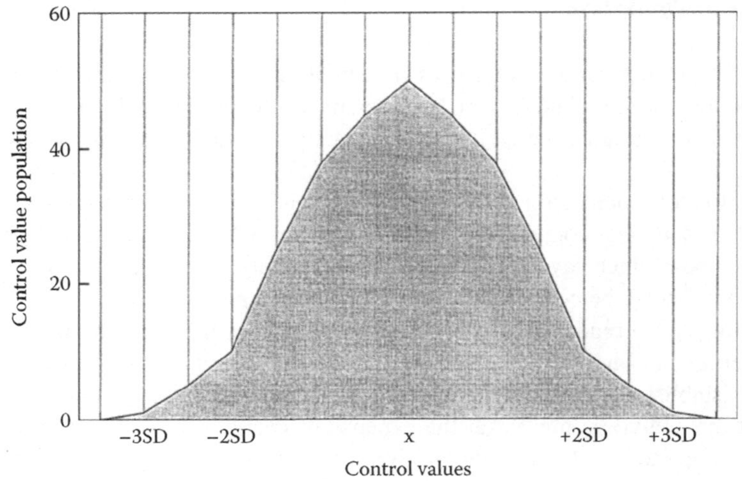

Figure 5.3 Gaussian curve.

laboratories, using comparable methods of data presentation and data handling, can be assumed to be the "true value."

5.8.1.5 Selectivity and Specificity

Selectivity refers to the ability of an analytical procedure to produce correct results for various components of a mixture without any mutual interference among the components. Specificity refers to the ability of an analytical procedure to discriminate between components in a mixture by their ability to produce a detector signal.

5.8.2 Qualitative Methods

Qualitative methods characterize the sample in terms of the identity of its toxic constituents. The identity can be specific, as produced by mass or infrared spectra, or nonspecific, as produced by immunoassays and spot tests.

Qualitative methods require that all analytes that can be detected or ruled out in the analysis be known. For nonspecific assays, such as thin-layer or gas chromatography, this can be an ever increasing list as new drugs are introduced.

With each assay, a negative control and a control representative of the analytes being tested should be analyzed. The positive control should contain the analytes near their respective limit of detection, and both should be prepared in a matrix similar to the samples. Interferences that can adversely affect the result should be indicated in the written procedure.

5.8.3 Quantitative Methods

Quantitative methods characterize the sample in terms of the quantity of its toxic constituents. The measured quantity carries with it an inherent uncertainty that must be known in order to appraise its reliability. The accepted thresholds of uncertainty, or limits of variation, are determined by quantifying the factors that affect the quality of the method. Therefore, each quantitative technique must be validated by determining its limit of detection, dynamic linear range, precision, and accuracy.

5.8.4 Method Development and Validation

Guidelines for method development instituted in a comprehensive procedures manual provide an effective way to tackle the analytical challenges that are frequently encountered in the forensic laboratory. The considerations listed below provide the basis upon which an analytical method can be implemented:

- Establishment of the intended purpose of the method
- Identification of chemical problems that must be addressed to fulfill the intended purpose of the method
- Search of the literature for existing methods that can fulfill the intended purpose and be accommodated by the laboratory

Appendix III provides literature sources for qualitative and quantitative assay procedures for most common drugs. The references should serve as a starting point for method development.

Once the basic characteristics of the method have been established, the method is developed by evaluating and documenting as much of the following information as possible:

- Analytical principle of the assay
- Brief description of toxic substances being analyzed
- Sample preparation requirements
- The sources of materials and the preparation of reagents, standards, and controls
- Quantitative statements about the stability of the reagents, standards, and controls
- Procedural steps to isolate and/or concentrate the analytes
- Instrumental requirements and settings
- Validation parameters; limit of detection and/or quantification, linear range, coefficient of variation, and recovery efficiency
- Interferences
- Data handling
- References to the source of the method

All analyses should be performed by the procedures set forth in the procedures manual, and carried out explicitly as described by the procedure whenever possible. Exceptions should be made only when special considerations are dictated by the character of the specimen (for example, interferences resulting from multidrug content). When modification to a method is necessary, the exercise of good analytical judgment and proper documentation are essential to impart confidence in the result.

5.9 INSTRUMENTS

In analytical chemistry, information about the chemical composition of a sample is obtained by measuring some chemical or physical property that is characteristic of the component of interest. These measurements are made by various analytical instruments designed to measure specific properties.

To apply instrumentation most efficiently to the problems, the analyst must understand the fundamental relations of chemical species to their physical and chemical properties. The analyst must know the scope, applicability, and limitations of physical property measurement with respect to qualitative and quantitative analysis. Knowing this, the analyst can call upon the instrumentation for the measurement of the desired properties with the needed accuracy and precision.[26,27]

The instrument is a device that converts chemical information to a form that is more readily observable. It accomplishes this function in several steps that may include (1) generation of a signal, (2) transduction (transformation of the signal to one of a different nature, such as electrical), (3) amplification of the transformed signal, and (4) presentation of the signal by a scale, recorder, integrator, or printout. Some instruments also prepare the sample to a form that can be analyzed or perform separation of components for increased specificity. It is common to find a combination of instruments working in tandem to produce the desired results.

To ensure that the instrumental data are reliable, steps must be taken to control the proper function of the instrument. This can be accomplished by establishing standard operating procedures that address proper installation guidelines, a preventive maintenance program, periodic performance evaluations, and preanalysis checklists.

All documentation concerning instrument maintenance and checks should be kept in bound notebooks specific to each instrument. These are to be kept near the instrument for easy access and inspection by all analysts. With time, a history of the instrument will develop that will impart a great insight for effective and timely troubleshooting.

5.9.1 Installation

An effort should be made to install the instrument in a manner that is commensurate with the recommendations of the manufacturer. These usually include environmental, energy, and safety requirements that are necessary for the proper function and longevity of the instrument.

5.9.2 Preventive Maintenance

A preventive maintenance program can reduce the frequency of instrument failure during analysis. It also reduces the likelihood of major breakdowns and extended downtime. Preventive maintenance requirements and procedures are usually specified in the instrument operation manual. The time interval required between preventive maintenance services is dictated by the amount of use and environmental factors. Therefore, laboratories must establish their own protocols according to their needs.

5.9.3 Pre-Analysis Checklist

A review of vital instrument parameters before processing samples assures that the correct settings have been chosen for the analysis and that the instrument is in good working order. This becomes especially important when the instrument is used for multiple procedures by multiple analysts. Use of a checklist is the most effective way to ensure that no parameter is overlooked and produces documentation that pre-analysis checks were performed. The specific parameters to be checked and their proper settings will vary with the instrument.

5.10 DATA

The American Academy of Forensic Sciences and the Society of Forensic Toxicologists recommend that before results are reported, each batch of analytical data should be reviewed by scientific personnel who are experienced with the analytical protocols used in the laboratory.[1] At a minimum this review should include chain of custody data, validity of analytical data and calculations, and quality control data. The review should be documented within the analytical record.

5.10.1 Chain-of-Custody Data

Review of the chain-of-custody documentation ensures that the analytical result represents the correct sample. The data necessary to accomplish this task include the dates and identification of individuals performing the sample collection and transportation to the laboratory; receipt; transfer of specimens or aliquots within the laboratory; chemical analysis; and analytical report.

5.10.2 Analytical Data

The first task of an analyst who wants to evaluate a procedure is to collect relevant data of measurements using that procedure. The second task is to reduce the number of measurements, remove irrelevant and erroneous data, and convert the measurements into statements pertaining to the condition of the procedure under control. To convert the data into a form that can be handled, data reduction procedures are applied.

Analytical instruments are usually equipped with data filters or data handlers that smooth and reduce the data collected, relieving the analyst of such arduous tasks. For this reason, the concepts of data production, information theory, data reduction, data handling, analysis of variance, pattern recognition, and system optimization are not discussed in this chapter. However, the analyst should have some understanding of how instruments perform data analysis. This knowledge will help the analyst identify corrupt data, correctly set thresholds for proper peak integration, and determine signal-to-noise ratios. A thorough discussion on data production and data reduction has been presented by Kateman and Pijpers.[28]

A thorough review by responsible supervisory personnel of the raw analytical data and the calculations derived therefrom should be performed before a report is issued.

5.10.3 Quality Control Data

A review of the results obtained from the analysis of control material is essential to evaluate the performance of the analysis. This is accomplished by deriving control charts for each control material so that control rules or decision criteria can be applied to determine whether the method performed within expected limits of variation.[29–32]

The control chart is a graphical representation of the arithmetic mean and the control limits calculated for the control material as described in Section 5.6.3. The *x*-axis is scaled to provide appropriate time period intervals. Horizontal lines are drawn corresponding to the mean (center) and multiples of the standard deviation above and below the mean, as shown in Figure 5.4. These graphs are sometimes referred to as Shewhart or Levey–Jennings charts.

The control rules or criteria described here are based on statistical properties arising from single control measurements, rather than replicate measurements, since they are more common. They provide a low level of false rejection, improved capability for detecting analytical errors, and some indication of the error type to aid in problem solving. Rejection of an analytical run occurs when the control value obtained violates one or more of the following rules, symbolized for brevity and convenience:

- (1_{3s}) A value outside 3 standard deviations
- (2_{2s}) Two consecutive values outside 2 standard deviations; one value outside 2 standard deviations should be considered a warning, requiring inspection of a second control
- (R_{4s}) Two consecutive values that differ by 4 standard deviations or more
- (4_{1s}) Four consecutive values on the same side of the mean that are more than 1 standard deviation from the mean
- (10_{x}) Ten consecutive values on the same side of the mean

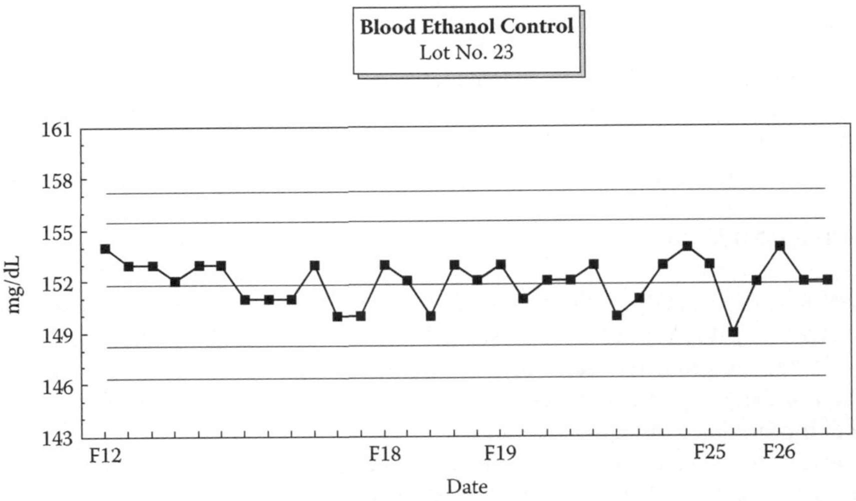

Figure 5.4 Quality control chart.

The particular rule violated may give some indication of the type of analytical error occurring. Random error will most often be detected by the 13s and R4s rules. Systematic error will usually be detected by the 22s, 41s, or 10× rules and, when very large, by the 13s rule. However, these rules may be difficult or impossible to properly apply in forensic toxicology work where, with the exception of ethanol and a small number of drugs, the frequency of analysis is relatively low.

5.11 REPORTS

Postmortem forensic laboratories are an integral part of, supported by, or associated with government agencies involved in medicolegal investigations. The laboratory must comply with the reporting requirements mandated by the agency to which the reports are submitted. Thus, a report format can be neither standardized nor recommended, since it will depend on the specific needs of the recipient. In general, however, the written report should include all information necessary to identify the case and its source, the test results, and the signature of the individual responsible for its contents. Forensic toxicology reporting is discussed in depth in the AAFS/SOFT Forensic Toxicology Laboratory Guidelines.[1]

5.12 PROFICIENCY PROGRAMS

In addition to the laboratory's effort in implementing a quality control program to impart confidence to its analytical results, there is a requirement to scrutinize the analytical process by independent evaluation against peer laboratories. A proficiency testing program established by accrediting organizations or independent consultants provides laboratories with such an evaluation mechanism.

The proficiency program provides laboratories with chemically fortified samples simulating those encountered routinely by the laboratory for analysis. The program derives statistical data on the results reported by the participating laboratories and issues a summary of useful information about the results. When the result of a chemical analysis is compared to the results obtained by other laboratories on the same sample, the laboratory can make a responsible determination of the strengths and weaknesses of its overall operation. This information can be used to focus resources on those areas that need improvement, be it personnel, training, equipment, method development, reference materials, or the like. It also builds confidence in the methods that yield reliable results.

Forensic toxicology laboratories must participate in external proficiency testing programs that evaluate as many of the analytical tests in as many specimen types as possible. These programs are the only independent way to evaluate the reliability of the methods used and the overall operating procedures of the laboratory.

5.13 ACCREDITATION PROGRAMS

Accreditation is playing an increasing role in the quality of work performed in forensic laboratories. It ensures that the laboratory has acceptable analytical methods, general procedures, and most important, that the standard operating procedures are followed. There are currently four organizations that offer accreditation in the field of forensic toxicology. The National Laboratory Certification Program (NLCP) is operated under private contract through the U.S. Substance Abuse and Mental Health Services Administration (SAMHSA).[33] That NLCP program applies only to U.S. federally regulated testing in the specific area of forensic urine drug testing for amphetamine and methamphetamine, cannabinoids, codeine and morphine, cocaine, and phencyclidine. The College of American Pathologists also operates a voluntary program for forensic urine drugs testing, but which covers a slightly greater range of drugs of abuse in urine.[34] However, the two major, broad-based accreditation programs that encompass forensic toxicology are run by the American Society of Crime Laboratory Directors Laboratory Accreditation Board (ASCLD/LAB) and the American Board of Forensic Toxicology (ABFT).[35,36] The ASCLD/LAB program covers all aspects of forensic laboratory management and operation, including forensic toxicology, whereas the ABFT program is focused on forensic toxicology, and specifically those laboratories performing postmortem toxicology and human performance drug testing (e.g., driving under the influence of drugs).

REFERENCES

1. Joint Committee of the American Academy of Forensic Sciences (AAFS) and the Society of Forensic Toxicologists, Inc. (SOFT), *Forensic Toxicology Laboratory Guidelines*, Colorado Springs, 2002. Available online from www.soft-tox.org.
2. Ayres, G.H., The analytical balance and its use, in *Quantitative Chemical Analysis*, 2nd ed., Harper & Row, New York, 1968, chap. 2.
3. Schenk, G.H., Hahn, R.B., and Hartkopf, A.V., Fundamentals of weighing and related measurements, in *Quantitative Analytical Chemistry — Principles and Life Science Applications*, Allyn & Bacon, Boston, 1977, chap. 6.
4. Blanke, R.V., Validation of the purity of standards, Publication 87-0175, Abbott Laboratories, Diagnostics Division, Irving, TX, 1989.
5. Williams, S., Ed., *Official Methods of Analysis of the Association of Official Analytical Chemists*, 14th ed., Association of Official Analytical Chemists, Arlington, VA, 1984, 1007.
6. Buttner, J., Borth, R., Boutwell, J.H., and Broughton, P.M.G., Provisional recommendation on quality control in clinical chemistry. I. General principles and terminology, International Federation of Clinical Chemistry, *Clin. Chem.*, 22, 532, 1976.
7. Ross, J.W., Control materials and calibration standards, *CRC Handbook of Clinical Chemistry*, Vol. 1, CRC Press, Boca Raton, FL, 1989, 359.
8. Foltz, R.L., Fentiman, A.F., and Foltz, R.B., GC/MS Assays for Abused Drugs in Body Fluids, Research Monograph Series 32, National Institute on Drug Abuse, Bethesda, MD, 1980, 9–12.
9. Samuelsson, B., Hamberg, M., and Sweely, C.C., *Anal. Biochem.*, 38, 301, 1970.
10. Lawson, N.S. and Haven, G.T., Analyte stability in control and reference materials, in *CRC Handbook of Clinical Chemistry*, Vol. 1, CRC Press, Boca Raton, FL, 1989, 371.

11. Bowers, G.N., Burnett, R.W., and McComb, R.B., Selected method: preparation and use of human serum control materials for monitoring precision in clinical chemistry, *Clin. Chem.*, 21, 1830, 1975.
12. Approved Standard: ASC-2, *Calibration Reference Materials and Control Materials in Clinical Chemistry*, National Committee for Clinical Laboratory Standards, Villanova, PA, 1975.
13. Anido, G., Preparation of quality control materials in clinical chemistry and hematology, *Proc. R. Soc. Med.*, 68, 624, 1975.
14. Klugerman, M.R. and Boutwell, J.H., Commercial control sera in the clinical chemistry laboratory, *Clin. Chem.*, 7, 185, 1961.
15. Logan, J.E. and Allen, R.H., Control serum preparations, *Clin. Chem.*, 14, 437, 1968.
16. Wilkins, D., Ph.D., Associate Toxicologist and Quality Control Manager, Center for Human Toxicology, personal communication, AAFS Meeting, New Orleans, February 1992.
17. Kateman, G. and Pijpers, F.W., Sampling, in *Quality Control in Analytical Chemistry*, Vol. 60, John Wiley & Sons, New York, 1981, chap. 2.
18. Toseland, P.A., Samples and sampling, *Clarke's Isolation and Identification of Drugs in Pharmaceuticals, Body Fluids, and Post-Mortem Material*, 2nd ed., Pharmaceutical Press, London, 1986, 111.
19. Committee on Hazardous Biological Substances in the Laboratory; Board on Chemical Sciences and Technology; Commission on Physical Sciences, Mathematics, and Resources; National Research Council, Biosafety in the Laboratory — Prudent Practices for the Handling and Disposal of Infectious Materials, National Academy Press, Washington, D.C., 1989.
20. Kateman, G. and Pijpers, F.W., Analysis, in *Quality Control in Analytical Chemistry*, Vol. 60, John Wiley & Sons, New York, 1981, chap. 3.
21. Ingle, J.D., *J. Chem. Ed.,* 51(2), 100, 1974.
22. Glaser, J.A., Foerst, D.L., McKee, G.D., Quave, S.A., and Budde, W.L., Trace analysis for wastewaters, *Environ. Sci. Technol.*, 15, 1426, 1981.
23. Code of Federal Regulations Part 100-136, Protection of Environment, Definition and Procedure for the Determination of the Method Detection Limit, Part 136, Appendix B, July 1992.
24. Analytical chemistry, *Anal. Chem.*, 47, 2527, 1975.
25. Youden, W.J. and Steiner, E.H., *Statistical Manual of the Association of Official Analytical Chemists*, Association of Official Analytical Chemists, Washington, D.C., 1975.
26. Sandell, E.B. and Elving, P.J., in *Treatise on Analytical Chemistry*, Part 1, Vol. 1, Kothoff, I.M. and Elving, P.J., Ed., Interscience Publishers, New York, 1959, 17.
27. Skoog, D.A. and West, D.M., *Principles of Instrumental Analysis*, Holt, Rinehart & Winston, New York, 1971.
28. Kateman, G. and Pijpers, F.W., Data processing, in *Quality Control in Analytical Chemistry*, Vol. 60, John Wiley & Sons, New York, 1981, chap. 4.
29. Westgard, J.O., Barry, P.L., and Hunt, M.R., A multi-rule Shewhart chart of quality control in clinical chemistry, *Clin. Chem.*, 27(3), 493–501, 1981.
30. Levey, S. and Jennings, E.R., The use of control charts in the clinical laboratories, *Am. J. Clin. Pathol.*, 20, 1059–1066, 1950.
31. Westgard, J.O., Groth, T., and Aronsson, T., Performance characteristics of rules for internal quality control: probabilities for false rejection and error detection, *Clin. Chem.*, 23, 1857–1867, 1977.
32. Westgard, J.O. and Groth, T., Power functions for statistical control rules, *Clin. Chem.*, 25, 863–869, 1979.
33. Substance and Mental Health Services Administration (SAMHSA): http://workplace.samhsa.gov.
34. College of American Pathologists: http://www.cap.org.
35. American Society of Crime Laboratory Directors/Laboratory Accreditation Board: http://www.ascld-lab.org.
36. American Board of Forensic Toxicology: http://www.abft.org.

CHAPTER 6

Interpretation of Postmortem Drug Levels

Graham R. Jones, Ph.D., DABFT
Office of the Chief Medical Examiner, Edmonton, Alberta, Canada

CONTENTS

6.1 Introduction 114
6.2 General Considerations 115
 6.2.1 The Analytical Result....115
 6.2.2 Postmortem Specimens 115
  6.2.2.1 Blood 115
  6.2.2.2 Vitreous Humor 116
  6.2.2.3 Liver....117
  6.2.2.4 Gastric Contents 117
  6.2.2.5 Urine....118
  6.2.2.6 Brain 118
  6.2.2.7 Other Soft Tissues 119
  6.2.2.8 Other Fluids....119
  6.2.2.9 Injection Sites, Nasal Swabs....119
  6.2.2.10 Hair....120
  6.2.2.11 Nails, Bone....120
  6.2.2.12 Paraphernalia: Syringes, Spoons, Glasses 120
6.3 Pharmacokinetics....121
 6.3.1 Absorption and Distribution 121
 6.3.2 Metabolism and Pharmacogenetics 122
 6.3.3 Calculation of Total Body Burden....122
 6.3.4 Estimation of Amount Ingested from Blood Levels 123
6.4 Postmortem Redistribution and Other Changes 123
 6.4.1 Incomplete Distribution 123
 6.4.2 Postmortem Redistribution and Postmortem Diffusion 124
6.5 Other Considerations....125
 6.5.1 Trauma....125
 6.5.2 Artifacts of Medication Delivery....126
 6.5.3 Additive and Synergistic Toxicity 126
 6.5.4 Adverse Reactions....127

6.5.5 Drug Instability 127
6.5.6 Interpretation Using Tables of Values....127
6.6 Conclusion....128
References....128

6.1 INTRODUCTION

In the early to mid-1900s, the practice of forensic toxicology was relatively limited in scope. Certainly, toxicologists could determine blood alcohol and a limited number of drugs with accuracy approaching that of today. However, the toxicological investigation was different in at least two respects. First, the sophistication of testing for drugs was limited, primarily relying on the efficiency of extraction techniques, followed by gravimetric and later spectrophotometric analysis. Second, with the exception of alcohol and a relatively limited number of drugs or poisons (e.g., salicylate, barbiturates, arsenic, heavy metals), there was a very limited database of reference drug concentrations available. The interpretation of quantitative results relied very heavily on the history and circumstances of the case, including the police investigation, witness accounts, and autopsy findings.

The development of gas chromatography (GC) and high-performance liquid chromatography (HPLC) during the early 1970s had a major influence on the development and growth of pharmacokinetics and therapeutic drug monitoring. As a result, the kinetics of drug absorption, distribution, metabolism, and excretion in clinical patients was easier to understand and predict. This coincided with a vast increase in the range of pure pharmaceuticals available, many of which were of lower absolute dosage compared with those previously available, for example, the replacement of barbiturates with low-dose benzodiazepines. It was logical that toxicologists started to use the pharmacokinetic data gained from living patients to interpret postmortem blood concentrations, for example, to predict whether a given blood drug concentration was "in the therapeutic range," whether the blood level was "fatal," or even to predict the amount ingested prior to death. Experience has since shown that postmortem drug concentrations must be interpreted from a perspective very different from those in living patients. Many processes occur after death that can change drug and alcohol concentrations, sometimes to a very large extent.

The period of enthusiasm in the late 1970s and 1980s has given way to the realization that there are many unique aspects of postmortem toxicology that must be considered when interpreting analytical results. It is no longer acceptable to interpret postmortem toxicology results from tables of so-called therapeutic, toxic, and fatal ranges, without taking into consideration the medical history, the immediate circumstances of the death, and the various processes that can affect drug concentrations both before and after death. It is probably fair to say that many toxicologists and pathologists are less confident about interpreting postmortem drug concentrations today — and with good reason — than they may have been 10 to 20 years ago.

It is important to remember that there are no "absolute" rules for the interpretation of toxicology results. The more information that is available to, and considered by, the interpreter, the more likely are the conclusions reached to be accurate. In the courtroom, lawyers, judges, and jurors often view all science, including the forensic subspecialties, in absolute terms. Certainly, if the toxicologist does his or her job properly, the laboratory findings will have the required accuracy. However, the subsequent interpretation is in part based on the scope of the toxicology testing (not least including the range of specimens tested), in part on the quantitative results, and perhaps, most importantly, on the history and circumstances surrounding the death. Attempts to interpret toxicology findings solely on the basis of so-called normal or reference ranges are irresponsible.

It is not the purpose of this chapter to teach anyone *how* to interpret postmortem drug concentrations, but rather to outline some of the pre-mortem and postmortem factors that should be taken into account when doing so.

6.2 GENERAL CONSIDERATIONS

6.2.1 The Analytical Result

It should be obvious that the interpretation of any toxicology test result will be no more reliable than the analytical result itself. The interpreter must be satisfied that the analysis is sufficiently accurate for the purpose, or at least know the limitations of the testing. Was the standard material used to prepare the calibrators pure and correctly identified? For example, was the salt or water of crystallization properly taken into account? Was the calibration properly prepared and valid in the range where the specimens were measured? Was the assay adequately verified by quality control samples? Was the assay sufficiently specific? Could endogenous substances or other drugs or metabolites have interfered with analysis of the specimen, either by obscuring the target analyte or by increasing the apparent concentration? If the specimen was analyzed only once, what was the potential for accidental contamination? Was there a matrix effect? For example, was recovery of the drug from the specimen the same, relatively, as from the calibrators? Using similar matrix calibrators (e.g., blood) is not necessarily a guarantee of that since postmortem blood, by its nature, is variable from case to case, or even from site to site within the same cadaver. The extraction efficiency of drug or metabolite or internal standard from animal or outdated blood bank blood may sometimes be markedly different from decomposed case blood. Although it is practically impossible to know the "absolute" or true concentration of drug in a postmortem specimen, the degree of confidence increases with the specificity of the analysis, with replication, or in some cases by applying multiple analytical methods of different physical or chemical principles.

The use of GC/mass spectrometry with multiple ion monitoring and stable isotope (e.g., deuterated) labeled internal standards will usually provide a higher degree of confidence in the accuracy of the analytical result than, say, use of an immunoassay procedure. The completeness of the analysis should also be considered. It is never possible to test for every single drug during routine screening tests. However, a careful review of the medications or other potential poisons available to the deceased should assist the laboratory in determining whether any of these substances would have been detected if present in significant concentrations.

6.2.2 Postmortem Specimens

Relying on a toxicology result from a single specimen can be misleading because of the postmortem changes that can occur. The most commonly used specimen, blood, is not a homogeneous fluid. It is good forensic practice to have multiple specimens available, or at least blood specimens from different sites in the body, because of the potential difficulties in interpreting postmortem toxicology results.

6.2.2.1 Blood

The concentrations of many drugs are affected by postmortem redistribution through the vascular system from the major organs, by direct postmortem diffusion from organ to organ, and sometimes by incomplete distribution. Sedimentation of blood after death may also affect the drug "blood" concentration obtained. For some drugs the distribution between blood and plasma is markedly uneven during life. However, toxicologists should be cautious about applying factors to "correct" for blood:plasma distribution unless it is known that the distribution is maintained after death. It may be found that the blood:plasma distribution that exists during life, due to active processes, decays after death occurs, for example, due to changes in pH and, therefore, protein binding.

Toxicologists should be cautious about inferring the exact source of a blood specimen from the labeled description. Blood, simply labeled as such, could come from almost anywhere, even collected as pooled blood at the scene. Most toxicologists and pathologists are well acquainted with the widely discouraged practice of drawing blood by a "blind stick" through the chest wall. Although such blood may be labeled as "heart blood," it may contain pericardial fluid, or worse, may be from the pleural cavity, and therefore potentially be contaminated by gastric contents, particularly if the death was traumatic or decomposition severe.[1] Even blood drawn from the "heart" after opening the body cavity at autopsy may contain blood from a number of sources. So-called "heart" blood may contain blood from one or more of the cardiac chambers — the ventricles and atria. However, it may equally contain blood that has drained from the pulmonary vein and artery (and hence the lungs), from the inferior vena cava (and hence from the liver), and from the aorta and subclavian veins. As a result, so-called heart blood is potentially one of the most nonhomogeneous specimens in the body. As described later, postmortem redistribution and other factors can cause the concentrations of many drugs to vary markedly from site to site.[2–4] Even drug concentrations in blood drawn from the same site, but simply placed into different collection vials, can also sometimes differ by severalfold.

It is generally recommended that to avoid the effects of postmortem redistribution or diffusion from the major organs, femoral blood should be sampled wherever possible. While this is certainly a good practice, interpreters should be cautioned that there is no such thing as "pure femoral blood"; it is simply blood drawn from the site of the femoral vein. Certainly, if the proximal part of the femoral vein is ligated prior to sampling, it is likely that much of the blood will be "peripheral" and therefore relatively uncontaminated by blood from the major organs. However, this is rarely the case. Femoral blood is typically drawn by a "stick" to the unligated femoral vein in the groin area, such that blood will be drawn from above and below the site of sampling. If the volume drawn is relatively small (e.g., 2 to 5 mL), it is unlikely that much blood will be drawn down from the central body cavity. However, with some skill, it is often possible to draw 50 mL or more of blood from a "femoral stick." Even with a limited knowledge of anatomy, it does not require much thought to realize that at least some of this blood will have been drawn down from the inferior vena cava, and hence from the liver. An alternative sampling technique is to cut the iliac vein at the side of the pelvis during autopsy, and only sample blood that is massaged out from the femoral vein directly into a test tube. Even if such a procedure ensures that the collected blood is from the femoral vein, some postmortem changes may just as well have happened in this blood, too, e.g., diffusion from vessel walls and skeletal muscle. Since blood concentrations of some drugs have the potential for marked postmortem change, it is good practice to analyze blood obtained from more than one site, plus tissue or other specimens where this may be useful.

6.2.2.2 Vitreous Humor

Vitreous humor, although limited in volume (e.g., 3 to 6 mL), is an extremely useful specimen. It has been used for years to verify postmortem blood concentrations of ethanol, since postmortem fermentation does not occur to any significant extent in the eye. However, vitreous humor has also been useful for a number of drugs. For example, it is well known that digoxin concentrations will rise after death in cardiac blood, due to postmortem redistribution from myocardial tissue, and possibly other organs. Consequently, vitreous digoxin concentrations are more likely to reflect those in ante-mortem plasma.[5] Vitreous humor has been used to analyze a large number of other drugs, including barbiturates, cocaine, morphine, tricyclic antidepressants, and benzodiazepines.[6–10] However, interpretation of vitreous drug concentrations is difficult, in part because very few studies have been published that relate blood concentrations to those in vitreous humor, and in part because the large *ad hoc* data on vitreous drug concentrations is fragmented in innumerable case reports. In general, however, those drugs that tend to be somewhat hydrophilic at physiological pH (e.g., digoxin, benzoylecgonine, acetaminophen, salicylate) are more likely to have concentrations approaching those in blood or plasma, than those drugs that are either highly protein bound (e.g., tricyclic antidepressants) or highly lipophilic (e.g., benzodiazepines). In fact, a significant negative correlation between the vitreous:blood concentration ratio and the degree of protein binding of different drugs has been reported.[11]

Because the eye is remote from the central body cavity and the abdominal organs, it has been suggested that vitreous may be a useful fluid for the determination of drugs that are subject to postmortem redistribution. That may hold true for many drugs such as digoxin. However, others have shown that some drugs, notably cocaine, may increase in concentration in the vitreous humor after death.[9] Postmortem diffusion of drugs to the vitreous from the brain, particularly in bodies lying in a prone position for an extended time, may be a possible source of error, and warrants systematic studies.

6.2.2.3 Liver

Many toxicologists rank the liver second only after blood in importance as a specimen of interpretive value in postmortem toxicology. It is particularly valuable for the tricyclic antidepressants and many other drugs that are very highly protein bound. It is useful for the phenothiazine neuroleptics which have a very large dosage range, and hence range in "therapeutic" blood concentrations. Liver tissue is also of value for interpreting postmortem concentrations of many other drugs where a sufficiently large database has been established, and particularly where blood is not available due to severe decomposition, fire, or exsanguination.

One other aspect of liver drug concentrations should be considered. It is known that postmortem diffusion from the stomach may artifactually elevate concentrations of the drug proximal to the stomach — for example, after an overdose, where both the concentration and absolute amount of drug in the stomach are high.[12,13] However, little appears to have been done to assess the kinetics of drugs in the liver after therapeutic doses. For example, common sense would suggest that drug concentrations in the liver, and particularly those that are strongly protein bound, would increase dramatically in the period after a dose was taken, compared with that at steady state. This might be particularly important for drugs with a relatively long half-life and that are often taken in single nighttime doses, or divided with a large portion of the dose at night. As for other specimens, liver concentrations are extremely valuable for assessing the role of many drugs in a death, but only in conjunction with other analytical findings and history.

6.2.2.4 Gastric Contents

Interpretation of the analytical findings of drugs in the gastric contents is largely dictated by common sense. It is the *amount* of drug or poison remaining in the gastric contents that is important; the concentration of the drug is generally of far less importance. The tricyclic antidepressants offer a good example. Most forensic toxicologists regard total tricyclic concentrations greater than 2 to 3 mg/L, even in postmortem "cardiac" blood, as at least potentially toxic or fatal. So what does a gastric tricyclic concentration of 1500 mg/L mean? The answer is, on its own, not much, except that the person may have consumed his or her medication a relatively short period prior to death. For example, 200 mg amitriptyline at night is a fairly common dosage. If the gastric volume was, say, 120 mL, then 1500 mg/L would be completely consistent with the person taking the normal dosage just prior to death — probably from unrelated causes. However, if in our example the gastric volume at autopsy were 900 mL, then a concentration of 1500 mg/L would calculate out to 1350 mg/900 mL in the stomach, and therefore almost certainly consistent with an overdose.

Conversely, a relatively low absolute amount of drug in the gastric contents, with or without a high concentration, does not rule out the possibility of an overdose. Numerous case histories have shown that it may take several hours for an individual to die from an intentional overdose, depending on the exact drugs or poisons ingested, the amounts, co-ingestion of alcohol, general state of health, and age. It is not unusual for people to die from an oral overdose with less than a single therapeutic dose remaining in the stomach, notwithstanding the fact that an overdose of drugs can be irritant to the stomach lining and therefore delay gastric emptying. Extensive vomiting before death can also reduce the amount of drug remaining in the stomach at the time death occurs.

Two other aspects of "gastric toxicology" should be mentioned. The simple presence of a drug in the gastric contents does not necessarily mean that the drug was recently consumed, or even prove that the drug was taken orally. Most drugs will be re-excreted into the gastric contents through the gastric juice, maintaining an equilibrium between the gastric fluid and the blood. This is especially so for drugs that are basic (alkaline) in nature. This can readily be demonstrated where it is known that a drug has only been administered intravenously under controlled conditions, and yet can be found later in small concentrations in the gastric contents. The same phenomenon can be seen with drug metabolites where, invariably, concentrations can be found in the gastric fluid. While it could be argued that microbial metabolism could have occurred in the stomach, it is more likely that the majority of the metabolites found were secreted into the stomach via the gastric juice. Conversely, the presence of "ghost" tablets in gastric contents has been reported for at least one type of slow-release analgesic, where overdose or abuse was not suspected. Apparently, the wax-resin matrix of these sustained release tablets may remain in the gastric contents long after the active ingredient has diffused out.[14]

More commonly, significant amounts of conglomerated, unabsorbed tablet or capsule residue can be found in the stomach many hours, or even a day or two, after a large overdose was consumed. These masses can occur after overdoses where large amounts of capsules or tablets may form a gelatinous mass, which is not readily dissolved or broken up, and which may lie slowly dissolving; they are called bezoars.[15] While the term can apply to unabsorbed masses of almost anything (e.g., hair balls), it is also applied to unabsorbed drug formulations. They occur, at least in part, because gastric emptying time is delayed significantly by irritants, including large amounts of undissolved drug residue. However, the phenomenon is also occasionally seen in patients where overdosage is extremely unlikely (e.g., controlled setting such as a hospital or nursing home), but where several unabsorbed tablets may be recovered from the stomach. This is more likely to occur where enteric-coated tablets are involved, which do not dissolve in the stomach, but may stick together to form a small mass of tablets. It is also more likely to happen in elderly individuals, or in other patients where gastric motility is abnormally slow.

6.2.2.5 Urine

It is almost universally accepted that, with few exceptions, there is very little correlation between urine and blood drug concentrations, and even less correlation between urine drug concentrations and pharmacological effect. So many factors affect urine concentration, such as fluid intake, rate of metabolism, glomerular clearance, urine pH, and the times of voiding relative to the dose, that any attempt to predict or even estimate a blood concentration from a urine concentration is pure folly. As always there are some exceptions. Urine alcohol concentrations can be used to estimate the approximate blood alcohol concentration, but only if the bladder is completely voided and the measurement made on the second void. Estimates of the body burden of some heavy metals are still made on 24-h urine collections.

6.2.2.6 Brain

The brain is the primary site of action of many forensically important drugs, such as the antidepressants, benzodiazepines, and narcotics. It is potentially a very useful specimen for the measurement and interpretation of drugs because it is remote from the stomach and other major organs in the body and would not be expected to be affected by postmortem diffusion and redistribution. However, although drug concentration data in brain tissue are not hard to find in the literature, it is largely fragmented into innumerable case reports that seldom specify what anatomic region of brain tissue was analyzed. The brain is an anatomically diverse organ such that concentrations of many drugs vary significantly from one region to another — up to about twofold.[2,4]

6.2.2.7 Other Soft Tissues

Most of the major organs such as the kidneys, lungs, spleen, and myocardial tissue have at some time been analyzed to estimate the degree of drug or poison exposure. However, for most drugs, adequate reference databases are not available in the literature, so the interpretive value of these measurements may be limited. Skeletal muscle has the potential to be one of the most useful specimens for drug or poison determination, particularly where the body is severely decomposed, or where postmortem redistribution or diffusion might affect measurement in blood or other organs. The problem is one of obtaining sufficient reference values for that drug in skeletal muscle in order to make a confident interpretation. Some studies have been published, but data are scattered and incomplete.[2,4,16]

The potential usefulness of bone marrow for the determination of both drugs and alcohol has been explored.[17–19] For drugs and other poisons at least, this could be very useful in cases where severe decomposition, fire, or the action of wild animals has made the major organs unavailable, but where bone marrow can still be harvested and analyzed. As for many other specimens, the problem is again one of establishing an adequate and reliable database of reference values.

6.2.2.8 Other Fluids

Bile has been used for decades as one of the primary specimens analyzed in the forensic toxicology laboratory, but mainly for the detection and measurement of morphine. However, the usefulness of bile has decreased in the past few years as sensitive immunoassays and mass spectrometry–based assays have been developed for whole blood. For most drugs, including morphine, the interpretive value of bile is limited. Biliary drug concentrations may also be influenced by postmortem diffusion from the liver and the stomach.

Cerebrospinal fluid (CSF) is also a potentially useful specimen for the measurement and interpretation of drugs, since it is the fluid that "bathes" the central nervous system, the brain, and spinal cord. Its limitation lies mainly in the fact that it is often more difficult to collect than blood postmortem, and as for many other specimens, there is a very limited database of reference values. As for the vitreous, drugs that are highly protein bound or those that are lipophilic will tend to have significantly lower concentrations than in the blood.

6.2.2.9 Injection Sites, Nasal Swabs

Suspect injection sites are periodically excised and submitted for analysis, to support evidence of that route of administration. Certainly, it is not difficult to perform such analyses. However, the simple qualitative detection or even quantitative measurement of a drug in a piece of skin is evidence only that the drug was taken or used, not that it was necessarily injected, let alone at that site. Sometimes it is forgotten that most drugs are distributed throughout the body from any route of administration, such that any piece of skin will contain some amount of the drug. For such measurements to be useful, a similar piece of skin from another part of the body, not suspected to be an injection site, must be analyzed for comparison. Only if the concentration in the suspect site is substantially higher than that in the reference site can meaningful conclusions be drawn. Even then, a perfect injection may not cause persistent elevated drug concentrations at the intravenous injection site, in contrast to an intramuscular or subcutaneous site. Similarly, the simple detection of a drug such as cocaine in a nasal swab does not prove that the drug was "snorted." Any fluid secreted by the body, including sweat, vaginal fluid, and nasal secretions, will contain some concentration of the drug. In this instance, quantitative determination is difficult and interpretation even more so unless the concentration of drug in the nasal secretions is extremely high relative to the blood.

6.2.2.10 Hair

Most drugs and poisons will be absorbed by bone, nails, and hair. Hair has long been used for the determination of arsenic and heavy metals, and by cutting the hair into sequential sections, for estimating the duration of exposure to the poison.[20] More recently, hair has been used for the determination of drugs of abuse in workplace and probation testing. Further, hair analysis can also be applied to estimate compliance in drug substitution programs and may also prove useful in therapeutic drug monitoring. In drug-facilitated crimes, the detection of a particular poison, such as GHB,[21] zopiclone,[22] and thiopental[23] in hair, has been used to document the exposure in several drug-facilitated crimes, but a negative finding can usually not exclude an exposure.[24] Finally, hair analysis has the potential to be useful in postmortem situations, for example, to estimate the duration of exposure to a drug or toxin, and hence provide information about the subject's previous drug use.[25–29]

The incorporation of drugs into hair is to a large extent due to melanin binding.[30] Hence, comparisons of levels between individuals is very risky. Even if the melanin content in the hair is measured, there are different types of melanin, and besides, a correction for total melanin content can only be applied to drugs where the drug-melanin binding characteristics have been firmly established. For most drugs, such information is lacking, and hence, the exact hair drug concentration per se is rarely informative.

6.2.2.11 Nails, Bone

One advantage of analysis of keratinized materials that should be emphasized is the stability of drugs in hair and nails, which means that such samples can be stored in room temperature for very long periods without major degradation of incorporated drugs. Drugs are incorporated into nails via both the root of the growing nail and via the nail bed.[31] This implies that during the growth of the nail, drugs follow the movement of the keratinized matrix both upward and forward. In addition, the growth of nails is variable and generally slow. Hence, a temporal mapping of previous drug intake using analysis of nails is hardly possible. On the other hand, nails are almost always available for analysis, whereas hair is not; some subjects may present with alopecia totalis, or have shaved the hair on many body parts. Despite the limitations as to the growth rate of nails, this matrix has the potential to be a useful source for information about the drug use history of the decedent.

Most drugs and poisons will be taken up in bone and therefore, unless volatile, will be detectable in skeletonized remains. The interpretation of concentrations of certain drugs or poisons is relatively easy since either the normal or reference values are well established (e.g., arsenic; heavy metals), or the substance should not be present in any concentration (e.g., strychnine). However, interpretation of specific concentrations of pharmaceutical drugs or drugs of abuse is problematic because of limited reference levels. In addition, it should be recognized that bone is continuously remodeled; hence, drugs incorporated in bone tissue over time will be liberated and re-delivered to the blood. This means that a negative detection in bone does not rule out an exposure and a positive detection will not give very much information as to the time for exposure.

6.2.2.12 Paraphernalia: Syringes, Spoons, Glasses

Most forensic toxicologists are willing to analyze potentially drug-related exhibits found at the scene of death. Syringes or spoons can provide a valuable confirmation of drugs that may have been used prior to death. For example, heroin is so rapidly broken down to morphine that little or no heroin, or even monoacetylmorphine, may be detectable in postmortem blood. The finding of morphine in, for example, blood could indicate either use of heroin or a morphine salt (or codeine, if it was also found). However, it should be borne in mind that most addicts reuse syringes and therefore the presence of a drug in a syringe found in the same room as a body does not necessarily mean that drugs contained therein were involved in the death, although it may provide circumstantial evidence. The use or abuse of insulin in a person without diabetes is exceptionally difficult to prove, since blood insulin concentrations are so variable, are difficult to determine accurately in postmortem blood, and even during life correlate poorly with blood glucose. Insulin abuse is uncommon,[32,33] but in those cases where it happens may be difficult to prove postmortem without a good clinical history. However, detection of insulin in a used syringe near someone who was not prescribed the drug can provide useful circumstantial evidence of abuse. The presence of drug residues in drinking glasses or cups can provide evidence of at least the route of ingestion and in most cases assist with the determination of manner of death, especially if the drug residue is large and obvious. Care would obviously have to be taken to distinguish, say, a multiple drug overdose mixed in a glass of water, from two or three hypnotic tablets introduced into an alcoholic beverage for the purposes of administering a "Mickey Finn."

6.3 PHARMACOKINETICS

In this section we review the basics of pharmacokinetics as it relates to postmortem interpretation. The kinetics of all drugs and poisons in the body are characterized by absorption, distribution, metabolism, and excretion. All these parameters affect the concentrations that will be found in the body after death, and therefore interpretation of analytical toxicology results.

6.3.1 Absorption and Distribution

Absorption may be via the oral route, parenteral (e.g., intravenous, intramuscular, subcutaneous), pulmonary, dermal, and, rarely, rectal. The route of absorption can be very important to the interpretation. For example, many drugs are extremely toxic via the intravenous route, especially if given rapidly. For example, heroin, barbiturates, and many other drugs can cause severe hypotension, and may be fatal if given rapidly, even though the total dose given is within the range normally considered "therapeutic." The resulting postmortem blood concentrations may be below those normally considered fatal. At the other extreme, dermal absorption of medication is probably the slowest, such that even therapeutic concentrations in blood may take several hours to reach. Moreover, absorption of the drug may continue for several hours after the source of the drug, for example, a transdermal patch, is removed, due to the depot of medication that accumulates in the upper layers of the skin. In these circumstances the dose is difficult to control, and if toxicity occurs, it is important that the patient be monitored for several hours after the patch is removed, in case of continued toxicity.[34]

Morphine provides a good and common example of why interpretation of blood concentrations alone in isolation from case history is difficult. First, opiate tolerance can vary tremendously between individuals and even within the same individual over a relatively short time span (days or weeks). Tolerance is an important consideration both clinically, where opiates may be chronically administered for pain, and in abuse situations where they are used for their euphoric effect. In clinical situations the issue of tolerance is complicated by the fact that patients in severe pain can tolerate higher doses of opioids than those in whom the pain is mild. It is also accepted that less opioid is required to prevent the recurrence of pain than to relieve it.[35] The form of the opioids will affect how rapidly the drug crosses the blood–brain barrier and, therefore, how potent it is. For example, heroin (diacetylmorphine) is at least twice as potent as morphine, probably because it is more lipid soluble and reaches the central nervous system faster than the more hydrophilic drug, morphine. It has been suggested that heroin may simply be a pro-drug for morphine, but one that reaches the site of action more efficiently. As a result, blood concentrations of morphine seen in heroin abuse deaths are frequently lower than concentrations resulting from the therapeutic administration of oral or parenteral morphine in clinical situations. The situation is complicated further because morphine is extensively metabolized by conjugation with glucuronic acid.

Originally it was assumed that this resulted in exclusively water-soluble metabolites, which were pharmacologically inactive. However, while morphine-3-glucuronide is devoid of narcotic activity, morphine-6-glucuronide, which is typically present in blood at higher concentrations than unconjugated morphine, is more potent than morphine itself.[36–38] Furthermore, much of the case data published in the clinical and forensic toxicology literature does not even distinguish between unconjugated and "total" morphine, let alone the 3- and 6-glucuronides, which are seldom measured routinely. With all these variables, it is no wonder unconjugated morphine blood concentrations correlate poorly with analgesic effect and central nervous system depression. A good example of this has been described where prolonged respiratory depression was observed in three patients in renal failure where morphine concentrations were extremely low, but where morphine-6-glucuronide had accumulated to toxic levels.[39]

6.3.2 Metabolism and Pharmacogenetics

A detailed treatise on the mechanisms of drug metabolism and the accumulation of drugs or metabolites due to impaired metabolism is beyond the scope of this chapter. However, it is worth pointing out at least three different scenarios where impaired metabolism can have a significant impact on the interpretation of results. Metabolism can be impaired by liver disease, such as advanced cirrhosis. However, not all metabolic pathways will be impaired equally by liver disease, and indeed some pathways may be affected little, if at all. Oxidative pathways, which are easily saturable, are likely to be affected more than others, such as glucuronidation. A person's metabolism may be genetically deficient, for example, in cytochrome P4502D6 (CYP2D6). This pathway is responsible for many oxidative transformations such as ring hydroxylation of the tricyclic antidepressants, and genetically poor metabolizers can be identified postmortem.[40] Third, co-ingested drugs can inhibit one or more drug metabolism pathways. For example, most or all of the selective serotonin-reuptake inhibitors (SSRIs) inhibit CYP2D6 and some are extremely potent in this regard. The degree of elevation of the drugs or metabolites affected depends very much on the respective dosages of the drugs involved and, not least, on the "metabolic reserve" of the individual patient. Some drug–drug interactions or genetic polymorphism may only result in slightly elevated drug or metabolite concentrations, perhaps necessitating lowering of dosage. However, in some circumstances the increases may be so dramatic as to cause life-threatening toxicity or death, particularly where the side effects were not sufficiently severe to alert the physician or patient that cardiotoxicity might be a problem. At least two cases involving probable impaired metabolism of imipramine have been described in the forensic literature.[41]

6.3.3 Calculation of Total Body Burden

Calculation of the total amount of drug ingested in self- or homicidal poisonings has been attempted many times over the years. This was attempted by the toxicologist who analyzed the remains found in the basement of Dr. Harvey Crippen, the renowned London poisoner who used hyoscine.[42] Calculations typically involve measurement of the drug or poison in the major organs including, where possible, skeletal muscle, and then taking into account the organ weights to arrive at a total estimate of the amount in the body. In some cases, the amounts have correlated very well with the available physical evidence (e.g., amount of drug in an empty injection vial or amount prescribed).[43,44] Doubtless, in some other examples attempted by toxicologists, correlation with the physical evidence was less convincing, or not possible. In order for such calculations to be meaningful, a number of factors must be assumed.

Perhaps most important, the particular part of the tissue or blood sample analyzed must be representative of the remainder of the organ or tissue. Since most organs are not homogeneous and because uneven postmortem diffusion (as discussed later) can lead to non-homogeneity of concentration, being sure of the average concentration of drug within any one organ may be difficult without analyzing that entire organ. While it is easy to know the weight of individual organs such as the heart, lungs, liver, kidneys, and brain, it is very difficult to reliably estimate the total amount of tissue into which most drugs readily distribute including the skeletal muscle. While the mass of skeletal muscle can be estimated from medical tables, given a person's height and weight, there is no assurance that the concentration of drug measured in one or two portions of skeletal muscle is representative of that in muscle from all other parts of the body.

Similar arguments apply to adipose tissue, where it is more difficult to obtain representative samples and accurately assay. It should also be borne in mind that for a person chronically taking a drug with a very large volume of distribution and long half-life, the equivalent of many times the total daily dose will be *normally* present in the body, even after therapeutic doses. Estimation of the total body burden of a drug may not be without value in all cases; it must be done with caution and the variables well understood and acknowledged. It is the rare cases of homicidal poisoning where significant weight may be erroneously placed on such calculations and where the stakes are the highest.

6.3.4 Estimation of Amount Ingested from Blood Levels

Given the foregoing discussion, it should go without saying that using pharmacokinetic calculations to try to estimate dosage, given a postmortem blood concentration, is of virtually no value and can be extremely misleading. Several factors make such calculations invalid. The blood drug concentration measured postmortem must be representative of that present at the time of death. As discussed elsewhere in this chapter, that is often not the case, and it is very difficult to predict whether any given postmortem drug concentration represents the concentration at the time of death, even for drugs for which postmortem redistribution is thought to be minimal. Any toxicologist who has routinely analyzed drugs in multiple blood samples from the same case knows how often those concentrations unexpectedly vary from sample to sample. Also, the drug must be at steady state at the time the person dies. By the very nature of drug-related deaths, that is rarely the case. Even if the gastric contents contain relatively little drug, much of the drug could still be present in the ileum, or at least not have attained equilibrium with muscle, adipose tissue, and the major organs. Finally, the rate of absorption, bioavailability, volume of distribution, half-life, rate of metabolism, and clearance are seldom known for any specific individual and can vary tremendously between subjects. The estimation of dose from postmortem blood concentrations is a practice of the foolhardy.

6.4 POSTMORTEM REDISTRIBUTION AND OTHER CHANGES

One question should be asked before attempting to interpret postmortem drug concentrations: Is the concentration found likely to represent, at least approximately, that present at the time of death? Unfortunately, the answer is often a flat no, or at least not necessarily. A number of factors need to be considered.

6.4.1 Incomplete Distribution

It is often the case that sudden deaths involving drugs are caused by abuse or suicidal drug overdose. Death will therefore usually occur before steady state has been reached. If a person is actively absorbing an overdose, it is likely that the concentration of the drug in blood leaving the liver (i.e., the inferior vena cava and right atrium) will have a somewhat higher concentration than, for example, venous blood returning from the peripheral vessels (e.g., femoral vein), for no other reason than a substantial amount of the drug will be absorbed during the course of circulation through the body. This has been demonstrated in living patients with concentration differences up to about twofold recorded between arterial and venous blood.[45,46] It is an open question if this is a practical issue in postmortem toxicology. In two cases of almost instantaneous death following heroin injection, the concentrations of morphine and codeine in blood collected from heart, brachial veins, and femoral veins were uniform, indicating a very rapid equilibrium.[47]

6.4.2 Postmortem Redistribution and Postmortem Diffusion

Postmortem redistribution and postmortem diffusion involve the movement of drug after death along a concentration gradient. Although the differentiation of these terms is not always clear in the literature, postmortem redistribution generally refers to the release of drugs from areas of higher concentration in organ tissues and subsequent diffusion into and through the capillaries and larger blood vessels of those organs. Postmortem diffusion generally refers to the diffusion of drug along a concentration gradient, from an area of high concentration to an area of low concentration. The usual scenario is where a high concentration of drug in the stomach contents (e.g., after an overdose) causes elevated concentrations of the drug in nearby tissue (e.g., proximal lobe of the liver) or blood.

Much is still unknown about the extent to which postmortem changes in drug concentration occur and the drugs affected; however, some generalizations can be made. Postmortem redistribution is likely to be most marked for drugs that are highly protein bound, but particularly those sequestered in the major organs such as the lungs and liver (e.g., tricyclic antidepressants, propoxyphene, chloroquine). Postmortem redistribution starts to occur within an hour after death and continues as the postmortem interval increases. The most important quantitative changes in blood drug concentration occur within the first 24 h and are highly site dependent. In general, increases will be greater in blood from "central" sites, such as the vessels near the major organs, than in more peripheral sites, such as the femoral veins. However, blood drug concentrations can vary fivefold or more between cardiac, hepatic, and pulmonary sites.[2,4] Given the very close proximity of these major vessels to one another and the organs they serve, it is impossible to even estimate peri-mortem drug concentrations based on the postmortem interval and site from which a blood sample was drawn. Even aside from the unpredictable nature of postmortem redistribution per se, blood from the "heart," if labeled as such, could have come from either of the cardiac atria or ventricles, the pulmonary vein or artery, the aorta, or the inferior vena cava.

Since it is known that many drug concentrations change after death, due to redistribution from the major organs, it is recommended that postmortem blood for drug and alcohol analysis be taken from a peripheral site such as the femoral vein. However, it should be emphasized that even if a "good" femoral blood sample is obtained, it is no guarantee that the drug concentrations subsequently measured will represent those present at the moment of death. In fact it is well established that femoral blood concentrations of many drugs can increase twofold or more after death. While it is possible that some of this increase is due to diffusion of released drug down the major vessels to the groin, it should be borne in mind that drug concentrations in skeletal muscle are often twofold or more higher than in the peri-mortem blood.[2,4] Given the mass of muscle surrounding these relatively small peripheral vessels, diffusion of drug directly into the blood across the vessel wall is very likely to occur. While in many of the published studies on postmortem redistribution the vessels have been carefully ligated prior to taking blood samples, this is rarely done during routine medicolegal autopsies. Consequently, blood labeled as "femoral" may contain blood drawn down from the inferior vena cava. This is particularly likely to be the case where large volumes (e.g., 30 to 50 mL) have been obtained from a supposedly femoral site. It should also be obvious that it does not matter whether the syringe needle is pointing down toward the leg!

The mechanisms for postmortem redistribution probably involve release of drug from protein-bound sites after death occurs, with subsequent diffusion into interstitial fluid, through the capillaries and into the larger blood vessels. Since this process appears to start within an hour or so of death, decomposition or putrefaction per se is not likely to play a role, at least in the early stages. It is more likely that cessation of active cellular processes and the rapid fall in blood and tissue pH that occurs after death would lead to changes in the conformation of proteins and therefore release of some proportion of drugs present from the protein-bound state. It is important to bear in mind that these changes start well before putrefaction and microbiological action is likely to play a role.

Other types of postmortem diffusion can occur. For example, it has been demonstrated that over a period of a day or more, significant changes in drug concentrations in the major organs can occur. This has been shown for the tricyclic antidepressants, where concentrations in the lungs tended to decrease, commensurate with an increase in concentration in the liver.[48] This study was done in such a manner as to show that these changes can occur due to direct diffusion from one organ to the other, independent of the residue of drug in the stomach. However, the magnitude of these changes is not likely to affect interpretation of tissue drug concentrations to a significant extent. It has also been demonstrated that postmortem diffusion of drug from the stomach can markedly increase drug concentrations in proximal lobes of the liver and lungs, as well as postmortem blood in some of the central vessels.[12,13] Ironically, when organ tissue was analyzed in previous decades, postmortem diffusion into the liver or lungs might have been less important since it was not uncommon to homogenize large amounts of organ tissue (e.g., 500 g), such that any local increases in concentration would be averaged out. However, today the tendency in many laboratories is to homogenize small amounts of tissue (e.g., 2 to 10 g), which could lead to a gross overestimation of the amount of drug in the organ if the sampled tissue were taken close to the stomach. The potential for postmortem diffusion of drugs in this manner has been known for decades, but recent work has brought the issue the attention it deserves and better quantified the potential changes.

Aspiration of gastric contents can provide one more important mechanism whereby postmortem blood concentrations can be artificially elevated.[49] This can occur agonally, as death is occurring, or after death, during transportation of the body. It is a factor that may more commonly occur after overdosage where the stomach contains a very concentrated cocktail of one or more drugs, with or without alcohol. However, it could also be very important to consider in deaths where therapeutic doses have been consumed and death occurs as a result of unrelated natural causes. It is not uncommon, for example, for tricyclic antidepressants to be taken as a single nightly dose, and in fact large doses of many antipsychotic drugs are taken at night. This can result in drug concentrations in the stomach of the order of grams per liter, which if aspirated could result in significant increases in some local postmortem blood concentrations. Not surprisingly, the pulmonary vein and artery blood concentrations are elevated to the greatest extent following simulated aspiration. This is more significant than it might seem because much of the so-called "heart blood," which is often sampled at autopsy, is in fact blood of pulmonary origin drawn from the major pulmonary vessels or the left atrium. A comprehensive discussion of the possible mechanisms for postmortem redistribution has been published.[50]

6.5 OTHER CONSIDERATIONS

6.5.1 Trauma

Severe trauma can affect the interpretation of both alcohol and drug concentrations. For example, it is not uncommon for severe motor vehicle accidents to result in rupture of the stomach and diaphragm. This can easily result in the release of gastric fluid into the body cavity. Because blood may be difficult to obtain from discrete vessels, pooled blood from the pleural cavity may be sampled. If an autopsy is performed, the origin and nature of the fluid so drawn should be obvious, and hopefully noted. However, if an autopsy is not performed and "blood" is sampled through the chest wall in an attempt to obtain cardiac blood, the coroner or medical examiner may be unaware that the sample is contaminated with gastric fluid. If even small, therapeutic amounts of drug remain unabsorbed in the gastric contents in these circumstances, it can result in what appears to be a grossly elevated "blood" drug (or alcohol) concentration. The release of microorganisms from the gastrointestinal tract and subsequent potential for fermentation are well-recognized problems.

Trauma causing extended blood loss may also affect blood drug levels, since the physiological reactions include, in addition to increased heart rate and peripheral vasoconstriction, plasma volume refill. Hence, blood levels may increase or drop, depending on their concentrations in the restoration fluid. Experimentally, codeine and morphine blood levels were found to increase significantly after controlled exsanguination in rats[51] and a similar study showed that the analgesic effect of morphine was elevated when given to rats with hemorrhagic shock.[52] Although further studies are needed to determine the impact of and conditions for such antemortem redistribution for several drugs with different pharmacokinetic properties, the phenomenon should be considered in trauma cases with longer duration of blood loss.

6.5.2 Artifacts of Medication Delivery

Artifacts of absorption and distribution must be recognized when interpreting postmortem blood concentrations. For example, it is quite common to find grossly elevated concentrations of lidocaine in cases where resuscitation has been unsuccessfully attempted. Concentrations may be two to five times those normally considered therapeutic when lidocaine is given by intravenous infusion for the treatment of cardiac arrhythmias. If lidocaine is administered as a bolus intracardiac injection and normal cardiac rhythm never established, very high local concentrations will result in the cardiac blood. These could be interpreted as "fatal" unless all the circumstances are considered.

Devices that automatically deliver medication by the parenteral route can lead to artificially high blood concentrations postmortem. Most of these devices will continue to periodically dispense medication, usually narcotics, into the vein after a person dies, unless they are switched off and disconnected quickly. This can result in extremely high local concentrations of drug, which may be misinterpreted as an overdose.

Transdermal patches left on a body after death will give rise to locally high concentrations of the drug (e.g., fentanyl). Since these patches rely primarily on passive diffusion across a rate-limiting membrane for drug delivery, the concentration of the medication in the local area will continue to rise after death, albeit at a slower rate. Since blood circulation through the skin obviously stops after death, the drug will no longer be transported away except by diffusion, allowing a local build-up of drug. However, such a high concentration gradient exists between the gel containing the medication in the patch and the skin, that even modest postmortem diffusion might be expected to raise the postmortem blood and tissue concentrations up to several inches away.

6.5.3 Additive and Synergistic Toxicity

When interpreting drug concentrations it is important to take into account the sum of the effects of all of the drugs detected. This is often an issue in drug abuse deaths, particularly those involving prescription drugs. Such deaths often involve multiple drugs of the same type (e.g., benzodiazepines or narcotics), individually present in "therapeutic" amounts, and often in combination with alcohol. Interpretation of blood drug concentrations in these cases has to take into account disease that may be present, and the total amounts of drugs and alcohol. In many cases, these effects may simply be additive, i.e., simply the sum of the individual effects of the drugs involved. In other cases, the effect may be truly synergistic, where the toxicity is greater than would be expected based on the pharmacology and concentrations of the individual drugs. Cases where multiple drugs are present, with or without alcohol, are probably the most difficult to interpret and rely heavily on the experience of the interpreter and a reliable and complete case history.

6.5.4 Adverse Reactions

A death attributed to neuroleptic malignant syndrome (NMS) resulting from therapy with phenothiazine or some other neuroleptics is a good example of a fatal adverse drug reaction.[53] Combinations of drugs can result in similar syndromes, such as combination of a tricyclic antidepressant and a monoamine oxidase inhibitor (MAOI) causing serotonin syndrome.[54] Although not always fatal, a serotonin reaction can result in death and might be considered where there is no other reasonable cause of death and especially where there are elevated concentrations of MAOIs and either tricyclic antidepressants or SSRIs. It should be borne in mind that by the very nature of drug–drug or other adverse reactions, blood concentrations of the drug(s) involved are seldom predictive of the outcome and are often well within the range normally expected from therapeutic doses. In the absence of clinical observations, such fatalities can be very difficult to diagnose accurately.

6.5.5 Drug Instability

It should not be overlooked that many drugs are unstable in any biological fluid. Cocaine is probably the most notable example. It is broken down in aqueous solution and enzymatically in blood or plasma to benzoylecgonine and methylecgonine, neither of which has much pharmacological activity. While cocaine may be stabilized to some extent by the addition of fluoride after the blood is collected, the extent of breakdown between death and autopsy must be considered. Unfortunately, there are many variables to consider. First, the toxicity of cocaine itself correlates only poorly with blood concentration, even in the living. There is good evidence that cocaine concentrations in postmortem blood can increase or decrease, depending on the exact site of collection.[55,56] There are probably competing effects due to variable breakdown in different areas of the body and true postmortem redistribution. The collection and measurement of cocaine in vitreous humor has been attempted to overcome these problems. However, it has been shown that cocaine will often, if irreproducible, increase in concentration with time in the vitreous humor. The mechanism for this has not been proved, but it likely involves postmortem redistribution from the brain, where cocaine is known to concentrate relative to the blood, into the eye via the optic nerve and other soft tissue. It is possible that time-dependent postmortem increases in vitreous concentrations may occur for other drugs where those drugs attain higher concentrations in the brain.

6.5.6 Interpretation Using Tables of Values

There probably is not a forensic toxicologist or pathologist alive who has not used published tables as a reference when trying to interpret postmortem blood concentrations. Tables of such values became a necessary evil due to the sheer volume of medical and forensic literature. However, they unfortunately perpetuate the myth that postmortem toxicology results can be interpreted solely using, or heavily relying on, so-called "therapeutic," "toxic," and "fatal" ranges. Although tables of drug concentrations can serve as a useful reference point, it should be borne in mind that many of the values in these tables are derived from serum or plasma data from living patients, that the ranges are seldom referenced to published cases, and that they may not take into account or state other variables such as postmortem redistribution, time of survival after intoxication, or the presence of other drugs, natural disease, or injury. Having stated that, one compilation has attempted to address some of these issues and indeed bases the postmortem values it lists exclusively on carefully collected femoral blood samples.[57] In that compilation, values are also provided for "controls," consisting of deceased subjects, who with certainty died of causes other than intoxication, and who were not incapacitated at the time for the demise. Such data are equally important as levels in fatal cases and additional compilations using this approach are encouraged.

6.6 CONCLUSION

In the final analysis, postmortem toxicology results must be interpreted with regard to all of the available information, including medical history, information from the scene, autopsy findings, nature and exact location of the postmortem samples collected, and the circumstances of the death. Only after weighing all of these variables can postmortem results be reliably interpreted. Even then, it must be admitted that *reliable* interpretation of some results is simply not possible based on the available information. In many respects, the desirable underlying approach to the interpretation of postmortem drug concentrations is not much different from that used a century ago: a good scene investigation, medical investigation, laboratory investigation, and the application of common sense. We hope we are also wiser now.

REFERENCES

1. Logan, B.K. and Lindholm, G., Gastric contamination of postmortem blood samples during blind-stick sample collection, *Am. J. Forensic Med. Pathol.*, 17, 109, 1996.
2. Jones, G.R. and Pounder, D.J., Site dependence of drug concentrations in postmortem blood — a case study, *J. Anal. Toxicol.*, 11, 186, 1987.
3. Prouty, R.W. and Anderson, W.H., The forensic implications of site and temporal differences on predicting blood-drug concentrations, *J. Forensic Sci.*, 35, 243, 1990.
4. Pounder, D.J. and Jones, G.R., Post-mortem drug redistribution — a toxicological nightmare, *Forensic Sci. Int.*, 45, 253, 1990.
5. Vorpahl, T.E. and Coe, J.I., Correlation of antemortem and postmortem digoxin levels, *J. Forensic Sci.*, 23, 329, 1978.
6. Ziminski, K.R., Wemyss, C.T., Bidanset, J.H., Manning, T.J., and Lukash, L., Comparative study of postmortem barbiturates, methadone, and morphine in vitreous humor, blood, and tissue, *J. Forensic Sci.,* 29, 903, 1984.
7. Worm, K. and Steentoft, A., A comparison of post-mortem concentrations of basic drugs in femoral whole blood and vitreous humor, in *Proceedings of the International Congress of Clinical Toxicology, Poison Control and Analytical Toxicology, Lux Tox '90, Societe des Sciences Medicales du Grand-Duche de Luxembourg,* Wennig, R., Ed., Luxembourg, 1990, 438.
8. Bermejo, A.M., Ramos, I., Fernandzez, P., Lopez-Rivadulla, M., Cruz, A., Chiarotti, M., Fucci, N., and Marsilli, R., Morphine determination by gas chromatography/mass spectrometry in human vitreous humor and comparison with radioimmunoassay, *J. Anal. Toxicol.*, 16, 372, 1992.
9. McKinney, P.E., Phillips, S., Gomez, H.F., Brent, J., MacIntyre, M.W., and Watson, W.A., Vitreous humor cocaine and metabolite concentrations: do postmortem specimens reflect blood levels at the time of death? *J. Forensic Sci.*, 40, 102, 1995.
10. Robertson, M.D. and Drummer, O.H., Benzodiazepine concentrations in vitreous humor, *Bull. Int. Assoc. Forensic Toxicol.*, 25, 28, 1995.
11. Holmgren, P., Druid, H., Holmgren, A., and Ahlner, J., Stability of drugs in stored femoral blood and vitreous humor, *J. Forensic Sci.,* 49, 820, 2004.
12. Pounder, D.J., Fuke, C., Cox, D.E., Smith, D., and Kuroda, N., Postmortem diffusion of drugs from gastric residue: an experimental study, *Am. J. Forensic Med. Pathol.*, 17, 1, 1996.
13. Pounder, D.J., Adams, E., Fuke, C., and Langford, A.M., Site to site variability of postmortem drug concentrations in liver and lung, *J. Forensic Sci.*, 41, 927, 1996.
14. Anderson, D.T., Fritz, K.L., and Muto, J.J., Oxycontin: the concept of a "ghost pill" and the postmortem tissue distribution of oxycodone in 36 cases, *J. Anal. Toxicol.*, 26, 448, 2002.

15. Ku, M.T., Bezoars, *Clin. Toxicol. Rev.*, 18, June 1996.
16. Christensen, H., Steentoft, A., and Worm, K., Muscle as an autopsy material for evaluation of fatal cases of drug overdose, *J. Forensic Sci. Soc.*, 25, 191, 1985.
17. Winek, C.L. and Esposito, F.M., Comparative study of ethanol levels in blood versus bone marrow, vitreous humor, bile and urine, *Forensic Sci. Int.*, 20, 1727, 1980.
18. Winek, C.L., Westwood, S.E., and Wahba, W.W., Plasma versus bone marrow desipramine: a comparative study, *Forensic Sci. Int.,* 48, 49–57, 1990.
19. Winek, C.L., Morris, E.M., and Wahba, W.W., The use of bone marrow in the study of postmortem redistribution of nortriptyline, *J. Anal. Toxicol.,* 17, 93–98, 1993.
20. Poklis, A. and Saady, J.J., Arsenic poisoning: acute or chronic? Suicide or murder? *Am. J. Forensic Med. Pathol.*, 11, 226, 1990.
21. Kintz, P., Cirimele, V., Jamey, C., and Ludes, B., Testing for GHB in hair by GC/MS/MS after a single exposure. Application to document sexual assault, *J. Forensic Sci.*, 48(1), 195–200, 2003.
22. Villain, M., Cheze, M., Tracqui, A., Ludes, B., and Kintz, P., Testing for zopiclone in hair application to drug-facilitated crimes, *Forensic Sci. Int.,* 145(2–3), 117–121, 2004.
23. Frison, G., Favretto, D., Tedeschi, L., and Ferrara, S.D., Detection of thiopental and pentobarbital in head and pubic hair in a case of drug-facilitated sexual assault, *Forensic Sci. Int.*, 133(1–2), 171–174, 2003.
24. Cheze, M., Duffort, G., Deveaux, M., and Pepin, G., Hair analysis by liquid chromatography-tandem mass spectrometry in toxicological investigation of drug-facilitated crimes: report of 128 cases over the period June 2003–May 2004 in metropolitan Paris, *Forensic Sci. Int.,* 153(1), 3–10, 2005.
25. Tagliaro, F., De Battisti, Z., Smith, F.P., and Marigo, M., Death from heroin overdose: findings from hair analysis, *Lancet,* 351(9120), 1923–1925, 1998.
26. Kronstrand, R., Grundin, R., and Jonsson, J., Incidence of opiates, amphetamines, and cocaine in hair and blood in fatal cases of heroin overdose, *Forensic Sci. Int.,* 92(1), 29–38, 1998.
27. Darke, S., Hall, W., Kaye, S., Ross, J., and Duflou, J., Hair morphine concentrations of fatal heroin overdose cases and living heroin users, *Addiction,* 97(8), 977–984, 2002.
28. Musshoff, F., Lachenmeier, K., Wollersen, H., Lichtermann, D., and Madea, B., Opiate concentrations in hair from subjects in a controlled heroin-maintenance program and from opiate-associated fatalities, *J. Anal. Toxicol.*, 29(5), 345–352, 2005.
29. Kronstrand, R., Nystrom, I., Strandberg, J., and Druid, H., Screening for drugs of abuse in hair with ion spray LC-MS-MS, *Forensic Sci. Int.,* 145(2–3), 183–190, 2004.
30. Cone, E.J., Mechanisms of drug incorporation into hair, *Ther. Drug Monit.*, 18(4), 438–443, 1996.
31. Palmeri, A., Pichini, S., Pacifici, R., Zuccaro, P., and Lopez, A., Drugs in nails: physiology, pharmacokinetics and forensic toxicology, *Clin. Pharmacokinet.*, 38(2), 95–110, 2000.
32. Odei, E.L.A., Insulin habituation and psychopathy, *Br. Med. J.,* 2, 346, 1968.
33. Retsas, S., Insulin abuse by a drug addict, *Br. Med. J.*, 2, 792, 1972.
34. Duragesic Monograph, Janssen Pharmaceutica, Titusville, NJ, April 1992.
35. Jaffe, J.H. and Martin, W.R., Opioid analgesics and antagonists, in *Goodman and Gilman's The Pharmacological Basis of Therapeutics*, Gilman, A.G., Rall, T.W., Nies, A.S., and Taylor, P., Eds., Pergamon Press, New York, 1990, chap. 21.
36. Shimomura, K., Kamata, O., Ueki., S., et al., Analgesic affects of morphine glucuronides, *Tohoku J. Exp. Med.*, 105, 45, 1971.
37. Yoshimura, H., Ida, S., Oguri, K., and Tsukamoto, H., Biochemical basis for analgesic activity of morphine-6-glucuronide. I. Penetration of morphine-6-glucuronide in the brain of rats, *Biochem. Pharmacol.*, 22, 1423, 1973.
38. Westerling, D., Persson, C., and Hoglund, P., Plasma concentrations of morphine, morphine-3-glucuronide, and morphine-6-glucuronide after intravenous and oral administration to healthy volunteers: relationship to nonanalgesic actions, *Ther. Drug Monit.*, 17, 287, 1995.
39. Osborne, R.J., Joel, S.P., and Slevin, M.L., Morphine intoxication in renal failure: the role of morphine-6-glucuronide, *Br. Med. J.*, 292, 1548, 1986.
40. Druid, H., Holmgren, P., Carlsson, B., and Ahlner, J., Cytochrome P450 2D6 (CYP2D6) genotyping on postmortem blood as a supplementary tool for interpretation of forensic toxicological results, *Forensic Sci. Int.,* 99(1), 25–34, 1999.

41. Swanson, J.R., Jones, G.R., Krasselt, W., Denmark, L.N., and Ratti, F., Death of two subjects due to chronic imipramine and desipramine metabolite accumulation during chronic therapy: a review of the literature and possible mechanisms, *J. Forensic Sci.*, 42, 335, 1997.
42. Anonymous, The Crippen trial: special report of the medical evidence, *Br. Med. J.*, 2, 1372, 1910.
43. Saady, J.J., Blanke, R.V., and Poklis, A., Estimation of the body burden of arsenic in a child fatally poisoned by arsenite weedkiller, *J. Anal. Toxicol.*, 13, 310, 1989.
44. Pounder, D.J. and Davies, J.I., Zopiclone poisoning: tissue distribution and potential for postmortem diffusion, *Forensic Sci. Int.*, 65, 177, 1994.
45. Baud, F.J., Buisine, A., Bismuth, C., Galliot, M., Vicaut, E., Bourdon, R., and Fournier, P.E., Arterio-venous plasma concentration differences in amitriptyline overdose, *J. Toxicol. Clin. Toxicol.*, 23, 391, 1985.
46. Sato, S., Baud, F.J., Bismuth, C., Galliot, M., Vicaut, E., and Buisine, A., Arterial-venous plasma concentration differences of meprobamate in acute human poisonings, *Hum. Toxicol.*, 5, 243, 1986.
47. Druid, H. and Holmgren, P., Fatal injections of heroin. Interpretation of toxicological findings in multiple specimens, *Int. J. Legal Med.*, 112(1), 62–66, 1999.
48. Hilberg, T., Morland, J., and Bjorneboe, A., Postmortem release of amitriptyline from the lungs; a mechanism of postmortem drug redistribution, *Forensic Sci. Int.*, 64, 47–55, 1994.
49. Pounder, D.J. and Yonemitsu, K., Postmortem absorption of drugs and ethanol from aspirated vomitus — an experimental model, *Forensic Sci. Int.*, 51, 189, 1991.
50. Pelissier-Alicot, A.L., Gaulier, J.M., Champsaur, P., and Marquet, P., Mechanisms underlying post-mortem redistribution of drugs: a review, *J. Anal. Toxicol.*, 27, 53, 2003.
51. Kugelberg, F.C., Holmgren, P., and Druid, H., Codeine and morphine blood concentrations increase during blood loss, *J. Forensic Sci.*, 48, 664, 2003.
52. De Paepe, P., Belpaire, F.M., Rosseel, M.T., and Buylaert, W.A., The influence of hemorrhagic shock on the pharmacokinetics and the analgesic effect of morphine in the rat, *Fundam. Clin. Pharmacol.*, 12, 624, 1998.
53. Laposata, E.A., Hale, P., Jr., and Poklis, A., Evaluation of sudden death in psychiatric patients with special reference to phenothiazine therapy: forensic pathology, *J. Forensic Sci.*, 33, 432, 1988.
54. Sternbach, H., The serotonin syndrome, *Am. J. Psychiatry*, 148, 705, 1991.
55. Hearn, W.L., Keran, E.E., Wei, H., and Hime, G., Site-dependent postmortem changes in blood cocaine concentrations, *J. Forensic Sci.*, 36, 673, 1991.
56. Logan, B.K., Smirnow, D., and Gullberg, R.G., Lack of predictable site-dependent differences and time-dependent changes in postmortem concentrations of cocaine, benzoylecgonine, and cocaethylene in humans, *J. Anal. Toxicol.*, 20, 23, 1997.
57. Druid, H. and Holmgren, P., A compilation of fatal and control concentration of drugs in postmortem femoral blood, *J. Forensic Sci.*, 42, 79, 1997.

APPENDIX I

Glossary of Terms in Forensic Toxicology

Compiled by H. Chip Walls, B.S.
Department of Pathology, Forensic Toxicology Laboratory, University of Miami, Miami, Florida

Absolute Method A method in which characterization is based on physically defined (absolute) standards.

Accreditation (l) A formal process by which a laboratory is evaluated, with respect to established criteria, for its competence to perform a specified kind(s) of measurement(s); (2) the decision based upon such a process; (3) formal recognition that a testing laboratory is competent to carry out specific tests or specific types of tests.

Accuracy Closeness of the agreement between the result of a measurement and a true value of the measured quantity.

Acetaldehyde The first product of ethanol metabolism.

Acute Severe, usually crucial, often dangerous in which relatively rapid changes are occurring. An acute exposure runs a comparatively short course.

Acute tolerance The development of tolerance within the course of a single exposure to a drug.

Alcohol dehydrogenase (ADH) The main enzyme that catalyzes the conversion of ethanol to acetaldehyde.

Aldehyde dehydrogenase (ALDH) The enzyme that converts acetaldehyde to acetate.

Aliquot (1) A divisor that does not divide a sample into a number of equal parts without leaving a remainder; (2) a sample resulting from such a divisor.

Analyte The specific component measured in a chemical analysis.

Analytical run (series) A set of measurements carried out successively by one analyst using the same measuring system, at the same location, under the same conditions, and during the same short period of time.

Analytical sensitivity The ability of a method or instrument to discriminate between samples having different concentrations or containing different amounts of the analyte. Slope of the analytical calibration function.

Analytical specificity Ability of a measurement procedure to determine solely the measurable quantity (desired substance) it purports to measure and not others.

Analytical wavelength Any wavelength at which an absorbance measurement is made for the purpose of the determination of a constituent of a sample.

Antemortem Before death, occurring before death.

Ascites An abnormal accumulation of fluid in the peritoneal cavity of the abdomen.

Assignable cause A cause believed to be responsible for an identifiable change in precision or accuracy of a measurement process.

Beer's law The absorbance of a homogeneous sample containing an absorbing substance is directly proportional to the concentration of the absorbing substance.

Bias A systematic error inherent in a method or caused by some artifact or idiosyncrasy of the measurement system. Temperature effects and extraction inefficiencies are examples of errors inherent in the method. Blanks, contamination, mechanical losses, and calibration errors are examples of artifact errors. Bias can be either positive or negative, and several kinds of error can exist concurrently. Therefore, net bias is all that can be evaluated.

Blank (1) The measured value obtained when a specified component of a sample is not present during the measurement. In such a case, the measured value (or signal) for the component is believed to be due to artifacts and should be deducted from a measured value to give a net value due solely to the component contained in the sample. The blank measurement must be made so that the correction process is valid. (2) Biological specimen with no detectable drugs added, routinely analyzed to ensure that no false-positive results are obtained.

Blind sample A control sample submitted for analysis as a routine specimen whose composition is known to the submitter but unknown to the analyst. A blind sample is one way to test the proficiency of a measurement process.

Calibrant Substance used to calibrate, or to establish the analytical response of, a measurement system.

Calibration Comparison of a measurement standard or instrument with another standard or instrument to report or eliminate, by adjustment, any variation or deviation in the accuracy of the item being compared.

Central line The long-term expected value of a variable displayed on a control chart.

Certification A written declaration that a particular product or service complies with stated criteria.

Certified reference material (CRM) A reference material one or more of whose property values are certified by a technically valid procedure, accompanied by or traceable to a certificate or other documentation that is issued by a certifying body. [ISO Guide 30: 1981 (E)]

Certified value The value that appears in a certificate as the best estimate of the value for a property of a certified reference material.

Chain of custody (COC) Handling samples in a way that supports legal testimony to prove that the sample integrity and identification of the sample have not been violated as well as the documentation describing these procedures.

Chance cause A cause for variability of a measurement process that occurs unpredictably, for unknown reasons, and is believed to happen by chance alone.

Check standard (in physical calibration) An artifact measured periodically, the results of which typically are plotted on a control chart to evaluate the measurement process.

Chronic Persistent, prolonged, repeated.

Chronic tolerance The gradual decrease in degree of effect produced at the same blood concentration in the course of repeated exposures to that drug.

Coefficient of variation The standard deviation divided by the value of the parameter measured.

Comparative method A method that is based on the intercomparison of the sample with a chemical standard.

Composite sample A sample composed of two or more components selected to represent a population of interest.

Concentration Amount of a drug in a unit volume of biological fluid, expressed as weight/volume. Urine concentrations are usually expressed either as nanograms per milliliter (ng/ml), micrograms per milliliter (μg/ml), or milligrams per liter (mg/l). (There are 28,000,000 micrograms in an ounce, and 1,000 nanograms in a microgram.)

Confidence interval That range of values, calculated from an estimate of the mean and the standard deviation, which is expected to include the population mean with a stated level of confidence. In the same manner, confidence intervals can also be calculated for standard deviations, lines, slopes, and points.

Confirmation A second test by an alternate chemical method to positively identify a drug or metabolite. Confirmations are carried out on presumptive positives from initial screens.

Control chart A graphical plot of test results with respect to time or sequence of measurement together with limits in which they are expected to lie when the system is in a state of statistical control.

Control limits The limits shown on a control chart beyond which it is highly improbable that a point could lie while the system remains in a state of statistical control.

Control sample A material of known composition that is analyzed concurrently with test samples to evaluate a measurement process. (See also Check standard.)

Correlation coefficient Measures the strength of the relation between two sets of numbers, such as instrument response and standard concentration.

Cross-reacting substances In immunoassays, refers to substances that react with antiserum produced specifically for other substances.

Cross-sensitivity A quantitative measure of the response for an undesired constituent or interferent as compared to that for a constituent of interest.

Cutoff level (threshold) Value serving as an administrative breakpoint (or cutoff point) for labeling a screening test result positive or negative.

Cytochrome P450 A detoxifying enzyme found in liver cells.

Detection limit or limit of detection (LOD) The lowest concentration of a drug that can reliably be detected. Smallest result of a measurement by a given measurement procedure that can be accepted with a stated confidence level as being different from the value of the measurable quantity obtained on blank material.

Double blind A sample, known by the submitter but supplied to an analyst in such a way that neither its composition nor its identification as a check sample or standard is known to the analyst.

Duplicate measurement A second measurement made on the same or identical sample of material to assist in the evaluation of measurement variance.

Endogenous Produced or originating within the body by natural processes such as intermediary metabolism.

Enzymes Proteins whose function is to drive the chemical reactions of the body — a catalyst of biochemical reactions.

False negative An erroneous result in an assay that indicates the absence of a drug that is actually present.

False-negative rate The proportion of true positive samples that give a negative result.

False positive An erroneous result in an assay that indicates the presence of a drug that is actually not present.

False-positive rate The proportion of true negative samples that give a positive test result.

Fume Gas-like emanation containing minute solid particles arising from the heating of a solid body such as lead, distinct from a gas or vapor. This physical change is often accompanied by a chemical reaction such as oxidation. Fumes flocculate and sometimes coalesce. Odorous gases and vapors are not fumes.

Hepatocyte Name given to cells within the liver.

Hyperglycemia An excessive amount of glucose in the blood.

Hypoglycemia An abnormally low concentration of glucose in the circulating blood.

Impairment Decreased ability to perform safely a given task.

Infrared Pertaining to the region of the electromagnetic spectrum from approximately 0.78 to 300 microns (780 to 300,000 nanometers).

Insulin A hormone produced in the islets of Langerhans in the pancreas as a response to elevated blood sugar levels. The hormone permits the metabolism and utilization of glucose.

Interferant A chemical compound or substance other than the substance of interest (e.g., ethanol) to which the measuring instrument responds to give a falsely elevated result.

Interfering substances Substances other than the analyte that give a similar analytical response or alter the analytical result.

Interindividual variation Distribution of the values of a type of quantity in individuals of a given set.

Intraindividual variation Distribution of the values of a type of quantity in a given individual.

Limit of quantification (LOQ) The lower limit of concentration or amount of substance that must be present before a method is considered to provide quantitative results. By convention, LOQ = 10 x so, where so = the estimate of the standard deviation at the lowest level of measurement.

Matrix The composition of the biological sample being analyzed, consisting of proteins, lipids, and other biomolecules that can affect analyte recovery.

Matrix effects Influence of a component in the analytical sample other than the component being investigated on the measurement being made.

MEOS The microsomal ethanol oxidizing system; an enzyme system in liver that converts ethanol to acetaldehyde.

Metabolite A compound produced from chemical changes of a drug in the body.

Microsomal enzymes Detoxifying enzymes associated with certain membranes (smooth endoplasmic reticulum) within cells.

Ordinal scale Ordered set of measurements consisting of words and/or numbers indicating the magnitude of the possible values that a type of quantity can take.

Outlier A value in a sample of values so far separated from the remainder as to suggest that it may be from a different population.

Perimortem At or near the time of death.

Pharmacodynamics The study of the relationship of drug concentration to drug effects.

Pharmacokinetics The study of the time course of the processes (absorption, distribution, metabolism, and excretion) a drug undergoes in the body.

Physical dependence A state that develops in parallel with chronic tolerance and is revealed by the occurrence of serious disturbances (abstinence syndrome) when drug intake is terminated.

Postmortem After death, occurring after death, of or pertaining to a postmortem examination, an autopsy.

Precision Closeness of agreement between independent results of measurements obtained by a measurement procedure under prescribed conditions (standard deviation).

Presumptive positive Sample that has been flagged as positive by screening but that has not been confirmed by an equally sensitive alternative chemical method.

Proficiency-testing specimen A specimen whose expected results are unknown to anyone in the laboratory, known only by an external agency, and later revealed to the laboratory as an aid to laboratory improvement and/or a condition of licensure.

Psycho Pertaining to the mind and mental processes.

Psychoactive Affecting the mind or mental processes.

Psychochemical A substance affecting the mind or mental processes.

Psychology The science of mental processes and behavior.

Psychomotor Of or pertaining to muscular activity associated with the mental process.

Psychomotor functions Matters of mental and motor function.

Psychosis Severe mental disorder, with or without organic damage, characterized by deterioration of normal intellectual and social functioning and by partial or complete withdrawal from reality.

Psychotomimetic Pertaining to or inducing symptoms of a psychotic state.

Psychotropic Having a mind-altering effect.

Qualitative test Chemical analysis to identify one or more components of a mixture.

Quality assurance (QA) Practices that assure accurate laboratory results.

Quality control (QC) Those techniques used to monitor errors that can cause a deterioration in the quality of laboratory results. Control material most often refers to a specimen, the expected results of which are known to the analyst, that is routinely analyzed to ensure that the expected results are obtained.

Quantitative test Chemical analysis to determine the amounts or concentrations of one or more components of a mixture.

Repeatability Closeness of agreement between the results of successive measurements during a short time (within run standard deviation).

Reproducibility Closeness of agreement between the results of measurements of the same measurable quantity on different occasions, made by different observers, using different calibrations, at different times (between run standard deviation).

Screen A series of initial tests designed to separate samples containing drugs at or above a particular minimum concentration from those below that minimum concentration (positive vs. negative).

Sensitivity The detection limit, expressed as a concentration of the analyte in the specimen.

Specificity Quality of an analytical technique that tends to exclude all substances but the analyte from affecting the result.

Split specimen Laboratory specimen that is divided and submitted to the analyst, unknown to him or her, as two different specimens with different identifications.

Standard Authentic sample of the analyte of known purity, or a solution of the analyte of a known concentration.

Substrate The substance (molecule) acted upon by an enzyme; its conversion to a particular product is catalyzed by a specific enzyme.

Tolerance A state that develops after long-term exposure to a drug. Metabolic tolerance infers a faster removal, oxidation by the liver. Functional tolerance infers a change in sensitivity of the organ to the effects of the drug.

Tolerance interval That range of values within which a specified percentage of individual values of a population, measurements, or sample are expected to lie with a stated level of confidence.

Ultraviolet Pertaining to the region of the electromagnetic spectrum from approximately 10 to 380 nm.

Visible Pertaining to radiant energy in the electromagnetic spectral range visible to the human eye, approximately 380 to 780 nm.

Wavelength A property of radiant energy, such as IR, visible, or UV. The distance measured along the line of propagation, between two points that are in phase on adjacent waves.

APPENDIX II

Common Abbreviations

Compiled by H. Chip Walls, B.S.
Department of Pathology, Forensic Toxicology Laboratory, University of Miami, Miami, Florida

ABS	Absorbance error (EMIT)
AM	Morning, antemortem
AMPH	Amphetamines
AP	Attending physician
APAP	Acetaminophen
ASA	Salicylates
ASCVD	Arteriosclerotic cardiovascular disease
ASHD	Arteriosclerotic heart disease
BAC	Blood alcohol concentration
BDS	Basic drug screen
BE	Benzoylecgonine
BENZO	Benzodiazepine(s)
Bld	Blood
BP	Blood pressure
BSV	Blue-stoppered vacutainer
CAP	College of American Pathologists
CBC	Complete blood count
CI	Chemical ionization (in mass spectrometry)
CID	Criminal investigation department
CN	Cyanide
CO	Carbon monoxide
Co	County
c/o	Complain(-ing), (-ed), (-t) of
COPD	Chronic obstructive pulmonary disease
DC	Death certificate
Decd	Decedent/deceased
DM	Diabetes melitus
DNR	Do not resuscitate
DOH	Department of Health
D/T	Due to
DUI	Driving under the influence
DUID	DUI for drugs
DWI	Driving while intoxicated
dx	Diagnosed
EB	Eastbound
ECD	Electron capture detector (GC)
EI	Electron impact ionization (in mass spectrometry)
EMIT	Enzyme-multiplied immunoassay testing
ER	Emergency room

ET	Evidence technician
EtOH	Ethanol/alcohol
Ext	Extract
Extn	Extraction
FH	Funeral home
FID	Flame ionization detector (GC)
FS	Fingerstick
FTD	Failed to detect
Fx	Fracture
g	Gram
g%	Gram percent
GC	Gastric contents, gas chromatography
GC/MS	Gas chromatography/mass spectrometry
gm	Gram
GSV	Gray-stoppered vacutainer
GSW	Gunshot wound
H_2O	Water
HCT	Hematocrit
Hgb	Hemoglobin
HIV	Human immunodeficiency virus
HPLC	High performance liquid chromatograph(y)
HTN	Hypertension
Hx	History
ICU	Intensive care unit
L, l	Liter
LLQ	Left lower quadrant
LUQ	Left upper quadrant
MC	Mixed volatiles
MCT	Micro color test
MCV	Mean cell volume
Meds	Medications
MEO	Medical Examiner's Office
MeOH	Methanol
mg	Milligram
ml, mL	Milliliter
MSDS	Material safety data sheet
MVA	Motor vehicle accident
n	Number
NB	Northbound
ND	None detected
NDD	No drugs detected
Neg	Negative
ng	Nanogram
NOK	Next of kin
NP	Nurse practitioner
NPD	Nitrogen phosphorus detector
NR	Not requested
O_2	Oxygen
OF	Ocular fluid (vitreous)
Opi	Opiates
p	After
P	Probation
Pb	Lead
PCC	Poison Control Center
PCP	Phencyclidine
pg	Picogram
PM	Postmortem, in the evening
PMH	Previous medical history
PO	Police officer, probation officer
Pos	Positive
PSV	Purple-stoppered vacutainer

p/u	Pick(ed) up
QA	Quality assurance
QC	Quality control
QNS	Quantity not sufficient
QS	Quantity sufficient
QS to _	Dilute to volume
R	Referral
RB	Reagent blank
RBC	Red blood cells
RIA	Radio immunoassay
RLQ	Right lower quadrant
R/O	Rule out
RSV	Red-stoppered vacutainer
RUQ	Right upper quadrant
Rx	Prescription
s	Without
S/A	Same address
SB	Southbound
SD	Standard deviation
Ser	Serum
SMA	Sympathomimetic amines
S/O	Sign-out
SOB	Shortness of breath
SOP	Standard operating procedure
Sp Gr	Specific gravity
SST	Serum separator tube
STD	Sexually transmitted disease
TAT	turn-around time
THC	Tetrahydrocannabinol
TLC	Thin-layer chromatography
Tx	Taken
U	Urine
VD	Venereal disease
VP	Venipuncture
w/	With
WAN	Weak acid/neutral
WB	Westbound
WBC	White blood cells
w/o	Without
x	Average
y/o	Year old
μL	Microliter (also uL)
μg	Microgram (also ug, ugm, μgm)
4-Br	Tetrabromophenolphthalein ethyl ester (a color test)
% sat	Percent saturation

APPENDIX III

References for Methods of Drug Quantitative Analysis

Drug Name	Class	Fraction	UV	GC	LC	GC/MS	General
11-Hydroxy delta-9-THC	3	B		[1]	[2]	[3–9]	[10–12]
delta-9-THC	3	B					[10–12]
Acebutolol	2	B			[13]	[14]	[15–17]
Acetaminophen	1	WAN	[18–20]		[21–24]		[25–29]
Acetazolamide	5	B		[30]			
Acetylcarbromal	3	WAN					
Acetylsalicyclic acid	1	A		[31–33]	[34,35]		[36–38]
Albuterol	2	B			[39]		[40]
Alfentanil	1	B		[41]		[42]	[43,44]
Allobarbital	3	WAN	[45]	[46–55]	[46,56–60]		
Allopurinol	5	WAN					
Alphaprodine	1	B					[61]
Alprazolam	3	B/N		[62,63]	[64,65]	[66]	
Amantadine	1	B					
Amiodarone	2	B		[67,68]			
Amitriptyline	3	B		[69,70]	[71–76]	[77–80]	
Amlodipine	3	B			[81]		
Amobarbital	3	WAN			[82–85]	[86,87]	
Amoxapine	3	B		[88–90]			
Amphetamine	3	B			[91–93]	[94–101]	
Amyl nitrite	3	G					[102–106]
Aprobarbital	3	WAN		[50]		[107]	
Astemizole	4	B					[108]
Atenolol	2	B			[109]		
Atracurium	3	Q					[110]
Atropine (Hyoscyamine-D,L)	3	B				[111,112]	[113]
Azatadine	3	B					
Baclofen	1	B			[114,115]		
Barbital	3	WAN			[116]	[117]	
Barbiturates	3	WAN			[118–123]		[51,120, 124–129]
Benzephetamine	3	B					[130–134]
Benzocaine	3	B					[135]
Benzoylecgonine	3	AMPHO			[136–139]		[140–145]
Benzphetamine	3	B				[146]	
Benztropine	3	B				[147]	
Bepridil	2	B					[67]
Betaxolol	2	B					
Biperiden	3	B					
Bisoprolol	3	B					

Drug Name	Class	Fraction	UV	GC	LC	GC/MS	General
Bretylium	2	O					
Bromazepam	3	B			[148]	[149]	
Bromocriptine	3	B				[150]	
Bromdiphen-hydramine	4	B		[151,152]		[153,154]	
Bupivacaine	3	B		[155–157]	[158]		[159–161]
Buprenorphine	1	B			[162,163]	[164–166]	[167–169]
Bupropion	3	B		[170]		[171,172]	[173,174]
Buspirone	3	B		[62]	[175]	[175]	
Butabarbital	3	WAN			[176]		
Butalbital	3	WAN				[86,107, 120,126]	
Butorphanol	1	B				[177]	[178]
Caffeine	3	WAN			[179–181]		[182–184]
Camazepam	3	B					
Carbamazepine	3	B		[185–187]	[188–190]		[191,192]
Carbinoxamine	3	B					
Carfentanil	1	B				[124,193]	[194]
Carisoprodol	3	WAN		[195]		[196]	
Chlopropamide	5	WAN	[197]		[198]		
Chloral Hydrate	3	O		[199–202]		[203]	
Chlordiazepoxide	3	B		[202,204–206]	[201,202]		
Chloropromazine	3	B		[207]	[208]	[209]	
Chloroquine	5	B			[210,211]		
Chlorpheniramine	3	B	[212]	[213]			
Chlorphentermine	3	B					
Chlorpromazine	3	B		[214,215]	[208,216]		
Chlorpropamide	5	WAN					[197]
Chlorprothixene	3	B					
Chlorzoxazone	3	WAN, B					
Cimetidine	5	B			[217]		
Clemastine	3	B					
Clobazam	3	B			[218,219]	[220]	
Clomipramine	3	B			[221–224]		
Clonazepam	3	B		[225–228]	[229–231]	[227]	
Clonidine	2	B				[232,233]	
Clorazepate	3	B		[234,235]		[236]	
Clotiazepam	3	B					
Clozapine	3	B		[237–239]	[240–243]		[244]
Cocaethylene	3	B			[245]	[140,245–248]	[138,249]
Cocaine	3	B		[248]	[250–253]	[140,145, 254–257]	
Codeine	1	B		[258]	[259]	[260–264]	[265]
Colchicine	5	B			[266,267]		
Cotinine	5	B		[268]		[269–271]	
Cyclizine	3	B				[272]	
Cyclobenzaprine	3	B			[72]	[73,273]	[274]
Cyclopane	5	WAN					
Cyproheptadine	3	B					[275]
delta-9-THC-Carboxylic acid	3	A			[276]	[3,7,10, 277–279]	
Demoxepam	3	B			[201,280, 281]	[202,282]	
Desalkylflurazepam	3	B			[283]	[284,285]	[286]
Desflurane	5	G				[287]	
Desipramine	3	B					
Dextromethorphan	4	B			[288,289]		
Dextrorphan	4	B			[288,289]		

Drug Name	Class	Fraction	UV	GC	LC	GC/MS	General
Diazepam	3	B		[234,235, 290]	[283,291, 292]	[236]	
Diclofenac	1	A			[293,294]		
Dicyclomine	5	B				[295]	
Diethylpropion	3	B					[296]
Diflunisal	1	WAN					[297]
Dihydrocodeine	1	B				[298,299]	
Diltiazem	2	B				[300]	
Diphenhydramine	4	B		[152]		[153]	
Diphenoxin	1	B			[301]		
Diphenoxylate	1	B			[301]		
Disopyramide	2	B			[302,303]	[304,305]	[300]
Doxepin	3	B			[306]		[307]
Doxylamine	4	B				[308]	
Ecgonine methyl ester	3	B			[250,251, 309–311]	[254,312–315]	
Encainide	2	B					[316,317]
Enflurane	5	G				[318]	[319]
Ephedrin	4	B			[320]	[183]	
Esmolol	2	B					
Estazolam	3	B			[321]	[149]	
Ethanol	5	G		[322–329]			
Ethchlorvynol	3	O		[330–334]			[335,336]
Ethinamate	3	WAN					
Ethosuximide	3	WAN			[337–339]		[340,341]
Ethylene	5	G					
Ethylflurazepam	3	B					
Etodolac	1	A					
Etomidate	3	WAN		[342]			
Famotidine	3	B				[343]	
Felbamate	3	WAN, B		[344]	[189,345, 346]		[347]
Felodipine	2	B		[348]			
Fenfluramine	3	B			[349]		
Fenoprofen	1	A			[350]		
Fentanyl	1	B		[351]		[124,193, 352–355]	[356]
Flecainide	2	B			[357–359]	[300]	
Flunitrazepam	3	B		[62,63]	[360–363]		
Fluoxetine	3	B		[364–367]	[368]	[369]	
Fluphenazine	3	B				[370]	
Flurazepam	3	B					
Flurbiprofen	1	A					
Freon	5	G					
Gasoline	5	G					
Glipizide	5	WAN			[371]		
Glutethimide	3	WAN		[372,373]			[374,375]
Glyburide	5	WAN			[371]		
Halazepam	3	B					
Haloperidol	3	B			[376–379]	[380–382]	
Hexobarbital	3	WAN		[129,383, 384]		[120,125, 126]	[385]
Hydrocodone	1	B					[386]
Hydromorphone	1	AMPHO			[387–389]	[264,390]	
Hydroxychloroquine	5	B			[211,391]		
Hydroxyzine	3	B		[392]			
Ibuprofen	1	WAN			[294,393]	[394–397]	
Imipramine	3	B		[398]	[398–401]	[402]	

Drug Name	Class	Fraction	UV	GC	LC	GC/MS	General
Indomethacin	1	WAN		[403,404]	[350,405–407]		
Insulin	5	O					[408–412]
Iso-metheptene	5	B					
Isoflurane	3	G				[318]	
Isopropanol	5	G					[413–419]
Isoxsuprine	2	B					
Isradipine	2	B					[420]
Ketamin	3	B		[421]	[422]	[423,424]	
Ketazolam	3	B					
Ketoprofen	1	WAN			[425–427]		
Ketorolac	1	B			[428–431]	[432]	
l-Methamphetamine	3	B				[433–435]	
Lamotrigine	3	B					[436–438]
Levallorphan	1	B				[439]	
Levodopa	5	O					
Levorphanol	1	AMPHO					[440]
Lidocaine	5,2	B			[155,156, 441]		
Lithium	3	O					
Loperamide	1	B					
Lorantadine	3	B					
Lorazepam	3	B			[281]	[442–444]	
Loxapine	3	B					
LSD	3	B			[445–447]	[448,449]	
Maprotiline	3	B				[450,451]	
Mazindol	3	B					
MDEA	3	B				[132]	
Meclizine	3	B					
Medazepam	3	B				[361]	
Mefenamic Acid	1	A					
Meperidine (Pethidine)	1	B				[157]	
Mephentermine	3	B					
Mephenytoin	3	B					
Mephobarbital	3	B					
Mepivacaine	3	B					
Meprobamate	3	WAN		[195,452]		[453]	[375,454, 455]
Mescaline (Peyote)	3	B					[456]
Mesoridazine	3	B			[457]		[458]
Methadone and metabolite	1	B		[459]		[460–462]	
Methamphetamine	3	B		[463]		[133,464, 465]	
Methanol	5	G		[418,466–468]			
Methapyrilene	3	B					
Methaqualone	3	WAN,B		[235,469]		[470]	
Methocarbamol	3	WAN					
Methohexital	3	WAN					
Methsuximide	3	WAN			[471]		[340]
Methylenedioxy amphetamine (MDA)	3	B				[132,472]	
Methylenedioxymethamphetamine (MDMA; Ecstasy)	3	B				[132,472]	
Methylphenidate	3	B					
Methyprylon	3	WAN					
Methysergide	3	B					
Metoclopramide	5	B					

Drug Name	Class	Fraction	UV	GC	LC	GC/MS	General
Metoprolol	2	B		[473]	[474]	[474]	
Mexiletine	2	B		[475]		[300,476]	
Midazolam	3	B			[422,477, 478]	[479]	
Molindone	1	B					
Monoacetylmorphine	1	B		[480]	[481]	299,482–484]	
Moricizine	2	B					
Morphine	3	AMPHO			[485–487]	[488–490]	
Morphine-3-glucuronide	3	AMPHO			[491–494]		
Nadolol	2	B					
Nalbuphine	1	B					[178,495]
Naproxen	1	WAN			[294]		
Nicotine	5	B			[496]	[269,497, 498]	
Nifedipine	2	B		[499]	[500,501]	[502]	
Nitrazepam	3	B			[149,321, 360,363]		
Nitrous oxide	3	G					
Nomifensine	3	B					
Nylidrin		B					
Orphenadrine	3	B					
Oxazepam	3	B			[292]	[503]	
Oxycodone	1	B				[504,505]	[506]
Oxymorphone	1	B				[505]	
Pancuraonium	3	Q					[507,508]
Papaverine	2	B				[509]	
Paradehyde	3	O					
Paroxetine	3	B					[510]
PCP	3	B		[511–513]		[514,515]	
Pemoline	3	B					[516]
Pentazocine	1	B		[517–519]			
Pentobarbital	3	WAN		[49,54]		[520]	[521–524]
Pergolide	3	B					[525]
Perphenazine	3	B					
Phendimetrazine	3	B					[526]
Phenelazine	3	B					
Phenobarbital	3	WAN			[189,339, 527–529]		
Phensuximide	3	WAN					
Phentermine	3	B			[530]	[134,531]	
Phenylpropanolamine	3	B		[532]			
Phenyltoloxamine	4	B					
Phenytoin (Diphenyl-hydantoin)	3	WAN			[528,533, 534,338]		
Piroxicam	1	A					
Prazepam	3	B			[62,321, 360,535]		
Primidone	3	WAN			[189,527, 529]	[536,537]	
Procainamide	2	B			[303]		[538,539]
Procaine	5	B					
Promazine	3	B					
Promethazine	3	B			[540]		
Propafenone	3	B			[541]		
Propanolol	2	B		[473]	[542–544]	[545,546]	
Propofol	3	B			[547]	[548]	
Propoxyphene	1	B		[469,549–552]		[553–556]	[557–559]

Drug Name	Class	Fraction	UV	GC	LC	GC/MS	General
Protriptyline	3	B			[74,222, 376,560]		[385,561–564]
Pseudoephedrine	4	B					[94,565]
Psycylobin	3	O					
Pyrilamine	4	B				[308,566]	
Quazepam	3	B		[567]	[568]		[569]
Quinidine	2	B			[570]		[538]
Quinine	5	B				[571]	
Ranitidine	5	B			[572,573]		
Risperidone	3	B			[574,575]		[576,577]
Scopolamine	3	B				[578,579]	
Secobarbital	3	WAN			[580]		[581]
Selegiline	3	B		[582]	[583]	[584,585]	[586]
Sertraline	3	B				[587]	[510]
Sotalol	2	B					
Strychnine	5	B					[588]
Succinylcholine	3	Q					[589,590]
Sufentanil	1	B					[193,591]
Sumatriptan	1	B					[592]
Talbutal	3	WAN				[86,593, 594]	
Temazepam	3	B			[595]		[596,597]
Terbutaline	4	B			[598]	[599,600]	
Terfenadine	4	B					
Tetracaine	5	B					[601]
Tetrazepam	3	B					
Theophylline	4	WAN			[83,338, 602,603]		[603–607]
Thiamylal	3	WAN			[608,609]		
Thiopental	3	WAN		[610]	[405]		
Thioridazine	3	B			[399,457]		
Thiothixene	3	B					
Tocainide	2	B					[300]
Tolazamide	3	WAN					
Tolmetin	1	WAN					[126]
Toluene	5	G		[611]		[612–614]	[615–617]
Tolutamide	3	WAN					
Tramadol	1	B					[618]
Tranylcypromine	3	B					
Trazodone	3	B		[619–621]			
Triazolam	3	B			[321]	[66,622–624]	
Trichloroethylene	5	G		[625]			
Trifluoperazine	3	B					[67]
Triflupromazine	3	B					
Trihexyphenidyl	3	B		[626]			
Trimethadione	3	WAN					[627]
Trimethobenzamide	3	B					[628,629]
Trimipramine	3	B		[398]	[630]	[402]	[631]
Tripelennamine	4	N		[517,518, 632]			
Triprolidine	4	N					
Tubocurarine	5	Q					
Valproic acid	3	WAN		[633–635]	[636,637]	[638]	[639]
Venlafaxine	3	B					[640,641]
Verapamil	2	N		[642–644]			[645,646]

Drug Name	Class	Fraction	UV	GC	LC	GC/MS	General
Xylene	5	G					[102,647–650]
Zolpidem	3	B			[651–655]		

KEY: Fraction (extraction): A = acid, B = Base, WAN = weak acid neutral, Ampho = amphoteric, Q = quantanary, O = Other

Pharmacological Classification	
1	**Analgesics and Anti-inflamatory**
	Nonsteroidal anti-inflammatories
	Opioids
	Central analgesics
2	**Cardiovascular/Diuretic Drugs**
	Antiarrhythmics
	Antihypertensives
	Beta blockers
	Calcium channel blockers
	Inotropic
	Nitrates
3	**Central Nervous System Drugs**
	Anticonvulsants
	Antiemetics/antivertigo
	Depressants
	Hallucinogens
	Psychotherapeutic agents
	Antianxiety
	Antidepressants
	Antipsychotics
	Sedatives and hypnotics
	General anesthetics
	Barbiturates
	Nonbarbiturates
	Gases
	Volatile liquids
	Muscle relaxants
	Parkinsonism drugs
	Stimulants
	Analeptics
	Amphetamines
	Anorexiants
4	**Respiratory Drugs**
	Antihistamines and antiallergics
	Bronchodilators
	Cough and cold
5	**Other**

REFERENCES

1. Ritchie, L. K., Caplan, Y. H., and Park, J., Delta-9-Tetrahydrocannabinol analysis in forensic blood specimens using capillary column gas chromatography with nitrogen sensitive detection, *Journal of Analytical Toxicology*, 11, 205–209, 1987.
2. Moffat, A. C., Williams, P. L., and King, L. J., Combined high-performance liquid chromatography and radioimmunoassay method for the analysis of delta 9-tetrahydrocannabinol and its metabolites in plasma and urine, *NIDA Research Monograph*, 42, 56–68, 1982.
3. Hattori, H., Detection of cannabinoids by GC/MS. I. Quantitation of delta-9-THC in human urine and blood plasma, *Nippon Hoigaku Zasshi*, 35, 67–72, 1981.

4. Huestis, M. A., Mitchell, J. M., and Cone, E. J., Detection times of marijuana metabolites in urine by immunoassay and GC-MS, *Journal of Analytical Toxicology*, 19, 443–449, 1995.
5. McCurdy, H. H., Lewellen, L. J., Callahan, L. S., and Childs, P. S., Evaluation of the Ion Trap Detector for the detection of 11-nor-delta 9-THC-9-carboxylic acid in urine after extraction by bonded-phase adsorption, *Journal of Analytical Toxicology*, 10, 175–177, 1986.
6. Clatworthy, A. J., Oon, M. C., Smith, R. N., and Whitehouse, M. J., Gas chromatographic-mass spectrometric confirmation of radioimmunoassay results for cannabinoids in blood and urine, *Forensic Science International*, 46, 219–230, 1990.
7. Wilkins, D., Haughey, H., Cone, E., Huestis, M., Foltz, R., and Rollins, D., Quantitative analysis of THC, 11-OH-THC, and THCCOOH in human hair by negative ion chemical ionization mass spectrometry, *Journal of Analytical Toxicology*, 19, 483–491, 1995.
8. Kudo, K., Nagata, T., Kimura, K., Imamura, T., and Jitsufuchi, N., Sensitive determination of delta-9-tetrahydrocannabinol in human tissue by GC/MS, *Journal of Analytical Toxicology*, 19, 87–90, 1995.
9. Moeller, M. R., Doerr, G., and Warth, S., Simultaneous quantitation of delta-9-tetrahydrocannabinol (THC) and 11-nor-9-carboxy-delta-9-tetrahydrocannabinol (THC-COOH) in serum by GC/MS using deuterated internal standards and its application to a smoking study and forensic cases, *Journal of Forensic Sciences*, 37, 969–983, 1992.
10. Huestis, M. A., Henningfield, J. E., and Cone, E. J., Blood cannabinoids. I. Absorption of THC and formation of 11-OH-THC and THCCOOH during and after smoking marijuana [see comments], *Journal of Analytical Toxicology*, 16, 276–282, 1992.
11. Huestis, M. A., Henningfield, J. E., and Cone, E. J., Blood cannabinoids. II. Models for the prediction of time of marijuana exposure from plasma concentrations of delta 9-tetrahydrocannabinol (THC) and 11-nor-9-carboxy-delta 9-tetrahydrocannabinol (THCCOOH) [see comments], *Journal of Analytical Toxicology*, 16, 283–290, 1992.
12. Kemp, P. M., Abukhalaf, I. K., Manno, J. E., Manno, B. R., Alford, D. D., and Abusada, G. A., Cannabinoids in humans, *Journal of Analytical Toxicology*, 19, 285–291, 1995.
13. Meffin, P. J., Harapat, S. R., Yee, Y. G., and Harrison, D. C., High-pressure liquid chromatographic analysis of drugs in biological fluids. V. Analysis of acebutolol and its major metabolite, *Journal of Chromatography*, 138, 183–191, 1977.
14. Siren, H., Saarinen, M., Hainari, S., Lukkari, P., and Riekkola, M., Screening of beta-blockers in human serum by ion-pair chromatography and their identification as methyl or acetyl derivatives by gas chromatography-mass spectrometry, *Journal of Chromatography*, 632, 215–227, 1993.
15. Leloux, M., Niessen, W., and van der Hoeven, R., Thermospray liquid chromatography/mass spectrometry of polar beta-blocking drugs: preliminary results, *Biological Mass Spectrometry*, 20, 647–649, 1991.
16. Ghanem, R., Bello, M. A., Callejon, M., and Guiraum, A., Determination of beta-blocker drugs in pharmaceutical preparations by non-suppressed ion chromatography, *Journal of Pharmaceutical & Biomedical Analysis*, 15, 383–388, 1996.
17. Segura, J., Pascual, J. A., Ventura, R., Ustaran, J. I., Cuevas, A., and Gonzalez, R., International cooperation in analytical chemistry: experience of antidoping control at the XI Pan American Games, *Clinical Chemistry*, 39, 836–845, 1993.
18. Davey, L. and Naidoo, D., Urinary screen for acetaminophen (paracetamol) in the presence of N-acetylcysteine, *Clinical Chemistry*, 39, 2348–2349, 1993.
19. Novotny, P. E. and Elser, R. C., Indophenol method for acetaminophen in serum examined, *Clinical Chemistry*, 30, 884–886, 1984.
20. Bailey, D. N., Colorimetry of serum acetaminophen (paracetamol) in uremia, *Clinical Chemistry*, 28, 187–190, 1982.
21. Wong, A. S., An evaluation of HPLC for the screening and quantitation of benzodiazepines and acetaminophen in post mortem blood, *Journal of Analytical Toxicology*, 7, 33–36, 1983.
22. West, J. C., Rapid HPLC analysis of paracetamol (acetaminophen) in blood and postmortem viscera, *Journal of Analytical Toxicology*, 5, 118–121, 1981.
23. Manno, B. R., Manno, J. E., Dempsey, C. A., and Wood, M. A., A high-pressure liquid chromatographic method for the determination of N-acetyl-p-aminophenol (acetaminophen) in serum or plasma using a direct injection technique, *Journal of Analytical Toxicology*, 5, 24–28, 1981.
24. Colin, P., Sirois, G., and Chakrabarti, S., Rapid high-performance liquid chromatographic assay of acetaminophen in serum and tissue homogenates, *Journal of Chromatography*, 413, 151–160, 1987.

25. Ashbourne, J. F., Olson, K. R., and Khayam-Bashi, H., Value of rapid screening for acetaminophen in all patients with intentional drug overdose, *Annals of Emergency Medicine*, 18, 1035–1038, 1989.
26. Campbell, R. S. and Price, C. P., Experience with an homogeneous immunoassay for paracetamol (acetaminophen), *Journal of Clinical Chemistry & Clinical Biochemistry*, 24, 155–159, 1986.
27. Dasgupta, A. and Kinnaman, G., Microwave-induced rapid hydrolysis of acetaminophen and its conjugates in urine for emergency toxicological screen, *Clinical Chemistry,* 39, 2349–2350, 1993.
28. Price, L. M., Poklis, A., and Johnson, D. E., Fatal acetaminophen poisoning with evidence of subendocardial necrosis of the heart, *Journal of Forensic Sciences*, 36, 930–935, 1991.
29. Slattery, J. T., Nelson, S. D., and Thummel, K. E., The complex interaction between ethanol and acetaminophen [review], *Clinical Pharmacology & Therapeutics*, 60, 241–246, 1996.
30. Wallace, S. M., Shah, V. P., and Riegelman, S., GLC analysis of acetazolamide in blood, plasma, and saliva following oral administration to normal subjects, *Journal of Pharmaceutical Sciences*, 66, 527–530, 1977.
31. Asselin, W. M. and Caughlin, J. D., A rapid and simple color test for detection of salicylate in whole hemolyzed blood, *Journal of Analytical Toxicology*, 14, 254–255, 1990.
32. Morris, H. C., Overton, P. D., Ramsay, J. R., Campbell, R. S., Hammond, P. M., Atkinson, T., et al., Development and validation of an automated, enzyme-mediated colorimetric assay of salicylate in serum, *Clinical Chemistry*, 36, 131–135, 1990.
33. Trinder, P., Rapid determination of salicylates in biological materials, *Biochemical Journal,* 57, 1954
34. Levine, B. and Caplan, Y. H., Liquid chromatographic determination of salicylate and methyl salicylate in blood and application to a postmortem case, *Journal of Analytical Toxicology*, 8, 239–241, 1984.
35. Dipietra, A. M., Gatti, R., Andrisano, V., and Cavrini, V., Application of high-performance liquid chromatography with diode-array detection and on-line post-column photochemical derivatization to the determination of analgesics, *Journal of Chromatography*, 729, 355–361, 1996.
36. Chan, T. Y., Chan, A. Y., Ho, C. S., and Critchley, J. A., The clinical value of screening for salicylates in acute poisoning, *Veterinary & Human Toxicology*, 37, 37–38, 1995.
37. Asselin, W. M. and Caughlin, J. D., A rapid and simple color test for detection of salicylate in whole hemolyzed blood, *Journal of Analytical Toxicology*, 14, 254–255, 1990.
38. Jammehdiabadi, M. and Tierney, M., Impact of toxicology screens in the diagnosis of a suspected overdose: salicylates, tricyclic antidepressants, and benzodiazepines, *Veterinary & Human Toxicology*, 33, 40–43, 1991.
39. Bland, R. E., Tanner, R. J., Chern, W. H., Lang, J. R., and Powell, J. R., Determination of albuterol concentrations in human plasma using solid-phase extraction and high-performance liquid chromatography with fluorescence detection, *Journal of Pharmaceutical & Biomedical Analysis*, 8, 591–596, 1990.
40. King, W. D., Holloway, M., and Palmisano, P. A., Albuterol overdose: a case report and differential diagnosis [review], *Pediatric Emergency Care*, 8, 268–271, 1992.
41. Bjorkman, S. and Stanski, D. R., Simultaneous determination of fentanyl and alfentanil in rat tissues by capillary column gas chromatography, *Journal of Chromatography*, 433, 95–104, 1988.
42. Mautz, D., Labroo, R., and Kharasch, E., Determination of alfentanil and noralfentanil in human plasma by gas chromatography-mass spectrometry, *Journal of Chromatography B: Biomedical Applications*, 658, 149–153, 1994.
43. Van, B. H., Van, P. A., Gasparini, R., Woestenborghs, R., Heykants, J., Noorduin, H., et al., Pharmacokinetics of alfentanil during and after a fixed rate infusion, *British Journal of Anaesthesia*, 62, 610–615, 1989.
44. Meistelman, C., Saint-Maurice, C., Lepaul, M., Levron, J., Loose, J., and Mac, G. K., A comparison of alfentanil pharmacokinetics in children and adults, *Anesthesiology*, 66, 13–16, 1987.
45. Schumann, G. B., Lauenstein, K., LeFever, D., and Henry, J. B., Ultraviolet spectrophotometric analysis of barbiturates, *American Journal of Clinical Pathology*, 66, 823–830, 1976.
46. Gill, R., Stead, A. H., and Moffat, A. C., Analytical aspects of barbiturate abuse: identification of drugs by the effective combination of gas-liquid, high-performance liquid and thin-layer chromatographic techniques, *Journal of Chromatography*, 204, 275–284, 1981.
47. Lillsunde, P., Michelson, L., Forsstrom, T., Korte, T., Schultz, E., Ariniemi, K., et al., Comprehensive drug screening in blood for detecting abused drugs or drugs potentially hazardous for traffic safety, *Forensic Science International*, 77, 191–210, 1996.

48. Mule, S. and Casella, G., Confirmation and quantitation of barbiturates in human urine by gas chromatography/mass spectrometry, *Journal of Analytical Toxicology*, 13, 13–16, 1989.
49. Wallace, J. E., Hall, L. R., and Harris, S. C., Determination of pentobarbital and certain other barbiturates by capillary gas-liquid chromatography, *Journal of Analytical Toxicology*, 7, 178–180, 1983.
50. Budd, R. D., Gas chromatographic properties of 1,3-dialkyl barbiturate derivatives, *Clinical Toxicology*, 17, 375–382, 1980.
51. Barbour, A. D., GC/MS analysis of propylated barbiturates, *Journal of Analytical Toxicology*, 15, 214–215, 1991.
52. Christophersen, A. S. and Rasmussen, K. E., Glass capillary column gas chromatography of barbiturates after flash-heater derivatization with dimethylformamide dimethylacetal, *Journal of Chromatography*, 192, 363–374, 1980.
53. Budd, R. D. and Mathis, D. F., GLC screening and confirmation of barbiturates in post mortem blood specimens, *Journal of Analytical Toxicology*, 6, 317–320, 1982.
54. Sun, S. R. and Hoffman, D. J., Rapid, sensitive GLC determination of pentobarbital and other barbiturates in serum using nitrogen-specific detector, *Journal of Pharmaceutical Sciences*, 68, 386–388, 1979.
55. Marigo, M., Ferrara, S. D., and Tedeschi, L., A sensitive method for gas-chromatographic assay of barbiturates in body fluids, *Archives of Toxicology*, 37, 107–112, 1977.
56. Gill, R., Lopes, A. A., and Moffat, A. C., Analysis of barbiturates in blood by high-performance liquid chromatography, *Journal of Chromatography*, 226, 117–123, 1981.
57. Drummer, O. H., Kotsos, A., and McIntyre, I. M., A class-independent drug screen in forensic toxicology using a photodiode array detector, *Journal of Analytical Toxicology*, 17, 225–229, 1993.
58. Chan, E. M. and Chan, S. C., Screening for acidic and neutral drugs by high performance liquid chromatography in post-mortem blood, *Journal of Analytical Toxicology*, 8, 173–176, 1984.
59. Ferrara, S. D., Tedeschi, L., Frison, G., and Castagna, F., Solid-phase extraction and HPLC-UV confirmation of drugs of abuse in urine, *Journal of Analytical Toxicology*, 16, 217–222, 1992.
60. Lehane, D. P., Menyharth, P., Lum, G., and Levy, A. L., Therapeutic drug monitoring: measurements of antiepileptic and barbiturate drug levels in blood by gas chromatography with nitrogen-selective detector, *Annals of Clinical & Laboratory Science*, 6, 404–410, 1976.
61. Van Vunakis, H., Freeman, D. S., and Gjika, H. B., Radioimmunoassay for anileridine, meperidine and other N-substituted phenylpiperidine carboxylic acid esters, *Research Communications in Chemical Pathology & Pharmacology*, 12, 379–387, 1975.
62. Gaillard, Y., Gay-Montchamp, J. P., and Ollagnier, M., Simultaneous screening and quantitation of alpidem, zolpidem, buspirone and benzodiazepines by dual-channel gas chromatography using electron-capture and nitrogen-phosphorus detection after solid-phase extraction, *Journal of Chromatography*, 622, 197–208, 1993.
63. Lillsunde, P. and Seppala, T., Simultaneous screening and quantitative analysis of benzodiazepines by dual-channel gas chromatography using electron-capture and nitrogen-phosphorus detection, *Journal of Chromatography*, 533, 97–110, 1990.
64. Akerman, K. K., Jolkkonen, J., Parviainen, M., and Penttila, I., Analysis of low-dose benzodiazepines by HPLC with automated solid-phase extraction, *Clinical Chemistry*, 42, 1412–1416, 1996.
65. Shimamine, M., Masunari, T., and Nakahara, Y., [Studies on identification of drugs of abuse by diode array detection. I. Screening-test and identification of benzodiazepines by HPLC-DAD with ICOS software system], *Eisei Shikenjo Hokoku—Bulletin of National Institute of Hygienic Sciences*, 47–56, 1993.
66. Cairns, E. R., Dent, B. R., Ouwerkerk, J. C., and Porter, L. J., Quantitative analysis of alprazolam and triazolam in hemolysed whole blood and liver digest by GC/MS/NICI with deuterated internal standards, *Journal of Analytical Toxicology*, 18, 1–6, 1994.
67. Pollak, P. T., A systematic review and critical comparison of internal standards for the routine liquid chromatographic assay of amiodarone and desethylamiodarone, *Therapeutic Drug Monitoring*, 18, 168–178, 1996.
68. Flanagan, R. J., Storey, G. C., and Holt, D. W., Rapid high-performance liquid chromatographic method for the measurement of amiodarone in blood plasma or serum at the concentrations attained during therapy, *Journal of Chromatography*, 187, 391–398, 1980.

69. Fernandez, G. S., Witherington, T. L., and Stafford, D. T., Effective column extraction from decomposed tissue in a suspected overdose case involving maprotiline and amitriptyline, *Journal of Analytical Toxicology*, 9, 230–231, 1985.
70. Bailey, D. N. and Jatlow, P. I., Gas-chromatographic analysis for therapeutic concentrations of amitriptyline and nortriptyline in plasma, with use of a nitrogen detector, *Clinical Chemistry*, 22, 777–781, 1976.
71. Vandel, S., Vincent, F., Prudhon, F., Nezelof, S., Bonin, B., and Bertschy, G., [Comparative study of two techniques for the determination of amitriptyline and nortriptyline: EMIT and gas chromatography]. [French], *Therapie*, 47, 41–45, 1992.
72. Poklis, A. and Edinboro, L. E., REMEDi drug profiling system readily distinguishes between cyclobenzaprine and amitriptyline in emergency toxicology urine specimens [letter], *Clinical Chemistry*, 38, 2349–2350, 1992.
73. Wong, E. C., Koenig, J., and Turk, J., Potential interference of cyclobenzaprine and norcyclobenzaprine with HPLC measurement of amitriptyline and nortriptyline: resolution by GC-MS analysis, *Journal of Analytical Toxicology*, 19, 218–224, 1995.
74. Attapolitou, J., Tsarpalis, K., and Koutselinis, A., A modified simple and rapid reversed phase high performance liquid chromatographic method for quantification of amitriptyline and nortriptyline in plasma, *Journal of Liquid Chromatography*, 17, 3969–3982, 1994.
75. Rop, P. P., Viala, A., Durand, A., and Conquy, T., Determination of citalopram, amitriptyline and clomipramine in plasma by reversed-phase high-performance liquid chromatography, *Journal of Chromatography*, 338, 171–178, 1985.
76. Hartter, S. and Hiemke, C., Column switching and high-performance liquid chromatography in the analysis of amitriptyline, nortriptyline and hydroxylated metabolites in human plasma or serum, *Journal of Chromatography*, 578, 273–282, 1992.
77. Oliver, J. S. and Smith, H., Amitriptyline and metabolites in biological fluids, *Forensic Science,* 3, 181–187, 1974.
78. Spiehler, V., Spiehler, E., and Osselton, M. D., Application of expert systems analysis to interpretation of fatal cases involving amitriptyline, *Journal of Analytical Toxicology*, 12, 216–224, 1988.
79. Bolster, M., Curran, J., and Busuttil, A., A five year review of fatal self-ingested overdoses involving amitriptyline in Edinburgh 1983–'87, *Human & Experimental Toxicology*, 13, 29–31, 1994.
80. Bailey, D. N. and Shaw, R. F., Interpretation of blood and tissue concentrations in fatal self-ingested overdose involving amitriptyline: an update (1978–1979), *Journal of Analytical Toxicology*, 4, 232–236, 1980.
81. Pandya, K. K., Satia, M., Gandhi, T. P., Modi, I. A., Modi, R. I., and Chakravarthy, B. K., Detection and determination of total amlodipine by high-performance thin-layer chromatography: a useful technique for pharmacokinetic studies, *Journal of Chromatography B: Biomedical Applications*, 667, 315–320, 1995.
82. Svinarov, D. A. and Dotchev, D. C., Simultaneous liquid-chromatographic determination of some bronchodilators, anticonvulsants, chloramphenicol, and hypnotic agents, with Chromosorb P columns used for sample preparation, *Clinical Chemistry*, 35, 1615–1618, 1989.
83. Meatherall, R. and Ford, D., Isocratic liquid chromatographic determination of theophylline, acetaminophen, chloramphenicol, caffeine, anticonvulsants, and barbiturates in serum, *Therapeutic Drug Monitoring*, 10, 101–115, 1988.
84. Kabra, P. M., Stafford, B. E., and Marton, L. J., Rapid method for screening toxic drugs in serum with liquid chromatography, *Journal of Analytical Toxicology*, 5, 177–182, 1981.
85. Kabra, P. M., Koo, H. Y., and Marton, L. J., Simultaneous liquid-chromatographic determination of 12 common sedatives and hypnotics in serum, *Clinical Chemistry*, 24, 657–662, 1978.
86. Liu, R. H., McKeehan, A. M., Edwards, C., Foster, G., Bensley, W. D., Langner, J. G., et al., Improved gas chromatography/mass spectrometry analysis of barbiturates in urine using centrifuge-based solid-phase extraction, methylation, with d5-pentobarbital as internal standard, *Journal of Forensic Sciences*, 39, 1504–1514, 1994.
87. Pocci, R., Dixit, V., and Dixit, V., Solid-phase extraction and GC/MS confirmation of barbiturates from human urine, *Journal of Analytical Toxicology*, 16, 45–47, 1992.
88. Osiewicz, R. J. and Middleberg, R., Detection of a novel compound after overdoses of aspirin and amoxapine, *Journal of Analytical Toxicology*, 13, 97–99, 1989.

89. Taylor, R. L., Crooks, C. R., and Caplan, Y. H., The determination of amoxapine in human fatal overdoses, *Journal of Analytical Toxicology*, 6, 309–311, 1982.
90. Wu Chen, N. B., Schaffer, M. I., Lin, R. L., Hadac, J. P., and Stein, R. J., Analysis of blood and tissue for amoxapine and trimipramine, *Journal of Forensic Sciences*, 28, 116–121, 1983.
91. Bourque, A. J., Krull, I. S., and Feibush, B., Automated HPLC analyses of drugs of abuse via direct injection of biological fluids followed by simultaneous solid-phase extraction and derivatization with fluorescence detection, *Biomedical Chromatography*, 8, 53–62, 1994.
92. Achilli, G., Cellerino, G. P., Deril, G. V. M., and Tagliaro, F., Determination of illicit drugs and related substances by high-performance liquid chromatography with an electrochemical coulometric-array detector, *Journal of Chromatography*, 729, 273–277, 1996.
93. Michel, R. E., Rege, A. B., and George, W. J., High-pressure liquid chromatography/electrochemical detection method for monitoring MDA and MDMA in whole blood and other biological tissues, *Journal of Neuroscience Methods*, 50, 61–66, 1993.
94. Paul, B. D., Past, M. R., McKinley, R. M., Foreman, J. D., McWhorter, L. K., and Snyder, J. J., Amphetamine as an artifact of methamphetamine during periodate degradation of interfering ephedrine, pseudoephedrine, and phenylpropanolamine: an improved procedure for accurate quantitation of amphetamines in urine, *Journal of Analytical Toxicology*, 18, 331–336, 1994.
95. Suzuki, S., Inoue, T., Hori, H., and Inayama, S., Analysis of methamphetamine in hair, nail, sweat, and saliva by mass fragmentography, *Journal of Analytical Toxicology*, 13, 176–178, 1989.
96. Hornbeck, C. L., Carrig, J. E., and Czarny, R. J., Detection of a GC/MS artifact peak as methamphetamine, *Journal of Analytical Toxicology*, 17, 257–263, 1993.
97. Nakahara, Y., Detection and diagnostic interpretation of amphetamines in hair [review], *Forensic Science International*, 70, 135–153, 1995.
98. Kalasinsky, K. S., Levine, B., Smith, M. L., Magluilo, J., Jr., and Schaefer, T., Detection of amphetamine and methamphetamine in urine by gas chromatography/Fourier transform infrared (GC/FTIR) spectroscopy, *Journal of Analytical Toxicology*, 17, 359–364, 1993.
99. Lillsunde, P. and Korte, T., Determination of ring- and N-substituted amphetamines as heptafluorobutyryl derivatives, *Forensic Science International*, 49, 205–213, 1991.
100. Logan, B. K., Methamphetamine and driving impairment [review], *Journal of Forensic Sciences*, 41, 457–464, 1996.
101. Rasmussen, S., Cole, R., and Spiehler, V., Methamphetamine in antemortem blood and urine by RIA and GC/MS, *Journal of Analytical Toxicology*, 13, 263–267, 1989.
102. Premel-Cabic, A., Cailleux, A., and Allain, P., [A gas chromatographic assay of fifteen volatile organic solvents in blood (author's transl)]. [French], *Clinica Chimica Acta*, 56, 5–11, 1974.
103. Astier, A., Chromatographic determination of volatile solvents and their metabolites in urine for monitoring occupational exposure, *Journal of Chromatography*, 643, 389–398, 1993.
104. Oliver, J. S. and Watson, J. M., Abuse of solvents "for kicks," *Lancet*, 1, 84–86, 1977.
105. Ghittori, S., Fiorentino, M. L., and Imbriani, M., [Use of gas chromatography with flame ionization (GC-FID) in the measurement of solvents in the urine], *Giornale Italiano di Medicina del Lavoro*, 9, 21–24, 1987.
106. Houghton, E., Teale, P., and Dumasia, M. C., Improved capillary GC/MS method for the determination of anabolic steroid and corticosteroid metabolites in horse urine using on-column injection with high-boiling solvents, *Analyst* (London), 109, 273–275, 1984.
107. Maurer, H. H., Identification and differentiation of barbiturates, other sedative-hypnotics and their metabolites in urine integrated in a general screening procedure using computerized gas chromatography-mass spectrometry, *Journal of Chromatography*, 530, 307–326, 1990.
108. Kingswood, J. C., Routledge, P. A., and Lazarus, J. H., A report of overdose with astemizole, *Human Toxicology*, 5, 43–44, 1986.
109. Law, B. and Weir, S., Fundamental studies in reversed-phase liquid-solid extraction of basic drugs. II. Hydrogen bonding effects, *Journal of Pharmaceutical & Biomedical Analysis*, 10, 181–186, 1992.
110. Logan, B. K. and Case, G. A., Identification of laudanosine, an atracurium metabolite, following a fatal drug-related shooting, *Journal of Analytical Toxicology*, 17, 117–119, 1993.
111. Xu, A., Havel, J., Linderholm, K., and Hulse, J., Development and validation of an LC/MS/MS method for the determination of L-hyoscyamine in human plasma, *Journal of Pharmaceutical & Biomedical Analysis*, 14, 33–42, 1995.

112. Saady, J. J. and Poklis, A., Determination of atropine in blood by gas chromatography/mass spectrometry, *Journal of Analytical Toxicology*, 13, 296–299, 1989.
113. Cugell, D. W., Clinical pharmacology and toxicology of ipratropium bromide. [Review], *American Journal of Medicine*, 81, 18–22, 1986.
114. Fraser, A. D., MacNeil, W., and Isner, A. F., Toxicological analysis of a fatal baclofen (Lioresal) ingestion, *Journal of Forensic Sciences*, 36, 1596–1602, 1991.
115. Millerioux, L., Brault, M., Gualano, V., and Mignot, A., High-performance liquid chromatographic determination of baclofen in human plasma, *Journal of Chromatography* 729, 309–314, 1996.
116. Bailey, D. N. and Jatlow, P. I., Barbital overdose and abuse, *American Journal of Clinical Pathology*, 64, 291–296, 1975.
117. Varin, F., Marchand, C., Larochelle, P., and Midha, K. K., GLC-mass spectrometric procedure with selected-ion monitoring for determination of plasma concentrations of unlabeled and labeled barbital following simultaneous oral and intravenous administration, *Journal of Pharmaceutical Sciences*, 69, 640–643, 1980.
118. Moriya, F. and Hashimoto, Y., Application of the Triage panel for drugs of abuse to forensic blood samples, *Nippon Hoigaku Zasshi—Japanese Journal of Legal Medicine*, 50, 50–56, 1996.
119. Chankvetadze, B., Chankvetadze, L., Sidamonidze, S., Yashima, E., and Okamoto, Y., High performance liquid chromatography enantioseparation of chiral pharmaceuticals using tris(chloro-methylphenylcarbamate)s of cellulose, *Journal of Pharmaceutical & Biomedical Analysis*, 14, 1295–1303, 1996.
120. Qiu, F. H., Liu, L., Guo, L., Luo, Y., and Lu, Y. Q., [Rapid identification and quantitation of barbiturates in plasma using solid-phase extraction combined with GC-FID and GC-MS method], *Yao Hsueh Hsueh Pao—Acta Pharmaceutica Sinica*, 30, 372–377, 1995.
121. Thormann, W., Meier, P., Marcolli, C., and Binder, F., Analysis of barbiturates in human serum and urine by high-performance capillary electrophoresis-micellar electrokinetic capillary chromatography with on-column multi-wavelength detection, *Journal of Chromatography*, 545, 445–460, 1991.
122. Minder, E. I., Schaubhut, R., and Vonderschmitt, D. J., Screening for drugs in clinical toxicology by high-performance liquid chromatography: identification of barbiturates by post-column ionization and detection by a multiplace photodiode array spectrophotometer, *Journal of Chromatography*, 428, 369–376, 1988.
123. Mangin, P., Lugnier, A. A., and Chaumont, A. J., A polyvalent method using HPLC for screening and quantification of 12 common barbiturates in various biological materials, *Journal of Analytical Toxicology*, 11, 27–30, 1987.
124. Cody, J. T. and Foltz, R. L., GC/MS analysis of body fluids for drugs of abuse, in *Forensic Applications of Mass Spectrometry*, Yinon, J., Ed., CRC Press, Boca Raton, FL, 1995, pp. 1–59.
125. Kojima, T., Taniguchi, T., Yashiki, M., Miyazaki, T., Iwasaki, Y., Mikami, T., et al., A rapid method for detecting barbiturates in serum using EI-SIM, *International Journal of Legal Medicine*, 107, 21–24, 1994.
126. Abadi, M. and Solomon, H. M., Detection of tolmetin and oxaprozin by a GC/MS method for barbiturates [letter], *Journal of Analytical Toxicology*, 18, 62, 1994.
127. Gibb, R. P., Cockerham, H., Goldfogel, G. A., Lawson, G. M., and Raisys, V. A., Substance abuse testing of urine by GC/MS in scanning mode evaluated by proficiency studies, TLC/GC, and EMIT, *Journal of Forensic Sciences*, 38, 124–133, 1993.
128. Pocci, R., Dixit, V., and Dixit, V. M., Solid-phase extraction and GC/MS confirmation of barbiturates from human urine, *Journal of Analytical Toxicology*, 16, 45–47, 1992.
129. Chen, X. H., Wijsbeek, J., van Veen, J., Franke, J. P., and de Zeeuw, R. A., Solid-phase extraction for the screening of acidic, neutral and basic drugs in plasma using a single-column procedure on Bond Elut Certify, *Journal of Chromatography*, 529, 161–166, 1990.
130. Logan, B. K., Methamphetamine and driving impairment. [Review] [37 refs], *Journal of Forensic Sciences*, 41, 457–464, 1996.
131. Long, C. and Crifasi, J., Methamphetamine identification in four forensic cases, *Journal of Forensic Sciences*, 41, 713–714, 1996.
132. Ensslin, H. K., Kovar, K. A., and Maurer, H. H., Toxicological detection of the designer drug 3,4-methylenedioxyethylamphetamine (Mde, Eve) and its metabolites in urine by gas chromatography mass spectrometry and fluorescence polarization immunoassay, *Journal of Chromatography B: Biomedical Applications*, 683, 189–197, 1996.

133. Valentine, J. L., Kearns, G. L., Sparks, C., Letzig, L. G., Valentine, C. R., Shappell, S. A., et al., GC-MS determination of amphetamine and methamphetamine in human urine for 12 hours following oral administration of dextro-methamphetamine: lack of evidence supporting the established forensic guidelines for methamphetamine confirmation, *Journal of Analytical Toxicology*, 19, 581–590, 1995.
134. Meatherall, R., Rapid GC-MS confirmation of urinary amphetamine and methamphetamine as their propylchloroformate derivatives, *Journal of Analytical Toxicology*, 19, 316–322, 1995.
135. Arufe-Martinez, M. I. and Romero-Palanco, J. L., Identification of cocaine in cocaine-lidocaine mixtures ("rock cocaine") and other illicit cocaine preparations using derivative absorption spectroscopy, *Journal of Analytical Toxicology*, 12, 192–196, 1988.
136. Clauwaert, K. M., Vanbocxlaer, J. F., Lambert, W. E., and Deleenheer, A. P., Analysis of cocaine, benzoylecgonine, and cocaethylene in urine by HPLC with diode array detection, *Analytical Chemistry*, 68, 3021–3028, 1996.
137. Fernandez, P., Lafuente, N., Bermejo, A. M., Lopezrivadulla, M., and Cruz, A., HPLC determination of cocaine and benzoylecgonine in plasma and urine from drug abusers, *Journal of Analytical Toxicology*, 20, 224–228, 1996.
138. Logan, B. K., Smirnow, D., and Gullberg, R. G., Lack of predictable site-dependent differences and time-dependent changes in postmortem concentrations of cocaine, benzoylecgonine, and cocaethylene in humans, *Journal of Analytical Toxicology*, 21, 23–31, 1997.
139. Sosnoff, C. S., Ann, Q., Bernert, J. T., Jr., Powell, M. K., Miller, B. B., Henderson, L. O., et al., Analysis of benzoylecgonine in dried blood spots by liquid chromatography—atmospheric pressure chemical ionization tandem mass spectrometry, *Journal of Analytical Toxicology*, 20, 179–184, 1996.
140. Thompson, W. C. and Dasgupta, A., Confirmation and quantitation of cocaine, benzoylecgonine, ecgonine methyl ester, and cocaethylene by gas chromatography/mass spectrometry, *American Journal of Clinical Pathology*, 104, 187–192, 1995.
141. Corburt, M. R. and Koves, E. M., Gas chromatography/mass spectrometry for the determination of cocaine and benzoylecgonine over a wide concentration range, *Journal of Forensic Sciences*, 39, 136–149, 1994.
142. Okeke, C. C., Wynn, J. E., and Patrick, K. S., Simultaneous analysis of cocaine, benzoylecgonine, methylecgonine, and ecgonine in plasma using an exchange resin and GC/MS, *Chromatographia*, 38, 52–56, 1994.
143. Gerlits, J., GC/MS quantitation of benzoylecgonine following liquid–liquid extraction of urine, *Journal of Forensic Sciences*, 38, 1210–1214, 1993.
144. Aderjan, R. E., Schmitt, G., Wu, M., and Meyer, C., Determination of cocaine and benzoylecgonine by derivatization with iodomethane-D3 or PFPA/HFIP in human blood and urine using GC/MS (EI or PCI mode), *Journal of Analytical Toxicology*, 17, 51–55, 1993.
145. Abusada, G. M., Abukhalaf, I. K., Alford, D. D., Vinzon-Bautista, I., Pramanik, A. K., Ansari, N. A., et al., Solid-phase extraction and GC/MS quantitation of cocaine, ecgonine methyl ester, benzoylecgonine, and cocaethylene from meconium, whole blood, and plasma, *Journal of Analytical Toxicology*, 17, 353–358, 1993.
146. Kikura, R. and Nakahara, Y., Hair analysis for drugs of abuse. XI. Disposition of benzphetamine and its metabolites into hair and comparison of benzphetamine use and methamphetamine use by hair analysis, *Biological & Pharmaceutical Bulletin*, 18, 1694–1699, 1995.
147. Rosano, T. G., Meola, J. M., Wolf, B. C., Guisti, L. W., and Jindal, S. P., Benztropine identification and quantitation in a suicidal overdose, *Journal of Analytical Toxicology*, 18, 348–353, 1994.
148. Le Solleu, H., Demotes-Mainard, F., Vincon, G., and Bannwarth, B., The determination of bromazepam in plasma by reversed-phase high-performance liquid chromatography, *Journal of Pharmaceutical & Biomedical Analysis*, 11, 771–775, 1993.
149. Yoshida, M., Watabiki, T., Tokiyasu, T., Saito, I., and Ishida, N., [Determination of benzodiazepines by thermospray liquid chromatograph-mass spectrometer. Part 1. Nitrazepam, estazolam, bromazepam, flunitrazepam]. [Japanese], *Nippon Hoigaku Zasshi Japanese Journal of Legal Medicine*, 47, 220–226, 1993.
150. Haring, N., Salama, Z., and Jaeger, H., Triple stage quadrupole mass spectrometric determination of bromocriptine in human plasma with negative ion chemical ionization, *Arzneimittel Forschung*, 38, 1529–1532, 1988.

151. Hindmarsh, K. W., Hamon, N. W., and LeGatt, D. F., Simultaneous identification and quantitation of diphenhydramine and methaqualone, *Clinical Toxicology*, 11, 245–255, 1977.
152. Meatherall, R. C. and Guay, D. R., Isothermal gas chromatographic analysis of diphenhydramine after direct injection onto a fused-silica capillary column, *Journal of Chromatography*, 307, 295–304, 1984.
153. Tonn, G. R., Mutlib, A., Abbott, F. S., Rurak, D. W., and Axelson, J. E., Simultaneous analysis of diphenhydramine and a stable isotope analog (2H10)diphenhydramine using capillary gas chromatography with mass selective detection in biological fluids from chronically instrumented pregnant ewes, *Biological Mass Spectrometry*, 22, 633–642, 1993.
154. Vycudilik, W. and Pollak, S., [Detection of diphenhydramine in autolytic brain tissue in poison-induced brain death syndrome], *Zeitschrift für Rechtsmedizin—Journal of Legal Medicine*, 95, 129–135, 1985.
155. Lorec, A. M., Bruguerolle, B., Attolini, L., and Roucoules, X., Rapid simultaneous determination of lidocaine, bupivacaine, and their two main metabolites using capillary gas-liquid chromatography with nitrogen phosphorus detector, *Therapeutic Drug Monitoring*, 16, 592–595, 1994.
156. Demedts, P., Wauters, A., Franck, F., and Neels, H., Simultaneous determination of lidocaine, bupivacaine, and their two main metabolites using gas chromatography and a nitrogen–phosphorus detector —selection of stationary phase and chromatographic conditions, *Therapeutic Drug Monitoring*, 18, 208–209, 1996.
157. Coyle, D. E. and Denson, D. D., Simultaneous measurement of bupivacaine, etidocaine, lidocaine, meperidine, mepivacaine, and methadone, *Therapeutic Drug Monitoring*, 8, 98–101, 1986.
158. Clark, B. J., Hamdi, A., Berrisford, R. G., Sabanathan, S., and Mearns, A. J., Reversed-phase and chiral high-performance liquid chromatographic assay of bupivacaine and its enantiomers in clinical samples after continuous extraplural infusion, *Journal of Chromatography*, 553, 383–390, 1991.
159. Zakowski, M. I., Ramanathan, S., Sharnick, S., and Turndorf, H., Uptake and distribution of bupivacaine and morphine after intrathecal administration in parturients: effects of epinephrine, *Anesthesia & Analgesia*, 74, 664–669, 1992.
160. Bailey, C. R., Ruggier, R., and Findley, I. L., Diamorphine-bupivacaine mixture compared with plain bupivacaine for analgesia, *British Journal of Anaesthesia*, 72, 58–61, 1994.
161. Martin, J. and Neill, R. S., Venous plasma (total) bupivacaine concentrations following lower abdominal field block, *British Journal of Anaesthesia*, 59, 1425–1430, 1987.
162. Kintz, P., Cirimele, V., Edel, Y., Jamey, C., and Mangin, P., Hair analysis for buprenorphine and its dealkylated metabolite by RIA and confirmation by LC/ECD, *Journal of Forensic Sciences*, 39, 1497–1503, 1994.
163. Debrabandere, L., Van Boven, M., and Daenens, P., Analysis of buprenorphine in urine specimens, *Journal of Forensic Sciences*, 37, 82–89, 1992.
164. Kuhlman, J. J., Magluilo, J., Cone, E., and Levine, B., Simultaneous assay of buprenorphine and norbuprenorphine by negative chemical ionization tandem mass spectrometry, *Journal of Analytical Toxicology*, 20, 229–235, 1996.
165. Shiraishi, Y., Sakai, S., Yokoyama, J., Hayatsu, K., Mochizuki, T., Moriwaki, G., et al., [The plasma concentration of buprenorphine during its continuous epidural infusion after catheterization at different vertebral levels], *Masui—Japanese Journal of Anesthesiology*, 42, 371–375, 1993.
166. Battah, A.-K. and Anderson, R. A., Comparison of silyl derivatives for GC/MS analysis of morphine and buprenorphine in blood, in 26th International Meeting of the International Association of Forensic Toxicologists, 1989, Glasgow, Scotland.
167. Kuhlman, J. J., Lalani, S., Magluilo, J., Levine, B., Darwin, W. D., Johnson, R. E., et al., Human pharmacokinetics of intravenous, sublingual, and buccal buprenorphine, *Journal of Analytical Toxicology*, 20, 369–378, 1996.
168. Ohtani, M., Kotaki, H., Uchino, K., Sawada, Y., and Iga, T., Pharmacokinetic analysis of enterohepatic circulation of buprenorphine and its active metabolite, norbuprenorphine, in rats, *Drug Metabolism & Disposition*, 22, 2–7, 1994.
169. San, L., Torrens, M., Castillo, C., Porta, M., and de la Torre, R., Consumption of buprenorphine and other drugs among heroin addicts under ambulatory treatment: results from cross-sectional studies in 1988 and 1990, *Addiction*, 88, 1341–1349, 1993.
170. Rohrig, T. P. and Ray, N. G., Tissue distribution of bupropion in a fatal overdose, *Journal of Analytical Toxicology*, 16, 343–345, 1992.

171. Fogel, P., Mamer, O. A., Chouinard, G., and Farrell, P. G., Determination of plasma bupropion and its relationship to therapeutic effect, *Biomedical Mass Spectrometry*, 11, 629–632, 1984.
172. Friel, P. N., Logan, B. K., and Fligner, C. L., Three fatal drug overdoses involving bupropion, *Journal of Analytical Toxicology*, 17, 436–438, 1993.
173. Spiller, H. A., Ramoska, E. A., Krenzelok, E. P., Sheen, S. R., Borys, D. J., Villalobos, D., et al., Bupropion overdose: a 3-year multi-center retrospective analysis, *American Journal of Emergency Medicine*, 12, 43–45, 1994.
174. Butz, R. F., Welch, R. M., and Findlay, J. W., Relationship between bupropion disposition and dopamine uptake inhibition in rats and mice, *Journal of Pharmacology & Experimental Therapeutics*, 221, 676–685, 1982.
175. Jajoo, H. K., Mayol, R. F., LaBudde, J. A., and Blair, I. A., Metabolism of the antianxiety drug buspirone in human subjects, *Drug Metabolism & Disposition*, 17, 634–640, 1989.
176. Scott, E. P., Application of postcolumn ionization in the high-performance liquid chromatographic analysis of butabarbital sodium elixir, *Journal of Pharmaceutical Sciences*, 72, 1089–1091, 1983.
177. Mulvana, D. E., Duncan, G. F., Shyu, W. C., Tay, L. K., and Barbhaiya, R. H., Quantitative determination of butorphanol and its metabolites in human plasma by gas chromatography electron capture negative-ion chemical ionization mass spectrometry, *Journal of Chromatography B: Biomedical Applications*, 682, 289–300, 1996.
178. Combie, J., Blake, J. W., Nugent, T. E., and Tobin, T., Furosemide, Patella vulgata beta-glucuronidase and drug analysis: conditions for enhancement of the TLC detection of apomorphine, butorphanol, hydromorphone, nalbuphine, oxymorphone and pentazocine in equine urine, *Research Communications in Chemical Pathology & Pharmacology*, 35, 27–41, 1982.
179. Rodopoulos, N. and Norman, A., Determination of caffeine and its metabolites in urine by high-performance liquid chromatography and capillary electrophoresis, *Scandinavian Journal of Clinical & Laboratory Investigation*, 54, 305–315, 1994.
180. Jin, X., Zhou, Z. H., He, X. F., Zhang, Z. H., and Wang, M. Z., [Solid-phase extraction and RP-HPLC screening procedure for diuretics, probenecid, caffeine and pemoline in urine], *Yao Hsueh Hsueh Pao —Acta Pharmaceutica Sinica*, 27, 875–880, 1992.
181. Leakey, T. E., Simultaneous analysis of theophylline, caffeine and eight of their metabolic products in human plasma by gradient high-performance liquid chromatography, *Journal of Chromatography*, 507, 199–220, 1990.
182. Fligner, C. L. and Opheim, K. E., Caffeine and its dimethylxanthine metabolites in two cases of caffeine overdose: a cause of falsely elevated theophylline concentrations in serum, *Journal of Analytical Toxicology*, 12, 339–343, 1988.
183. Garriott, J. C., Simmons, L. M., Poklis, A., and Mackell, M. A., Five cases of fatal overdose from caffeine-containing "look-alike" drugs, *Journal of Analytical Toxicology*, 9, 141–143, 1985.
184. Miceli, J. N., Aravind, M. K., and Ferrell, W. J., Analysis of caffeine: comparison of the manual enzyme multiplied immunoassay (EMIT), automated EMIT, and high-performance liquid chromatography procedures, *Therapeutic Drug Monitoring*, 6, 344–347, 1984.
185. Lensmeyer, G. L., Isothermal gas chromatographic method for the rapid determination of carbamazepine ("tegretol") as its TMS derivative, *Clinical Toxicology*, 11, 443–454, 1977.
186. Schwertner, H. A., Hamilton, H. E., and Wallace, J. E., Analysis for carbamazepine in serum by electron-capture gas chromatography, *Clinical Chemistry*, 24, 895–899, 1978.
187. Toseland, P. A., Grove, J., and Berry, D. J., An isothermal GLC determination of the plasma levels of carbamazepine, diphenylhydantoin, phenobarbitone and primidone, *Clinica Chimica Acta*, 38, 321–328, 1972.
188. Martens, J. and Banditt, P., Validation of the analysis of carbamazepine and its 10,11-epoxide metabolite by high-performance liquid chromatography from plasma: comparison with gas chromatography and the enzyme-multiplied immunoassay technique, *Journal of Chromatography*, 620, 169–173, 1993.
189. Romanyshyn, L. A., Wichmann, J. K., Kucharczyk, N., Shumaker, R. C., Ward, D., and Sofia, R. D., Simultaneous determination of felbamate, primidone, phenobarbital, carbamazepine, two carbamazepine metabolites, phenytoin, and one phenytoin metabolite in human plasma by high-performance liquid chromatography, *Therapeutic Drug Monitoring*, 16, 90–99, 1994.

190. Rainbow, S. J., Dawson, C. M., and Tickner, T. R., Direct serum injection high-performance liquid chromatographic method for the simultaneous determination of phenobarbital, carbamazepine and phenytoin, *Journal of Chromatography*, 527, 389–396, 1990.
191. Schmidt, S. and Schmitz-Buhl, M., Signs and symptoms of carbamazepine overdose, *Journal of Neurology*, 242, 169–173, 1995.
192. Chai, C. and Killeen, A. A., Carbamazepine measurement in samples from the emergency room, *Therapeutic Drug Monitoring*, 16, 407–412, 1994.
193. Schwartz, J. G., Garriott, J. C., Somerset, J. S., Igler, E. J., Rodriguez, R., and Orr, M. D., Measurements of fentanyl and sufentanil in blood and urine after surgical application. Implication in detection of abuse, *American Journal of Forensic Medicine & Pathology*, 15, 236–241, 1994.
194. Tobin, T., Kwiatkowski, S., Watt, D., Tai, H., Tai, C., Woods, W., et al., Immunoassay detection of drugs in racing horses. XI. ELISA and RIA detection of fentanyl, alfentanil, sufentanil and carfentanil in equine blood and urine, *Research Communications in Chemical Pathology & Pharmacology*, 63, 129–152, 1989.
195. Kintz, P., Mangin, P., Lugnier, A. A., and Chaumont, A. J., A rapid and sensitive gas chromatographic analysis of meprobamate or carisoprodol in urine and plasma, *Journal of Analytical Toxicology*, 12, 73–74, 1988.
196. Backer, R. C., Zumwalt, R., McFeeley, P., Veasey, S., and Wohlenberg, N., Carisoprodol concentrations from different anatomical sites: three overdose cases, *Journal of Analytical Toxicology*, 14, 332–334, 1990.
197. Kaistha, K. K., Selective assay procedure for chlorpropamide in the presence of its decomposition products, *Journal of Pharmaceutical Sciences*, 58, 235–237, 1969.
198. Meatherall, R. C., Green, P. T., Kenick, S., and Donen, N., Diazoxide in the management of chlorpropamide overdose, *Journal of Analytical Toxicology*, 5, 287–291, 1981.
199. Levine, B., Park, J., Smith, T. D., and Caplan, Y. H., Chloral hydrate: unusually high concentrations in a fatal overdose, *Journal of Analytical Toxicology*, 9, 232–233, 1985.
200. Meyer, E., Van Bocxlaer, J. F., Lambert, W. E., Piette, M., and De Leenheer, A. P., Determination of chloral hydrate and metabolites in a fatal intoxication, *Journal of Analytical Toxicology*, 19, 124–126, 1995.
201. Lister, R. G., Abernethy, D. R., Greenblatt, D. J., and File, S. E., Methods for the determination of lorazepam and chlordiazepoxide and metabolites in brain tissue, *Journal of Chromatography*, 277, 201–208, 1983.
202. Song, D., Zhang, S., and Kohlhof, K., Determination of chlordiazepoxide in mouse plasma by gas chromatography-negative-ion chemical ionization mass spectrometry, *Journal of Chromatography B: Biomedical Applications*, 660, 95–101, 1994.
203. Heller, P. F., Goldberger, B. A., and Caplan, Y. H., Chloral hydrate overdose: trichloroethanol detection by gas chromatography/mass spectrometry, *Forensic Science International*, 52, 231–234, 1992.
204. Bailey, D. N., Blood concentrations and clinical findings following overdose of chlordiazepoxide alone and chlordiazepoxide plus ethanol, *Journal of Toxicology—Clinical Toxicology*, 22, 433–446, 1984.
205. Dixon, R., Brooks, M. A., Postma, E., Hackman, M. R., Spector, S., Moore, J. D., et al., N-desmethyldiazepam: a new metabolite of chlordiazepoxide in man, *Clinical Pharmacology & Therapeutics*, 20, 450–457, 1976.
206. Stronjny, N., Bratin, K., Brooks, M. A., and de Silva, J. A., Determination of chlordiazepoxide, diazepam, and their major metabolites in blood or plasma by spectrophotodensitometry, *Journal of Chromatography*, 143, 363–374, 1977.
207. Bailey, D. N. and Guba, J. J., Gas-chromatographic analysis for chlorpromazine and some of its metabolites in human serum, with use of a nitrogen detector, *Clinical Chemistry*, 25, 1211–1215, 1979.
208. Ohkubo, T., Shimoyama, R., and Sugawara, K., Determination of chlorpromazine in human breast milk and serum by high-performance liquid chromatography, *Journal of Chromatography*, 614, 328–332, 1993.
209. Nishigami, J., Takayasu, T., and Ohshima, T., Toxicological analysis of the psychotropic drugs chlorpromazine and diazepam using chemically fixed organ tissues, *International Journal of Legal Medicine*, 107, 165–170, 1995.

210. Walker, O. and Ademowo, O. G., A rapid, cost-effective liquid chromatographic method for the determination of chloroquine and desethylchloroquine in biological fluids, *Therapeutic Drug Monitoring*, 18, 92–96, 1996.
211. Volin, P., Simple and specific reversed-phase liquid chromatographic method with diode-array detection for simultaneous determination of serum hydroxychloroquine, chloroquine and some corticosteroids, *Journal of Chromatography B: Biomedical Applications*, 666, 347–353, 1995.
212. Murtha, J. L., Julian, T. N., and Radebaugh, G. W., Simultaneous determination of pseudoephedrine hydrochloride, chlorpheniramine maleate, and dextromethorphan hydrobromide by second-derivative photodiode array spectroscopy, *Journal of Pharmaceutical Sciences*, 77, 715–718, 1988.
213. Masumoto, K., Tashiro, Y., Matsumoto, K., Yoshida, A., Hirayama, M., and Hayashi, S., Simultaneous determination of codeine and chlorpheniramine in human plasma by capillary column gas chromatography, *Journal of Chromatography*, 381, 323–329, 1986.
214. Bailey, D. N. and Guba, J. J., Gas-chromatographic analysis for chlorpromazine and some of its metabolites in human serum, with use of a nitrogen detector, *Clinical Chemistry*, 25, 1211–1215, 1979.
215. Garriott, J. C. and Stolman, A., Detection of some psychotherapeutic drugs and their metabolites in urine, *Clinical Toxicology*, 4, 225–243, 1971.
216. Fenimore, D. C., Meyer, C. J., Davis, C. M., Hsu, F., and Zlatkis, A., High-performance thin-layer chromatographic determination of psychopharmacologic agents in blood serum, *Journal of Chromatography*, 142, 399–409, 1977.
217. Lin, Q., Lensmeyer, G. L., and Larson, F. C., Quantitation of cimetidine and cimetidine sulfoxide in serum by solid-phase extraction and solvent-recycled liquid chromatography, *Journal of Analytical Toxicology*, 9, 161–166, 1985.
218. Borel, A. G. and Abbott, F. S., Metabolic profiling of clobazam, a 1,5-benzodiazepine, in rats, *Drug Metabolism & Disposition*, 21, 415–427, 1993.
219. Streete, J. M., Berry, D. J., and Newbery, J. E., The analysis of clobazam and its metabolite desmethylclobazam by high-performance liquid chromatography, *Therapeutic Drug Monitoring*, 13, 339–344, 1991.
220. Schutz, H., [A screening test for Nor-clobazam, a principal metabolite of the new 1,5 benzodiazepine clobazam (Frisium)], *Archiv für Kriminologie*, 163, 91–94, 1979.
221. Coudore, F., Hourcade, F., Moliniermanoukian, C., Eschalier, A., and Lavarenne, E., Application of HPLC with silica-phase and reversed-phase eluents for the determination of clomipramine and demethylated and 8-hydroxylated metabolites, *Journal of Analytical Toxicology*, 20, 101–105, 1996.
222. Altieri, I., Pichini, S., Pacifici, R., and Zuccaro, P., Improved clean-up procedure for the high-performance liquid chromatographic assay of clomipramine and its demethylated metabolite in human plasma, *Journal of Chromatography B: Biomedical Applications*, 669, 416–417, 1995.
223. McIntyre, I. M., King, C. V., Cordner, S. M., and Drummer, O. H., Postmortem clomipramine: therapeutic or toxic concentrations? *Journal of Forensic Sciences*, 39, 486–493, 1994.
224. Nielsen, K. K. and Brosen, K., High-performance liquid chromatography of clomipramine and metabolites in human plasma and urine, *Therapeutic Drug Monitoring*, 15, 122–128, 1993.
225. Marliac, Y. and Barazi, S., [Determination of unchanged clonazepam in plasma by gas-liquid chromatography]. [French], *Annales de Biologie Clinique*, 47, 503–506, 1989.
226. Miller, L. G., Friedman, H., and Greenblatt, D. J., Measurement of clonazepam by electron-capture gas-liquid chromatography with application to single-dose pharmacokinetics, *Journal of Analytical Toxicology*, 11, 55–57, 1987.
227. Wilson, J. M., Friel, P. N., Wilensky, A. J., and Raisys, V. A., A methods comparison: clonazepam by GC-electron capture and GC/MS, *Therapeutic Drug Monitoring*, 1, 387–397, 1979.
228. Petters, I., Peng, D. R., and Rane, A., Quantitation of clonazepam and its 7-amino and 7-acetamido metabolites in plasma by high-performance liquid chromatography, *Journal of Chromatography*, 306, 241–248, 1984.
229. Shaw, W., Long, G., and McHan, J., An HPLC method for analysis of clonazepam in serum, *Journal of Analytical Toxicology*, 7, 119–122, 1983.
230. Haver, V. M., Porter, W. H., Dorie, L. D., and Lea, J. R., Simplified high performance liquid chromatographic method for the determination of clonazepam and other benzodiazepines in serum, *Therapeutic Drug Monitoring*, 8, 352–357, 1986.

231. Doran, T. C., Liquid chromatographic assay for serum clonazepam, *Therapeutic Drug Monitoring*, 10, 474–479, 1988.
232. Haering, N., Salama, Z., Reif, G., and Jaeger, H., GC/MS determination of clonidine in body fluids. Application to pharmacokinetics, *Arzneimittel-Forschung*, 38, 404–407, 1988.
233. Arrendale, R. F., Stewart, J. T., and Tackett, R. L., Determination of clonidine in human plasma by cold on-column injection capillary GC/MS, *Journal of Chromatography*, 432, 165–175, 1988.
234. Linnoila, M. and Dorrity, F., Jr., Rapid gas chromatographic assay of serum diazepam, N-desmethyldiazepam, and N-desalkylflurazepam, *Acta Pharmacologica et Toxicologica*, 41, 458–464, 1977.
235. McCurdy, H. H., Lewellen, L. J., Cagle, J. C., and Solomons, E. T., A rapid procedure for the screening and quantitation of barbiturates, diazepam, desmethyldiazepam and methaqualone, *Journal of Analytical Toxicology*, 5, 253–257, 1981.
236. Kudo, K., Nagata, T., Kimura, K., Imamura, T., and Noda, M., Sensitive determination of diazepam and N-desmethyldiazepam in human material using capillary GC/MS, *Journal of Chromatography*, 431, 353–359, 1988.
237. Lovdahl, M. J., Perry, P. J., and Miller, D. D., The assay of clozapine and N-desmethylclozapine in human plasma by high-performance liquid chromatography, *Therapeutic Drug Monitoring*, 13, 69–72, 1991.
238. Jennison, T. A., Brown, P., Crossett, J., Kushnir, M., and Urry, F. M., A rapid gas chromatographic method quantitating clozapine in human plasma or serum for the purpose of therapeutic monitoring, *Journal of Analytical Toxicology*, 19, 537–541, 1995.
239. Lin, G., McKay, G., Hubbard, J. W., and Midha, K. K., Decomposition of clozapine N-oxide in the qualitative and quantitative analysis of clozapine and its metabolites, *Journal of Pharmaceutical Sciences*, 83, 1412–1417, 1994.
240. McCarthy, P. T., Hughes, S., and Paton, C., Measurement of clozapine and norclozapine in plasma/serum by high performance liquid chromatography with ultraviolet detection, *Biomedical Chromatography*, 9, 36–41, 1995.
241. Gupta, R. N., Column liquid chromatographic determination of clozapine and N-desmethylclozapine in human serum using solid-phase extraction, *Journal of Chromatography B: Biomedical Applications*, 673, 311–315, 1995.
242. Olesen, O. V. and Poulsen, B., On-line fully automated determination of clozapine and desmethylclozapine in human serum by solid-phase extraction on exchangeable cartridges and liquid chromatography using a methanol buffer mobile phase on unmodified silica, *Journal of Chromatography*, 622, 39–46, 1993.
243. Chung, M. C., Lin, S. K., Chang, W. H., and Jann, M. W., Determination of clozapine and desmethylclozapine in human plasma by high-performance liquid chromatography with ultraviolet detection, *Journal of Chromatography*, 613, 168–173, 1993.
244. Liu, H. C., Chang, W. H., Wei, F. C., Lin, S. K., Lin, S. K., and Jann, M. W., Monitoring of plasma clozapine levels and its metabolites in refractory schizophrenic patients, *Therapeutic Drug Monitoring*, 18, 200–207, 1996.
245. Clauwaert, K. M., Van Bocxlaer, J. F., Lambert, W. E., and De Leenheer, A. P., Analysis of cocaine, benzoylecgonine, and cocaethylene in urine by HPLC with diode array detection, *Analytical Chemistry*, 68, 3021–3028, 1996.
246. Bailey, D. N., Cocaethylene (ethylcocaine) detection during toxicological screening of a university medical center patient population, *Journal of Analytical Toxicology*, 19, 247–250, 1995.
247. Cone, E. J., Hillsgrove, M., and Darwin, W. D., Simultaneous measurement of cocaine, cocaethylene, their metabolites, and "crack" pyrolysis products by gas chromatography-mass spectrometry, *Clinical Chemistry*, 40, 1299–1305, 1994.
248. Hime, G. W., Hearn, W. L., Rose, S., and Cofino, J., Analysis of cocaine and cocaethylene in blood and tissues by GC-NPD and GC-ion trap mass spectrometry, *Journal of Analytical Toxicology*, 15, 241–245, 1991.
249. Bailey, D. N., Comprehensive review of cocaethylene and cocaine concentrations in patients, *American Journal of Clinical Pathology*, 106, 701–704, 1996.
250. Nishikawa, M., Nakajima, K., Tatsuno, M., Kasuya, F., Igarashi, K., Fukui, M., et al., The analysis of cocaine and its metabolites by liquid chromatography/atmospheric pressure chemical ionization-mass spectrometry (LC/APCI-MS), *Forensic Science International*, 66, 149–158, 1994.

251. Peterson, K. L., Logan, B. K., Christian, G. D., and Ruzicka, J., Analysis of polar cocaine metabolites in urine and spinal fluid, in 46th Annual Meeting of the American Academy of Forensic Sciences, San Antonio, TX, 1994.
252. Logan, B. K. and Stafford, D. T., High-performance liquid chromatography with column switching for the determination of cocaine and benzoylecgonine concentrations in vitreous humor, *Journal of Forensic Sciences*, 35, 1303–1309, 1990.
253. Masoud, A. N. and Krupski, D. M., High-performance liquid chromatographic analysis of cocaine in human plasma, *Journal of Analytical Toxicology*, 4, 305–310, 1980.
254. Thompson, W. C. and Dasgupta, A., Confirmation and quantitation of cocaine, benzoylecgonine, ecgonine methyl ester, and cocaethylene by gas chromatography/mass spectrometry. Use of microwave irradiation for rapid preparation of trimethylsilyl and T-butyldimethylsilyl derivatives [see comments], *American Journal of Clinical Pathology*, 104, 187–192, 1995.
255. Cardenas, S., Gallego, M., and Valcarcel, M., An automated preconcentration-derivatization system for the determination of cocaine and its metabolites in urine and illicit cocaine samples by gas chromatography/mass spectrometry, *Rapid Communications in Mass Spectrometry*, 10, 631–636, 1996.
256. Kintz, P. and Mangin, P., Simultaneous determination of opiates, cocaine and major metabolites of cocaine in human hair by gas chromotography/mass spectrometry (GC/MS), *Forensic Science International*, 73, 93–100, 1995.
257. Hearn, W. L., Keran, E. E., Wei, H. A., and Hime, G., Site-dependent postmortem changes in blood cocaine concentrations, *Journal of Forensic Sciences*, 36, 673–684, 1991.
258. Delbeke, F. T. and Debackere, M., Influence of hydrolysis procedures on the urinary concentrations of codeine and morphine in relation to doping analysis, *Journal of Pharmaceutical & Biomedical Analysis*, 11, 339–343, 1993.
259. Posey, B. L. and Kimble, S. N., High-performance liquid chromatographic study of codeine, norcodeine, and morphine as indicators of codeine ingestion, *Journal of Analytical Toxicology*, 8, 68–74, 1984.
260. Vu-Duc, T. and Vernay, A., Simultaneous detection and quantitation of O6-monoacetylmorphine, morphine and codeine in urine by gas chromatography with nitrogen specific and/or flame ionization detection, *Biomedical Chromatography*, 4, 65–69, 1990.
261. Bowie, L. J. and Kirkpatrick, P. B., Simultaneous determination of monoacetylmorphine, morphine, codeine, and other opiates by GC/MS, *Journal of Analytical Toxicology*, 13, 326–329, 1989.
262. elSohly, H. N., Stanford, D. F., Jones, A. B., elSohly, M. A., Snyder, H., and Pedersen, C., Gas chromatographic/mass spectrometric analysis of morphine and codeine in human urine of poppy seed eaters, *Journal of Forensic Sciences*, 33, 347–356, 1988.
263. Wu Chen, N. B., Schaffer, M. I., Lin, R. L., and Stein, R. J., Simultaneous quantitation of morphine and codeine in biological samples by electron impact mass fragmentography, *Journal of Analytical Toxicology*, 6, 231–234, 1982.
264. Saady, J. J., Narasimhachari, N., and Blanke, R. V., Rapid, simultaneous quantification of morphine, codeine, and hydromorphone by GC/MS, *Journal of Analytical Toxicology*, 6, 235–237, 1982.
265. Gygi, S. P., Colon, F., Raftogianis, R. B., Galinsky, R. E., Wilkins, D. G., and Rollins, D. E., Dose-related distribution of codeine and its metabolites into rat hair, *Drug Metabolism & Disposition*, 24, 282–287, 1996.
266. Tracqui, A., Kintz, P., Ludes, B., Rouge, C., Douibi, H., and Mangin, P., High-performance liquid chromatography coupled to ion spray mass spectrometry for the determination of colchicine at ppb levels in human biofluids, *Journal of Chromatography B: Biomedical Applications*, 675, 235–242, 1996.
267. Clevenger, C. V., August, T. F., and Shaw, L. M., Colchicine poisoning: report of a fatal case with body fluid analysis by GC/MS and histopathologic examination of postmortem tissues, *Journal of Analytical Toxicology*, 15, 151–154, 1991.
268. Thompson, J. A., Ho, M. S., and Petersen, D. R., Analysis of nicotine and cotinine in tissues by capillary GC and GC/MS, *Journal of Chromatography*, 231, 53–63, 1982.
269. Urakawa, N., Nagata, T., Kudo, K., Kimura, K., and Imamura, T., Simultaneous determination of nicotine and cotinine in various human tissues using capillary gas chromatography/mass spectrometry, *International Journal of Legal Medicine*, 106, 232–236, 1994.

270. Deutsch, J., Hegedus, L., Greig, N. H., Rapoport, S. I., and Soncrant, T. T., Electron-impact and chemical ionization detection of nicotine and cotinine by gas chromatography-mass spectrometry in rat plasma and brain, *Journal of Chromatography*, 579, 93–98, 1992.
271. Jacob, P. D., Yu, L., Wilson, M., and Benowitz, N. L., Selected ion monitoring method for determination of nicotine, cotinine and deuterium-labeled analogs: absence of an isotope effect in the clearance of (S)-nicotine-3′,3′-d2 in humans, *Biological Mass Spectrometry*, 20, 247–252, 1991.
272. Backer, R. C., McFeeley, P., and Wohlenberg, N., Fatality resulting from cyclizine overdose, *Journal of Analytical Toxicology*, 13, 308–309, 1989.
273. Tasset, J. J., Schroeder, T. J., and Pesce, A. J., Cyclobenzaprine overdose: the importance of a clinical history in analytical toxicology [letter], *Journal of Analytical Toxicology*, 10, 258, 1986.
274. Levine, B., Jones, R., Smith, M. L., Gudewicz, T. M., and Peterson, B., A multiple drug intoxication involving cyclobenzaprine and ibuprofen, *American Journal of Forensic Medicine & Pathology*, 14, 246–248, 1993.
275. Baehr, G. R., Romano, M., and Young, J. M., An unusual case of cyproheptadine (Periactin) overdose in an adolescent female, *Pediatric Emergency Care*, 2, 183–185, 1986.
276. Law, B., Mason, P. A., Moffat, A. C., Gleadle, R. I., and King, L. J., Forensic aspects of the metabolism and excretion of cannabinoids following oral ingestion of cannabis resin, *Journal of Pharmacy and Pharmacology*, 36, 289–294, 1983.
277. elSohly, M. A., Little, T. L., Jr., and Stanford, D. F., Hexadeutero-11-nor-delta 9-tetrahydrocannabinol-9-carboxylic acid: a superior internal standard for the GC/MS analysis of delta 9-THC acid metabolite in biological specimens, *Journal of Analytical Toxicology*, 16, 188–191, 1992.
278. Moeller, M., Doerr, G., and Warth, S., Simultaneous quantitation of delta-9-tetrahydrocannabinol (THC) and 11-nor-9-carboxy-delta-9-tetrahydrocannabinol (THC-COOH) in serum by GC/MS using deuterated internal standards and its application to a smoking study and forensic cases, *Journal of Forensic Sciences*, 37, 969–983, 1992.
279. Kemp, P. M., Abukhalaf, I. K., Manno, J. E., Manno, B. R., Alford, D. D., McWilliams, M. E., et al., Cannabinoids in humans. II. The influence of three methods of hydrolysis on the concentration of THC and two metabolites in urine, *Journal of Analytical Toxicology*, 19, 292–298, 1995.
280. Wolff, K., Garretty, D., and Hay, A. W. M., Micro-extraction of commonly abused benzodiazepines for urinary screening by liquid chromatography, *Annals of Clinical Biochemistry*, 34, 61–67, 1997.
281. Tanaka, E., Terada, M., Misawa, S., and Wakasugi, C., Simultaneous determination of twelve benzodiazepines in human serum using a new reversed-phase chromatographic column on a 2-mu-m porous microspherical silica gel, *Journal of Chromatography B: Biomedical Applications*, 682, 173–178, 1996.
282. Needleman, S. B. and Porvaznik, M., Identification of parent benzodiazepines by gas chromotography/mass spectroscopy (GC/MS) from urinary extracts treated with B-glucuronidase, *Forensic Science International*, 73, 49–60, 1995.
283. Peat, M. A. and Kopjak, L., The screening and quantitation of diazepam, flurazepam, chloridazepoxide, and their metabolites in blood and plasma by electron-capture gas chromatography and high pressure liquid chromatography, *Journal of Forensic Sciences*, 24, 46–54, 1979.
284. Song, D., Zhang, S., and Kohlhof, K., Gas chromatographic-mass spectrometric method for the determination of flurazepam and its major metabolites in mouse and rat plasma, *Journal of Chromatography B: Biomedical Applications*, 658, 142–148, 1994.
285. Clatworthy, A. J., Jones, L. V., and Whitehouse, M. J., The GC/MS of the major metabolites of flurazepam., *Biomedical Mass Spectronomy*, 4, 248–254, 1977.
286. Aderjan, R. and Mattern, R., [A fatal monointoxication by flurazepam (Dalmadorm). Problems of the toxicological interpretation (author's transl.)]. [German], *Archives of Toxicology*, 43, 69–75, 1979.
287. Abel, M. and Eisenkraft, J. B., Erroneous mass spectrometer readings caused by desflurane and sevoflurane, *Journal of Clinical Monitoring*, 11, 152–158, 1995.
288. Hartter, S., Baier, D., Dingemanse, J., Ziegler, G., and Hiemke, C., Automated determination of dextromethorphan and its main metabolites in human plasma by high-performance liquid chromatography and column switching, *Therapeutic Drug Monitoring*, 18, 297–303, 1996.
289. Lam, Y. W. and Rodriguez, S. Y., High-performance liquid chromatography determination of dextromethorphan and dextrorphan for oxidation phenotyping by fluorescence and ultraviolet detection, *Therapeutic Drug Monitoring*, 15, 300–304, 1993.

290. Wallace, J. E., Schwertner, H. A., and Shimek, E. L. J., Analysis for diazepam and nordiazepam by electron-capture gas chromatography and by liquid chromatography, *Clinical Chemistry*, 25, 1296–1300, 1979.
291. St-Pierre, M. V. and Pang, K. S., Determination of diazepam and its metabolites by high-performance liquid chromatography and thin-layer chromatography, *Journal of Chromatography*, 421, 291–307, 1987.
292. MacKichan, J. J., Jusko, W. J., Duffner, P. K., and Cohen, M. E., Liquid-chromatographic assay of diazepam and its major metabolites in plasma, *Clinical Chemistry*, 25, 856–859, 1979.
293. Plavsic, F. and Culig, J., Determination of serum diclofenac by high-performance liquid chromatography by electromechanical detection, *Human Toxicology*, 4, 317–322, 1985.
294. Blagbrough, I. S., Daykin, M. M., Doherty, M., Pattrick, M., and Shaw, P. N., High-performance liquid chromatographic determination of naproxen, ibuprofen and diclofenac in plasma and synovial fluid in man, *Journal of Chromatography*, 578, 251–257, 1992.
295. Garriott, J. C., Rodriquez, R., and Norton, L. E., Two cases of death involving dicyclomine in infants, *Journal of Toxicology—Clinical Toxicology*, 22, 455–462, 1984.
296. Shimamine, M., Takahashi, K., and Nakahara, Y., [Studies on the identification of psychotropic substances], *Eisei Shikenjo Hokoku—Bulletin of National Institute of Hygienic Sciences*, 67–73, 1992.
297. Levine, B., Smyth, D., and Caplan, Y., A diflunisal related fatality: a case report, *Forensic Science International*, 35, 45–50, 1987.
298. Hofmann, U., Fromm, M. F., Johnson, S., and Mikus, G., Simultaneous determination of dihydrocodeine and dihydromorphine in serum by gas chromatography-tandem mass spectrometry, *Journal of Chromatography B: Biomedical Applications*, 663, 59–65, 1995.
299. Musshoff, F. and Daldrup, T., Evaluation of a method for simultaneous quantification of codeine, dihydrocodeine, morphine, and 6-monoacetylmorphine in serum, blood, and postmortem blood, *International Journal of Legal Medicine*, 106, 107–109, 1993.
300. Maurer, H. H., Identification of antiarrhythmic drugs and their metabolites in urine, *Archives of Toxicology*, 64, 218–230, 1990.
301. Pierce, T. L., Murray, A. G., and Hope, W., Determination of methadone and its metabolites by high performance liquid chromatography following solid-phase extraction in rat plasma, *Journal of Chromatographic Science*, 30, 443–447, 1992.
302. Angelo, H. R., Bonde, J., Kampmann, J. P., and Kastrup, J., A HPLC method for the simultaneous determination of disopyramide, lidocaine and their monodealkylated metabolites, *Scandinavian Journal of Clinical & Laboratory Investigation*, 46, 623–627, 1986.
303. Proelss, H. F. and Townsend, T. B., Simultaneous liquid-chromatographic determination of five antiarrhythmic drugs and their major active metabolites in serum, *Clinical Chemistry*, 32, 1311–1317, 1986.
304. Anderson, W. H., Stafford, D. T., and Bell, J. S., Disopyramide (Norpace) distribution at autopsy of an overdose case, *Journal of Forensic Sciences*, 25, 33–39, 1980.
305. Kapil, R. P., Abbott, F. S., Kerr, C. R., Edwards, D. J., Lalka, D., and Axelson, J. E., Simultaneous quantitation of disopyramide and its mono-dealkylated metabolite in human plasma by fused-silica capillary gas chromatography using nitrogen-phosphorus specific detection, *Journal of Chromatography*, 307, 305–321, 1984.
306. McIntyre, I. M., King, C. V., Skafidis, S., and Drummer, O. H., Dual ultraviolet wavelength high-performance liquid chromatographic method for the forensic or clinical analysis of seventeen antidepressants and some selected metabolites, *Journal of Chromatography*, 621, 215–223, 1993.
307. Pounder, D. J. and Jones, G. R., Post-mortem drug redistribution—a toxicological nightmare, *Forensic Science International*, 45, 253–263, 1990.
308. Wu Chen, N. B., Schaffer, M. I., Lin, R. L., Kurland, M. L., Donoghue, E. R., Jr., and Stein, R. J., The general toxicology unknown. II. A case report: doxylamine and pyrilamine intoxication, *Journal of Forensic Sciences*, 28, 398–403, 1983.
309. Virag, L., Mets, B., and Jamdar, S., Determination of cocaine, norcocaine, benzoylecgonine and ecgonine methyl ester in rat plasma by high-performance liquid chromatography with ultraviolet detection, *Journal of Chromatography B: Biomedical Applications*, 681, 263–269, 1996.
310. Peterson, K. L., Logan, B. K., and Christian, G. D., Detection of cocaine and its polar transformation products and metabolites in human urine, *Forensic Science International*, 73, 183–196, 1995.

311. Balikova, M. and Vecerkova, J., High-performance liquid chromatographic confirmation of cocaine and benzoylecgonine in biological samples using photodiode-array detection after toxicological screening, *Journal of Chromatography B: Biomedical Applications*, 656, 267–273, 1994.
312. Crouch, D. J., Alburges, M. E., Spanbauer, A. C., Rollins, D. E., and Moody, D. E., Analysis of cocaine and its metabolites from biological specimens using solid-phase extraction and positive ion chemical ionization mass spectrometry, *Journal of Analytical Toxicology*, 19, 352–358, 1995.
313. Wang, W. L., Darwin, W. D., and Cone, E. J., Simultaneous assay of cocaine, heroin and metabolites in hair, plasma, saliva and urine by gas chromatography-mass spectrometry, *Journal of Chromatography B: Biomedical Applications*, 660, 279–290, 1994.
314. Mule, S. J. and Casella, G. A., Confirmation and quantitation of cocaine, benzoylecgonine, ecgonine methyl ester in human urine by GC/MS, *Journal of Analytical Toxicology*, 12, 153–155, 1988.
315. Matsubara, K., Maseda, C., and Fukui, Y., Quantitation of cocaine, benzoylecgonine and ecgonine methyl ester by GC-CI-SIM after Extrelut extraction, *Forensic Science International*, 26, 181–192, 1984.
316. Ahnoff, M., Ervik, M., Lagerstrom, P. O., Persson, B. A., and Vessman, J., Drug level monitoring: cardiovascular drugs. [Review], *Journal of Chromatography*, 340, 73–138, 1985.
317. Braggio, S., Sartori, S., Angeri, F., and Pellegatti, M., Automation and validation of the high-performance liquid chromatographic-radioimmunoassay method for the determination of lacidipine in plasma, *Journal of Chromatography B: Biomedical Applications*, 669, 383–389, 1995.
318. Saito, K., Takayasu, T., Nishigami, J., Kondo, T., Ohtsuji, M., Lin, Z., et al., Determination of the volatile anesthetics halothane, enflurane, isoflurane, and sevoflurane in biological specimens by pulse-heating GC-MS, *Journal of Analytical Toxicology*, 19, 115–119, 1995.
319. Heusler, H., Quantitative analysis of common anaesthetic agents, *Journal of Chromatography*, 340, 273–319, 1985.
320. Ohtsuji, M., Lai, J. S., Binder, S. R., Kondo, T., Takayasu, T., and Ohshima, T., Use of REMEDi HS in emergency toxicology for a rapid estimate of drug concentrations in urine, serum, and gastric samples, *Journal of Forensic Sciences*, 41, 881–886, 1996.
321. Boukhabza, A., Lugnier, A. A., Kintz, P., and Mangin, P., Simultaneous HPLC analysis of the hypnotic benzodiazepines nitrazepam, estazolam, flunitrazepam, and triazolam in plasma, *Journal of Analytical Toxicology*, 15, 319–322, 1991.
322. Charlebois, R. C., Corbett, M. R., and Wigmore, J. G., Comparison of ethanol concentrations in blood, serum, and blood cells for forensic application, *Journal of Analytical Toxicology*, 20, 171–178, 1996.
323. O' Neal, C., Wolf, C. E., II, Levine, B., Kunsman, G., and Poklis, A., Gas chromatographic procedures for determination of ethanol in postmortem blood using t-butanol and methyl ethyl ketone as internal standards, *Forensic Science International*, 83, 31–38, 1996.
324. Macchia, T., Mancinelli, R., Gentili, S., Lugaresi, E. C., Raponi, A., and Taggi, F., Ethanol in biological fluids: headspace GC measurement, *Journal of Analytical Toxicology*, 19, 241–246, 1995.
325. Skrupskii, V. A., [Gas chromatographic analysis of ethanol and acetone in the air exhaled by patients]. [in Russian], *Klinicheskaia Laboratornaia Diagnostika*, 4, 35–38, 1995.
326. Jones, A. W., Edman-Falkensson, M., and Nilsson, L., Reliability of blood alcohol determinations at clinical chemistry laboratories in Sweden, *Scandinavian Journal of Clinical & Laboratory Investigation*, 55, 463–468, 1995.
327. Clerc, Y., Huart, B., Charotte, J. M., and Pailler, F. M., Validation of blood ethanol determination method by gas chromatography (letter) [in French], *Annales de Biologie Clinique*, 53, 233–238, 1995.
328. Cox, R. A. and Crifasi, J. A., A comparison of a commercial microdiffusion method and gas chromatography for ethanol analysis, *Journal of Analytical Toxicology*, 14, 211–212, 1990.
329. Jones, A. W. and Schuberth, J., Computer-aided headspace gas chromatography applied to blood-alcohol analysis: importance of online process control, *Journal of Forensic Sciences*, 34, 1116–1127, 1989.
330. Bridges, R. R. and Jennison, T. A., Analysis of ethchlorvynol (Placidyl): evaluation of a comparison performed in a clinical laboratory, *Journal of Analytical Toxicology*, 8, 263–268, 1984.
331. Winek, C. L., Wahba, W. W., Rozin, L., and Winek, C. L., Jr., Determination of ethchlorvynol in body tissues and fluids after embalmment, *Forensic Science International*, 37, 161–166, 1988.
332. Winek, C. L., Wahba, W. W., and Winek, C. L., Jr., Body distribution of ethchlorvynol, *Journal of Forensic Sciences*, 34, 687–690, 1989.

333. Flanagan, R. J., Lee, T. D., and Rutherford, D. M., Analysis of chlormethiazole, ethchlorvynol and trichloroethanol in biological fluids by gas-liquid chromatography as an aid to the diagnosis of acute poisoning, *Journal of Chromatography*, 153, 473–479, 1978.
334. Flanagan, R. J. and Lee, T. D., Rapid micro-method for the measurement of ethchlorvynol in blood plasma and in urine by gas-liquid chromatography, *Journal of Chromatography*, 137, 119–126, 1977.
335. Bailey, D. N. and Shaw, R. F., Ethchlorvynol ingestion in San Diego County: a 14-year review of cases with blood concentrations and findings. [Review], *Journal of Analytical Toxicology*, 14, 348–352, 1990.
336. Kelner, M. J. and Bailey, D. N., Ethchlorvynol ingestion: interpretation of blood concentrations and clinical findings, *Journal of Toxicology—Clinical Toxicology*, 21, 399–408, 1983.
337. Berry, D. J. and Clarke, L. A., Gas chromatographic analysis of ethosuximide (2-ethyl-2-methyl succinimide) in plasma at therapeutic concentrations, *Journal of Chromatography*, 150, 537–541, 1978.
338. Richard, L., Leducq, B., Baty, C., and Jambou, J., [Plasma determination of 7 common drugs by high performance liquid chromatography], *Annales de Biologie Clinique*, 47, 79–84, 1989.
339. Schmutz, A. and Thormann, W., Determination of phenobarbital, ethosuximide, and primidone in human serum by micellar electrokinetic capillary chromatography with direct sample injection, *Therapeutic Drug Monitoring*, 15, 310–316, 1993.
340. Miles, M. V., Howlett, C. M., Tennison, M. B., Greenwood, R. S., and Cross, R. E., Determination of N-desmethylmethsuximide serum concentrations using enzyme-multiplied and fluorescence polarization immunoassays, *Therapeutic Drug Monitoring*, 11, 337–342, 1989.
341. Stewart, C. F. and Bottorff, M. B., Fluorescence polarization immunoassay for ethosuximide evaluated and compared with two other immunoassay techniques, *Clinical Chemistry*, 32, 1781–1783, 1986.
342. Haring, C. M., Dijkhuis, I. C., and van Dijk, B., A rapid method of determining serum levels of etomidate by gas chromatography with the aid of a nitrogen detector, *Acta Anaesthesiologica Belgica*, 31, 107–112, 1980.
343. Qin, X. Z., Ip, D. P., Chang, K. H., Dradransky, P. M., Brooks, M. A., and Sakuma, T., Pharmaceutical application of LC-MS. I. Characterization of a famotidine degradate in a package screening study by LC-APCI MS, *Journal of Pharmaceutical & Biomedical Analysis*, 12, 221–233, 1994.
344. Poquette, M. A., Isothermal gas chromatographic method for the rapid determination of felbamate concentration in human serum, *Therapeutic Drug Monitoring*, 17, 168–173, 1995.
345. Wong, S. H. Y., Sasse, E. A., Schroeder, J. M., Rodgers, J. K., Pearson, M. L., Neicheril, J. C., et al., Totally automated analysis by robotized prepstation and liquid chromatography—direct-sample analysis of felbamate, *Therapeutic Drug Monitoring*, 18, 573–580, 1996.
346. Annesley, T. M. and Clayton, L. T., Determination of felbamate in human serum by high-performance liquid chromatography, *Therapeutic Drug Monitoring*, 16, 419–424, 1994.
347. Friel, P. N., Formoso, E. J., and Logan, B. K., GC/MS analysis of felbamate, a new antiepileptic drug, in postmortem specimens, in American Academy of Forensic Science, Seattle, WA, 1995.
348. Nishioka, R., Umeda, I., Oi, N., Tabata, S., and Uno, K., Determination of felodipine and its metabolites in plasma using capillary gas chromatography with electron-capture detection and their identification by gas chromatography-mass spectrometry, *Journal of Chromatography*, 565, 237–246, 1991.
349. Ferretti, R., Gallinella, B., Latorre, F., and Lusi, A., Direct high-performance liquid chromatography resolution on a chiral column of dexfenfluramine and its impurities, in bulk raw drug and pharmaceutical formulations, *Journal of Chromatography*, 731(1–2): 340–345, 1996.
350. Moore, C. M. and Tebbett, I. R., Rapid extraction of anti-inflammatory drugs in whole blood for HPLC analysis, *Forensic Science International*, 34, 155–158, 1987.
351. Watts, V. and Caplan, Y., Determination of fentanyl in whole blood at subnanogram concentrations by dual capillary column gas chromatography with nitrogen sensitive detectors and gas chromatography/mass spectrometry, *Journal of Analytical Toxicology*, 12, 246–254, 1988.
352. Mautz, D. S., Labroo, R., and Kharasch, E. D., Determination of alfentanil and noralfentanil in human plasma by gas chromatography-mass spectrometry, *Journal of Chromatography B: Biomedical Applications*, 658, 149–153, 1994.
353. Smialek, J. E., Levine, B., Chin, L., Wu, S. C., and Jenkins, A. J., A fentanyl epidemic in Maryland 1992, *Journal of Forensic Sciences*, 39, 159–164, 1994.

354. Levine, B., Goodin, J. C., and Caplan, Y. H., A fentanyl fatality involving midazolam, *Forensic Science International*, 45, 247–251, 1990.
355. Ferslew, K., Hagardorn, A., and McCormick, W., Postmortem determination of the biological distribution of sufentanil and midazolam after an acute intoxication, *Journal of Forensic Sciences*, 34, 249–257, 1989.
356. Poklis, A., Fentanyl: A review for clinical and analytical toxicologists [Review], *Journal of Toxicology Clinical Toxicology*, 33, 439–447, 1995.
357. Hoppe, U., Krudewagen, B., Stein, H., Hertrampf, R., and Gundert-Remy, U., Comparison of fluorescence polarisation immunoassay (FPIA) and high performance liquid chromatography (HPLC) methods for the measurement of flecainide in human plasma, *International Journal of Clinical Pharmacology, Therapy, & Toxicology*, 31, 142–147, 1993.
358. Stas, C. M., Jacqmin, P. A., and Pellegrin, P. L., Comparison of gas-liquid chromatography and fluorescence polarization immunoassay for therapeutic drug monitoring of flecainide acetate, *Journal of Pharmaceutical & Biomedical Analysis*, 7, 1651–1656, 1989.
359. Straka, R. J., Hoon, T. J., Lalonde, R. L., Pieper, J. A., and Bottorff, M. B., Liquid chromatography and fluorescence polarization immunoassay methods compared for measuring flecainide acetate in serum, *Clinical Chemistry*, 33, 1898–1900, 1987.
360. Berthault, F., Kintz, P., and Mangin, P., Simultaneous high-performance liquid chromatographic analysis of flunitrazepam and four metabolites in serum, *Journal of Chromatography B: Biomedical Applications*, 685, 383–387, 1996.
361. Kleinschnitz, M., Herderich, M., and Schreier, P., Determination of 1,4-benzodiazepines by high-performance liquid chromatography electrospray tandem mass spectrometry, *Journal of Chromatography B: Biomedical Applications*, 676, 61–67, 1996.
362. Robertson, M. D. and Drummer, O. H., High-performance liquid chromatographic procedure for the measurement of nitrobenzodiazepines and their 7-amino metabolites in blood, *Journal of Chromatography B: Biomedical Applications*, 667, 179–184, 1995.
363. Benhamou-Batut, F., Demotes-Mainard, F., Labat, L., Vincon, G., and Bannwarth, B., Determination of flunitrazepam in plasma by liquid chromatography, *Journal of Pharmaceutical & Biomedical Analysis*, 12, 931–936, 1994.
364. Lantz, R. J., Farid, K. Z., Koons, J., Tenbarge, J. B., and Bopp, R. J., Determination of fluoxetine and norfluoxetine in human plasma by capillary gas chromatography with electron-capture detection, *Journal of Chromatography*, 614, 175–179, 1993.
365. Rohrig, T. P. and Prouty, R. W., Fluoxetine overdose: a case report [published erratum appears in *Journal of Analytical Toxicology*, 14, 63, 1990], *Journal of Analytical Toxicology*, 13, 305–307, 1989.
366. Orsulak, P. J., Kenney, J. T., Debus, J. R., Crowley, G., and Wittman, P. D., Determination of the antidepressant fluoxetine and its metabolite norfluoxetine in serum by reversed-phase HPLC with ultraviolet detection, *Clinical Chemistry*, 34, 1875–1878, 1988.
367. Nash, J. F., Bopp, R. J., Carmichael, R. H., Farid, K. Z., and Lemberger, L., Determination of fluoxetine and norfluoxetine in plasma by gas chromatography with electron-capture detection, *Clinical Chemistry*, 28, 2100–2102, 1982.
368. Nichols, J. H., Charlson, J. R., and Lawson, G. M., Automated HPLC assay of fluoxetine and norfluoxetine in serum, *Clinical Chemistry*, 40, 1312–1316, 1994.
369. Eap, C. B., Gaillard, N., Powell, K., and Baumann, P., Simultaneous determination of plasma levels of fluvoxamine and of the enantiomers of fluoxetine and norfluoxetine by gas chromatography mass spectrometry, *Journal of Chromatography B: Biomedical Applications*, 682, 265–272, 1996.
370. Miller, R. S., Peterson, G. M., McLean, S., Westhead, T. T., and Gillies, P., Monitoring plasma levels of fluphenazine during chronic therapy with fluphenazine decanoate, *Journal of Clinical Pharmacy & Therapeutics*, 20, 55–62, 1995.
371. Sener, A., Akkan, A. G., and Malaisse, W. J., Standardized procedure for the assay and identification of hypoglycemic sulfonylureas in human plasma, *Acta Diabetologica*, 32, 64–68, 1995.
372. Flanagan, R. J. and Withers, G., A rapid micro-method for the screening and measurement of barbiturates and related compounds in plasma by gas-liquid chromatography, *Journal of Clinical Pathology*, 25, 899–904, 1972.

373. Shipe, J. R. and Savory, J., A comprehensive gas chromatography procedure for measurement of drugs in biological materials, *Annals of Clinical & Laboratory Science*, 5, 57–64, 1975.
374. Bailey, D. N. and Shaw, R. F., Blood concentrations and clinical findings in nonfatal and fatal intoxications involving glutethimide and codeine, *Journal of Toxicology Clinical Toxicology*, 23, 557–570, 1985.
375. Bailey, D. N. and Shaw, R. F., Interpretation of blood glutethimide, meprobamate, and methyprylon concentrations in nonfatal and fatal intoxications involving a single drug, *Journal of Toxicology Clinical Toxicology*, 20, 133–145, 1983.
376. Hoffman, D. W. and Edkins, R. D., Solid-phase extraction and high-performance liquid chromatography for therapeutic monitoring of haloperidol levels, *Therapeutic Drug Monitoring*, 16, 504–508, 1994.
377. Aravagiri, M., Marder, S. R., Van Putten, T., and Marshall, B. D., Simultaneous determination of plasma haloperidol and its metabolite reduced haloperidol by liquid chromatography with electrochemical detection. Plasma levels in schizophrenic patients treated with oral or intramuscular depot haloperidol, *Journal of Chromatography B: Biomedical Applications*, 656, 373–381, 1994.
378. Jann, M. W., Chang, W. H., Lam, Y. W., Hwu, H. G., Lin, H. N., Chen, H., et al., Comparison of haloperidol and reduced haloperidol plasma levels in four different ethnic populations, *Progress in Neuro Psychopharmacology & Biological Psychiatry*, 16, 193–202, 1992.
379. Park, K. H., Lee, M. H., and Lee, M. G., Simultaneous determination of haloperidol and its metabolite, reduced haloperidol, in plasma, blood, urine and tissue homogenates by high-performance liquid chromatography, *Journal of Chromatography*, 572, 259–267, 1991.
380. Haering, N., Salama, Z., Todesko, L., and Jaeger, H., GC/MS determination of haloperidol in plasma. Application to pharmacokinetics, *Arzneimittel-Forschung*, 37, 1402–1404, 1987.
381. van Leeuwen, P. A., Improved GC/MS assay for haloperidol utilizing ammonia CI and SIM, *Journal of Chromatography and Biomedical Applications*, 40, 321–330, 1985.
382. Hornbeck, C. L., Griffiths, J. C., Neborsky, R. J., and Faulkner, M. A., GC/MS chemical ionization assay for haloperidol with SIM, *Biomedical Mass Spectrometry*, 6, 427–430, 1979.
383. Coudore, F., Alazard, J. M., Paire, M., Andraud, G., and Lavarenne, J., Rapid toxicological screening of barbiturates in plasma by wide-bore capillary gas chromatography and nitrogen-phosphorus detection, *Journal of Analytical Toxicology*, 17, 109–113, 1993.
384. Soo, V. A., Bergert, R. J., and Deutsch, D. G., Screening and quantification of hypnotic sedatives in serum by capillary gas chromatography with a nitrogen-phosphorus detector, and confirmation by capillary gas chromatography-mass spectrometry, *Clinical Chemistry*, 32, 325–328, 1986.
385. Mahoney, J. D., Gross, P. L., Stern, T. A., Browne, B. J., Pollack, M. H., Reder, V., et al., Quantitative serum toxic screening in the management of suspected drug overdose, *American Journal of Emergency Medicine*, 8, 16–22, 1990.
386. Meeker, J. E., Som, C. W., Macapagal, E. C., and Benson, P. A., Zolpidem tissue concentrations in a multiple drug related death involving Ambien, *Journal of Analytical Toxicology*, 19, 531–534, 1995.
387. Bouquillon, A. I., Freeman, D., and Moulin, D. E., Simultaneous solid-phase extraction and chromatographic analysis of morphine and hydromorphone in plasma by high-performance liquid chromatography with electrochemical detection, *Journal of Chromatography*, 577, 354–357, 1992.
388. Sawyer, W. R., Waterhouse, G. A., Doedens, D. J., and Forney, R. B., Heroin, morphine, and hydromorphone determination in postmortem material by high performance liquid chromatography [see comments], *Journal of Forensic Sciences*, 33, 1146–1155, 1988.
389. O' Connor, E. F., Cheng, S. W., and North, W. G., Simultaneous extraction and chromatographic analysis of morphine, dilaudid, naltrexone and naloxone in biological fluids by high-performance liquid chromatography with electrochemical detection, *Journal of Chromatography*, 491, 240–247, 1989.
390. Cone, E. J. and Darwin, W. D., Simultaneous determination of hydromorphone, hydrocodone and their 6alpha- and 6beta-hydroxy metabolites in urine using selected ion recording with methane chemical ionization, *Biomedical Mass Spectrometry*, 5, 291, 1978.
391. Croes, K., McCarthy, P. T., and Flanagan, R. J., Simple and rapid HPLC of quinine, hydroxychloroquine, chloroquine, and desethylchloroquine in serum, whole blood, and filter paper–adsorbed dry blood, *Journal of Analytical Toxicology*, 18, 255–260, 1994.

392. Kintz, P., Godelar, B., and Mangin, P., Gas chromatographic identification and quantification of hydroxyzine: application in a fatal self-poisoning, *Forensic Science International*, 48, 139–143, 1990.
393. Naidong, W. and Lee, J. W., Development and validation of a liquid chromatographic method for the quantitation of ibuprofen enantiomers in human plasma, *Journal of Pharmaceutical & Biomedical Analysis*, 12, 551–556, 1994.
394. Maurer, H. H., Kraemer, T., and Weber, A., Toxicological detection of ibuprofen and its metabolites in urine using gas chromatography-mass spectrometry (GC-MS), *Pharmazie*, 49, 148–155, 1994.
395. Zhao, M. J., Peter, C., Holtz, M. C., Hugenell, N., Koffel, J. C., and Jung, L., GC/MS determination of ibuprofen enantiomers in human plasma using r(-)-2,2,2-trifluoro-1-(9-anthryl)ethanol as derivatizing reagent, *Journal of Chromatography B: Biomedical Applications*, 656, 441–446, 1994.
396. Seideman, P., Lohrer, F., Graham, G. G., Duncan, M. W., Williams, K. M., and Day, R. O., The stereoselective disposition of the enantiomers of ibuprofen in blood, blister and synovial fluid, *British Journal of Clinical Pharmacology*, 38, 221–227, 1994.
397. Theis, D. L., Halstead, G. W., and Halm, K. A., Development of capillary GC/MS methodology for the simultaneous determination of ibuprofen and deuterated ibuprofen in serum, *Journal of Chromatography*, 380, 77–87, 1986.
398. Jourdil, N., Pinteur, B., Vincent, F., Marka, C., and Bessard, G., Simultaneous determination of trimipramine and desmethyl- and hydroxytrimipramine in plasma and red blood cells by capillary gas chromatography with nitrogen-selective detection, *Journal of Chromatography*, 613, 59–65, 1993.
399. Maynard, G. L. and Soni, P., Thioridazine interferences with imipramine metabolism and measurement, *Therapeutic Drug Monitoring*, 18, 729–731, 1996.
400. Nielsen, K. K. and Brosen, K., High-performance liquid chromatography of imipramine and six metabolites in human plasma and urine, *Journal of Chromatography*, 612, 87–94, 1993.
401. Koyama, E., Kikuchi, Y., Echizen, H., Chiba, K., and Ishizaki, T., Simultaneous high-performance liquid chromatography-electrochemical detection determination of imipramine, desipramine, their 2-hydroxylated metabolites, and imipramine N-oxide in human plasma and urine: preliminary application to oxidation pharmacogenetics, *Therapeutic Drug Monitoring*, 15, 224–235, 1993.
402. Eap, C. B., Koeb, L., and Baumann, P., Determination of trimipramine and its demethylated and hydroxylated metabolites in plasma by gas chromatography-mass spectrometry, *Journal of Chromatography*, 652, 97–103, 1994.
403. Hunt, J. P., Haywood, P. E., and Moss, M. S., A gas chromatographic screening procedure for the detection of non-steroidal anti-inflammatory drugs in horse urine, *Equine Veterinary Journal*, 11, 259–263, 1979.
404. Sibeon, R. G., Baty, J. D., Baber, N., Chan, K., and Orme, M. L., Quantitative gas-liquid chromatographic method for the determination of indomethacin in biological fluids, *Journal of Chromatography*, 153, 189–194, 1978.
405. Hannak, D., Scharbert, F., and Kattermann, R., Stepwise binary gradient high-performance liquid chromatographic system for routine drug monitoring, *Journal of Chromatography A*, 728, 307–310, 1996.
406. Caturla, M. C. and Cusido, E., Solid-phase extraction for the high-performance liquid chromatographic determination of indomethacin, suxibuzone, phenylbutazone and oxyphenbutazone in plasma, avoiding degradation of compounds, *Journal of Chromatography*, 581, 101–107, 1992.
407. Cosolo, W., Drummer, O. H., and Christophidis, N., Comparison of high-performance liquid chromatography and the Abbott fluorescent polarization radioimmunoassay in the measurement of methotrexate, *Journal of Chromatography*, 494, 201–208, 1989.
408. Bauernfeind, M. and Wood, W. G., Evaluation of a fully mechanised immunoassay—Enzymun-Test System ES 300—and comparison with in-house methods for 8 analytes, *European Journal of Clinical Chemistry & Clinical Biochemistry*, 31, 165–172, 1993.
409. Patel, F., Fatal self-induced hyperinsulinaemia: a delayed post-mortem analytical detection, *Medicine, Science & the Law*, 32, 151–159, 1992.
410. Fletcher, S. M., Insulin. A forensic primer. [Review], *Journal Forensic Science Society*, 23, 5–17, 1983.
411. Heyndrickx, A., Van Peteghem, C., Majelyne, W., and Timperman, J., Detection of insulin in cadavers, *Acta Pharmaceutica Hungarica*, 50, 201–206, 1980.

412. Dickson, S. J., Cairns, E. R., and Blazey, N. D., The isolation and quantitation of insulin in postmortem specimens—a case report, *Forensic Science,* 9, 37–42, 1977.
413. Jones, A. W., Severe isopropanolemia without acetonemia: contamination of specimens during venipuncture? [letter; comment], *Clinical Chemistry,* 41, 123–124, 1995.
414. Chan, K. M., Wong, E. T., and Matthews, W. S., Severe isopropanolemia without acetonemia or clinical manifestations of isopropanol intoxication [see comments], *Clinical Chemistry,* 39, 1922–1925, 1993.
415. Jerrard, D., Verdile, V., Yealy, D., Krenzelok, E., and Menegazzi, J., Serum determinations in toxic isopropanol ingestion, *American Journal of Emergency Medicine*, 10, 200–202, 1992.
416. Davis, P. L., Dal Cortivo, L. A., and Maturo, J., Endogenous isopropanol: forensic and biochemical implications, *Journal of Analytical Toxicology,* 8, 209–212, 1984.
417. Kelner, M. and Bailey, D. N., Isopropanol ingestion: interpretation of blood concentrations and clinical findings, *Journal of Toxicology Clinical Toxicology,* 20, 497–507, 1983.
418. Baker, R. N., Alenty, A. L., and Zack, J. F., Jr., Toxic volatiles in alcoholic coma. A report of simultaneous determination of blood methanol, ethanol, isopropanol, acetaldehyde and acetone by gas chromatography, *Bulletin of the Los Angeles Neurological Societies*, 33, 140–144, 1968.
419. Alexander, C. B., McBay, A. J., and Hudson, R. P., Isopropanol and isopropanol deaths — ten years' experience, *Journal of Forensic Sciences*, 27, 541–548, 1982.
420. Brogden, R. N. and Sorkin, E. M., Isradipine. An update of its pharmacodynamic and pharmacokinetic properties and therapeutic efficacy in the treatment of mild to moderate hypertension. [Review], *Drugs*, 49, 618–649, 1995.
421. Kochhar, M. M., Bavda, L. T., and Bhushan, R. S., Thin-layer and gas chromatographic determination of ketamine and its biotransformed products in biological fluids, *Research Communications in Chemical Pathology & Pharmacology,* 14, 367–376, 1976.
422. Adams, H. A., Weber, B., Bachmann, M. B., Guerin, M., and Hempelmann, G., [The simultaneous determination of ketamine and midazolam using high pressure liquid chromatography and UV detection (HPLC/UV)], *Anaesthesist*, 41, 619–624, 1992.
423. Feng, N., Vollenweider, F. X., Minder, E. I., Rentsch, K., Grampp, T., and Vonderschmitt, D. J., Development of a gas chromatography-mass spectrometry method for determination of ketamine in plasma and its application to human samples, *Therapeutic Drug Monitoring*, 17, 95–100, 1995.
424. Lau, S. S. and Domino, E. F., Gas chromatography mass spectrometry assay for ketamine and its metabolites in plasma, *Biomedical Mass Spectrometry,* 4, 317–321, 1977.
425. Carr, R. A., Caille, G., Ngoc, A. H., and Foster, R. T., Stereospecific high-performance liquid chromatographic assay of ketoprofen in human plasma and urine, *Journal of Chromatography B: Biomedical Applications*, 668, 175–181, 1995.
426. Lovlin, R., Vakily, M., and Jamali, F., Rapid, sensitive and direct chiral high-performance liquid chromatographic method for ketoprofen enantiomers, *Journal of Chromatography B: Biomedical Applications*, 679, 196–198, 1996.
427. Palylyk, E. L. and Jamali, F., Simultaneous determination of ketoprofen enantiomers and probenecid in plasma and urine by high-performance liquid chromatography, *Journal of Chromatography,* 568, 187–196, 1991.
428. Chun, I. K., Kang, H. H., and Gwak, H. S., Determination of ketorolac in human serum by high-performance liquid chromatography, *Archives of Pharmacal Research*, 19, 529–534, 1996,
429. Tsina, I., Tam, Y. L., Boyd, A., Rocha, C., Massey, I., and Tarnowski, T., An indirect (derivatization) and a direct hplc method for the determination of the enantiomers of ketorolac in plasma, *Journal of Pharmaceutical & Biomedical Analysis*, 15, 403–417, 1996.
430. Tsina, I., Chu, F., Kaloostian, M., Pettibone, M., and Wu, A., HPLC method for the determination of ketorolac in human plasma, *Journal of Liquid Chromatography & Related Technologies*, 19, 957–967, 1996.
431. Sola, J., Prunonosa, J., Colom, H., Peraire, C., and Obach, R., Determination of ketorolac in human plasma by high performance liquid chromatography after automated online solid phase extraction, *Journal of Liquid Chromatography & Related Technologies*, 19, 89–99, 1996.
432. Logan, B. K., Friel, P. N., Peterson, K. L., and Predmore, D. B., Analysis of ketorolac in postmortem blood, *Journal of Analytical Toxicology,* 19, 61–64, 1995.

433. Sievert, H. J. P., Determination of amphetamine and methamphetamine enantiomers by chiral derivatization and GC/MS as a test case for an automated sample preparation system, *Chirality*, 6, 295–301, 1994.
434. Cooke, B. J., Chirality of methamphetamine and amphetamine from workplace urine samples, *Journal of Analytical Toxicology*, 18, 49–51, 1994.
435. Nagai, T., Kamiyama, S., Kurosu, A., and Iwamoto, F., [Identification of optical isomers of methamphetamine and its application to forensic medicine]. [Japanese], *Nippon Hoigaku Zasshi Japanese Journal of Legal Medicine*, 46, 244–253, 1992.
436. Wallace, S. J., Lamotrigine—a clinical overview, *Seizure*, 3, 47–51, 1994.
437. Rambeck, B. and Wolf, P., Lamotrigine clinical pharmacokinetics. [Review], *Clinical Pharmacokinetics*, 25, 433–443, 1993.
438. May, T. W., Rambeck, B., and Jurgens, U., Serum concentrations of lamotrigine in epileptic patients —the influence of dose and comedication, *Therapeutic Drug Monitoring*, 18, 523–531, 1996.
439. Kintz, P., Flesch, F., Jaeger, A., and Mangin, P., GC-MS procedure for the analysis of zipeprol, *Journal of Pharmaceutical & Biomedical Analysis*, 11, 335–338, 1993.
440. Xu, Y. Q., Fang, H. J., Xu, Y. X., Duan, H. J., and Wu, Y., [Studies on the analysis of anileridine, levorphanol, nalbuphine and ethamivan in urine], *Yao Hsueh Hsueh Pao—Acta Pharmaceutica Sinica*, 26, 606–610, 1991.
441. Benko, A. and Kimura, K., Toxicological analysis of lidocaine in biological materials by using HPLC, *Forensic Science International*, 49, 65–73, 1991.
442. Cirimele, V., Kintz, P., and Mangin, P., Detection and quantification of lorazepam in human hair by GC-MS/NCI in a case of traffic accident, *International Journal of Legal Medicine*, 108, 265–267, 1996.
443. Higuchi, S., Urabe, H., and Shiobara, Y., Simplified determination of lorazepam and oxazepam in biological fluids by gas chromatography-mass spectrometry, *Journal of Chromatography*, 164, 55–61, 1979.
444. Koves, E. M. and Yen, B., The use of gas chromatography/negative ion chemical ionization mass spectrometry for the determination of lorazepam in whole blood, *Journal of Analytical Toxicology*, 13, 69–72, 1989.
445. Twitchett, P. J., Fletcher, S. M., Sullivan, A. T., and Moffat, A. C., Analysis of LSD in human body fluids by high-performance liquid chromatography, fluorescence spectroscopy and radioimmunoassay, *Journal of Chromatography*, 150, 73–84, 1978.
446. Veress, T., Study of the extraction of LSD from illicit blotters for HPLC determination, *Journal of Forensic Sciences*, 38, 1105–1110, 1993.
447. Cai, J. and Henion, J., On-line immunoaffinity extraction-coupled column capillary liquid chromatography/tandem mass spectrometry: trace analysis of LSD analogs and metabolites in human urine, *Analytical Chemistry*, 68, 72–78, 1996.
448. Nelson, C. C. and Foltz, R. L., Determination of lysergic acid diethylamide (LSD), iso-LSD, and N-demethyl-LSD in body fluids by gas chromatography/tandem mass spectrometry, *Analytical Chemistry*, 64, 1578–1585, 1992.
449. Bukowski, N. and Eaton, A. N., The confirmation and quantitation of LSD in urine using GC/MS, *Rapid Communication Mass Spectrometry*, 7, 106–108, 1993.
450. Ackermann, R., Kaiser, G., Schueller, F., and Dieterle, W., Determination of the antidepressant levoprotiline and its N-desmethyl metabolite in biological fluids by gas chromatography/mass spectrometry, *Biological Mass Spectrometry*, 20, 709–716, 1991.
451. Alkalay, D., Carlsen, S., Khemani, L., and Bartlett, M. F., Selected ion monitoring assay for the antidepressant maprotiline, *Biomedical Mass Spectrometry*, 6, 435–438, 1979.
452. Stidman, J., Taylor, E. H., Simmons, H. F., Gandy, J., and Pappas, A. A., Determination of meprobamate in serum by alkaline hydrolysis, trimethylsilyl derivatization and detection by GC/MS, *Journal of Chromatography*, 494, 318–323, 1989.
453. Kintz, P. and Mangin, P., Determination of meprobamate in human plasma, urine, and hair by gas chromatography and electron impact mass spectrometry, *Journal of Analytical Toxicology*, 17, 408–410, 1993.
454. Bailey, D. N., The present status of meprobamate ingestion. A five-year review of cases with serum concentrations and clinical findings, *American Journal of Clinical Pathology*, 75, 102–106, 1981.

455. Hamman, B., Meprobamate, in *Methodology for Analytical Toxicology: Volume I*, Sunshine, I., Ed., CRC Press, Boca Raton, FL, 1984, 219–221.
456. Foltz, R. L., Fentiman, A. F., Jr., and Foltz, R. B., GC/MS assays for abused drugs in body fluids. [Review], *NIDA Research Monograph,* 32, 1–198, 1980.
457. Poklis, A., Wells, C. E., and Juenge, E. C., Thioridazine and its metabolites in post mortem blood, including two stereoisomeric ring sulfoxides, *Journal of Analytical Toxicology*, 6, 250–252, 1982.
458. Schurch, F., Meier, P. J., and Wyss, P. A., Acute poisoning with thioridazine [in German], *Deutsche Medizinische Wochenschrift*, 121, 1003–1008, 1996.
459. Kintz, P., Mangin, P., Lugnier, A. A., and Chaumont, A. J., A rapid and sensitive gas chromatographic analysis of methadone and its primary metabolite, *Journal de Toxicologie Clinique et Experimentale*, 10, 15–20, 1990.
460. Alburges, M. E., Huang, W., Foltz, R. L., and Moody, D. E., Determination of methadone and its N-demethylation metabolites in biological specimens by GC-PICI-MS, *Journal of Analytical Toxicology*, 20, 362–368, 1996.
461. Wilkins, D. G., Nagasawa, P. R., Gygi, S. P., Foltz, R. L., and Rollins, D. E., Quantitative analysis of methadone and two major metabolites in hair by positive chemical ionization ion trap mass spectrometry, *Journal of Analytical Toxicology*, 20, 355–361, 1996.
462. Baugh, L. D., Liu, R. H., and Walia, A. S., Simultaneous gas chromatography/mass spectrometry assay of methadone and 2-ethyl-1,5-dimethyl-3,3-diphenylpyrrolidine (EDDP) in urine, *Journal of Forensic Sciences*, 36, 548–555, 1991.
463. Jacob, P., III, Tisdale, E. C., Panganiban, K., Cannon, D., Zabel, K., Mendelson, J. E., et al., Gas chromatographic determination of methamphetamine and its metabolite amphetamine in human plasma and urine following conversion to N-propyl derivatives, *Journal of Chromatography B: Biomedical Applications*, 664, 449–457, 1995.
464. Dallakian, P., Budzikiewicz, H., and Brzezinka, H., Detection and quantitation of amphetamine and methamphetamine—electron impact and chemical ionization with ammonia-comparative investigation on Shimadzu Qp 5000 GC-MS System, *Journal of Analytical Toxicology*, 20, 255–261, 1996.
465. Valtier, S. and Cody, J. T., Evaluation of internal standards for the analysis of amphetamine and methamphetamine, *Journal of Analytical Toxicology*, 19, 375–380, 1995.
466. Wu, A. H., Kelly, T., McKay, C., Ostheimer, D., Forte, E., and Hill, D., Definitive identification of an exceptionally high methanol concentration in an intoxication of a surviving infant: methanol metabolism by first-order elimination kinetics, *Journal of Forensic Sciences*, 40, 315–320, 1995.
467. Pla, A., Hernandez, A. F., Gil, F., Garcia-Alonso, M., and Villanueva, E., A fatal case of oral ingestion of methanol. Distribution in postmortem tissues and fluids including pericardial fluid and vitreous humor, *Forensic Science International*, 49, 193–196, 1991.
468. Winkel, D. R. and Hendrick, S. A., Detection limits for a GC determination of methanol and methylene chloride residues on film-coated tablets, *Journal of Pharmaceutical Sciences*, 73, 115–117, 1984.
469. Kintz, P., Tracqui, A., Mangin, P., Lugnier, A. A., and Chaumont, A. A., Simultaneous determination of dextropropoxyphene, norpropoxyphene and methaqualone in plasma by gas chromatography with selective nitrogen detection, *Journal de Toxicologie Clinique et Experimentale*, 10, 89–94, 1990.
470. Liu, F., Liu, Y. T., Feng, C. L., and Luo, Y., Determination of methaqualone and its metabolites in urine and blood by UV, GC/FID and GC/MS, *Yao Hsueh Hsueh Pao Acta Pharmaceutica Sinica*, 29, 610–616, 1994.
471. Streete, J. M., Berry, D. J., Clarke, L. A., and Newbery, J. E., Analysis of desmethylmethsuximide using high-performance liquid chromatography, *Therapeutic Drug Monitoring,* 17, 280–286, 1995.
472. Poklis, A., Mackell, M. A., and Drake, W. K., Fatal intoxication from 3,4-methylenedioxyamphetamine, *Journal of Forensic Science*, 24, 70–75, 1979.
473. Quaglio, M. P., Bellini, A. M., and Minozzi, L., Simultaneous determination of propranolol or metoprolol in the presence of benzodiazepines in the plasma by gas chromatography, *Farmaco*, 47, 799–809, 1992.
474. Li, F., Cooper, S. F., and Cote, M., Determination of the enantiomers of metoprolol and its major acidic metabolite in human urine by high-performance liquid chromatography with fluorescence detection, *Journal of Chromatography B: Biomedical Applications*, 668, 67–75, 1995.

475. Holt, D. W., Flanagan, R. J., Hayler, A. M., and Loizou, M., Simple gas-liquid chromatographic method for the measurement of mexiletine and lignocaine in blood-plasma or serum, *Journal of Chromatography*, 169, 295–301, 1979.
476. Minnigh, M. B., Alvin, J. D., and Zemaitis, M. A., Determination of plasma mexiletine levels with gas chromatography-mass spectrometry and selected-ion monitoring, *Journal of Chromatography B: Biomedical Applications*, 662, 118–22, 1994.
477. Bourget, P., Bouton, V., Lesnehulin, A., Amstutz, P., Benayed, M., Benhamou, D., et al., Comparison of high-performance liquid chromatography and polyclonal fluorescence polarization immunoassay for the monitoring of midazolam in the plasma of intensive care unit patients, *Therapeutic Drug Monitoring*, 18, 610–619, 1996.
478. Mastey, V., Panneton, A. C., Donati, F., and Varin, F., Determination of midazolam and two of its metabolites in human plasma by high-performance liquid chromatography, *Journal of Chromatography B: Biomedical Applications*, 655, 305–310, 1994.
479. de Vries, J. X., Rudi, J., Walter-Sack, I., and Conradi, R., The determination of total and unbound midazolam in human plasma, *Biomedical Chromatography*, 4, 28–33, 1990.
480. Vu-Duc, T. and Vernay, A., Simultaneous detection and quantitation of O_6-monoacetylmorphine, morphine and codeine in urine by gas chromatography with nitrogen specific and/or flame ionization detection, *Biomedical Chromatography*, 4, 65–69, 1990.
481. Hanisch, W. and Meyer, L. V., Determination of the heroin metabolite 6-monoacetyl-morphine in urine by high-performance liquid chromatography with electrochemical detection, *Journal of Analytical Toxicology*, 17, 48–50, 1993.
482. Kintz, P., Mangin, P., Lugnier, A. A., and Chaumont, A. J., Identification by GC/MS of 6-monoacetylmorphine as an indicator of heroin abuse, *European Journal of Clinical Pharmacology*, 37, 531–532, 1989.
483. Schuberth, J. and Schuberth, J., GC/MS determination of morphine, codeine and 6-monoacetylmorphine in blood extracted by solid phase, *Journal of Chromatography*, 490, 444–449, 1989.
484. Wasels, R. and Belleville, F., Gas chromatographic-mass spectrometric procedures used for the identification and determination of morphine, codeine and 6-monoacetylmorphine, *Journal of Chromatography A*, 674, 225–234, 1994.
485. Rotshteyn, Y. and Weingarten, B., A highly sensitive assay for the simultaneous determination of morphine, morphine-3-glucuronide, and morphine-6-glucuronide in human plasma by high-performance liquid chromatography with electrochemical and fluorescence detection, *Therapeutic Drug Monitoring*, 18, 179–188, 1996.
486. Pacifici, R., Pichini, S., Altieri, I., Caronna, A., Passa, A. R., and Zuccaro, P., HPLC electrospray mass spectrometric determination of morphine and its 3- and 6-glucuronides: application to pharmacokinetic studies, *Journal of Chromatography B: Biomedical Applications*, 664, 329–334, 1995.
487. Pacifici, R., Pichini, S., Altieri, I., Caronna, A., Passa, A. R., and Zuccaro, P., High-performance liquid chromatographic-electrospray mass spectrometric determination of morphine and its 3- and 6-glucuronides: application to pharmacokinetic studies, *Journal of Chromatography B: Biomedical Applications*, 664, 329–334, 1995.
488. Tyrefors, N., Hyllbrant, B., Ekman, L., Johansson, M., and Langstrom, B., Determination of morphine, morphine-3-glucuronide and morphine-6-glucuronide in human serum by solid-phase extraction and liquid chromatography mass spectrometry with electrospray ionisation, *Journal of Chromatography*, 729, 279–285, 1996.
489. Moeller, M. R. and Mueller, C., The detection of 6-monoacetylmorphine in urine, serum and hair by GC/MS and RIA, *Forensic Science International*, 70, 125–133, 1995.
490. Levine, B., Wu, S., Dixon, A., and Smialek, J., An unusual morphine fatality, *Forensic Science International*, 65, 7–11, 1994.
491. Romberg, R. W. and Lee, L., Comparison of the hydrolysis rates of morphine-3-glucuronide and morphine-6-glucuronide with acid and beta-glucuronidase, *Journal of Analytical Toxicology*, 19, 157–162, 1995.
492. Aderjan, R., Hofmann, S., Schmitt, G., and Skopp, G., Morphine and morphine glucuronides in serum of heroin consumers and in heroin-related deaths determined by HPLC with native fluorescence detection, *Journal of Analytical Toxicology*, 19, 163–168, 1995.

493. Wright, A. W., Watt, J. A., Kennedy, M., Cramond, T., and Smith, M. T., Quantitation of morphine, morphine-3-glucuronide, and morphine-6-glucuronide in plasma and cerebrospinal fluid using solid-phase extraction and high-performance liquid chromatography with electrochemical detection, *Therapeutic Drug Monitoring*, 16, 200–208, 1994.
494. Rop, P. P., Grimaldi, F., Burle, J., De Saint Leger, M. N., and Viala, A., Determination of 6-monoacetylmorphine and morphine in plasma, whole blood and urine using high-performance liquid chromatography with electrochemical detection, *Journal of Chromatography B: Biomedical Applications*, 661, 245–253, 1994.
495. Yoo, Y. C., Chung, H. S., Kim, I. S., Jin, W. T., and Kim, M. K., Determination of nalbuphine in drug abusers' urine, *Journal of Analytical Toxicology*, 19, 120–123, 1995.
496. McManus, K. T., deBethizy, J. D., Garteiz, D. A., Kyerematen, G. A., and Vesell, E. S., A new quantitative thermospray LC-MS method for nicotine and its metabolites in biological fluids, *Journal of Chromatographic Science*, 28, 510–516, 1990.
497. Cooper, D. A. and Moore, J. M., Femtogram on-column detection of nicotine by isotope dilution gas chromatography/negative ion detection mass spectrometry, *Biological Mass Spectrometry*, 22, 590–594, 1993.
498. Deutsch, J., Hegedus, L., Greig, N. H., Rapoport, S. I., and Soncrant, T. T., Electron-impact and chemical ionization detection of nicotine and cotinine by gas chromatography-mass spectrometry in rat plasma and brain, *Journal of Chromatography*, 579, 93–98, 1992.
499. Lesko, L. and Miller, A., Rapid GC method for quantitation of nifedipine in serum using electron-capture detection, *Journal of Chromatographic Science*, 21, 415–419, 1983.
500. Ohkubo, T., Noro, H., and Sugawara, K., High-performance liquid chromatographic determination of nifedipine and a trace photodegradation product in hospital prescriptions, *Journal of Pharmaceutical & Biomedical Analysis*, 10, 67–70, 1992.
501. Nitsche, V., Schuetz, H., and Eichinger, A., Rapid high-performance liquid chromatographic determination of nifedipine in plasma with on-line precolumn solid-phase extraction, *Journal of Chromatography*, 420, 207–211, 1987.
502. Martens, J., Banditt, P., and Meyer, F. P., Determination of nifedipine in human serum by gas chromatography-mass spectrometry: validation of the method and its use in bioavailability studies, *Journal of Chromatography B: Biomedical Applications*, 660, 297–302, 1994.
503. Kintz, P., Cirimele, V., Vayssette, F., and Mangin, P., Hair analysis for nordiazepam and oxazepam by gas chromatography—negative-ion chemical ionization mass spectrometry, *Journal of Chromatography B: Biomedical Applications*, 677, 241–244, 1996.
504. Dickson, P. H., Lind, A., Studts, P., Nipper, H. C., Makoid, M., and Therkildsen, D., The routine analysis of breast milk for drugs of abuse in a clinical toxicology laboratory, *Journal of Forensic Sciences*, 39, 207–214, 1994.
505. Smith, M. L., Hughes, R. O., Levine, B., Dickerson, S., Darwin, W. D., and Cone, E. J., Forensic drug testing for opiates. VI. Urine testing for hydromorphone, hydrocodone, oxymorphone, and oxycodone with commercial opiate immunoassays and gas chromatography-mass spectrometry, *Journal of Analytical Toxicology*, 19, 18–26, 1995.
506. Drummer, O. H., Syrjanen, M. L., Phelan, M., and Cordner, S. M., A study of deaths involving oxycodone, *Journal of Forensic Sciences,* 39, 1069–1075, 1994.
507. Poklis, A. and Melanson, E. G., A suicide by pancuronium bromide injection: evaluation of the fluorometric determination of pancuronium in postmortem blood, serum and urine, *Journal of Analytical Toxicology,* 4, 275–280, 1980.
508. Briglia, E. J., Davis, P. L., Katz, M., and Dal Cortivo, L. A., Attempted murder with pancuronium, *Journal of Forensic Sciences*, 35, 1468–1476, 1990.
509. Paul, B. D., Dreka, C., Knight, E. S., and Smith, M. L., Gas chromatographic mass spectrometric detection of narcotine, papaverine, and thebaine in seeds of *Papaver somniferum*, *Planta Medica*, 62, 544–547, 1996.
510. Eap, C. B. and Baumann, P., Analytical methods for the quantitative determination of selective serotonin reuptake inhibitors for therapeutic drug monitoring purposes in patients [Review], *Journal of Chromatography B: Biomedical Applications*, 686, 51–63, 1996.

511. Miceli, J. N., Bowman, D. B., and Aravind, M. K., An improved method for the quantitation of phencyclidine (PCP) in biological samples utilizing nitrogen-detection gas chromatography, *Journal of Analytical Toxicology*, 5, 29–32, 1981.
512. Kintz, P., Tracqui, A., Lugnier, A. J., Mangin, P., and Chaumont, A. A., Simultaneous screening and quantification of several nonopiate narcotic analgesics and phencyclidine in human plasma using capillary gas chromatography, *Methods & Findings in Experimental & Clinical Pharmacology*, 12, 193–196, 1990.
513. Holsztynska, E. J. and Domino, E. F., Quantitation of phencyclidine, its metabolites, and derivatives by gas chromatography with nitrogen-phosphorus detection: application for in vivo and in vitro biotransformation studies, *Journal of Analytical Toxicology*, 10, 107–115, 1986.
514. Slawson, M. H., Wilkins, D. G., Foltz, R. L., and Rollins, D. E., Quantitative determination of phencyclidine in pigmented and nonpigmented hair by ion-trap mass spectrometry, *Journal of Analytical Toxicology*, 20, 350–354, 1996.
515. Kidwell, D. A., Analysis of phencyclidine and cocaine in human hair by tandem mass spectrometry, *Journal of Forensic Sciences*, 38, 272–284, 1993.
516. Jin, X., Zhou, Z. H., He, X. F., Zhang, Z. H., and Wang, M. Z., [Solid-phase extraction and RP-HPLC screening procedure for diuretics, probenecid, caffeine and pemoline in urine]. [Chinese], *Yao Hsueh Hsueh Pao—Acta Pharmaceutica Sinica*, 27, 875–880, 1992.
517. Mackell, M. A. and Poklis, A., Determination of pentazocine and tripelennamine in blood of T's and Blue addicts by gas-liquid chromatography with a nitrogen detector, *Journal of Chromatography*, 235, 445–452, 1982.
518. Poklis, A. and Mackell, M. A., Pentazocine and tripelennamine (T's and Blues) abuse: toxicological findings in 39 cases, *Journal of Analytical Toxicology*, 6, 109–114, 1982.
519. Poklis, A. and Mackell, M. A., Toxicological findings in deaths due to ingestion of pentazocine: a report of two cases, *Forensic Science International*, 20, 89–95, 1982.
520. Liu, R. H., McKeehan, A. M., Edwards, C., Foster, G., Bensley, W. D., Langner, J. G., et al., Improved GC/MS analysis of barbiturates in urine using centrifuge-based solid-phase extraction, methylation, with d5-pentobarbital as internal standard, *Journal of Forensic Science*, 39, 1504–1514, 1994.
521. Turley, C. P., Pentobarbital quantitation using immunoassays in Reye's syndrome patient serum, *Therapeutic Drug Monitoring*, 11, 343–346, 1989.
522. Earl, R., Sobeski, L., Timko, D., and Markin, R., Pentobarbital quantification in the presence of phenobarbital by fluorescence polarization immunoassay, *Clinical Chemistry*, 37, 1774–1777, 1991.
523. Li, P. K., Lee, J. T., and Schreiber, R. M., Rapid quantification of pentobarbital in serum by fluorescence polarization immunoassay, *Clinical Chemistry*, 30, 307–308, 1984.
524. Sarandis, S., Pichon, R., Miyada, D., and Pirkle, H., Quantitation of pentobarbital in serum by enzyme immunoassay, *Journal of Analytical Toxicology*, 8, 59–60, 1984.
525. Bowsher, R. R., Apathy, J. M., Compton, J. A., Wolen, R. L., Carlson, K. H., and DeSante, K. A., Sensitive, specific radioimmunoassay for quantifying pergolide in plasma, *Clinical Chemistry*, 38, 1975–1980, 1992.
526. Shimamine, M., Takahashi, K., and Nakahara, Y., [Studies on the identification of psychotropic substances. IX. Preparation and various analytical data of reference standard of new psychotropic substances, N-ethyl methylenedioxyamphetamine, N-hydroxy methylenedioxyamphetamine, mecloqualone, 4-methylaminorex, phendimetrazine and phenmetrazine], *Eisei Shikenjo Hokoku—Bulletin of National Institute of Hygienic Sciences*, 66–74, 1993.
527. Moriyama, M., Furuno, K., Oishi, R., and Gomita, Y., Simultaneous determination of primidone and its active metabolites in rat plasma by high-performance liquid chromatography using a solid-phase extraction technique, *Journal of Pharmaceutical Sciences*, 83, 1751–1753, 1994.
528. Kouno, Y., Ishikura, C., Homma, M., and Oka, K., Simple and accurate high-performance liquid chromatographic method for the measurement of three antiepileptics in therapeutic drug monitoring, *Journal of Chromatography*, 622, 47–52, 1993.
529. Liu, H., Delgado, M., Forman, L. J., Eggers, C. M., and Montoya, J. L., Simultaneous determination of carbamazepine, phenytoin, phenobarbital, primidone and their principal metabolites by high-performance liquid chromatography with photodiode-array detection, *Journal of Chromatography*, 616, 105–115, 1993.

530. Binder, S. R., Adams, A. K., Regalia, M., Essien, H., and Rosenblum, R., Standardization of a multi-wavelength UV detector for liquid chromatography-based toxicological analysis, *Journal of Chromatography*, 550, 449–459, 1991.
531. Wu, A. H., Onigbinde, T. A., Wong, S. S., and Johnson, K. G., Identification of methamphetamines and over-the-counter sympathometic amines by full-scan GC-ion trap MS with electron impact and chemical ionization, *Journal of Analytical Toxicology*, 16, 137–141, 1992.
532. Cui, J. F., Zhou, Y., Cui, K. R., Li, L., and Zhou, T. H., [Study on metabolism of phenmetrazine-like drugs and their metabolites], *Yao Hsueh Hsueh Pao—Acta Pharmaceutica Sinica*, 25, 632–636, 1990.
533. Rambeck, B., May, T. W., Jurgens, M. U., Blankenhorn, V., Jurges, U., Korn-Merker, E., et al., Comparison of phenytoin and carbamazepine serum concentrations measured by high-performance liquid chromatography, the standard TDx assay, the enzyme multiplied immunoassay technique, and a new patient-side immunoassay cartridge system, *Therapeutic Drug Monitoring*, 16, 608–612, 1994.
534. Logan, B. K. and Stafford, D. T., Direct analysis of anticonvulsant drugs in vitreous humour by HPLC using a column switching technique, *Forensic Science International*, 41, 125–134, 1989.
535. Lensmeyer, G. L., Rajani, C., and Evenson, M. A., Liquid-chromatographic procedure for simultaneous analysis for eight benzodiazepines in serum, *Clinical Chemistry*, 28, 2274–2278, 1982.
536. Eadie, M. J., Formation of active metabolites of anticonvulsant drugs. A review of their pharmacokinetic and therapeutic significance. [Review] [86 refs.], *Clinical Pharmacokinetics*, 21, 27–41, 1991.
537. Streete, J. M. and Berry, D. J., Gas chromatographic analysis of phenylethylmalonamide in human plasma, *Journal of Chromatography*, 416, 281–291, 1987.
538. Kim, S. Y. and Benowitz, N. L., Poisoning due to class IA antiarrhythmic drugs. Quinidine, procainamide and disopyramide. [Review], *Drug Safety*, 5, 393–420, 1990.
539. Sonsalla, P. K., Bridges, R. R., Jennison, T. A., and Smith, C. M., An evaluation of the TDX fluorescence polarization immunoassays for procainamide and n-acetylprocainamide, *Journal of Analytical Toxicology*, 9, 152–155, 1985.
540. Bagli, M., Rao, M. L., and Hoflich, G., Quantification of chlorprothixene, levomepromazine and promethazine in human serum using high-performance liquid chromatography with coulometric electrochemical detection, *Journal of Chromatography B: Biomedical Applications*, 657, 141–148, 1994.
541. Bohm, R., Ellrich, R., and Koytchev, R., Quantitation of R- and S-propafenone and of the main metabolite in plasma, *Pharmazie*, 50, 542–545, 1995.
542. Botterblom, M. H., Feenstra, M. G., and Erdtsieck-Ernste, E. B., Determination of propranolol, labetalol and clenbuterol in rat brain by high-performance liquid chromatography, *Journal of Chromatography*, 613, 121–126, 1993.
543. Kwong, E. C. and Shen, D. D., Versatile isocratic high-performance liquid chromatographic assay for propranolol and its basic, neutral and acidic metabolites in biological fluids, *Journal of Chromatography*, 414, 365–379, 1987.
544. Lindner, W., Rath, M., Stoschitzky, K., and Uray, G., Enantioselective drug monitoring of (R)- and (S)-propranolol in human plasma via derivatization with optically active (R,R)-O,O-diacetyl tartaric acid anhydride, *Journal of Chromatography*, 487, 375–383, 1989.
545. Ehrsson, H., Identification of diastereomeric propranolol-o-glucuronides by GC/MS, *Journal of Pharmacy and Pharmacology*, 27, 971–973, 1975.
546. Ehrsson, H., Simultaneous determination of (–)- and (+)-propranolol by GC/MS using a deuterium labeling technique, *Journal of Pharmacy and Pharmacology*, 28, 662, 1976.
547. Altmayer, P., Buch, U., Buch, H. P., and Larsen, R., Rapid and sensitive pre-column extraction high-performance liquid chromatographic assay for propofol in biological fluids, *Journal of Chromatography*, 612, 326–330, 1993.
548. Guitton, J., Desage, M., Lepape, A., Degoute, C. S., Manchon, M., and Brazier, J. L., Quantitation of propofol in whole blood by gas chromatography-mass spectrometry, *Journal of Chromatography B: Biomedical Applications*, 669, 358–365, 1995.
549. Amalfitano, G., Bessard, J., Vincent, F., Eysseric, H., and Bessard, G., Gas chromatographic quantitation of dextropropoxyphene and norpropoxyphene in urine after solid-phase extraction, *Journal of Analytical Toxicology*, 20, 547–554, 1996.
550. Margot, P. A., Crouch, D. J., Finkle, B. S., Johnson, J. R., and Deyman, M. E., Capillary and packed column GC determination of propoxyphene and norpropoxyphene in biological specimens: analytical problems and improvements, *Journal of Chromatographic Science*, 21, 201–204, 1983.

551. Wolen, R. L., Gruber, C. M., Jr., Baptisti, A., Jr., and Scholz, N. E., The concentration of propoxyphene in the plasma and analgesia scores in postpartum patients, *Toxicology & Applied Pharmacology*, 19, 498–503, 1971.
552. Wolen, R. L. and Gruber, C. M., Jr., Determination of propoxyphene in human plasma by gas chromatography, *Analytical Chemistry*, 40, 1243–1246, 1968.
553. Wolen, R. L., Obermeyer, B. D., Ziege, E. A., Black, H. R., and Gruber, C. M., Jr., Drug metabolism and pharmacokinetic studies in man utilising nitrogen-15- and deuterium-labelled drugs: the metabolic fate of cinoxacin and the metabolism and pharmacokinetics of propoxyphene, in *Stable Isotopes*, Baillie, T. A., Ed., University Park Press, Baltimore, 1978, 20.
554. Wolen, R. L., Ziege, E. A., and Gruber, C., Jr., Determination of propoxyphene and norpropoxyphene by chemical ionization mass fragmentography, *Clinical Pharmacology & Therapeutics*, 17, 15–20, 1975.
555. Nash, J. F., Bennett, I. F., Bopp, R. J., Brunson, M. K., and Sullivan, H. R., Quantitation of propoxyphene and its major metabolites in heroin addict plasma after large dose administration of propoxyphene napsylate, *Journal of Pharmaceutical Sciences*, 64, 429–433, 1975.
556. Wolen, R. L., Ziege, E. A., and Gruber, C. M., Determination of propoxyphene and norpropoxyphene by chemical ionization mass fragmentography, *Clinical Pharmacological Therapy*, 17, 15–20, 1974.
557. Flanagan, R. J., Johnston, A., White, A. S., and Crome, P., Pharmacokinetics of dextropropoxyphene and nordextropropoxyphene in young and elderly volunteers after single and multiple dextropropoxyphene dosage, *British Journal of Clinical Pharmacology*, 28, 463–469, 1989.
558. Kaa, E. and Dalgaard, J. B., Fatal dextropropoxyphene poisonings in Jutland, Denmark, *Zeitschrift für Rechtsmedizin—Journal of Legal Medicine*, 102, 107–115, 1989.
559. Kintz, P. and Mangin, P., Abbott propoxyphene assay: evaluation and comparison of TDx FPIA and GC/MS methods, *Journal of Analytical Toxicology*, 17, 222–224, 1993.
560. Preskorn, S. H. and Fast, G. A., Therapeutic drug monitoring for antidepressants: efficacy, safety, and cost effectiveness [published erratum appears in *Journal of Clinical Psychiatry*, 52, 353, 1992]. [Review], *Journal of Clinical Psychiatry*, 52, 23–33, 1991.
561. Power, B. M., Hackett, L. P., Dusci, L. J., and Ilett, K. F., Antidepressant toxicity and the need for identification and concentration monitoring in overdose. [Review], *Clinical Pharmacokinetics*, 29, 154–171, 1995.
562. Henry, J. A., Alexander, C. A., and Sener, E. K., Relative mortality from overdose of antidepressants [see comments] [published erratum appears in *British Medical Journal*, 8, 310(6984), 911, 1995], *British Medical Journal*, 310, 221–224, 1995.
563. Rao, M. L., Staberock, U., Baumann, P., Hiemke, C., Deister, A., Cuendet, C., et al., Monitoring tricyclic antidepressant concentrations in serum by fluorescence polarization immunoassay compared with gas chromatography and HPLC, *Clinical Chemistry*, 40, 929–933, 1994.
564. Poklis, A., Soghoian, D., Crooks, C. R., and Saady, J. J., Evaluation of the Abbott ADx total serum tricyclic immunoassay, *Journal of Toxicology Clinical Toxicology*, 28, 235–248, 1990.
565. Brooks, K. E. and Smith, N. S., Lack of formation of methamphetamine-like artifacts by the monoacetates of pseudoephedrine and related compounds in the GC/MS analysis of urine extracts [letter], *Journal of Analytical Toxicology*, 17, 441–442, 1993.
566. Yeh, S. Y., N-depyridination and N-dedimethylaminoethylation of tripelennamine and pyrilamine in the rat, *Drug Metabolism & Disposition*, 18, 453–461, 1990.
567. Bun, H., Coassolo, P., Ba, B., Aubert, C., and Cano, J. P., Plasma quantification of quazepam and its 2-oxo and N-desmethyl metabolites by capillary gas chromatography, *Journal of Chromatography*, 378, 137–145, 1986.
568. Gupta, S. K. and Ellinwood, E. H., Jr., Liquid chromatographic assay and pharmacokinetics of quazepam and its metabolites following sublingual administration of quazepam, *Pharmaceutical Research*, 5, 365–368, 1988.
569. Kales, A., Quazepam: hypnotic efficacy and side effects. [Review] [137 refs.], *Pharmacotherapy*, 10, 1–10, 1990.
570. Brandsteterova, E., Romanova, D., Kralikova, D., Bozekova, L., and Kriska, M., Automatic solid-phase extraction and high-performance liquid chromatographic determination of quinidine in plasma, *Journal of Chromatography A*, 665, 101–104, 1994.
571. Cosbey, S. H., Craig, I., and Gill, R., Novel solid-phase extraction strategy for the isolation of basic drugs from whole blood, *Journal of Chromatography B: Biomedical Applications*, 669, 229–235, 1995.

572. Lloyd, T. L., Perschy, T. B., Gooding, A. E., and Tomlinson, J. J., Robotic solid phase extraction and high performance liquid chromatographic analysis of ranitidine in serum or plasma, *Biomedical Chromatography*, 6, 311–316, 1992.
573. Karnes, H. T., Opong-Mensah, K., Farthing, D., and Beightol, L. A., Automated solid-phase extraction and high-performance liquid chromatographic determination of ranitidine from urine, plasma and peritoneal dialysate, *Journal of Chromatography*, 422, 165–173, 1987.
574. Aravagiri, M., Marder, S. R., Van Putten, T., and Midha, K. K., Determination of risperidone in plasma by high-performance liquid chromatography with electrochemical detection: application to therapeutic drug monitoring in schizophrenic patients, *Journal of Pharmaceutical Sciences*, 82, 447–449, 1993.
575. Le Moing, J. P., Edouard, S., and Levron, J. C., Determination of risperidone and 9-hydroxyrisperidone in human plasma by high-performance liquid chromatography with electrochemical detection, *Journal of Chromatography*, 614, 333–339, 1993.
576. Borison, R. L., Diamond, B., Pathiraja, A., and Meibach, R. C., Pharmacokinetics of risperidone in chronic schizophrenic patients, *Psychopharmacology Bulletin*, 30, 193–197, 1994.
577. Springfield, A. C. and Bodiford, E., An overdose of risperidone, *Journal of Analytical Toxicology*, 20, 202–203, 1996.
578. Deutsch, J., Soncrant, T. T., Greig, N. H., and Rapoport, S. I., Electron-impact ionization detection of scopolamine by gas chromatography-mass spectrometry in rat plasma and brain, *Journal of Chromatography*, 528, 325–331, 1990.
579. Oertel, R., Richter, K., Ebert, U., and Kirch, W., Determination of scopolamine in human serum by gas chromatography ion trap tandem mass spectrometry, *Journal of Chromatography B: Biomedical Applications*, 682, 259–264, 1996.
580. Quatrehomme, G., Bourret, F., Zhioua, M., Lapalus, P., and Ollier, A., Post mortem kinetics of secobarbital, *Forensic Science International*, 44, 117–123, 1990.
581. Sharp, M. E., Wallace, S. M., Hindmarsh, K. W., and Peel, H. W., Monitoring saliva concentrations of methaqualone, codeine, secobarbital, diphenhydramine and diazepam after single oral doses, *Journal of Analytical Toxicology*, 7, 11–14, 1983.
582. Paetsch, P. R., Baker, G. B., Caffaro, L. E., Greenshaw, A. J., Rauw, G. A., and Coutts, R. T., Electron-capture gas chromatographic procedure for simultaneous determination of amphetamine and N-methylamphetamine, *Journal of Chromatography*, 573, 313–317, 1992.
583. La Croix, R., Pianezzola, E., and Strolin Benedetti, M., Sensitive high-performance liquid chromatographic method for the determination of the three main metabolites of selegiline (L-deprenyl) in human plasma, *Journal of Chromatography B: Biomedical Applications*, 656, 251–258, 1994.
584. Maurer, H. H. and Kraemer, T., Toxicological detection of selegiline and its metabolites in urine using fluorescence polarization immunoassay (FPIA) and gas chromatography-mass spectrometry (GC-MS) and differentiation by enantioselective GC-MS of the intake of selegiline from abuse of methamphetamine or amphetamine, *Archives of Toxicology*, 66, 675–678, 1992.
585. Reimer, M. L., Mamer, O. A., Zavitsanos, A. P., Siddiqui, A. W., and Dadgar, D., Determination of amphetamine, methamphetamine and desmethyldeprenyl in human plasma by gas chromatography/negative ion chemical ionization mass spectrometry, *Biological Mass Spectrometry*, 22, 235–242, 1993,
586. Meeker, J. E. and Reynolds, P. C., Postmortem tissue methamphetamine concentrations following selegiline administration, *Journal of Analytical Toxicology*, 14, 330–331, 1990.
587. Rogowsky, D., Marr, M., Long, G., and Moore, C., Determination of sertraline and desmethylsertraline in human serum using copolymeric bonded-phase extraction, liquid chromatography and GC/MS, *Journal of Chromatography B: Biomedical Applications*, 655, 138–141, 1994.
588. De Saqui-Sannes, P., Nups, P., Le Bars, P., and Burgat, V., Evaluation of an HPTLC method for the determination of strychnine and crimidine in biological samples, *Journal of Analytical Toxicology*, 20, 185–188, 1996.
589. Stevens, H. M. and Moffat, A. C., A rapid screening procedure for quaternary ammonium compounds in fluids and tissues with special reference to suxamethonium (succinylcholine), *Journal of the Forensic Science Society*, 14, 141–148, 1974.
590. Forney, R. B., Jr., Carroll, F. T., Nordgren, I. K., Pettersson, B. M., and Holmstedt, B., Extraction, identification and quantitation of succinylcholine in embalmed tissue, *Journal of Analytical Toxicology*, 6, 115–119, 1982.

591. Woestenborghs, R. J., Timmerman, P. M., Cornelissen, M. L., Van Rompaey, F. A., Gepts, E., Camu, F., et al., Assay methods for sufentanil in plasma. Radioimmunoassay versus gas chromatography-mass spectrometry, *Anesthesiology*, 80, 666–670, 1994.
592. Rochholz, G., Ahrens, B., Konig, F., Schutz, H. W., Schutz, H., and Seno, H., Screening and identification of sumatriptan and its main metabolite by means of thin-layer chromatography, ultraviolet spectroscopy and gas chromatography/mass spectrometry, *Arzneimittel-Forschung*, 45, 941–946, 1995.
593. Qiu, F. H., Liu, L., Guo, L., Luo, Y., and Lu, Y. Q., [Rapid identification and quantitation of barbiturates in plasma using solid-phase extraction combined with GC-FID and GC-MS method]. [Chinese], *Yao Hsueh Hsueh Pao—Acta Pharmaceutica Sinica*, 30, 372–377, 1995.
594. Laakkonen, U. M., Leinonen, A., and Savonen, L., Screening of non-steroidal anti-inflammatory drugs, barbiturates and methyl xanthines in equine urine by gas chromatography-mass spectrometry, *Analyst*, 119, 2695–2696, 1994.
595. Tjaden, U. R., Meeles, M. T., Thys, C. P., and van der Kaay, M., Determination of some benzodiazepines and metabolites in serum, urine and saliva by high-performance liquid chromatography, *Journal of Chromatography*, 181, 227–241, 1980.
596. Pounder, D. J., Adams, E., Fuke, C., and Langford, A. M., Site to site variability of postmortem drug concentrations in liver and lung, *Journal of Forensic Sciences*, 41, 927–932, 1996.
597. Walash, M. I., Belal, F., Metwally, M. E., and Hefnawy, M. M., A selective fluorimetric method for the determination of some 1,4-benzodiazepine drugs containing a hydroxyl group at C-3, *Journal of Pharmaceutical & Biomedical Analysis*, 12, 1417–1423, 1994.
598. McCarthy, P., Atwal, S., Sykes, A., and Ayres, J., Measurement of terbutaline and salbutamol in plasma by high performance liquid chromatography with fluorescence detection, *Biomedical Chromatography*, 7, 25–28, 1993.
599. Van Vyncht, G., Preece, S., Gaspar, P., Maghuin-Rogister, G., and DePauw, E., Gas and liquid chromatography coupled to tandem mass spectrometry for the multiresidue analysis of beta-agonists in biological matrices, *Journal of Chromatography A*, 750, 43–49, 1996.
600. Lindberg, C., Paulson, J., and Blomqvist, A., Evaluation of an automated thermospray liquid chromatography-mass spectrometry system for quantitative use in bioanalytical chemistry, *Journal of Chromatography*, 554, 215–226, 1991.
601. Altieri, M., Bogema, S., and Schwartz, R. H., TAC topical anesthesia produces positive urine tests for cocaine, *Annals of Emergency Medicine*, 19, 577–579, 1990.
602. Hannak, D., Haux, P., Scharbert, F., and Kattermann, R., Liquid chromatographic analysis of phenobarbital, phenytoin, and theophylline, *Wiener Klinische Wochenschrift. Supplementum*, 191, 27–31, 1992.
603. Mounie, J., Richard, L., Ribon, B., Hersant, J., Sarmini, H., Houin, G., et al., Methods of theophylline assay and therapeutic monitoring of this drug [published erratum appears in *Annales de Biologie Clinique* (Paris) 48, 447, 1990]. [Review], *Annales de Biologie Clinique*, 48, 287–293, 1990.
604. Zaninotto, M., Secchiero, S., Paleari, C. D., and Burlina, A., Performance of a fluorescence polarization immunoassay system evaluated by therapeutic monitoring of four drugs, *Therapeutic Drug Monitoring*, 14, 301–305, 1992.
605. Jones, L. A., Gonzalez, E. R., Venitz, J., Edinboro, L. E., and Poklis, A., Evaluation of the Vision Theophylline assays in the emergency department setting, *Annals of Emergency Medicine*, 21, 777–781, 1992.
606. Sessler, C. N., Theophylline toxicity: clinical features of 116 consecutive cases. [Review], *American Journal of Medicine*, 88, 567–576, 1990.
607. el-Sayed, Y. M. and Islam, S. I., Comparison of fluorescence polarization immunoassay and HPLC for the determination of theophylline in serum, *Journal of Clinical Pharmacy & Therapeutics*, 14, 127–134, 1989.
608. Costantino, A. G., Caplan, Y. H., Levine, B. S., Dixon, A. M., and Smialek, J. E., Thiamylal: review of the literature and report of a suicide, *Journal of Forensic Sciences*, 35, 89–96, 1990.
609. Stockham, T. L., McGee, M. P., and Stajic, M., Report of a fatal thiamylal intoxication, *Journal of Analytical Toxicology*, 15, 155–156, 1991.
610. Yashiki, M., Kojima, T., and Okamoto, I., Toxicological study on intravenous thiopental anesthesia—interrelation between rate of injection and distribution of thiopental, *Forensic Science International*, 33, 169–175, 1987.

611. Garriott, J. C., Foerster, E., Juarez, L., de la Garza, F., Mendiola, I., and Curoe, J., Measurement of toluene in blood and breath in cases of solvent abuse, *Clinical Toxicology*, 18, 471–479, 1981.
612. Inoue, H., Iwasa, M., Maeno, Y., Koyama, H., Sato, Y., and Matoba, R., Detection of toluene in an adipoceratous body, *Forensic Science International*, 78, 119–124, 1996.
613. Kawai, T., Mizunuma, K., Yasugi, T., Horiguchi, S., and Ikeda, M., Toluene in blood as a marker of choice for low-level exposure to toluene, *International Archives of Occupational & Environmental Health*, 66, 309–315, 1994.
614. Jones, A. D., Dunlap, M. R., and Gospe, S. M., Jr., Stable-isotope dilution GC-MS for determination of toluene in submilliliter volumes of whole blood, *Journal of Analytical Toxicology*, 18, 251–254, 1994.
615. Von Burg, R., Toluene. [Review] [85 refs.], *Journal of Applied Toxicology*, 13, 441–446, 1993.
616. Lof, A., Wigaeus Hjelm, E., Colmsjo, A., Lundmark, B. O., Norstrom, A., and Sato, A., Toxicokinetics of toluene and urinary excretion of hippuric acid after human exposure to 2H8-toluene, *British Journal of Industrial Medicine*, 50, 55–59, 1993.
617. Saker, E. G., Eskew, A. E., and Panter, J. W., Stability of toluene in blood: its forensic relevance, *Journal of Analytical Toxicology*, 15, 246–249, 1991.
618. Xu, Y. X., Xu, Y. Q., Zhang, C. J., and Shen, L., [Analysis of tramadol and its metabolites in human urine]. [Chinese], *Yao Hsueh Hsueh Pao—Acta Pharmaceutica Sinica*, 28, 379–383, 1993.
619. Anderson, W. H. and Archuleta, M. M., The capillary gas chromatographic determination of trazodone in biological specimens, *Journal of Analytical Toxicology*, 8, 217–219, 1984.
620. Caccia, S., Ballabio, M., Fanelli, R., Guiso, G., and Zanini, M. G., Determination of plasma and brain concentrations of trazodone and its metabolite, 1-m-chlorophenylpiperazine, by gas-liquid chromatography, *Journal of Chromatography*, 210, 311–318, 1981.
621. Lambert, W., Van Bocxlaer, J., Piette, M., and De Leenheer, A., A fatal case of trazodone and dothiepin poisoning: toxicological findings, *Journal of Analytical Toxicology*, 18, 176–179, 1994.
622. Senda, N., Kohta, K., Takahashi, T., Shizukuishi, K., Mimura, T., Fujita, T., et al., A highly sensitive method to quantify triazolam and its metabolites with liquid chromatography—mass spectrometry, *Biomedical Chromatography*, 9, 48–51, 1995.
623. Joynt, B. P., Triazolam blood concentrations in forensic cases in Canada, *Journal of Analytical Toxicology*, 17, 171–177, 1993.
624. Koves, G. and Wells, J., The quantitation of triazolam in postmortem blood by gas chromatography/negative ion chemical ionization mass spectrometry, *Journal of Analytical Toxicology*, 10, 241–244, 1986.
625. Kostrzewski, P., Jakubowski, M., and Kolacinski, Z., Kinetics of trichloroethylene elimination from venous blood after acute inhalation poisoning, *Journal of Toxicology—Clinical Toxicology*, 31, 353–363, 1993.
626. Kintz, P., Godelar, B., Mangin, P., Chaumont, A. J., and Lugnier, A. A., Identification and quantification of trihexyphenidyl and its hydroxylated metabolite by gas chromatography with nitrogen-phosphorus detection, *Journal of Analytical Toxicology*, 13, 47–49, 1989.
627. Maurer, H. H., Detection of anticonvulsants and their metabolites in urine within a "general unknown" analytical procedure using computerized GC/MS, *Archives of Toxicology*, 64, 554–561, 1990.
628. Jones, R., Klette, K., Kuhlman, J. J., Levine, B., Smith, M. L., Watson, C. V., et al., Trimethobenzamide cross-reacts in immunoassays of amphetamine/methamphetamine [letter; see comments], *Clinical Chemistry*, 39, 699–700, 1993.
629. Colbert, D. L., Possible explanation for trimethobenzamide cross-reaction in immunoassays of amphetamine/methamphetamine [letter; comment], *Clinical Chemistry*, 40, 948–949, 1994.
630. Pok Phak, R., Conquy, T., Gouezo, F., Viala, A., and Grimaldi, F., Determination of metapramine, imipramine, trimipramine and their major metabolites in plasma by reversed-phase column liquid chromatography, *Journal of Chromatography*, 375, 339–347, 1986.
631. Fraser, A. D., Isner, A. F., and Perry, R. A., Distribution of trimipramine and its major metabolites in a fatal overdose case, *Journal of Analytical Toxicology*, 11, 168–170, 1987.
632. Poklis, A., Case, M. E., and Ridenour, G. C., Abuse of pentazocine/tripelennamine combination. Ts and Blues in the city of St. Louis, *Missouri Medicine*, 80, 21–23, 1983.
633. Pokrajac, M., Miljkovic, B., Spiridonovic, D., and Varagic, V. M., An improved gas chromatographic determination of valproic acid and valpromide in plasma, *Pharmaceutica Acta Helvetiae*, 67, 237–240, 1992.

634. Vajda, F. J., Drummer, O. H., Morris, P. M., McNeil, J. J., and Bladin, P. F., Gas chromatographic measurement of plasma levels of sodium valproate: tentative therapeutic range of a new anticonvulsant in the treatment of refractory epileptics, *Clinical & Experimental Pharmacology & Physiology*, 5, 67–73, 1978.
635. Berry, D. J. and Clarke, L. A., Determination of valproic acid (dipropylacetic acid) in plasma by gas-liquid chromatography, *Journal of Chromatography*, 156, 301–307, 1978.
636. Liu, H., Montoya, J. L., Forman, L. J., Eggers, C. M., Barham, C. F., and Delgado, M., Determination of free valproic acid: evaluation of the Centrifree system and comparison between high-performance liquid chromatography and enzyme immunoassay, *Therapeutic Drug Monitoring*, 14, 513–521, 1992.
637. Liu, H., Forman, L. J., Montoya, J., Eggers, C., Barham, C., and Delgado, M., Determination of valproic acid by high-performance liquid chromatography with photodiode-array and fluorescence detection, *Journal of Chromatography*, 576, 163–169, 1992.
638. Yu, D., Gordon, J. D., Zheng, J., Panesar, S. K., Riggs, K. W., Rurak, D. W., et al., Determination of valproic acid and its metabolites using gas chromatography with mass-selective detection: application to serum and urine samples from sheep, *Journal of Chromatography B: Biomedical Applications*, 666, 269–281, 1995.
639. Dupuis, R. E., Lichtman, S. N., and Pollack, G. M., Acute valproic acid overdose, *Drug Safety*, 5, 65–71, 1990.
640. Levine, B., Jenkins, A. J., Queen, M., Jufer, R., and Smialek, J. E., Distribution of venlafaxine in three postmortem cases, *Journal of Analytical Toxicology*, 20, 502–505, 1996.
641. Parsons, A. T., Anthony, R. M., and Meeker, J. E., Two fatal cases of venlafaxine poisoning, *Journal of Analytical Toxicology*, 20, 266–268, 1996.
642. Shin, H. S., Ohshin, Y. S., Kim, H. J., and Kang, Y. K., Sensitive assay for verapamil in plasma using gas-liquid chromatography with nitrogen-phosphorus detection, *Journal of Chromatography B: Biomedical Applications*, 677, 369–373, 1996.
643. Levine, B., Jones, R., Klette, K., Smith, M. L., and Kilbane, E., An intoxication involving BRON and verapamil, *Journal of Analytical Toxicology*, 17, 381–383, 1993.
644. Crouch, D. J., Crompton, C., Rollins, D. E., Peat, M. A., and Francom, P., Toxicological findings in a fatal overdose of verapamil, *Journal of Forensic Sciences*, 31, 1505–1508, 1986.
645. Ashraf, M., Chaudhary, K., Nelson, J., and Thompson, W., Massive overdose of sustained-release verapamil—a case report and review of literature, *American Journal of the Medical Sciences*, 310, 258–263, 1995.
646. Brogden, R. N. and Benfield, P., Verapamil—a review of its pharmacological properties and therapeutic use in coronary artery disease [review], *Drugs*, 51, 792–819, 1996.
647. Akisu, M., Mir, S., Genc, B., and Cura, A., Severe acute thinner intoxication, *Turkish Journal of Pediatrics*, 38, 223–225, 1996.
648. Etzel, R. A. and Ashley, D. L., Volatile organic compounds in the blood of persons in Kuwait during the oil fires, *International Archives of Occupational & Environmental Health*, 66, 125–129, 1994.
649. Mannino, D. M., Schreiber, J., Aldous, K., Ashley, D., Moolenaar, R., and Almaguer, D., Human exposure to volatile organic compounds: a comparison of organic vapor monitoring badge levels with blood levels, *International Archives of Occupational & Environmental Health*, 67, 59–64, 1995.
650. Ramsey, J., Anderson, H. R., Bloor, K., and Flanagan, R. J., An introduction to the practice, prevalence and chemical toxicology of volatile substance abuse, *Human Toxicology*, 8, 261–269, 1989.
651. Stanke, F., Jourdil, N., Lauby, V., and Bessard, G., Zopiclone and zolpidem quantification in human plasma by high performance liquid chromatography with photodiode-array detection, *Journal of Liquid Chromatography & Related Technologies*, 19, 2623–2633, 1996.
652. Meeker, J. E., Som, C. W., Macapagal, E. C., and Benson, P. A., Zolpidem tissue concentrations in a multiple drug related death involving Ambien, *Journal of Analytical Toxicology*, 19, 531–534, 1995.
653. Ahrens, B., Schutz, H., Seno, H., and Weiler, G., Screening, identification and determination of the two new hypnotics zolpidem and zopiclone, *Arzneimittel-Forschung*, 44, 799–802, 1994.
654. Tracqui, A., Kintz, P., and Mangin, P., High-performance liquid chromatographic assay with diode-array detection for toxicological screening of zopiclone, zolpidem, suriclone and alpidem in human plasma, *Journal of Chromatography*, 616, 95–103, 1993.
655. Debailleul, G., Khalil, F. A., and Lheureux, P., HPLC quantification of zolpidem and prothipendyl in a voluntary intoxication, *Journal of Analytical Toxicology*, 15, 35–37, 1991.

APPENDIX IV

Sample Calculations

Barry K. Logan, Ph.D.[1] **and Alan Wayne Jones, D.Sc.**[2]
[1] Director, Washington State Toxicology Laboratory, Department of Laboratory Medicine, University of Washington, Seattle, Washington
[2] Department of Forensic Toxicology, University Hospital, Linköping, Sweden

This section presents some typical scenarios based on authentic DUI cases. Bear in mind that statutory "per se" alcohol limits are somewhat arbitrary, and that a person's driving might be influenced below the so-called "legal limit." For this reason, the quantitative measurement of blood or breath alcohol, and related calculations, should be one element of any DUI case, and not the entire case.

Example 1. The defendant (male, 175 lb) had been drinking for 3 h, but gulps down a "double vodka" (assumed to be 2 oz of 40% v/v) immediately before leaving the bar, and is arrested for DUI 15 min later. His BrAC 30 min after arrest is 0.10 g/210 L. Could his BrAC have been below 0.08 at the time of driving?

This question relates to the significance of the last drink as a factor in raising the BrAC. Since this pattern of drinking represents a small bolus on top of a pre-existing BrAC, it is likely that the last drink was substantially absorbed within 15 min, i.e., at the time of the arrest. The small amount of alcohol unabsorbed would not be enough to account for the difference between 0.08 and 0.10 g/210 L. Note that no allowance was made for alcohol metabolism (often called burn-off) in this example. Assuming some alcohol elimination occurred between the time of the arrest and the breath test, this would make it even less likely that the BrAC at the time of the arrest was below 0.08 g/210 L.

It is possible to construct a scenario whereby the defendant's version could be supported, and might involve some kind of delayed gastric emptying, an unusually low volume of distribution for the alcohol, and a low alcohol elimination rate. This latter scenario, however, is much less likely than the former, and needs to be evaluated in the context of other available information in the case. For example, what was the reason for the driver being stopped in the first place? These situations require the application of some scientific common sense, and the principle of Occam's razor, namely, that the fewer assumptions one has to invoke to explain a set of facts, the more likely that explanation is. Note also that intra-individual variations in absorption and elimination of alcohol make any kind of reconstruction or repeat of the circumstances in question of dubious value.

Example 2. The defendant (male, 230 lb) claims he consumed ten 12-oz beers of 4.2% v/v alcohol content in 1 h, then drove immediately afterward, and was arrested 10 min after his last drink. The BrAC was 0.17 g/210 L, 1 h later. Could the suspect's BrAC have been below 0.10 g/210 L at the time of driving?

In this scenario, one has to make fewer assumptions in order for the defendant's BrAC to be below 0.10 g/210 L at the time of driving. Absorption of alcohol after drinking so much beer could result in a delayed peak. The drinking pattern is unusual; however, based on Widmark's formula it could account for the measured BrAC. Credible corroboration of the defendant's story would be important in presenting this case to the jury, and would have to be considered in the context of other evidence of his behavior, his driving, his statements at the time of arrest, etc. It has to be said that even if true, this pattern of drinking followed by driving is not likely to engender much sympathy from the jury.

Example 3. The defendant (male, 150 lb) admits to having a few drinks before an accident, but alleges he drank 4 oz of 40% v/v whisky to steady his nerves after the accident. His BAC at the time of blood sampling about 1 h later was 0.15 g/dL. Could his BAC at the time of the accident have been below 0.08 g/dL?

This scenario relates to whether the contribution from post-accident drinking can account for the difference between the measured BAC and an administrative legal limit. According to Widmark's formula, the contribution to BAC from the post-accident drinking would be approximately 0.08 g/dL. Given the uncertainty in this estimate (~0.06 to 0.09 g/dL), there is a significant possibility that he could have been below 0.08 g/dL at the time of the accident. Important factors to consider would be the accuracy of the estimate of how much post-accident drinking actually took place (if indeed it did), the actual times of the accident and blood sampling, and some corroboration of the pre-accident drinking pattern. A large amount of drinking immediately before the accident could further raise the likelihood of the BAC being below 0.08 at the time of the accident. In some countries, drinking within a certain time period after an accident is itself considered a punishable offense, and certainly displays poor judgment on the part of the defendant.

Example 4. Defendant (male, 230 lb) is arrested and an evidential breath test shows 0.21 g/210 L. He claims he only consumed two 16-oz beers over a 3-h period. Application of Widmark's formula shows that the volume of beer required to produce this BrAC is about 230 oz of 3.5% v/v beer. How can this discrepancy be resolved?

The defendant maintains that the discrepancy suggests a malfunction in the breath test instrument. This comes down to an evaluation of the credibility of the defendant's story against the accuracy and reliability of the breath test. Safeguards followed when conducting the breath test, such as duplicate testing, room air blank tests, and simulator control tests with each subject test, will help to validate the accuracy of the result. Again, other factors such as the defendant's driving pattern, performance in field sobriety tests, and behavior at the time of the arrest will either help or hurt his story. It is the experience of most people working in this field that defendants will invariably underestimate their actual consumption, and may not recall the brand of beer or liquor they were drinking.

Example 5. The defendant (female 120 lb) leaves the scene of an accident, but is eventually arrested and a blood sample is collected 4 h later. Her BAC at the time of sampling is 0.05 g/dL. What was her BAC at the time of the accident?

This is a clear-cut case regarding the validity of retrograde extrapolation, or estimating back. If one assumes that the defendant was fully post-absorptive at the time of the accident, estimating back 4 h and allowing a mean burn-off rate of 0.019 g/dL/h (with a range from 0.009 g/dL/h to 0.030 g/dL/h) would produce a most likely BAC of 0.126 g/dL (range 0.086 to 0.170 g/dL). However, since a BAC plateau might have occurred, especially with food in the stomach, the validity of this assumption of a decreasing blood alcohol curve for 4 h is perhaps open to question.

Another approach, which is more defensible, can be applied if there is a statutory time limit that applies to the measured BAC. For example, there may be a presumption in the law that a BAC within 2 h of driving is representative of the BAC at the time of driving. In this case, estimating back only 2 h, to place the defendant within the 2-h statutory window, is more reliable and produces a most likely BAC of 0.088 g/dL within a range of 0.068 to 0.110 g/dL.

The larger question in this case would be whether the woman was under the influence of alcohol at the time of the accident, and the estimated BAC is only one element of that determination.

Example 6. The defendant has a breath alcohol concentration of 0.16 g/210L. An expert called by the defense claims that the suspect's elevated body temperature (102.9°F) resulting from a fever raised his breath level over his blood level by 20%. He claims that the defendant held his breath before exhaling into the instrument, raising his BrAC by 10%. He claims that the defendant may have had some acetone on his breath, but not enough to trigger the interference detector on the instrument, resulting in up to 0.009 g/dL apparent ethanol response from acetone. He notes the "margin of error" on the instrument is 0.01 g/210 L. He also claims that alcohol from the defendant's upper airways was picked up by his breath during the expiration, suggesting that the alcohol entering the instrument did not come from alveoli, or deep lung regions of the airway. The net effect is that the defendant's "actual" BrAC could have been as low as 0.08 g/210 L.

This shotgun approach, perhaps tied to one of the other rising BAC scenarios discussed above, is very common in DUI litigation, as it seeks to present a barrage of details attacking the validity of breath testing in general, and this defendant's test in particular. The various assertions need to be evaluated individually. First, if the jurisdiction has separate blood and breath statutes, the blood/breath ratio resulting from elevated temperature is not relevant. Breath holding will elevate breath alcohol concentrations compared with rapid, repeated inspiration and expiration. However, breath holding is not part of the breath test protocol, and a well-documented 15-min observation period can challenge this assertion. The amount of acetone required to produce an apparent BrAC of 0.009 g/210 L would result only from extreme fasting (including abstinence from alcoholic beverages) or diabetes, which is not a transient condition. The defendant's medical records can determine whether he or she is diabetic. The "margin of error" issue is frequently raised when the result is close to the legal limit. What "margin of error" means is not clear; it is certainly not a scientific term. Most instrument protocols that include a control with each breath test will require that the control is within ±0.01 g/210 L of a reference value; however, these same instruments will also include optical controls which typically must meet much more stringent parameters. The kinetics of alcohol deposition and evaporation from the airways during inspiration and expiration have been alluded to in other books; however, the bottom line is that breath testing is recognized as a valid measurement of impairment, and breath alcohol concentration, regardless of the complexity of the respiration physiology, is a valid indicator of intoxication. The best approach in these cases is again to contrast the contrived circumstances that are required for the defendant's version to be valid, with the generally more straightforward explanation that the defendant had consumed too much alcohol, was arrested because of impaired driving, failed field sobriety tests, and gave a breath test that reflects his true breath alcohol concentration and is consistent with his impairment.

Example 7. The defendant has a BrAC of 0.05 g/210 L, and performs field sobriety tests well. To what extent was the subject's driving affected?

One can say with some confidence that certain elements of the driving task are influenced at fairly low BrAC levels even in experienced drinkers. However, certain kinds of driving tasks are more likely to be affected than others. Driving down a straight, country road with no other traffic, in good weather, during daylight hours requires less skill than driving on a busy city street at night, in the rain, with pedestrians around, and distractions in the car such as intoxicated companions or loud music. In a case such as this, one must look at the driver's actual driving performance and determine first if it was impaired, then second if other explanations exist for that impairment besides drinking, including possibly fatigue, drug use, or inattention. This BrAC on its own says relatively little about the extent of driving impairment.

APPENDIX V

Predicted Normal Heart Weight (g) as a Function of Body Height in 392 Women and 373 Men[a]

Body height		Women			Men		
(cm)	(in.)	L95	P	U95	L95	P	U95
130	51	133	204	314	164	232	327
132	52	135	207	319	167	236	333
134	53	137	210	324	170	240	338
136	54	139	214	329	173	243	344
138	54	141	217	334	175	247	349
140	55	143	220	338	178	251	355
142	56	145	223	343	181	255	361
144	57	147	226	348	184	259	366
146	57	149	229	353	187	263	372
148	58	151	232	358	189	267	378
150	59	153	236	363	192	271	383
152	60	155	239	368	195	275	389
154	61	157	242	372	198	280	395
156	61	159	245	377	201	284	400
158	62	161	248	382	204	288	406
160	63	163	251	387	207	292	412
162	64	165	254	392	209	296	417
164	65	167	258	397	212	300	423
166	65	169	261	401	215	304	429
168	66	171	264	406	218	308	435
170	67	173	267	411	221	312	440
172	68	176	270	416	224	316	446
174	69	178	273	421	227	320	452
176	69	180	277	426	230	324	458
178	70	182	280	431	233	328	463
180	71	184	283	435	235	332	469
182	72	186	286	440	238	336	475
184	72	188	289	445	241	341	481
186	73	190	292	450	244	345	487
188	74	192	295	455	247	349	492
190	75	194	299	460	250	353	498
192	76	196	302	465	253	357	504
194	76	198	305	469	256	361	510
196	77	200	308	474	259	365	516
198	78	202	311	479	262	369	522
200	79	204	314	484	265	374	527

Body height (cm)	Women				Men		
	(in.)	L95	P	U95	L95	P	U95
202	80	206	318	489	268	378	533
204	80	208	321	494	271	382	539
206	81	210	324	499	274	386	545
208	82	212	327	508	276	394	557
210	83	214	330	508	279	394	557

[a] P = predicted normal heart weight; L95 = lower 95% confidence limit; U95 = upper 95% confidence limit.

From Kitzman, D. et al., Age related changes in normal human hearts during the first 10 decades of life. Part II (Maturity): A quantitive anatomic study of 765 specimens from subjects 20 to 99 years old, *Mayo Clinic Proc.*, 63, 137–146, 1988. With permission.

Index

A

Abbreviations, 137–139
Abdollo studies, 95–111
Abdominal cavity blood, 17
Abdominal muscle, 24
Absolute interpretation, 114
Absorption, drug level interpretation, 121–122
Accidents, 6, 82
Accreditation programs, 111
Acebutolol, 141
Acetaldehyde, 16
Acetaminophen
  chemical tests, 33
  comprehensive toxicology screening, 8
  confirmation, 78
  forensic pathologist role, 4
  gastric contents, 72–73
  quantitative analysis references, 141
  vitreous humor, 116
Acetazolamide, 141
Acetylcarbromal, 141
6-acetylmorphine, 21–22
Acetylsalicylic acid, 34, 141
Acidic drugs, 41–42
Additive toxicity, 126–127
Adverse reactions, 127
Aerosol containers, 26
Aircraft crashes, *see* Accidents
Airplane glue, 22
Albuterol, 141
Alcohol
  bone and bone marrow, 119
  gas chromatography, 42
  suicides, 5
  vitreous humor, 21
Alfentanil, 141
Alkali, 35
Allobarbital, 141
Allpurinol, 141
Alphaprodine, 141
Alprazolam, 38, 141
Amantadine, 141
Amides, 42
Amiodarone, 141
Amitriptyline
  confirmation, 77–78
  gastric contents, 117
  immunoassays, 39
  quantitative analysis references, 141
Amlodipine, 141
Amobarbital, 38, 141
Amoxapine, 141
Amphetamines
  immunoassays, 38
  investigation strategies, 70
  pharmacological classification, 147
  quantitative analysis references, 141
  screening immunoassays, 38
Amphoteric drugs, 48
Amyl nitrite, 141
Analeptics, 147
Analgesics
  pH adjustment, extraction, 48
  pharmacological classification, 147
  suicides, 5
Analysis, drug level interpretation, 115
Analytical chemistry, 32–33, *33*
Analytical data, 109
Analytical methods and procedures, 104–107
Anesthetics, 83, 147
Anorexiants, 147
Antiallergics, 147
Antianxiety drugs, 147
Antiarrhythmics, 48, 147
Anticoagulants, 15–16
Anticonvulsants, 82, 147
Antidepressants, *see also* Tricyclic antidepressants
  bone and bone marrow specimen selection, 23
  brain, 118
  comprehensive toxicology screening, 8
  fly larvae, 24
  gas chromatography-mass spectrometry, 80
  pH adjustment, extraction, 48
  pharmacological classification, 147
  suicides, 5
Antiemetics, 147
Antifreeze, 26
Antihistamines
  pH adjustment, extraction, 48
  pharmacological classification, 147
  quantification, 82

Antihypertensives, 147
Antimony, 35
Antipsychotics, 147
Antivertigo drugs, 147
APCI, *see* Atmospheric pressure-chemical ionization (APCI)
API-ES, *see* Atmospheric pressure-positive electrospray ionization (API-ES)
Applications, extractions, 49
Aprobarbital, 141
Arsenic, 23, 35
Artifacts, medication delivery, 126
Aspirin, 72
Astemizole, 141
Atenolol, 141
Atmospheric pressure-chemical ionization (APCI), 81
Atmospheric pressure-positive electrospray ionization (API-ES), 81
Atracurium, 141
Atropine
  confirmation, 78
  quantification, 82
  quantitative analysis references, 141
Autopsy findings, 74
Azatadine, 141

B

BAC, *see* Blood alcohol content (BAC)
Back-extraction, 83
Baclofen, 141
Barbital, 141
Barbiturates
  bone and bone marrow specimen selection, 23
  drug level interpretation, 116
  flame ionization detector, 42
  fly larvae, 24
  gastric contents, 72–73
  investigation strategies, 70–71
  pH adjustment, extraction, 48
  pharmacological classification, 147
  quantitative analysis references, 141
  screening immunoassays, 38
  solid phase extraction, 48
  vitreous humor, 116
Basements, 26
Benzephetamine, 141
Benzocaine, 141
Benzodiazepines
  bile specimen selection, 21
  bone and bone marrow specimen selection, 23
  brain, 118
  confirmation, 77
  electron capture detector, 42
  fly larvae, 24
  gastric contents, 72–73
  investigation strategies, 71
  liquid chromatography-mass spectrometry, 81
  pH adjustment, extraction, 48
  screening immunoassays, 38–39
  suicides, 5
  vitreous humor, 116
Benzoylecgonine
  cocaine, 71
  gastric contents, 72
  pH adjustment, extraction, 48
  quantification, 82
  quantitative analysis references, 141
  screening immunoassays, 39
  vitreous humor, 116
Benzphetamine, 141
Benztropine, 141
Bepridil, 141
Beta blockers, 81, 147
Betaxolol, 141
Bezoars, 118
Bhongs, 25
Bile
  collection techniques, 17–18
  drug level interpretation, 119
  specimen selection, 19, 21
Biperiden, 141
Bismuth, 35
Bisoprolol, 141
Bladder, *see* Urine
Blood, *see also blood from specific location, such as heart blood;* Whole blood
  collection techniques, 16–17
  drug level interpretation, 115–116
  gas chromatography-mass spectrometry, 80
  gastric contents, 72–73
  ingestion estimation, 123
  preservatives, 15–16
  quantification preparation, 83
  specimen selection, 20, 25
Blood alcohol content (BAC), 181–183
Blood clots, 17, 20
Blood volatiles, 78
Blowflies, 24
Boating accidents, *see* Accidents
Body burden calculation, total, 122–123
Body secretions, 119
Bone and bone marrow
  drug level interpretation, 119–120
  specimen selection, 23–24
Bovine blood, 103
Brain
  blood specimen selection, 20
  drug level interpretation, 118–119
  specimen selection, 22
  tissue specimen selection, 23
Bretylium, 142
Bromate, 34
Bromazepam, 142
Bromdiphen-hydramine, 142
Bromocriptine, 142
Bronchodilators, 147
Bupivacaine, 142
Buprenorphine, 142
Bupropion, 142

Burden calculation, total body, 122–123
Buspirone, 142
Butabarbital, 142
Butalbital, 38, 142
Butane lighters, 25
Butorphanol, 142

C

Cabinets, under-sink, 26
Caffeine, 82, 142
Calcium channel blockers, 147
Calculations, sample scenarios, 181–183
Calibrators, 98–100
Callphorid genus, 24
Camazepam, 142
Camphor, 35
Cannabinoids, 39, 71
Capsules, 25–26, 35, *see also* Tablets
Carbamates, 33
Carbamazepine, 48, 142
Carbinoximine, 142
Carbon monoxide
  quantification, 82–83
  tests, 35
  tissue specimen selection, 23
Carbon tetrachloride, 34
Delta-9-THC-carboxylic acid, 142
Carboxylic acids, 42
Cardiac blood, *see* Heart blood
Cardiac glycosides, 83
Carfentanil, 142
Carisoprodol, 142
Carrots, 22
Case histories, 74
Case reviews, 8–9
Caustics, 26
CEDIA assays, 37
Central analgesics, 147
Cerebrospinal fluid, 22, 119
Certification of death, 4, 7
Chain of custody
  fundamentals, 14
  hospital admission specimens, 19
  quality assurance, 109
  specimen collection, 4
Chemical tests, 33–34
Child abuse, 6, *see also* Infants
Chlopropamide, 142
Chloral hydrate, 72, 142
Chlorate, 34
Chlordiazepoxide, 38, 142
Chloride, 22
Chlorinated hydrocarbons, 23
Chloropromazine, 142
Chloroquine, 142
Chlorpheniramine, 142
Chlorphentermine, 142
Chlorpromazine, 39, 142
Chlorpropamide, 142
Chlorprothixene, 142
Chlorzoxazone, 142
Chromate, 34
Chromatography, 39–45, 72
Cimetidine, 142
Classifications, 2, 147
Cleaning fluid, 22
Cleanliness, 16
Clemastine, 142
Clobazam, 142
Clomipramine, 39, 142
Clonazepam, 142
Clonidine, 142
Clorazepate, 142
Clothing blood stains, 25
Clotiazepam, 142
Clozapine, 142
Cocaethylene, 142
Cocaine
  comprehensive toxicology screening, 8
  confirmation, 78
  drug instability, 127
  fly larvae, 24
  forensic pathologist role, 4
  immunoassays, 39
  internal standards, 101
  investigation strategies, 71
  nasal swabs, 119
  pH adjustment, extraction, 48
  preservatives, 15
  quantification, 82–83
  quantitative analysis references, 142
  skeletal muscle specimen selection, 24
  tissue specimen selection, 23
  vitreous humor, 116
Codeine
  immunoassays, 39
  investigation, 71
  quantitative analysis references, 142
  ToxiLab systems, 71
Cody and Foltz studies, 79
Colchicine, 142
Cold and cough remedies, 147
Collection techniques, *see also* Samples and sampling; Specimen collection
  bile, 17–18
  blood, 16–17
  fundamentals, 16, *17*
  gastric contents, 18
  hair, 18–19
  labeling, 19
  tissues, 19
  urine, 17
  vitreous humor, 18
Color-blindness, 40
Color tests, 33–35
Common methods, postmortem toxicology
  analytical chemistry, 32–33, *33*
  applications, 49
  carbon monoxide, 35

- chemical tests, 33–34
- chromatography, 39–45
- color and color tests, 34–35
- cyanide test, 35
- dip-stick tests, 35
- enzyme immunoassays, 37
- extraction methods, 46–48
- fluoresence polarization immunoassay, 37–38
- gas chromatography, 41–42
- gas chromatography-mass spectrometry, 42–43
- gastric contents, 35
- glucose strips, 35
- heavy metals, 34–35
- high-performance liquid chromatography, 44–45
- hydrolysis, 48–49
- immunoassays, 35–39
- ketone strips, 35
- kinetic interaction, microparticles, 38
- metaloids, 46
- microdiffusion tests, 35
- odor, 35
- pH, 35
- protein test dip-sticks, 35
- radioimmunoassay, 38
- Reinsch test, 34–35
- sample preparation, 46–49
- screening immunoassays, 38–39
- test dip-sticks, 35
- thin-layer chromatography, 40–41
- toxic metals and metaloids, 46
- ultraviolet-visible spectrophotometry, 45–46

Comprehensive toxicology screening, 8
Confirmation, 75–78
Containers, 15
Continuing education, 97
Controls, 102–104
Cookers, 25
Cotinine, 142
Cough and cold remedies, 147
Court
- absolute interpretation, 114
- confirmation, 75, 77
- findings usage, 5

Crashes, *see* Accidents
Creatinine, 22
Cremation ash, 25
Cresol, 35
Crippen, Harvey, 122
Cyanide
- forensic pathologist role, 4
- odor, gastric contents, 22, 35
- quantification, 82
- test, common methods, 35
- tissue specimen selection, 23

Cyclic antidepressants, 39, *see also* Tricyclic antidepressants
Cyclizine, 142
Cyclobenzaprine
- confirmation, 77
- immunoassays, 39
- quantitative analysis references, 142

Cyclopane, 142
CYP2D6, 122
Cyproheptadine, 142
Cytochrome P4502D6, 122

D

Data, quality assurance, 108–110
DAWN, *see* Drug Abuse Warning Network (DAWN)
Death
- certification, 4, 7
- classifications of manner, 2
- investigation process, 2, *2*
- location, unknowns guidance, 75
- toxicology issue identification, *5*

Decomposed body cases
- controls, 102
- specimen selection, 20, 25

Dehydration, 22
DELTA-9-THC, 141
Delta-9-THC-carboxylic acid, 142
Demoxepam, 142
Depressants, 147
Desalkylflurazepam, 142
Desflurane, 142
Desipramine, 39, 142
Devices, medication delivery, 126
Dextromethorphan, 142
Dextrorphan, 142
Diabetes, 22, *see also* Insulin
Diazepam, 38, 143
Dichromate, 34
Diclofenac, 143
Dicyclomine, 143
Diethylpropion, 143
Diffusion, postmortem, 124–125
Diflunisal, 143
Difluorococaine, 101
Digoxin
- quantification, 83
- vitreous humor, 21, 116–117

Dihydrocodeine, 143
Diltiazem, 143
Diode array detectors, 44
Diphenhydramine, 82, 143
Diphenoxin, 143
Diphenoxylate, 143
Diphenylamine test, 34
Diphenylhydantoin (phenytoin), 145
Dip-stick tests, 35
Disopyramide, 143
Distribution, 121–124
Documentation, 14, 96
Double indemnity clauses, 6
Doxepin, 39, 143
Doxylamine, 143
Drownings, *see* Accidents
Drug Abuse Warning Network (DAWN), 74
Drug Epidemiology Network, 74

Drug instability, 127
Drug level interpretation
  absorption, 121–122
  additive toxicity, 126–127
  adverse reactions, 127
  analytical results, 115
  artifacts, medication delivery, 126
  blood, 115–116, 123
  bone, 120
  brain, 118–119
  diffusion, postmortem, 124–125
  distribution, 121–124
  drug instability, 127
  fluids, 119
  fundamentals, 114, 128
  gastric contents, 117–118
  glasses, 120–121
  hair, 120
  incomplete distribution, 123–124
  ingestion estimation, 123
  injection sites, 119
  instability of drugs, 127
  liver, 117
  medication delivery artifacts, 126
  metabolism, 122
  nails, 120
  nasal swabs, 119
  paraphernalia, 120–121
  pharmacogenetics, 122
  pharmacokinetics, 121–123
  postmortem redistribution, 123–125
  postmortem specimens, 115–121
  redistribution, postmortem, 124–125
  soft tissues, 119
  spoons, 120–121
  synergistic toxicity, 126–127
  syringes, 120–121
  tables of values, 127–128
  total body burden calculation, 122–123
  trauma, 125–126
  urine, 118
  virteous humor, 116–117
Drug quantification
  analysis, 141–147
  investigation strategies, 81–84
Drug uptake, vitreous humor, 21
Druid studies, 67–84

E

ECD, *see* Electron capture detector (ECD)
Ecgonine methyl ester, 39, 143
Ecstasy, *see* Methylenedioxymethamphetamine (MDMA; Ecstacy)
Edema, 7
EDTA, 15
Elderly, 71, 118
Electrocutions, *see* Accidents
Electrolyte balance, 22
Electron capture detector (ECD), 42
ELISA assays, 37
Embalmed cases, 20
Encainide, 143
Enflurane, 143
Entrance wounds, 83
Enzyme immunoassays, 37
Ephedrin, 143
Ephedrine, 38
Esmolol, 143
Estazolam, 143
Ester alcohols, 42
Esters, preservatives, 15
Ethanol
  blood specimen selection, 20
  comprehensive toxicology screening, 8
  odor, gastric contents, 35
  preservatives, 15–16
  quality control data, 110
  quantitative analysis references, 143
Ethchlorvynol
  chemical tests, 33
  gastric content tests, 35
  odor, gastric contents, 22
  quantitative analysis references, 143
  test, 34
  ToxiLab system alternatives, 72
Ethinamate, 143
Ethosuximide, 143
Ethyl alcohol, 23–24
Ethylene, 143
Ethylene glycol, 22
Ethylflurazepam, 143
Etodolac, 143
Etomidate, 143
Evidence, chain of custody, 14
Examination, postmortem toxicology, 7–9
Exit wounds, 83
Extraction methods, 46–48
Eyes, *see* Vitreous humor

F

Falls, *see* Accidents
False-positives, 77
Famotidine, 143
Felbamate, 143
Felodipine, 143
Femoral blood
  digoxin toxicity, 21
  drug level interpretation, 116
  redistribution, postmortem, 124
Fenfluramine, 143
Fenoprofen, 143
Fentanyl, 143
FID, *see* Flame ionization detector (FID)
Findings, court use, 5
Fires, *see* Accidents
Flame ionization detector (FID), 42

Flecainide, 143
Flow of information, case reviews, 8–9
Fluids, drug level interpretation, 119
Flunitrazepam, 38, 143
Fluoresence detectors, 44
Fluoresence polarization immunoassay, 37–38
Fluoxetine, 143
Fluphenazine, 143
Flurazepam, 38, 143
Fluribiprofen, 143
Foltz, Cody and, studies, 79
Foltz studies, 80
Forensic pathologist role, 3–4
Freon
  nonbiological evidence, 26
  quantitative analysis references, 143
  tissue specimen selection, 23
Fujiwara test, 34

G

Gallbladder, *see* Bile
Garage, nonbiological evidence, 26
Garlic odor, 22
Gas chromatography (GC)
  amphetamines, 70
  barbiturates, 71
  cocaine, 71
  immunoassays, 71
  investigation strategies, 73–74
  phencyclidine, 71
  quantification, 83
  tests, common methods, 41–42
Gas chromatography-mass spectrometry (GC-MS)
  barbiturates, 71
  benzodiazepines, 71
  internal standards, 101
  investigation strategies, 78–80
  opiates, 71
  quantification, 83
  tests, common methods, 42–43
Gas chromatography-mass spectrometry with selected ion monitoring (GC-MS-SIM), 79–80
Gases, 98, 147
Gasoline, 143
Gas scrubbers, 98
Gastric contents
  collection techniques, 18
  color, 35
  diffusion, postmortem, 125
  drug level interpretation, 116–118
  gas chromatography-mass spectrometry, 80
  investigation strategies, 72–73
  odor, 35
  pH, 35
  quantification preparation, 83
  redistribution, postmortem, 125
  specimen selection, 19, 22
  tests, 35
  thin-layer chromatography, 40
  ToxiLab A, 72
  Trinder's reagent, 34
GC, *see* Gas chromatography (GC)
GC-MS, *see* Gas chromatography-mass spectrometry (GC-MS)
GC-MS-SIM, *see* Gas chromatography-mass spectrometry with selected ion monitoring (GC-MS-SIM)
General unknowns, investigation strategies, 74–75, *76*
GHB, 120
Glass containers, 15
Glasses, 120–121
Glipizide, 143
Glossary, 131–135
Glucose, 22, 35
Glue odor, 22
Glutethimide, 48, 143
Glyburide, 143
Glycosides, cardiac, 83

H

Hair
  collection techniques, 18–19
  controls, 102
  drug level interpretation, 120
  gas chromatography-mass spectrometry, 80
  solid phase extraction, 48
  specimen selection, 23
Halazepam, 143
Hallucinogens, 147
Halogenated hydrocarbons, 22
Haloperidol, 143
Hearn studies
  investigation strategies, 67–84
  postmortem toxicology fundamentals, 1–9
  tests, common methods, 31–49
Heart blood, *see also* Blood
  drug level interpretation, 116
  redistribution, postmortem, 124–125
  sampling, 16
  skeletal muscle specimen selection, 24
  specimen selection, 19–20, 22
Heart weight, 185–186
Heavy metals
  quantification, 82
  specimen selection, 22
  tests, 34–35
Hepler studies, 13–26
Heroin
  drug paraphernalia, 120–121
  immunoassays, 39
  vitreous humor, 21–22
Hexobarbital, 143
High-performance liquid chromatography (HPLC)
  barbiturates, 71
  liquid chromatography, 74
  quantification, 83
  tests, common methods, 44–45

Highway crashes, *see* Accidents
Home, unknowns guidance, 75
Homemade controls, 103
Homicides, 4–6
Hospice, 6–7
Hospital admission specimens, 19
HPLC, *see* High-performance liquid chromatography (HPLC)
Hydration, vitreous humor, 22
Hydrocodone
  immunoassays, 39
  investigation, 71
  quantitative analysis references, 143
  ToxiLab systems, 71
Hydrolysis, 48–49
Hydromorphone
  immunoassays, 39
  investigation, 71
  quantitative analysis references, 143
Hydroxychloroquine, 143
Hydroxyzine, 143
Hyoscine, 122
Hypnotics
  comprehensive toxicology screening, 8
  liquid chromatography-mass spectrometry, 81
  pharmacological classification, 147
  suicides, 5
Hypochlorite, 34
11-Hyroxy delta-9-THC, 141

I

Ibuprofen, 143
Imipramine
  chemical tests, 33
  immunoassays, 39
  metabolism, 122
  quantitative analysis references, 143
Immunoassays
  enzyme type, 37
  fluoresence polarization type, 37–38
  fundamentals, 35–36
  kinetic interactions, microparticles, 38
  radioimmunoassays, 38
  screening, 38–39
Inactive metabolites, 82
Incomplete distribution, 123–124
Indomethacin, 144
Infants, 25, 71, *see also* Child abuse
Information, case reviews, 8–9
Ingestion estimation, blood levels, 123
Injection sites, 119
Inotropics, 147
Insecticides, 26
Instability of drugs, 127
Installation, 108
Instruments, 83, 107–108
Insulin, 121, 144
Insurance policies, 6
Internal standards, 84, 101–102
Intrepretation, postmortem toxicology, 9–10
Investigation strategies
  amphetamines, 70
  barbiturates, 70–71
  benzodiazepines, 71
  chromatographic methods, 72
  cocaine, 71
  confirmation, 75–78
  drug quantification, 81–84
  fundamentals, 68–74, *69–70*
  gas chromatography, 73–74
  gas chromatography-mass spectrometry, 78–80
  gastric contents, 72–73
  general unknown, 74–75, *76*
  liquid chromatography, 74
  liquid chromatography-mass spectrometry, 80–81
  method validation, 81
  opiates, 71
  pending toxicology conference, 84
  phencyclidine, 71
  poisons quantification, 81–84
  review process, 84
  screening, 68
  selective ion monitoring, 79–80
  urine, 72–73
Iodate, 34
Ionic strength, 74
Iron salts, 35
Isenschmid studies, 13–26
Isoflurane, 144
Iso-metheptene, 144
Isopropanol, 144
Isoxsuprine, 144
Isradipine, 144

J

Jones, A.W., studies, 181–183
Jones, G.R., studies, 113–128

K

Kateman and Pijpers studies, 104, 109
Keratin, 23
Ketamin, 144
Ketazolam, 144
Ketone test dip-sticks, 35
Ketoprofen, 144
Ketorolac, 144
Kidney
  drug level interpretation, 119
  skeletal muscle specimen selection, 24
  specimen selection, 22
Kinetic interaction, microparticles, 38

L

Labeling, 19
Lamotrigine, 144
Larvae, 24–25
LC, *see* Liquid chromatography (LC)
LC-MS, *see* Liquid chromatography-mass spectrometry (LC-MS)
LC-MS-MS, *see* Tandem liquid chromatography-mass spectrometry (LC-MS-MS)
LC-MS-MS-TOF, *see* Tandem liquid chromatography-mass spectrometry time of flight (LC-MS-MS-TOF)
Lead, 23, 34
Leg veins, blood, 17
Levallorphan, 144
Levey-Jennings chart, 109
Levodopa, 144
Levorphanol, 144
Lidocaine
    confirmation, 78
    quantification, 82
    quantitative analysis references, 144
Lighters, butane, 25
Linear dynamic range, 105
Liquid chromatography (LC), 74
Liquid chromatography-mass spectrometry (LC-MS)
    benzodiazepines, 71
    investigation strategies, 80–81
    opiates, 71
    quantification, 83
Liquid-liquid extraction, 46–47, 49, 83
Lithium, 144
Liver
    bile, 119
    diffusion, postmortem, 125
    drug level interpretation, 117
    skeletal muscle specimen selection, 24
    specimen selection, 19, 22
L-methamphetamine, 144
Logan studies, 181–183
Loperamide, 144
Lorantadine, 144
Lorazepam, 38, 144
Loxapine, 144
LSD, 71, 144
Lungs
    diffusion, postmortem, 125
    drug level interpretation, 119
    specimen selection, 22
    tissue specimen selection, 23
Lyophilized serum, 102

M

Malathion, 24
Manganese, 34
MAOI, *see* Monoamine oxidase inhibitor (MAOI)
Maprotiline, 144
Marijuana, 78, 83
Mazindol, 144
MDA, *see* Methylene amphetamine (MDA)
MDEA, 144
MDMA, *see* Methylenedioxymethamphetamine (MDMA; Ecstacy)
Measuring devices, 97
Meclizine, 144
Meconium, 25
Medazepam, 144
Medical examiner investigator role, 3
Medical records, 74
Medication delivery, 126
Medicine vials, 25–26
Medicolegal death investigation, 1–4, *2*
Mefenamic acid, 144
Meperidine, 39, 144
Mephenytoin, 144
Mephetermine, 144
Mephobarbital, 144
Mepivacaine, 144
Meprobamate, 48, 144
Mercury, 23, 35
Mescaline (peyote), 144
Mesoridazine, 144
Metabolism, 122
Metaloids, 46
Metals and metaloids, toxic, 46
Methadone
    immunoassays, 39, 71
    quantitative analysis references, 144
Methamphetamine
    confirmation, 78
    immunoassays, 38
    quantitative analysis references, 144
Methanol, 144
Methapryilene, 144
Methaqualone, 71, 144
Methocarbamol, 144
Methods, postmortem toxicology
    analytical chemistry, 32–33, *33*
    applications, 49
    carbon monoxide, 35
    chemical tests, 33–34
    chromatography, 39–45
    color and color tests, 34–35
    cyanide test, 35
    dip-stick tests, 35
    enzyme immunoassays, 37
    extraction methods, 46–48
    fluoresence polarization immunoassay, 37–38
    gas chromatography, 41–42
    gas chromatography-mass spectrometry, 42–43
    gastric contents, 35
    glucose strips, 35
    heavy metals, 34–35
    high-performance liquid chromatography, 44–45
    hydrolysis, 48–49
    immunoassays, 35–39
    ketone strips, 35
    kinetic interaction, microparticles, 38

metaloids, 46
microdiffusion tests, 35
odor, 35
pH, 35
protein test dip-sticks, 35
radioimmunoassay, 38
Reinsch test, 34–35
sample preparation, 46–49
screening immunoassays, 38–39
test dip-sticks, 35
thin-layer chromatography, 40–41
toxic metals and metaloids, 46
ultraviolet-visible spectrophotometry, 45–46
Method validation, 81
Methohexital, 144
Methsuximide, 144
Methylene amphetamine (MDA), 144
Methylenedioxymethamphetamine (MDMA; Ecstacy), 38, 144
Methylphenidate, 144
Methyl salicylate, 35
Methyprylon, 144
Methysergide, 144
Metoclopramide, 144
Metoprolol, 145
Mexiletine, 145
Microdiffusion tests, 35
Midazolam, 145
Molindone, 145
Monoacetylmorphine, 71, 145
Monoamine oxidase inhibitor (MAOI), 127
Moricizine, 145
Morphine
bile, 21, 119
drug level interpretation, 121–122
immunoassays, 39
investigation, 71
pH adjustment, extraction, 48
quantitative analysis references, 145
vitreous humor, 116
Morphine-3-glucuronide, 39, 145
Murder, 4–6
Muscle relaxants, 147
Myocardial tissue, 119

N

Nadolol, 145
Nails
controls, 102
drug level interpretation, 120
gas chromatography-mass spectrometry, 80
hair specimen selection, 23
Nalbuphine, 145
Nalgene containers, 15
Naproxen, 145
Narcotic analgesics, 48
Narcotics, 118
Nasal swabs, 119
National Laboratory Certification Program (NLCP), 111
Natural deaths, 6–7
Neonates, *see* Infants
Neuroleptic malignant syndrome (NMS), 127
Neutral drugs, 41–42
Nicotine
pH adjustment, extraction, 48
quantification, 82
quantitative analysis references, 145
Nifedipine, 145
Nitrates, 34, 147
Nitrazepam, 145
Nitrites, 34
Nitrogen/phosphorus detector (NPD), 42, 72
Nitrous oxide, 145
NLCP, *see* National Laboratory Certification Program (NLCP)
NMS, *see* Neuroleptic malignant syndrome (NMS)
Nomifensine, 145
Nonbiological evidence, 25–26
Nonsteroidal antiinflammatories, 147
Norpropoxyphene, 39
Nortriptyline, 39
NPD, *see* Nitrogen/phosphorus detector (NPD)
Nylidrin, 145

O

Odors, 22, 35
Opiates and opioids
bile specimen selection, 21
comprehensive toxicology screening, 8
confirmation, 77
fly larvae, 24
gastric contents, 72
investigation strategies, 71
pharmacological classification, 147
screening immunoassays, 39
ToxiLab systems, 41
Oral ingestion, drug administration, 22
Organic bases, 48
Organic solvents, 35
Organic volatiles, 23
Organophosphates
fly larvae, 24
odor, gastric contents, 22
solid phase extraction, 48
Orphenadrine, 145
Otto, Stas and, studies, 46
Overdoses, 7, 22
Over-the-counter medicines, 78
Oxazepam, 38, 145
Oxidizing agents, 34
Oxycodone
immunoassays, 39
investigation, 71
quantitative analysis references, 145
ToxiLab systems, 71
Oxymorphone, 145

P

Pain medication, 25
Pancuraonium, 145
Papaverine, 145
Paradehyde, 35, 145
Paraphernalia, 25, 120–121
Parkinsonism drugs, 147
Paroxetine, 145
PCP, *see* Phencyclidine (PCP)
Pemoline, 145
Pending causes, deaths, 7
Pending toxicology conference, 84
Pentazocine, 145
Pentobarbital, 38, 145
Pergolide, 145
Peripheral blood, 17, 19–20
Permanganate, 34
Perphenazine, 145
Personnel, quality assurance, 97
Pest killers, 26
Peyote (mescaline), 144
pH
  blood drug level interpretation, 115
  extraction adjustment, 48
  gastric contents, 35
  liquid chromatography, 74
  liquid-liquid extraction, 47
  preservatives, 15
  test dip-sticks, 35
  vitreous humor, 116
Pharmacogenetics, 122
Pharmacokinetics, 121–123
Pharmacological classifications, 147
Phencyclidine (PCP)
  confirmation, 78
  investigation strategies, 71
  pH adjustment, extraction, 48
  quantitative analysis references, 145
  screening immunoassays, 39
Phendimetrazine, 145
Phenelazine, 145
Phenobarbital
  fly larvae, 24
  immunoassays, 38
  quantitative analysis references, 145
Phenols, 42
Phenothiazines
  adverse reactions, 127
  chemical tests, 33
  immunoassays, 39
  pH adjustment, extraction, 48
  Trinder's reagent, 34
Phensuximide, 145
Phentermine, 38, 145
Phenylpropanolmine, 38, 145
Phenyltoloxamine, 145
Phenytoin (diphenylhydantoin), 48, 145
Phosphorus detector, *see* Nitrogen/phosphorus detector (NPD)
Pijpers, Kateman and, studies, 104, 109
Piroxicam, 145
Placidyl test, 34
Plasma
  controls, 102–103
  fluoresence polarization immunoassay, 38
  gastric contents, 72
  REMEDi HS HPLC system, 45
Plasticizer contaminants, 15
Poisons
  autopsy, pending toxicology, 7
  investigation strategies, 81–84
  terminally ill patients, 6–7
  toxicology examination, 8
Police role, 3
Poppers, 25
Postmortem specimens, 115–121
Postmortem toxicology
  accidents, 6
  case review, 8–9
  comprehensive toxicology screening, 8
  death certification, 4
  examination, 7–9
  forensic pathologist role, 3–4
  homicides, 4–5
  intrepretation, 9–10
  medical examiner investigator role, 3
  medicolegal death investigation, 1–4, *2*
  natural deaths, 6–7
  overdose, death, 7
  pending causes, deaths, 7
  poisons, 8
  police role, 3
  quality assurance, 9
  report, 9
  role of toxicology, 4–7, *5*
  screening methods, 8
  suicides, 5
  toxicology role, 4–7, *5*
  unclassified deaths, 7
  undetermined deaths, 7
Potassium oxalate, 15–16
Prazepam, 145
Pre-analysis checklist, 108
Predicted normal heart weight, 185–186
Prescription drugs, 78
Preservatives, specimens, 15–16
Preventative maintenance, 108
Primidone, 48, 145
Procainamide, 145
Procaine, 145
Proficiency programs, 110–111
Promazine, 145
Promethazine, 145
Propafenone, 145
Propanolol, 145
Propellant canisters, 25
Propofol, 145
Propoxyphene
  immunoassays, 71
  quantitative analysis references, 145
  screening immunoassays, 39

Propylbenzoylecgonine, 101
Protein-free filtrates, 33
Protein test dip-sticks, 35
Protriptyline, 39, 146
Pseudoephedrine, 38, 146
Psychotherapeutic agents, 147
Psycylobin, 146
Pulmonary congestion, 7
Pyrilamine, 146

Q

Quality assurance
- accreditation programs, 111
- analysis, 104–107, 109
- calibrators, 98–100
- chain-of-custody data, 109
- continuing education, 97
- controls, 102–104
- data, 108–110
- fundamentals, 9, 96
- installation, 108
- instruments, 107–108
- internal standards, 101–102
- measuring devices, 97
- personnel, 97
- pre-analysis checklist, 108
- preventative maintenance, 108
- proficiency programs, 110–111
- quality control data, 109–110, *110*
- reagents, 97–98
- reference materials, 98–104
- reports, 110
- samples and sampling, 104
- standard operating procedures, 96–97

Quality control data, 109–110, *110*
Quantitative analysis, 141–147
Quazepam, 146
Quinidine, 146
Quinine, 146

R

Radioimmunoassay, 38
Ranitidine, 146
Reagents, 97–98
Redistribution, postmortem, 116, 124–125
Reference materials, 98–104
Reinsch test, 34–35
REMEDi HS HPLC system, 45
Renal function, 22
Reports
- police, scene documentation, 3
- quality assurance, 110
- toxicology, 9

Review process, 84
Risperidone, 146

S

Salicylates
- chemical tests, 33
- comprehensive toxicology screening, 8
- confirmation, 78
- gastric contents, 72–73
- ToxiLab system alternatives, 72
- vitreous humor, 116

Salicylic acid, 34
Samples and sampling, *see also* Specimen collection
- bile, 17–18
- blood, 16–17
- collection, 16, *17*
- fundamentals, 16
- gastric contents, 18
- hair, 18–19
- investigation strategies, 83
- labeling, 19
- preparation, 46–49, 83
- quality assurance, 104
- tests, common methods, 46–49
- tissues, 19
- urine, 17
- vitreous humor, 18

Sample scenario calculations, 181–183
Scenario calculations, 181–183
Scene documentation, 3
Scopolamine, 146
Screening, investigation strategies, 8, 68
Screening immunoassays, methods, 38–39
Secobarbital, 38, 146
Sedatives, 8, 147
Selection of specimens
- bile, 21
- blood, 20
- bone and bone marrow, 23–24
- fundamentals, 19–20
- gastric contents, 22
- hair, 23
- larvae, 24–25
- meconium, 25
- nonbiological evidence, 25–26
- skeletal muscle, 24
- tissues, 22–23
- urine, 20–21
- vitreous humor, 21–22

Selective ion monitoring, 79–80
Selective serotonin-reuptake inhibitors (SSRIs), 122, 127
Selegiline, 146
Selenium, 35
Serotonin syndrome, 127, *see also* Selective serotonin-reuptake inhibitors (SSRIs)
Sertraline, 146
Serum
- controls, 102
- fluoresence polarization immunoassay, 38
- REMEDi HS HPLC system, 45
- thin-layer chromatography, 40
- Trinder's reagent, 34

Shewhart charts, 109

Sink cabinets, 26
Skeletal muscle, 24
Skeleton cases, 20, 25
Sodium, 22
Sodium citrate, 15–16
Soft tissues, 119, *see also* Tissues
Soil samples, 25
Solid-phase dynamic extraction (SPDE), 48
Solid phase extraction (SPE), 47–49, 83
Solvents, 23, 26, 35
Sotalol, 146
SPDE, *see* Solid-phase dynamic extraction (SPDE)
SPE, *see* Solid phase extraction (SPE)
Specimen collection, 4, 14–16, *see also* Samples and sampling
Specimen selection
  bile, 21
  blood, 20
  bone and bone marrow, 23–24
  fundamentals, 19–20
  gastric contents, 22
  hair, 23
  larvae, 24–25
  meconium, 25
  nonbiological evidence, 25–26
  skeletal muscle, 24
  tissues, 22–23
  urine, 20–21
  vitreous humor, 21–22
Spillage, sampling, 16
Spleen
  drug level interpretation, 119
  specimen selection, 22
  tissue specimen selection, 23
Spoons, 25, 120–121
Spot tests, 33, 77
SSRIs, *see* Selective serotonin-reuptake inhibitors (SSRIs)
Standard operating procedures, 96–97
Stas and Otto studies, 46
Stimulants, 147
Stock solutions, 103
Stomach contents
  enzyme immunoassays, 37
  REMEDi HS HPLC system, 45
  ToxiLab systems, 41
Strychnine, 146
Succinylcholine, 146
Sudden infant death syndrome (SIDS), 6
Sufentanil, 146
Suicides
  confirmation, 78
  fundamentals, postmortem toxicology, 5
  nonbiological evidence, 26
Sulfur, 35
Sumatriptan, 146
Sympathomimetic amines, 48
Synergistic toxicity, 126–127
Syringes, 25, 120–121

T

Tables of values, 127–128
Tablets
  gastric contents, 35, 118
  nonbiological evidence, 25–26
Talbutal, 146
Tandem liquid chromatography-mass spectrometry (LC-MS-MS), 32, 81
Tandem liquid chromatography-mass spectrometry time of flight (LC-MS-MS-TOF), 71
Tellurium, 35
Temazepam, 146
Terbutaline, 146
Terfenadine, 146
Terminal illness, 6–7
Test dip-sticks, 35
Tetracaine, 146
Tetrahydrocannabinol (THC), 39, 41
Tetrazepam, 146
Theophylline, 82, 146
Therapeutic drug analysis and monitoring
  ethchlorvynol test, 34
  fundamentals, 8
  hair specimen selection, 23
  quantification, 83
  REMEDi HS HPLC system, 45
  ultraviolet-visible spectrophotometry, 45
Thiamylal, 146
Thigh muscle, 24
Thin-layer chromatography (TLC)
  gas chromatography, 74
  phencyclidine, 71
  tests, common methods, 40–41
Thiopental
  hair, 120
  immunoassays, 38
  quantitative analysis references, 146
Thioridazine, 146
Thiothixene, 146
Thoracic blood, 17
Tissues
  collection techniques, 19
  controls, 103
  enzyme immunoassays, 37
  REMEDi HS HPLC system, 45
  soft, 119
  specimen selection, 19, 22–23
TLC, *see* Thin-layer chromatography (TLC)
Tocainide, 146
Tolazamide, 146
Tolmetin, 146
Toluene
  confirmation, 78
  odor, gastric contents, 22
  quantitative analysis references, 146
Tolutamide, 146
Total body burden calculation, 122–123
Toxic metals and metaloids, 46
Toxicology role, 4–7, *5*

ToxiLab systems
amphetamines, 70
barbiturates, 71
benzodiazepines, 71
chromatographic methods, 72
cocaine, 71
fundamentals, 40–41
immunoassays, 71
Tracheal air, 25
Tramadol, 146
Tranquilizers, 25
Transdermal patches, 126
Tranylcypromine, 146
Trauma, 125–126
Trazodone, 146
Triazolam, 38, 146
Trichloro compounds, 34, 78
Trichloroethane, 78
Trichloroethylene, 146
Tricyclic antidepressants, *see also* Antidepressants
adverse reactions, 127
bone and bone marrow specimen selection, 23
diffusion, postmortem, 125
fly larvae, 24
gas chromatography-mass spectrometry, 80
gastric contents, 117
quantification, 83
vitreous humor, 116
Trifluoperazine, 146
Triflupromazine, 146
Trihexypehnidyl, 146
Trimethadione, 146
Trimethobenzamide, 146
Trimipramine, 146
Trinder's reagent, 34, 72
Tripelennamine, 146
Triprolidine, 146
True values, 105
Tubocurarine, 146

U

Ultraviolet absorption detectors, 44
Ultraviolet-visible spectrophotometry, 45–46
Unclassified deaths, 7
Under-sink cabinets, 26
Undetermined deaths, 7
Unlabeled containers, 26
Unstable analytes, 102
Urea nitrogen, 22
Uric acid, 22
Urine
amphetamines, 38
barbiturates, 38
benzodiazepines, 39
benzoylecgonine, 39
cannabinoids, 39
chemical tests, 33
collection techniques, 17
controls, 102–103
cyclic antidepressants, 39
drug level interpretation, 118
enzyme immunoassays, 37
fluoresence polarization immunoassay, 38
investigation strategies, 72–73
opiates, 39
phencyclidine, 39
REMEDi HS HPLC system, 45
specimen selection, 19–21
thin-layer chromatography, 40
ToxiLab systems, 41, 72
Trinder's reagent, 34

V

Valproic acid, 146
Vanadate, 34
Venlafaxine, 146
Verapamil, 146
Vitreous humor
collection techniques, 18
drug level interpretation, 116–117, 119
gastric contents, 72–73
specimen selection, 19, 21–22
Volatile compounds
pharmacological classification, 147
quantification, 83
tissue specimen selection, 23
Volatiles, blood, 78

W

Walls studies
abbreviations, 137–139
postmortem toxicology fundamentals, 1–9
terms glossary, 131–135
tests, common methods, 31–49
Whipped cream propellant canisters, 25
Whole blood, *see also* Blood; Heart blood
controls, 103
ELISA, 37
enzyme immunoassays, 37
fluoresence polarization immunoassay, 38
gastric contents, 72–73
REMEDi HS HPLC system, 45
Witnesses, unknowns guidance, 75
Workplace accidents, *see* Accidents
Workplace drug testing, 23

X

Xylene, 22, 147